P9-CRO-740

INFORMATION AND COGNITION IN ORGANIZATIONS

INFORMATION AND COGNITION IN ORGANIZATIONS

Edited by

L.L. CUMMINGS
University of Minnesota

BARRY M. STAW
University of California, Berkeley

JAI PRESS INC.
Greenwich, Connecticut London, England

Library of Congress Cataloging-in-Publication Data

Information and cognition in organizations / edited by L.L. Cummings,
Barry M. Staw.
p. cm.
ISBN 1-55938-218-X
1. Organizational behavior. 2. Decision-making. I. Cummings, Larry L.
II. Staw, Barry M.
HD58.7.I54 1990
658.4'03—dc20 90-4523
CIP

Copyright © 1990 JAI PRESS INC.
55 Old Post Road, No. 2
Greenwich, Connecticut 06836

JAI PRESS LTD.
118 Pentonville Road
London N1 9JN
England

All rights reserved. No part of this publication may be reproduced, stored on a retrieval system, or transmitted in any form or by any means, electronic, mechanical photocopying, filming, recording or otherwise without prior permission in writing from the publisher.

Manufactured in the United States of America

CONTENTS

LIST OF CONTRIBUTORS

Max H. Bazerman
Northwestern University

John S. Carroll
Massachusetts Institute of Technology

Richard L. Daft
Vanderbilt University

Steven G. Green
Purdue University

Robert H. Lengel
University of Texas at San Antonio

Terence R. Mitchell
University of Washington

Charles A. O'Reilly, III
University of California, Berkeley

Jeffrey Pfeffer
Stanford University

Barry M. Staw
University of California, Berkeley

Philip E. Tetlock
University of California, Berkeley

Karl E. Weick
Cornell University

Robert Wood
Australian Graduate School of Management

PREFACE

One of the major recent trends in organizational behavior is the emphasis on cognitive skills and cognitive complexity of human actors in organizations. This has been accompanied by a central interest in the information processing capacities and limitations of decision makers and of the organizational contexts within which they make decisions and solve problems.

This volume brings together eight selections from *Research in Organizational Behavior* that have emphasized and illustrated this theme over nine years of the development of the series.

We begin with a chapter by Jeffrey Pfeffer that highlights the central role played by *cognitions* in models of managerial action and accountability. Pfeffer argues that both managerial action and organizational processes can be viewed as systems of shared meaning and beliefs. Managers, argues Pfeffer, in large part construct meanings for others through the use of language, symbolism, and ritual. These symbolic tools are argued to enhance compliance and commitment to shared systems of norms and to a common understanding of organizational culture.

Barry Staw continues the cognitive theme by arguing that rationality and justification are powerful images through which to view and understand action in organizations. He offers new hypotheses derived from the creative tension between rationality on the one hand and post-decision justification on the other. Staw's essay vividly illustrates the value of conceiving of these two cognitive processes at multiple levels of analysis (individual and organizational) simultaneously.

Charles O'Reilly integrates much of the literature on informational processes in decision making and offers propositions that can guide future research. O'Reilly reviews the biases and misinterpretations that managers are subject to in their cognitive processing of decisions. Particular emphasis is given to the selective nature of perception and recall as biasing influences on decision. making in organizations. The propositions offered by O'Reilly can serve to guide both our interpretation of those biases and ourfuture research aimed at understanding the preventing their operation.

Negotiations represent a form of decision making and are, thus, subject to many of the same cognitive processes and biases articulated by O'Reilly. Max Bazerman and John Carroll present a systematic integration of the literature on the effect of the cognitive characteristics and processes of negotiators on the negotiating process and outcomes. Their work incorporates many of the current developments in cognitive psychology as these relate to bargaining behavior in conflict resolution settings. Their chapter is rich with suggestions for future research that would take the study of cognition in negotiations well beyond the typical, rational economic person assumptions that tend to present a misleadingly narrow concept of negotiations.

Philip Tetlock places our analysis of cognitions squarely in the context of organizations. He does this by emphasizing the understudied role of accountability in decision making. He traces the history of research on decision making and judgment, thereby advocating that attention be given to the organizational and political context of individual judgment and choice. Such an analysis demands that we consider the effects of individual accountability on judgment and decision outcomes. Accountability is treated as both a motive at the individual level and as a social constraint on judgment at the organizational level.

Terence Mitchell, Steven Green, and Robert Wood apply a particular form of information processing (attributional process) to an understanding of leadership reactions to poor performance by subordinates. They examine the information clues used by leaders to make causal attributions about the reasons for the poor performance of a subordinate. The cognitive analysis is then extended to include the reasoning used by leaders in deciding how to respond, given a causal attribution. They review both theoretical and empirical work done on the model and offer suggestions for future research.

Richard Daft and Robert Lengel present a model of information processing within organizations that attempts to balance the richness of most informational environments and the demands for clarity and simplicity needed for an organization to attempt to function rationally. It is the tension between sufficient information and uncertainty and equivocality reduction that must be managed by organizational mechanisms and managerial behavior. Uncertainty and overload are presented as the two forces in tension around which effective balance needs to be attained.

Finally, Karl Weick provides a broad conceptualization of organizations *as* composed bodies of thought and as ways of thinking. Organizations are seen as basically cognitive in character. The symbolic and schematic nature of organizations is emphasized. In turn, organizations as thought systems are seen as influencing the interpretation and transmission of cognitions by organizational participants. Thus, organizations become both substance and method; in both cases bounded by and subject to their essentially cognitive nature.

Many of the chapters in this volume have attained recognition as contributions already. It is our intent in bringing them together to encourage their use in courses that focus on cognitive and information processing within organizations and to add emphasis to a central theme in the contemporary study of organizations.

L.L. CUMMINGS
Minneapolis, Minnesota

B M. STAW
Berkeley, California

MANAGEMENT AS SYMBOLIC ACTION:
THE CREATION AND MAINTENANCE OF ORGANIZATIONAL PARADIGMS

Jeffrey Pfeffer

ABSTRACT

The analysis of management or leadership in organizations must proceed on two levels. On the level of substantive actions and results, decisions are largely the result of external constraint and power-dependence relations. On the expressive or symbolic level, the use of political language and symbolic action serves to legitimate and rationalize organizational decisions and policies. Organizations are viewed as systems of shared meanings and beliefs, in which a critical administrative activity involves the construction and maintenance of belief systems which assure continued compliance, commitment, and positive affect on the part of participants regardless of how they fare in the contest for resources. Language, symbolism, and ritual are important in this management activity which is effective in part because members find it difficult to precisely assess what they are obtaining from the organization. Administrative interventions are successful in enhancing positive sentiments and compliance to the extent that they build shared beliefs using political language and symbolic acts to cause action to be interpreted in a way compatible with the emergent norms and values.

There is evidence of dualism in the literature of organizational behavior involving the extent to which behavior is externally controlled versus proactively constructed in a quasi-rational fashion. This dualism is apparent at all levels of analysis and frequently within the same work. Thus, for example, Pfeffer and Sanancik (1978) write about the external control of organizations, arguing, particularly in the first chapter, that environmental constraints deriving from conditions of resource interdependence dictated actions and structures of the organization. At the same time, they wrote about managing interdependence and managing the environment through strategic actions such as mergers, joint ventures, and board of director interlocks. The role of the individual was down-played as the manager was viewed as a symbol (Ch. 1), but at the same time one of the mechanisms through which environmental effects were hypothesized to affect the organization was executive succession (Ch. 9). This dualism is apparent also in the literature on organizational design. Some research suggests that organizational structures are results of the interplay of the effects of size, technology, and environmental uncertainty, while other authors (Galbraith, 1973) suggest that structures can be rationally designed to optimize performance. One of the reasons that Child's (1972) article on the role of strategic choice in organizational structuring has received so much attention is that it focused attention on this dual approach in organizational theorizing, and the conflict between the positions of external determinism and internal direction, strategic choice, and rational decision making.

This dualism appears in the more psychologically oriented organizational literature as well. The field of psychology has been plagued for years by the controversy over the relative theoretical utility of proceeding from an emphasis on the situation (S), individual characteristics of the person (P), or some interaction of the two (P × S) (Sarason, Smith, and Diener, 1975). The literature on motivation has been confronted with the controversy between those stressing the external, operant control of behavior (Luthans and Kreitner, 1975; Nord, 1969) and those stressing an internal, cognitive approach to motivation (Oldham, 1976; Maslow, 1943; Locke, 1968). Both Nord and Luthans and Kreitner made this distinction between an external and internal perspective in their overviews of the motivation literature. And, as a final example, the literature on leadership has been divided into those who believe that leaders have few effects on organizations as their behaviors are largely constrained by the social system in which they find themselves (Pfeffer and Salancik, 1975; Pfeffer, 1977a), and the vast majority who continue to emphasize the role of leadership in organizational functioning (e.g., House and Baetz, 1979).

Another distinction has been emerging between a cognitive perspective on organizations (Weick, 1979; Pondy and Boje, 1976; Pondy, 1978;

Brown, 1978) and more traditional research approaches which have tended to emphasize social actions, behaviors, and social facts. The cognitive perspective has emphasized the importance of language and symbols in organizations, and has proceeded from the premise that reality was, in large measure, socially constructed. Traditional approaches to the study of organizations, by contrast, have emphasized observable, measurable social facts. The division between the two approaches has at times revolved around the type of scientific procedures employed in testing and developing knowledge. The cognitive researchers have, for the most part, been essayistic, conceptual, and not concerned much of the time with developing testable empirical predictions (however, see Pondy, 1977, as an exception). When data have been employed, it has been frequently in a case-study style of argument (e.g., Gephart, 1978). By contrast, the traditional approach to organizational research has employed more comparative, quantitative data and more statistically rigorous analytical procedures. The distinct differences in research styles had led to the neglect both of the usefulness of the theoretical ideas and of the data generated by one school of thought by the other.

These dualisms in the organizations literature are a healthy source of controversy and consequently energy. Moreover, it is not clear that there is enough theory or research in place to resolve these issues even if we wanted to. However, there is some benefit in examining one possible approach to resolving these dual perspectives. The purpose of this chapter is to explore the role of management and the conduct of the administrative process considering the symbolic content of such activity. One goal is to illustrate how testable propositions can emerge from considering the symbolic nature of administrative action. A second purpose is to try to place these various positions on the analysis and study of organizations in some perspective. Indeed, to consider management as symbolic action, it is first necessary to consider the place of this argument in the larger context of organizational theory.

UNDERSTANDING ORGANIZATIONS ON TWO LEVELS

One way of addressing the dualism between external constraint on activity and the effects of individual social actors acting independently involves recognizing the fact that a given social entity can be at once influenced by its social context and at the same time have effects on that social environment. The analogy can be drawn to physics and the law of gravity. Just as the moon is constrained in its orbit by the gravity or force of the earth, so it also has effects on the earth and its movement in the solar system. In the same way a manager might be said to be constrained by the demands of subordinates, peers, and supervisors (Pfeffer and Salancik, 1975) while at the same time influencing these other actors through his or her own behaviors and preferences.

But such an approach, although probably valid, misses something also. Organizations are more than systems of mutual constraint in which actors with various amounts of power or force mutually constrain and influence each other. They are also social systems populated by individuals who come to the system with norms, values, and expectations and with the necessity of developing understandings of the world around them so there can be enough predictability for them to take some action. Just as one could not drive an automobile if the various controls randomly changed in both content and operation from one moment to the next, so one could not navigate through the social world without some understanding of action that made this action predictable from one instance to the next. This is what motivates, in part, the development of interlocked cycles of collective behavior (Weick, 1969).

But because of the norms, values, and expectations that individuals bring with them from the larger society into the organization, they are not indifferent about the type of explanations and predictions that arise to make sense and meaning of the world around them. For instance, in the literature on attribution theory, Kelley (1971) has noted that persons seek to develop causal schemata which are not only accurate but also provide an illusion or feeling of control over events. Thus, a preference or bias in favor of interpretations of power and personal efficacy will color the explanations of action developed and held within organizations. Gergen (1969), in a chapter commenting on the criteria for the acceptance of social theories, noted that although consistency with the data was desirable, theories have continued to exist in contradiction of data and that tastes, preferences or values also governed which theories of social behavior would be held. Thus, organizations are systems of patterned or structured activity in which the participants attempt to develop causal explanations and rationalizations for these patterns of activity, with the explanations being constrained to be legitimate and acceptable in the social context and with the further preference for explanations that provide a feeling of control over events.

Then, it can be argued that it is the task of management to provide explanations, rationalizations, and legitimation for the activities undertaken in the organization. These terms have been defined previously in reference to the development of a social information processing perspective on job attitudes:

> The term "rationalize" refers to any situation in which a person's action is described with reference to some supporting reason or cause. The term "legitimate" refers to one criterion by which rationalizations are selected from the many possible explana-

> tions for action. Justifications or rationalizations are selected primarily when they are acceptable explanations in a given social context. This means they fit with the facts as known according to the rules of behavior generally followed (Salancik and Pfeffer, 1978: 231).

Management provides rationalizations or reasons that make sense of and thereby explain the organization's activities. These rationalizations or explanations for behavior are constructed so as to legitimate the organization to its constituents both within and outside its boundaries, in that the explanations for activity provide reasons for organizational action that are consistent with social norms, values, and expectations for the organization. This legitimation occurs to ensure support not only from the organization's environment but also to ensure the continued participation and, indeed, acquiescence, enthusiasm, and commitment for the organization on the part of its employees or members.

Note that the task of management, in this perspective, has been defined in terms of rationalizing and legitimating action. The actions themselves, it can be argued, are principally the result of fundamental resource interdependencies and other environmental imperatives confronting the organization. Thus, substantive organizational actions such as resource allocations are predicted from conditions of power and dependence. Management's task is to rationalize and legitimate these actions.

In this sense, there is a clear parallel between the analysis of management actions in formal organizations, which can be viewed as coalitions (March, 1962; Cyert and March, 1963), and political analysis more generally. As Edelman has noted (1964: 12):

> Political analysis must, then, proceed on two levels simultaneously. It must examine how political actions get some groups the tangible things they want from government and at the same time it must explore what these same actions mean to the mass public and how it is placated or aroused by them. In Himmelstrand's terms, political actions are both instrumental and expressive.

The argument advanced here is that management's effect is primarily with respect to expressive or symbolic actions; management has less, although still some, discretionary impact on instrumental action. Thus, the argument that leadership does not matter (Pfeffer, 1977a) was based on considering leadership effects on profits, sales, profit margins, capital budgets and other allocations, and budget expenditures in cities (Salancik and Pfeffer, 1977a). These are all tangible, real outcomes of organizational activities. A very different answer on the effect of leadership might be derived if one examined the consequences of managerial activity for the sentiments, beliefs, attitudes, or commitment of the organizational participants. In analyses of tangible outcomes of the political process such as expenditures, taxation policies, and public works, resource-based political power is relatively more predictive of the observed outcomes. At the same time, symbolic political language may lead to a different distribution of perceived benefits and satisfaction so that a different set of interests may feel well served by the political process. A similar outcome occurs in formal organizations in which power and dependence can profitably be used to account for resource allocations (e.g., Pfeffer and Salancik, 1974), but the language and symbolism surrounding the allocation process may be able to produce a somewhat different distribution of satisfaction with those outcomes.

The symbolic and instrumental aspects of organizational activity are clearly linked, but at the same time it is likely that the coupling between them is loose. A parallel argument can be made to that developed to explain the relationship between attitudes and behavior. First, the activity or decisions may precede the justification, just as behavior frequently precedes the attitude that is constructed so as to be consistent with that behavior (Bem, 1972). Second, the linkage between justifications and rationalizations and organizational action can be loose, just as there is far less than perfect correspondence between attitudes and behavior even after the behavior has occurred. Of course, under external prompting (Salancik and Conway, 1975), behaviors can be recalled and thereby one can force a closer correspondence between the attitudes and the behaviors. Similarly, under external prompting or pressure, management may invest more effort in making sense of and legitimating organizational actions, and in so doing create greater correspondence between the organization's activities and the language by which it describes what it is about. However, in both cases, in the absence of external demands, the correspondence between actions or outcomes and attitudes is likely to be moderate to low.

In Figure 1, the relationship described between symbolic and substantive action and management control and external, environmental control is displayed. The argument is that management action operates largely with and on symbolic outcomes, and that external constraints affect primarily substantive actions and outcomes in formal organizations. One problem in the organizational behavior literature has been a tendency to confuse or to mix the two. In particular, symbolic outcomes such as attitudes and other sentiments have been used as dependent variables as proxies for substantive results. And, the confusion between symbolic outcomes and actual patterns of resource allocation has clouded the issue of the effects of management in organizations. What the figure suggests is that, as Edelman has argued, analysis should proceed on two levels simultaneously, but the two levels have different dependent variables, different processes, and are themselves only imperfectly linked. Indeed,

Figure 1. The Relationship Between Substantive and Symbolic Outcomes and Management Versus External Control

	SUBSTANTIVE OUTCOMES (ALLOCATIONS OR DECISIONS WITH PHYSICAL REFERENTS)	SYMBOLIC OUTCOMES (ATTITUDES, SENTIMENTS, VALUES, PERCEPTIONS)
EXTERNAL CONTROL BASED ON POWER, DEPENDENCE	LARGE EFFECT PREDICTED BY RESOURCE DEPENDENCE, NATURAL SELECTION, AND OPERANT CONDITIONING APPROACHES.	SMALL EFFECT.
MANAGEMENT CONTROL DERIVED FROM LANGUAGE AND SYMBOLIC ACTION	SMALL EFFECT BECAUSE OF ENVIRONMENTAL CONSTRAINTS AND SOCIAL SYSTEM SIZE AND COMPLEXITY.	LARGE EFFECT PREDICTED BY THEORIES OF ATTITUDE FORMATION CHANGE AND APPROACHES EMPHASIZING THE SOCIAL CONSTRUCTION OF REALITY.

one important research issue is the extent and conditions of linkage between symbolic and substantive outcomes in organizations.

One potentially troublesome theoretical issue in this argument about two levels of analysis involves the ability to distinguish substantive outcomes from symbolic results. It might be argued, for instance, that if a group is satisfied with a symbolic gesture, then the gesture or symbol itself is of substantive importance to the group and cannot be distinguished from any other outcome. Such an approach, however, confuses an attitude (the satisfaction of some social actor) with a behavior (the allocation of some resource, for example). The argument would seek to define a potentially objectively measurable quantity in terms of how it is perceived. The whole thrust of the position taken here is that the two levels of analysis are only loosely linked. Thus, substantive outcomes refer to actions, activities, tangible, measurable results—salary allocations, capital or operating budget allocations, the allocation of chief executive positions. Symbolic outcomes are, in contrast, assessed by sentiments of affect, by satisfaction, by values, and by beliefs. The fact that an allocation of resources can at once be consistent with the organization's power-dependence relations but still leave those who have received less well satisfied speaks to the capacity of management to legitimate and rationalize actions, but should not be confused with analyses of actual allocation outcomes.

What is being suggested is that there are two distinct levels of analysis of organizations. One level involves the prediction of actions taken within the organization—decisions that have observable, substantive outcomes in the sense of having objective, physical referents. The second level involves predicting and understanding how such organizational activities are perceived, interpreted, and legitimated. The study of organizational activity at each level is itself a useful undertaking. It is important to understand how organizational benefits and resources get allocated. At the same time, it is important to understand how such allocation patterns become perceived and justified by the organizational participants. In such analyses, however, care must be taken to keep the two perspectives as loosely linked in theory as they undoubtedly are in actual ongoing organizations.

The cognitive approach to the study of organizations, then, appears to be fruitful for examining the process by which the management of meaning is accomplished. It is this management task of meaning creation and maintenance that will be explored in greater detail below. At the same time, perspectives stressing external constraints and resource dependencies (Pfeffer and Salancik, 1978) are probably more useful for understanding substantive outcomes in organizations. And, because there is some connection between the two levels even though weak, further analysis is required to delineate the relationship between symbolic action and substantive outcomes.

ELEMENTS OF A COGNITIVE THEORY OF MANAGERIAL ACTION

The basic argument of a cognitive approach to the analysis of administrative action is: 1) social and organizational realities are, in part, outcomes of processes of social construction; 2) organizations, among other social entities, can be viewed as systems of shared meanings, entities in which there exists a shared consensus concerning the social construction of reality; 3) one of the tasks of management and a critical administrative activity involves the construction and maintenance of systems of shared meanings, shared paradigms, and shared languages and cultures; 4) language, symbolism, and ritual are important elements in the process of developing shared systems of belief and meaning, and become the focus and object of much administrative work; 5) a given organizational system's meanings are in contact, competition, and conflict with alternative views and belief systems held by other groups and in other organizations; which implies that 6) one of the elements of competition and conflict among social organizations involves the conflict between paradigms, defined as systems of beliefs or points of view. In the sections that follow, we provide some explication and evidence for each of these parts of the argument.

The Social Nature of Organizational Realities

Numerous authors from a variety of disciplines have noted the inherently social nature of much of organizational reality. Although physical factors of the organization, such as the hours employees work, the amount of money they are paid, the location and content of task activities, the resources that are exchanged within and across organizational boundaries, constrain the extent to which events can be reinterpreted and reconstructed, such physical realities are far from binding in the determination of beliefs and attitudes.

The examples of social effects on perceptions of reality are numerous, and those reviewed here are selected primarily to highlight certain important theoretical and empirical issues that remain to be developed and explored in analyzing the processes by which reality becomes socially constructed. Social effects refer to the processes by which individual attitudes and perceptions are impacted by others in the environment. One important form of social effect on perception is informational social influence (Festinger, 1954), in which an individual, confronted by a situation of ambiguity, uses the perception and beliefs of others as anchors and as referents.

In reviewing the extant literature on task design and its effects on motivation and in proposing an alternative formulation, Salancik and Pfeffer (1977b; 1978) noted that the content and dimensions of jobs were partly the result of perceptions that were subject to social influences. First, the individual's social environment may provide cues as to which dimensions might be used to characterize the work environment. Whether one characterizes jobs using dimensions such as variety, autonomy, feedback, and skill required or dimensions such as pay, social usefulness, effort required, and physical surroundings is in part under the control of a social environment in which some dimensions become talked about and other dimensions are ignored and thus are not as salient. Second, the social environment may provide information concerning how the individual should weight the various dimensions—whether autonomy is more or less important than variety of skill, whether pay is more or less important than social usefulness or worth. Third, the social context provides cues concerning how others have come to evaluate the work environment on each of the selected dimensions. Whether a given job situation provides or does not provide autonomy, variety, or high pay is as much a matter of social perception as it is a function of the specific job. And fourth, it is possible that the social context provides direct evaluation of the work setting along positive or negative dimensions, leaving it to the individual to construct a rationale to make sense of the generally shared affective reaction.

Several experimental studies have begun the process of exploring the social construction of work. O'Reilly and Caldwell (1979), for instance, gave students two conditions of a task involving the processing of admissions files. In the unenriched condition, the students merely recorded information. In the enriched condition, students had more decision-making authority. The authors were able to show with a set of control subjects that the two tasks did significantly differ according to the Hackman and Oldham (1975) dimensions. In the experiment, subjects randomly assigned to either the enriched or unenriched condition were exposed to information from another that indicated that the task was either interesting and challenging or was not. O'Reilly and Caldwell reported that job perceptions and affective reactions to the job were affected more strongly by the presumed social information than by the task itself. White and Mitchell (1979), in a replication of this study, obtained similar results.

The fact that social cues were important in affecting perceptions of tasks is supportive of the position that realities are socially constructed. But, substantial additional work remains to be done. One issue concerns the dimensions of work environments that are more or less susceptible to the form of informational social influence exemplified in these studies. Festinger (1954) argued that a process of social communication would be particularly used when physical reality was not available for anchoring one's beliefs or judgments. In these studies, relatively nonspecific task dimensions were subject to social cueing. After all, the very concepts of variety, autonomy, and so forth are matters of judgment and perception—there are clearly few objective or physical referents to address the issue of how much autonomy a job has. Issues such as pay, the level of physical or mental effort required, the physical comfort of the work environment, may be somewhat less subject to the type of social influence observed. A second issue concerns the relative effect of various types of social influence. As noted above, the social context can provide a person with information about what dimensions should be used to characterize a setting, which of these dimensions are more important, the value of the environment along those dimensions, and the general affective reaction to be expected in the environment. In the studies described, several of these components were present simultaneously. Thus, an important study would involve separating these four effects and estimating their relative importance in the process of socially constructing definitions and evaluations of contexts.

Another important class of variables has to do with the degree of consensus characterizing social perceptions. In the landmark conformity experiments (Asch, 1958), it was found that the presence of even one person who took the subject's position dramatically reduced conformity. In the present instance, it is informational social influence that is operating (Smith, 1973), but similar questions can be raised: what is the effect of varying degrees of uniformity of perception on the social construction process?

It is clear that noting social effects on perceptions of reality is insufficient for the long run. Much more explication is needed to assess how such socially constructed realities are created and the importance of information salience, evaluations, consensus, and characteristics of the dimensions being constructed in this process.

Although we have thus far focused on the task-attribute literature, there are other examples in the research literature illustrating the importance of the social context in developing definitions of the situation. For instance, the literature on pay equity (Adams, 1965; Goodman and Friedman, 1971) has argued that perceptions of fair, overpaid, or underpaid conditions result from a process of social comparison, so that definitions of equitable treatment are socially anchored if not socially derived. Theories of aspiration level (e.g., March and Simon, 1958: 183) have maintained that one determinant of a person's level of aspiration, which in turn determines the experiencing of psychological success or failure, is the amount received by others in the individual's environment. And, the extensive literature on relative deprivation (e.g., Stouffer *et al.*, 1949) also indicates the importance of the social context for anchoring and defining individuals' perceptions of their own situations (also see the chapter by Martin in this volume).

The focus on the social processes involved in perceptions of the world can provide insights which may potentially resolve some troublesome empirical results. Organizational researchers have focused on environmental uncertainty as an important determinant of organizational structure and decision processes. One of the controversies characterizing this literature is how uncertainty is to be measured—whether in terms of perceived environmental uncertainty or in terms of some presumably more objective characteristics of the environment such as the amount of change or variability. One of the more troubling results has been the finding that neither Lawrence and Lorsch's instruments (1967) nor Duncan's (1972) scales can be validated using external criteria (Tosi, Aldag, and Storey, 1973; Downey, Hellriegel, and Slocum, 1975). Two points can be made about this literature. The first is that it is scarcely surprising that there is any less convergence between perceived and externally defined characteristics of the environment than there is between perceived and externally defined job dimensions. It is likely that the amount of environmental uncertainty registered is partially a function of the amount of uncertainty socially constructed. And it is particularly important to note that most of the studies of perceived environmental uncertainty have used single respondents per organization or operating unit. It is likely that environmental uncertainty is defined through a process of social construction, and attempts to understand the determinants of perceived uncertainty might well begin by focusing on processes of social consensus and social definition of situations in much the same way as others have done for the task characteristics and motivation literature.

Organizations as Systems of Shared Meanings

If reality is socially constructed (Berger and Luckmann, 1967), then one of the important defining characteristics of organizations is that within an organization, there are consensually shared perceptions and definitions of the world. The earliest definitions of organizations stressed the importance of goals as an integral, defining characteristic. Thus, for example, Zedeck and Blood (1974), Blau and Scott (1962), and Parsons (1956) all distinguished organizations from other social entities by the emphasis on coordinated activity to accomplish some purpose or set of purposes. Thompson and Tuden (1959) have pointed out that there are two elements of organized decision making: 1) whether there is consensus about goals or values; and 2) whether there is consensus about beliefs concerning cause-effect relations, or the organization's technology. It is maintained here that it is possible that either or both forms of agreement may define an organization, but that for a variety of reasons, consensus about cause-effect relations may be easier to attain and hence constitute a more fundamental property of organizations. Certainly, there is ample literature to document the lack of goal consensus within organizations (e.g., March, 1962; Pfeffer and Salancik, 1978). Different organizational participants or subunits may have different values or objectives, but as long as the inducements offered to these participants are greater than the contributions demanded (March and Simon, 1958), the organizational coalition will be viable (Cyert and March, 1963).

Yet another way of defining organizations is by focusing on the extent of consensus on identity and organizational boundaries. Aldrich (1971), for instance, has argued that boundaries and boundary maintenance are fundamental for organizations. Agreement or disagreement on inclusion, exclusion, and the degree of membership of various social actors, as well as the control the organization has over such exclusion or inclusion are important properties. One way in which identity and inclusion become known and developed is through the articulation of an ideology or world view and the acceptance of that view, at least to some degree, by those included in the organization.

Boundaries can be defined and measured in a number of different ways, including the frequency of contact and communication (Deutsch, 1953), the extent to which behavior of a social actor is under the organization's control (Pfeffer and Salancik, 1978), and now, it is being suggested, by the degree of acceptance of a distinguishing ideology, perception of the world, or distinctive organizational paradigm. One of the results of more frequent communication intensity is likely to be the development, through informational social influence, of a more common set of understandings about the organization and its environment. These understandings, these shared meanings, provide organizational participants with a sense of belonging and identity as well as demarcating the organization from its environment and assisting in the control and commitment of those within the organization.

Though organizations are described in global terms, it is important to recognize that organizations have subunits which may have their own ideologies, shared meanings, and subparadigms. Thus, just as communication or the extent of control can define subunit boundaries as well as larger social system boundaries, so can commonalities in paradigm or shared definitions of the situation define and distinguish organizational subunits. Although the point will not be repeated, it should be clear that the arguments made for total organizations can be made, though to a lesser degree, with respect to subunits within those organizations.

Brown (1978: 373) has explicitly defined the organization using the concept of paradigm:

> . . . may lie in the concept of the organization as a paradigm. By paradigm we refer to those sets of assumptions, usually implicit, about what sort of things make up the world, how they act, how they hang together, and how they may be known. In actual practice, such paradigms function as a means of imposing control as well as a resource that dissidents may use in organizing their awareness and action. . . . In a similar fashion, organizational paradigms provide roles to be enacted in particular ways, in particular settings, and in particular relation to other roles.

In science, the concept of paradigm refers to shared exemplars, shared perceptions of research methodologies (ways of discovering knowledge) and shared perceptions of the organization of knowledge and what gaps in understanding exist (e.g., Lodahl and Gordon, 1972). Organizations also have shared exemplars, as in Wilkins' (1978) analysis of organizational stories and myths, and shared definitions of the technology for making organizational decisions and shared understandings of causality. Thus, organizations may be bound together more by a common perception of reality than by common values or preferences. As Weick (1979) has noted, an organization can be viewed as a body of jargon available for attachment to experience, which is to say, as a socially shared way of making sense of the environment.

In addition to the goal approach to conceptualizing organizations, another perspective has viewed organizations as cycles of interlocked or structured behaviors (Weick, 1969). The argument advanced here is that it is information and shared meanings which become structured in organizations, as well as behaviors. Indeed, it is through the development of shared meaning and understanding that the cycles of interlocked behaviors themselves become sensible and meaningful. Shared understandings may not be necessary for interlocked behaviors to emerge. Behaviors may become structured initially because of mutual interdependence. Shared understandings are likely to emerge to rationalize the patterns of behavior that develop, and in the absence of such rationalization and meaning creation, the structured patterns of behavior are likely to be less stable and persistent.

Weick noted that such interlocked cycles of behavior had to be renewed in order for the structuring of activities to persist over time. In an analogous fashion, the existence of a shared perspective within the organization also must be continually maintained, and the social concensus and shared beliefs which constitute the organization must be renewed and reconstituted. It might be predicted that shifts in power and control occur, and the organizational coalition becomes unstable or begins to fall apart primarily when social reality construction and sense-making activities have been neglected and ignored within the organization.

The conceptualization of organizations as shared systems of meaning and belief, characterized by a common paradigm raises three issues: 1) why might it be easier to organize activity around a shared definition of technology rather than around shared preferences; 2) how can the degree of paradigm consensus within organizations or organizational subunits be empirically assessed; and 3) what are some consequences of shared social realities for organizational action. These issues will be considered in turn.

We have already noted that Thompson and Tuden (1959) have distinguished decision-making situations according to their degree of consensus on goal and on action-consequence sequences. The argument advanced here is that consensus on technology is more readily achieved than consensus on values and preferences, at least in this culture. There are several reasons why this might be so. First, as Parsons and Smelser (1956) have noted, rationality is more than a description of a decision-making procedure, it is a valued social ideal. Educational organizations socialize individuals to learn from data, to explore and experiment to resolve questions, in short, to act as lay scientists. Recourse to facts, analysis, and expertise provides not only a basis of social power (French and Raven, 1968) but is also the inculcated mode of conducting choice. By contrast, values and preferences are taught to be matters of personal taste and individual discretion. Therefore, although it is not appropriate for me to argue with you about whether you prefer some outcome, it is both appropriate and expected that you should be convinced if I can produce data that indicate that a given course of action will produce some desired outcome. Power is developed and employed not merely by selectively advocating the use of criteria that favor one's position (Pfeffer, 1977b), but also by demonstrating that the course of action one is advocating is the most effective strategy for attaining the values and preferences of others involved in the decision process. In this endeavor, data and analysis demonstrating the effects of courses of action are crucial. The argument is that the very social norms governing rationality and choice processes make it more feasible to organize around definitions of technology rather than shared preferences which are deemed to be individual in nature.

Second, definitions of the situation are more malleable than preferences and values, though the latter can be changed. We know what we like with somewhat more certainty than we know how to achieve what we like. Informational social influence is particularly potent in resolving ambiguity and uncertainty about the state of events. Indeed, the irony is that when confronted with an uncertain and ambiguous choice situation, individuals actively engage in a process of informal social communication that will inevitably lead to their being influenced by the emerging social consensus they experience. It is, for example, more likely that one can be influenced by a social consensus concerning the characteristics of a job candidate than one can be influenced concerning the characteristics deemed to be most critical and important. Thus, in a situation of interpersonal influence, one might expect to see attempts made to claim that a given choice accomplishes or provides what the individual wants, rather than a strategy which directly attempts to change the preferences or values of the person.

Third, influencing perceptions of reality through informational influence is probably easier than attempting to produce consensus on preferences, which may develop from shared paradigms and perceptions in any event. One of the important aspects of organizations is that individuals in them are in a structured informational environment. The concept of structure implies a patterning of interaction (Thompson, 1967), which in turn implies that access to information is restricted and controlled. Organizations develop and implement information systems, reporting forms, and accounting conventions that determine what is measured and how the world is analyzed and viewed. These information systems and structures determine to some degree how causality is perceived and what elements of the environment are noticed (Pfeffer and Salancik, 1978: Ch. 4). This control over the presentation and definition of information, and the control over interaction patterns, renders organizational members more likely to develop shared perceptions and belief systems about the environment in which they operate. Therefore, for reasons of social legitimacy, ease of influence, and because of the very nature of what organizations control—information and interaction—it is likely that organizing around common perceptions of cause-effect relations will be more readily accomplished than organizing around shared values and preferences. This may be why there are more utilitarian than normative organizations (Etzioni, 1961).

Measurement of the Level of Paradigm Consensus

Although all organizations probably have some degree of paradigm consensus, it is likely that as in the case of scientific disciplines, some organizations are characterized by more or less such consensus. Lodahl and Gordon (1972; 1973) found that the degree of paradigm development or consensus characterizing a scientific discipline had numerous effects on the organization and operation of departments representing these various disciplines. Others have also found that the differences in paradigm development are related to differences in decision making (Yoels,

1974; Pfeffer, Salancik, and Leblebici, 1976; Pfeffer, Leong, and Strehl, 1977). Differences in the degree of organizational paradigm consensus may lead to similar differences in decision making and operations. In order to explore such differences, measures of consensus need to be developed. Lodahl and Gordon (1972) employed a questionnaire in which consensus was assessed directly. A similar process might be employed in organizations, in which consensus in definitions of major issues, beliefs about causality, and beliefs about data and data sources could be measured. Such a process, however, is time-consuming and costly and relies to some extent on a subjectively perceived level of social consensus.

Recently, Pfeffer, Salancik, and Moore (1979) developed archival indicators of paradigm development for scientific fields. The two types of indicators employed were: 1) parsimony in communication (measured in the specific case by the length of dissertations and dissertation abstracts), and 2) the level of integration and interdependence of activity (measured by the length of the longest sequence of prerequisite courses in the department). The rationales underlying the two types of indicators are reasonably straightforward. Scientific disciplines in which there is greater agreement on the underlying paradigm of the field should be characterized by briefer scientific communication. With a shared set of understandings about the definition of concepts, important research problems, and research methodologies, less time and space must be devoted to explicating definitions, developing theoretical arguments, and defining and justifying variables and their measurement. By contrast, in fields in which there is less paradigm consensus, each author must justify the importance of his or her particular research, must explicate the concepts and their measurement in greater detail, and must provide more rationale for the arguments advanced as well as more examples. Beyer (1978), in a study of the operation of journals in two social sciences and two physical sciences, observed that the average length of journal articles was less in the two physical sciences. Pfeffer, Salancik, and Moore (1979) employed the dissertation and the dissertation abstract as two examples of standardized communication in scientific disciplines. Their index of paradigm development correlated highly with the ranking produced by the perceptual measures used by Lodahl and Gordon (1972).

The second indicator, the level of integration of knowledge, measured by the length of the longest chain of prerequisite courses, reflects the ability of those working within the field to agree on an elaborated set of educational stages involved in developing knowledge of the discipline. Such agreement on a longer chain of prerequisite courses requires and presumes a higher degree of consensus on the content of the field and its appropriate sequencing. In fields characterized by less highly developed paradigms, it would be difficult to obtain agreement even on the content of the discipline, let alone on a long chain of sequenced educational activities to produce a level of competence in the discipline. Pfeffer, Salancik, and Moore (1979) observed excellent convergence between the indicator of knowledge integration and the indicators of language parsimony, providing further confidence in the validity of the indicators of the level of paradigm development.

In applying these concepts to business firms and other nonacademic organizations, the issue is one of finding equivalent measures. With respect to the indicator of language parsimony, it is necessary to uncover standard, recurring written communication activities such as budget requests, performance reports, requests for personnel, and so forth. Organizations in which there are shared beliefs about the relevant data, analyses, and about the technology that governs the organization's operations should be characterized by briefer communications because much of what might otherwise require explication is taken for granted and known as part of the organization's shared culture. In addition to language parsimony, the shared culture may be indexed by the number and frequency of use of terms which are known within the organization but not familiar to those outside. Most people are familiar with the fact that military and government agency personnel speak and write using abbeviations and acronyms for agencies and programs. Similarly, one of the functions of socialization into various professions is to provide the entrant with terminology that enables him or her to communicate efficiently with others within the profession in language which is less accessible to those not in the profession. Law and medicine are clearly excellent examples of this specialized language and its socialization effects.

It is important to distinguish between the parsimony or efficiency of communication and the amount of communication. Although shared cultures and a common paradigm may be characterized by briefer and more specialized communication, at the same time communication frequency may be actually higher than in social systems in which beliefs are not as widely shared. The frequency of communication is itself one way in which a common culture and set of beliefs develop, and these shared beliefs in turn facilitate communication among the members of the organization.

The level of integration of activity in a nonacademic organization poses an even more difficult problem of generalizing the indicator used in the academic context. The existence of a shared culture, it might be suggested, is indexed jointly by the degree of differentiation and integration present within the organization. Specialization and the division of labor require some basic agreement on the components of the task and how these components are interrelated. Without consensus on the nature and technology of the organization's work, differentiation and specialization of function are less feasible. At the same time, without a high degree of integration within the organization, this division of labor may represent the development of subparadigms within the organization rather than a common understanding shared among organizational participants. Lawrence and Lorsch (1967) have suggested that differentiation and integration are independent concepts. The indicator of the degree of paradigm development suggested would be the extent to which the organization scored high on both indicators.

Wilkins (1978) used stories, myths, and sagas to measure the degree of shared culture within two business firms. Certainly the extent to which common stories and exemplars are used and the extent to which there are shared perceptions about causality and about the organization and its relation to the environment would evidence paradigm consensus. Bougon, Weick, and Binkhorst (1977) developed the concept of the causal map as a way of empirically representing perceptions of reality. In their study of a jazz orchestra, the causal maps were assessed by asking individuals to indicate the relationship among concepts and events. A measure of shared paradigms, then, is the extent to which the causal maps within the organization are similar.

What seems to be required are empirical studies in which the various indicators of organizational paradigm consensus—parsimony in communication, common stories and myths, similar causal maps, a high level of differentiation and integration—are compared to validate the concept. Then, with some general indicators, it is possible to explore the ways in which paradigm consensus affects organizational variables such as the type of control employed, forms and outcomes of decision making, and organizational structures.

Institutionalization as a Consequence of Shared Paradigms

One way of measuring the extent to which paradigms are shared within an organization is by the consequences of such consensus, and one important consequence involves the institutionalization of beliefs, structures, and activities. Kuhn's (1970) description of paradigm change in the sciences may be quite descriptive of organizational change as well. Once a paradigm is established, it requires a lot of disconfirmation and challenge to undo the established patterns of analysis, data collection, and choice of activities. Similarly, organizations which have well-developed paradigms may have more institutionalized structures and activities, less adaptable to shifts in organizational environments or contingencies.

The institutionalization of beliefs and activities has not been frequently empirically examined. But Zucker (1977) in an innovative experimental study illustrated the concept of institutionalization in a manner quite consistent with the argument developed here. Jacobs and Campbell (1961) had employed the mechanism of the autokinetic effect used by Sherif

(1935) to study conformity to examine the persistence of cultures over experimental generations. Using a varying number of initial confederates in an experimental group, Jacobs and Campbell established initially extreme estimates of the distance an actually stationary point of light appeared to move. In successive generations, one of the confederates was replaced by a new, naive subject, and the replacement continued sequentially until all new subjects were in the group providing the distance estimations. Jacobs and Campbell found that the initial estimates of light movement decayed fairly rapidly to the estimates provided by subjects performing the task by themselves.

Zucker, in addition to replicating the basic Jacobs and Campbell design, also used two additional conditions. In the organizational context condition, the following was added to the instructions (Zucker, 1977: 732): "This study involves problem solving in model organizations. You will be participating with another organizational member. . . ." In the office condition, the organizational context instructions were supplemented with: "Large organizations also place members in different positions. . . . The model organization in which you will participate also has this feature . . . the member who has spent the most time in the organization will be the Light Operator." Zucker found that the transmission and maintenance of cultural understandings, represented by distance estimates, as well as the resistance of these understandings to change was higher in the organizational context condition than in the standard condition and higher still in the office condition.

Zucker (1977: 726) argued:

> . . . social knowledge once institutionalized exists as a fact, as part of objective reality, and can be transmitted directly on that basis. For highly institutionalized acts, it is sufficient for one person simply to tell another that this is how things are done. Each individual is motivated to comply because otherwise his actions and those of others in the system cannot be understood. . . .

What her experiment demonstrates is that identifying action with the concept of organization, and even more so with the concept of office or position, institutionalizes the action. Zucker called attention to the fact that the institutionalization of meaning was a variable. And the results of the experiments indicate what is meant by the concept of organization as a system of shared meanings and beliefs.

In analyzing why structures of interlocked behaviors, once established, were relatively stable, Weick (1969) argued that such structures of behavior provided certainty and predictability for the social actors so interstructured. A similar argument can be made for why meaning structures, once established, become resistant to change. The system of meaning, through the organizational paradigm, provides a way of understanding the world for those within the organization. This understanding is shared with others and thus binds the individual to the collectivity and at the same time this sharing provides reassurance for the veracity of the beliefs. If such understandings are consonant with the shared structures of behavior, either shaping such behaviors or being shaped by them, then a challenge to the shared system of beliefs both challenges the actions taken within the social structure and threatens to introduce increased uncertainty and ambiguity into the situation. Given the certainty and social cohesion they facilitate, it is quite understandable why shared paradigms or systems of meaning and belief come to have great stability and resistance to change.

The Task of Management

If organizations are systems of shared meanings and beliefs, and if they are organized through the development of shared paradigms, then clearly one important administrative activity is the development of such understandings within organizations. Weick (1979) has made a similar argument when he noted that managerial work could be viewed as managing myths, symbols, and images and when he argued that the manager may be more evangelist than accountant. Pondy (1978), writing about leadership, has explicitly developed the argument that leadership (or management or administration) involves a large component of symbolic activity. One of the tasks of a manager or leader is to provide a label and an explanation for organizational activity:

> . . . the effectiveness of a leader lies in his ability to make activity meaningful for those in his role set—not to change behavior but to give others a sense of understanding what they are doing and especially to articulate it so they can communicate about the meaning of their behavior. . . . If in addition the leader *can put it into words*, then the meaning of what the group is doing becomes a *social* fact. . . . This dual capacity . . . to make sense of things *and* to put them into language meaningful to large numbers of people gives the person who has it enormous leverage (Pondy, 1978: 94–95).

The activity of management is viewed as making what is going on in the organization meaningful and sensible to the organizational participants, and furthermore developing a social consensus and social definition around the activities being undertaken. Management involves more than labeling or sense making—it involves the development of a social consensus around those labels and the definition of activity.

This task of management is directed both internally, to produce organized collective action, and externally, as part of a process of legitimating the organization in its larger social context (e.g., Dowling, 1978). One of the important ways of generating external support for a given organization is to make that organization's operations and outcomes appear to be consonant with prevailing social values and useful to the larger social system. Such external legitimation can be accomplished through explicating an organizational paradigm in a way that makes it consonant with prevailing social expectations, as well as through identification of the organization with socially valued and accepted individuals, institutions, and methods of operation (Dowling and Pfeffer, 1975).

This discussion of the task of management is necessarily abstract, as the argument being developed is a general one. However, three concrete examples can be provided to illustrate what the concept in action entails. The first two involve a school of business administration that has perceived itself and is perceived by others as being more research-oriented, more quantitative and theoretical, and somewhat less professional and applied than many other such schools. Also, the school, because of previous decisions to remain as one of the social sciences on campus, does not have a separate salary scale and so suffers in comparison with the salaries offered at other schools of business.

The first example deals with the change in the orientation of the school. Because of the need to attract increasing amounts of resources from alumni and the business community, it became necessary for the school to shift, to some degree, its curriculum, values, criteria for promotion, and activities to undertake actions that would be more responsive and consonant with the criteria used by the business community in contrast to the academic community in evaluating the organization. In changing the thrust of the organization, it was necessary to develop a paradigm that would both legitimate the organization's new role to its external environment as well as to forestall internal opposition to the change. One professor in the school developed the term, "theory-based professionalism," to describe what the school was about. Note that this conception retains the historical emphasis on theory and scholarship, incorporates the notion of professionalism, and can serve as a device for making sense of activities within and outside of the particular organization. The development of a language and concept that makes sense out of the activities the school needed to undertake is, it seems, an important if not critical part of the management task. The successful development of a new paradigm both provides external legitimation and hence support as well as serving to motivate and direct internal action.

The second example deals with how the salary situation was managed. Given a relatively cosmopolitan faculty and severe salary differentials, it was scarcely feasible to argue that the school's salaries were not, in fact, lower. But the fact of lower salaries can have many meanings. It may mean that the school is in a relatively lower power position with respect to the campus or those who make salary decisions. It may mean that earlier decisions that created this position were incorrect. It may mean that the present inability to remedy the salary situation calls into question the administrative competence of the current leaders of the school. It may mean that the school is going to face a situation of imminent decline. However, it was a somewhat different social definition of the situation that was developed within the school. The social consensus emerged that the school had a uniquely favorable intellectual environment which stimulated research and creative thought. This environment was a product of the school's unique relationship with the rest of the campus, enhanced by its comparable, low salaries, and by its emphasis on research and scholarship to the neglect of consulting and fund raising. This social definition was developed through continually articulating stories which illustrated its reality and by a constant repetition of the theme. In the best traditions of the insufficient justification literature (Staw, 1974), the argument was made that if persons were joining and remaining in an organization that demonstrably offered fewer extrinsic rewards, it must be the unique, intrinsically rewarding atmosphere which served as an attraction. And, in contrast to the unmanaged insufficient justification experiments, leaders within the organization took pains, at every opportunity, to make just this argument. Thus, commitment to the institution was managed by managing a social definition of the situation.

Note that the interpretation provided might be a conscious and strategic reinterpretation (or, perhaps, misinterpretation) of cause-effect relations. The real cause of the lower turnover in the presence of poor salaries could be geographic area and not any intrinsic quality of the school. But by providing a specific interpretation of the observed reality, the administration of the school was able to legitimate and enhance the school's position to those both inside and outside of the organization.

The third example deals with a failure of a set of administrators to effectively explicate the organizational subunit's paradigm. After a great deal of controversy, the recommendation was made in 1974 to close the School of Criminology on the campus of the University of California at Berkeley, and after some demonstrations and protests, the school was subsequently closed. Many reasons might be given for the closing, including the failure of the school to develop a professional constituency, its radical faculty and students, and its record of perceived research and scholarship problems. But of the three reasons given in a report on the closing of the school, one of the reasons relates directly to the failure to develop a defined and consensually shared definition and identity of the subunit:

> Second, the faculty of Criminology has been unable to agree on its educational objectives or to provide a stable and systematic curriculum that reflects a broadly

shared view of the field. These weaknesses may be attributable to the state of criminology generally, but it appears that continuing disagreement within the faculty has prevented the establishment of common goals and would continue to do so (Committee on Educational Policy, 1974: 2).

The other two reasons given in the report have to do with the failure to develop linkages with the practicing professionals in the field and issues of scholarship. The explanation for the demise of the school is probably that the failure to develop a paradigm interacted with the other two issues to make the elimination of the subunit more easily accomplished. In the absence of a consensually shared paradigm but with a professional constituency and with perceived research stature, the issue of eliminating the school would probably not have arisen. But once the issue did arise, the presence of a developed paradigm within the school would probably have made the task of abolishing this subunit more difficult. Thus, the management task of developing a shared paradigm and system of beliefs within the organization can be, in the presence of external threats, critical to the survival of the organization.

The Role of Language in the Social Construction of Reality

In the management activity of developing shared systems of belief and meaning within the organization, the use of language is important. As noted in a frequently quoted passage, "Sharing a language with other persons provides the subtlest and most powerful of all tools for controlling the behavior of these other persons to one's advantage" (Morris, 1949: 214). Pondy has argued, "Language is after all one of the key tools of social influence" (1978: 91). In examples just employed, the importance of language and labeling is evident. The development of the terminology, "theory-based professionalism," was critical in justifying and explaining to those within and outside the organization the sense of the organization's activities. And, the labeling of a resource-poor environment as intellectually stimulating facilitated those in that environment coming to terms with their commitments.

Indeed, it is possible to argue that one of the ways in which shared beliefs, paradigms, and cultures are manifest and created is through shared language. It is possible to think of organizations as entities in which language is shared, and through this shared language, a common set of beliefs and understandings. The use of specialized language to develop a common identity in the socialization process is clearly visible in the professions. There is no reason to believe that a similar use of language is not part of the socialization process in organizations more generally. In this process, the individual is inculturated into the paradigms and meanings shared within the organization.

Perhaps no other analyst has devoted the amount of attention to the role of language in the administrative process as has Edelman. The view of organizations taken in this chapter is that organizations are coalitions and politics is one of the most prominent and important processes of organizational activity. If the political nature of organizations is accepted, then Edelman's work on the use of language in broader political contexts becomes quite relevant. Edelman (1964: Ch. 6) saw language as a catalyst for focusing and developing interests and points of view. He wrote, "Political argument, when it is effective, calls the attention of a group with shared interests to those aspects of their situation which make an argued-for line of action seem consistent with the furthering of their interests" (p. 123). If management is the activity of rationalizing and making sense of activity, then language is a vehicle through which such rationalization occurs.

Edelman made two other points about language which are important for understanding administrative action. First, language is an important substitute for the use of raw power or brute force. "Force signals weakness in politics, as rape does in sex. Talk, on the other hand, involves a competitive exchange of symbols, referential and evocative, through which values are shared and assigned and coexistence attained" (1964: 114). Language is used to provide meanings and justifications for desired behaviors that render them more likely to occur without the reactance the use of force might engender.

Second, Edelman saw political language as obfuscating and clouding analytical processes. Political language was viewed as symbolic language, evocative and motivating, but not producing an accurate assessment of self-interest. He argued that political speech was a ritual which dulled the critical faculties rather than sharpening them (1964: 124). Thus, the use of language in the administrative process was viewed as a way of providing symbols rather than substance to participants not closely involved in the political process. This analysis emerges quite clearly in his treatise on the war-on-poverty programs (Edelman, 1977) in which the general thesis was developed that social policies served primarily symbolic value while substantive activities continued to serve those with real power. Edelman saw the political process in terms of two sets of actors, those with a dominant position and clearly defined self-interest, and those more removed from the centers of authority and control with limited interest in and knowledge of political activities. The substance of programs served the former group, while the latter was placated with symbolic language and ritualized actions. The parallel to formal organizations is direct, with the dominant coalition (Thompson, 1967) being the vested interests, and the general employees, shareholders, customers, and public being those who receive primarily symbolic outputs from the organization.

It should be possible to trace the rise and diffusion of language and symbols across organizations as well as the frequency of their use. Such analyses can trace the integration and disintegration of organizations and sets of organizations, as well as providing information on the use of various symbols over time and across contexts.

One example of such an analysis would involve examining the annual reports of corporations in various industries and over time. For instance, one could examine what proportion of those pictures included in the report (not of officers and directors) include women or ethnic minorities. Such symbols of corporate concern for equal employment opportunity might be expected to increase over time as pressure for equal employment has intensified, and to vary by industry according to how strongly the industry relies on regulation and social legitimacy for its profits. It was shortly after the Bank of America signed a consent decree establishing a multimillion-dollar trust fund for the training and educational enrichment of female employees that their annual report featured a picture of a young woman who was working for the bank part-time and attending the Berkeley MBA program in part supported by these funds. Similarly, one might examine the language used in the reports (Lentz and Tschirgi, 1963) to describe and justify the corporation's activities. Content analyses are likely to reveal interesting differences in references to issues of social legitimacy such as pollution, equal employment, public service, and the level of profits both across industries and over time. Within a given industry, such as electric utilities, one can trace the diffusion of sections in the annual reports dealing with environmental concerns across companies. The analysis of language and symbols provides evidence on the origination and diffusion of various concerns and organizational responses to these concerns.

Causes of Interunit Conflict

The final part of the cognitive argument involves the examination of the interaction of separate organizational entities. One of the areas in which organizations compete is in which organization's paradigm or world view is to prevail. Every organization has an interest in seeing its definition of reality accepted in the larger social context, for such acceptance is an integral part of the legitimation of the organization and the development of assured resources. The basic prediction made is that organizations are more likely to be in conflict to the extent their paradigms differ. Organizations with basically similar perceptions should find it easier to transact with each other and to engage in various forms of cooperative activity, such as the exchange of personnel or engaging in joint ventures or joining the same interorganizational association. Conversely, such forms of cooperation should be less prevalent among organizations with differing paradigms.

One important empirical issue highlighted by this argument is the development of measures and metrics to assess similarity and differences in paradigms. The measures of language parsimony, activity interdependence, or shared beliefs all measure the extent to which paradigms are developed, or the extent of consensus concerning appropriate activities and methods. None of these measures, however, measures the specific content of the paradigm about which there is more or less agreement. Conflicts about competing paradigms are likely to be defined in terms of central issues concerning the operation of the organization, involving basic beliefs about the connections between actions and results. In this assessment, the causal map methodology (Bougon *et al.*, 1977) may be particularly useful.

In the educational context, paradigms might be defined in terms of the technology of education used, for instance, experiential, case, or lecture-discussion styles of presentation, or the distinction between theoretical sophistication versus practical relevance. If such distinctions were important to organizational belief systems, then one might predict more personnel movement and interorganizational cooperation among units that shared the same beliefs about educational technology. In business-firm settings, paradigms might involve the form and use of strategic planning methodologies, control and accounting systems, capital budgeting decision rules, or the reliance on mathematical operations research techniques for decision making. The prediction would again be that transactions of various kinds occur more frequently and more easily among organizations with similar paradigms or belief systems. This argument parallels Meyer and Rowan's (1977) discussion of institutionalized organizations. They argued that organizations that adopted the socially sanctioned practices and structures would be more successful in attracting resources from the environment. The difference in the argument developed here is that in some cases beliefs and standards of practice may not be fully shared among organizations—there may be disagreements about the usefulness of open classrooms, the case method, or linear programming. When such disagreements do occur, organizations that share critical beliefs about technology are more likely to transact with each other.

It is important to note that the form of conflict being described involves a conflict emanating from differences in perceptions of reality. Such conflict is likely to be waged through the mustering of data, expertise, and analysis to support the particular position favored. Such a conflict is likely to appear to be more restrained than conflict emanating from differences in fundamental values and preferences. In fact, differences in perceptions of reality may result from different preference and value systems, but this is probably not apparent. Consequently, the arguments can go on interminably, as each side musters new evidence and argumentation to support its position. The continuing debate between the Keynesian and monetarist economists illustrates this point.

WHY SYMBOLIC ACTION IS POSSIBLE

In the previous section, the argument was developed that reality was socially constructed and that one of the principal tasks of management was to construct and maintain systems of shared beliefs and meanings. Management involves the taking of symbolic action, and as Edelman has suggested in the case of political programs, some persons receive tangible benefits and others receive only symbolic outcomes from organizations. This suggests that, simply put, much organizational action is ritual and ceremony. For this to be true, it must be the case that at least some substantial portion of persons interested in the organization, including employees, customers and clients, and others must be unable to discern with any certainty whether or what they are obtaining from the organization. In other words, symbolic outcomes will suffice if those in contact with the organization are unable to discriminate reality from symbol. It is often the case that the outcomes received from the organization are difficult to assess precisely. Thus, symbolic action becomes possible and effective. Symbolic actions taken by management can be effective because 1) individuals or groups in contact with the organization may have uncertain, unstable, or undefined preferences; 2) organizations may systematically seek to avoid taking actions or providing data that might facilitate assessment; 3) individuals or groups in contact with the organization may be unable to discern what outcomes they are obtaining or the value of such outcomes; and 4) symbolic outcomes may be all that are desired by those making demands of the organization.

The Nature of Preferences for Organizational Actions

One reason why symbolic administrative action may be both appropriate and sufficient is that parties in contact with the organization may have unclear or unstable preferences for organizational actions or outcomes. March (1978) has expanded the critique of the rational decision-making literature from a concern with cognitive information processing limits to rationality to a concern with the nature of preferences. In contrast to theories of choice that dominate the economics and decision sciences literature, March argued that preferences may emerge as a consequence of action rather than guiding such action *a priori,* a point found also in Weick's (1969) discussion of retrospective rationality. Preferences may be discovered and uncovered through actions. Analogously, preferences may be discovered through what one obtains from an organization. An individual may not know whether he or she prefers work with variety, or a product with certain characteristics, or a certain rate of return on investment until such outcomes are received. If preferences are either unstable or unformed, it will be difficult for social actors to readily assess whether or not the organization, through its policies and outcomes, is fulfilling those preferences. Given an unclear idea of what is wanted, it may be difficult to discriminate symbolic from substantive action.

Avoidance of Assessment

Even if preferences are reasonably well formed, organizations may be able to get by with symbolic action if assessment of the action is difficult. One of the interesting aspects of many organizations is the efforts undertaken to systematically avoid assessment, especially assessment of outcomes that are of potential interest to various groups or individuals in contact with the organization.

Meyer and Rowan (1977) have noted, for instance, that educational organizations such as public school systems have systematically avoided assessment of the educational product. Publication of test scores by school on standardized reading and mathematics tests was, at least in California, initiated by the legislature over the opposition of the educational establishment. Assessment at the level of the individual teacher or classroom has still been resisted, as of this writing. Schools are scarcely the only organizations that have taken pains to avoid the collection and dissemination of data that would make assessment of real outcomes feasible or easy. Hospitals avoid the publication of mortality and morbidity figures, universities steadfastly avoided for some years collecting placement data for doctoral students in the humanities and social sciences, and police departments seldom widely publicize the proportion of serious crimes in their jurisdictions that are solved.

Nor are nonprofit or governmental organizations the only ones that engage in such behavior. Meyer and Rowan (1977) argued that the avoidance of assessment was part of a process involving the decoupling of the organization's internal activities from the external constraints on what its operations should look like, a characteristic of institutionalized organizations which had uncertain or unknown technologies. However, business firms also engage in similar avoidance of assessment, so that it is not clear that such practices are as limited as the Meyer and Rowan argument might suggest. One could do an interesting case study of the implementation of various Securities and Exchange Commission reporting requirements for business over time, with business opposing these disclosures at each stage. Things such as line of business reporting, making 10-K reports available to shareholders, the publication of historical and quarterly data in annual reports, the inclusion of lease and other long-term obligations, and fuller disclosure of adverse legal actions are all relatively recent inclusions in required financial disclosures.

One strategy of avoiding assessment, then, is simply keeping secret the information that might be necessary or useful for evaluating organizational results. However, since assessment is likely to be desired, a related strategy involves the selective release of information which is a) defined along criteria more favorable to the organization, b) measured along criteria which are more readily controlled by the organization, and c) acceptable to those interested in the organization. One example of such a strategy is the release of numerous indicators of inputs at the same time information about process and particularly outcomes is not released. For instance, hospitals, while refusing to divulge risk-adjusted mortality or morbidity, are willing to display figures on staffing ratios, capital equipment ratios, the proportion of board-certified physicians, the number of services provided, and so forth. Schools will report results in terms of the proportion of teachers with advanced (typically master's) degrees, the average per pupil expenditure, equipment per pupil, and similar indicators of input resource intensity. Note that in these cases, it is easier for the organization to manage the input resources than to actually affect results, which may require a knowledge of technology (the connections between actions and results) which is simply not possessed. Such indicators are likely to be acceptable to those in contact with the organization. This is because in the absence of defined preferences or clearly measured outcomes, organizations may be assessed in terms of the espoused goals or apparent effort. Edelman has written, "Willingness to cope is evidently central. Any action substitutes personal responsibility for impersonal causal chains and chance" (1964: 79). And George Gallup, quoted in Edelman (1964: 78), noted, "People tend to judge a man by his goals, by what he's trying to do, and not necessarily by what he accomplishes or by how well he succeeds." Organizations are also judged by what they apparently are attempting to do. An organization that tries to provide the best and most plentiful input resources can scarcely be faulted (or perhaps, even assessed) by what those resources actually accomplish.

Assessing organizations by reference to organizational inputs also occurs because those in contact with the organization probably can more readily control inputs as contrasted with attempting to control organizational processes or outcomes. In addition, many in contact with the organization come to believe that the organization knows its technology and has some expertise in understanding the transformation process from inputs to results. As Meyer and Rowan (1977) suggested, it is in almost no one's interest to test this latter assumption. Clearly, the organization and its management maintains discretion by promoting the belief that it possesses understanding of the technology of its operations, and has some comparative advantage with respect to knowledge about that technology. At the same time, belief in the organization's expertise provides those in contact with the organization a sense of security and psychological well-being. To know that the organization comprehends its own technology imperfectly is a prospect that is frightening because those in contact with the organization probably know and can readily learn very little more about the technology. Thus, the discrediting of the organization's knowledge can lead, in some instances, to a general loss of feeling of control over the organization's activities.

The use of secrecy and restriction of access to some information while at the same time providing other, more controllable and more favorable data, are practices that are buttressed by the development of various rationalizing mythologies which justify the policies. Myths are generally unquestioned, widely taught, and shared within the social context. The myths that justify the nonrelease of outcome or results data are numerous, and tend to be custom tailored to the situation. Release of student achievement data or the use of such data in evaluation, it is maintained, will tend to direct the educational process to teach to the tests, rather than to produce broadly trained young citizens. The release of salary data so that social equity comparisons can be made might engender unnecessary and unwanted internal competition and status hierarchies. The release of medical outcome data fails to take into account the complexity and uncertainty of medical service delivery technology. Each release or non-release of information can and customarily is justified by the development of some socially sanctioned explanation.

Uncertainty About Results

Related to the problems of undefined preferences and avoidance of assessment is the problem of ambiguity concerning what is being obtained from the organization and the value of that output. Such ambiguity may result from a social definition of expertise and professionalism which maintains that the client, customer, or member is not qualified either to determine what he or she wants or to evaluate the quality of the product or service delivered. That such professionalization is fundamentally a political process which accrues power to the organization or occupation so professionalized because it places the definition of satisfaction in the hands of those being evaluated has been recognized by other researchers (e.g., Benson, 1973). Expert or professionalized power can convey to those who are deemed to have such expertise or professional acumen the right and indeed the duty to define acceptable services or outcomes and by so doing, define for those evaluating the organization what their evaluations are.

Even in the absence of such professionalization, evaluation of what is being received may be difficult because organizational products may have multiple attributes. A product or service may have price as well as quality, and quality itself may be measured along many dimensions. Education both costs resources and has, as its results, levels of reading, mathematics, and skills in other subjects, as well as socialization into widely shared values and patterns of conduct. The multi-attribute nature of the assessment process inevitably makes assessment difficult. Medical care has both cost and quality components, and quality may have physiological and psychological components, at a minimum. The evaluation of business firms can occur along both long-run and short-run perspectives, and may depend upon the weighting given to market share, profits, social legitimacy, or the likelihood of future growth.

Of course, such uncertainty concerning the evaluation of organizations is exacerbated by the presence of undefined or ambiguous preferences and by the organization's ability to selectively define and present information relevant to its operations. But even in the absence of these two factors, the multi-attribute nature of organizational activities and outputs may make assessment more difficult than the average person or group, with limited contact and limited dependence on the organization, can or will deal with.

The Value of Symbolic Results

If evaluation is problematic because preferences are uncertain, data are hard to obtain and, even if obtained, require the making of complex multidimensional trade-offs, then a reasonable course of action may be to rely on surrogate measures of organizational benefits. Such surrogate measures may be the symbolic actions taken by organizational administrations. Symbolic responses may be desirable either because that is all those in contact with the organization really desire, or because of limited time and information, they are unwilling or incapable of discerning symbol from substance.

Downs (1957), in an effort to explain why small but committed and organized interests could get policies implemented that were inconsistent with the majority view, argued that for most people the policies in question were of little enough concern so that voting and other expressions of political preference would not be primarily affected by politicians' responses on that single issue. However, such was not the case for the smaller, but more interested group for whom the political policy adopted might have substantial economic consequences. Downs was able to derive, using a rational, economic approach, the result that it was not just the number of people who favored or opposed the issue, but also the intensity of concern that affected the adoption of policy in a democratic process. Edelman, using a different mode of analysis, came to the same conclusion. "The fact that large numbers of people are objectively affected by a governmental program may actually serve in some contexts to weaken their capacity to exert a political claim upon tangible values" (Edelman, 1964: 43). Both Downs and Edelman maintained that a large number of persons who share some but limited concern in the outcomes received are probably going to be unwilling to invest the time and energy required to monitor outcomes and to attempt to exert influence. For such social actors, symbolic responses may be sufficient to assure quiescence, as there is little incentive to look beyond the symbol given the limited concern over the outcome in question.

A similar argument is applicable in an organizational context. A consumer who buys an inexpensive product on an infrequent basis may well be satisfied by symbolic responses to complaints about product quality. The person has neither the reason nor the resources to invest in ascertaining whether the organization has really changed production or distribution practices. A letter of apology and perhaps a free sample or coupon is sufficient to assuage feelings of being wronged. Assessing organizational actions is an activity that takes resources and attention. It is unlikely to be undertaken except by those who stand to be significantly affected by what the organization actually does. Since most people are not so profoundly impacted, for most people, symbolic responses are sufficient given their limited involvement in knowing the organization.

Symbolic responses may also be sufficient because in the absence of the ability to specify precisely what is desired or to assess the multiple dimensions of organizational outputs, parties in contact with the organization may desire only some reassurance that their interests are being seriously considered within the organization. In this case, a symbolic response conveys information that the organization is responsive to the demands being made, and this symbolic gesture may be sufficiently reassuring.

Most students, for instance, have neither the time nor the inclination to get heavily involved in the running of universities, and have no interest in getting bogged down in the myriad details of administration. When they protest against investment policies, faculty evaluation policies, or resource allocation practices, a symbolic response which reaffirms their power in and importance to the university can convey a sense of efficacy that reassures them that their concerns will be heeded. The symbol, in this case, may be a surrogate for the substance, and may suffice to provide ratification of the importance of some constituent group, which may be what that group is primarily seeking.

Thus, symbolic action is possible because preferences are undefined or ambiguous, organizations may successfully avoid assessment, there may be uncertainty about what is being received from the organization and how to evaluate it, and symbolic outcomes may be sufficient given the limited aims or the limited interest of social actors in the organization. These factors, taken together, suggest that symbolic administrative responses may, in fact, be sufficient in most instances. Thus, a symbolic response may be reasonable given the situation confronted. Groups which make demands on the organization may be satisfied by the taking of symbolic action that leaves the manager with discretion over the allocation of actual resources within the organization. "It is not uncommon to give the rhetoric to one side and the decision to the other" (Edelman, 1964: 39).

THE CONSEQUENCES OF SYMBOLIC ACTION

All may not be illusion—or at least, the large component of managerial action that is symbolic can have real consequences. Individuals respond on the basis of perceptions, regardless of the veracity of these perceptions. The symbols and perceptions of reality once created and socially shared and institutionalized can become a basis on which decisions are made and actions are taken. Symbolic action can have consequences for the motivation and mobilization of support, for the diversion or satisfaction of demands, and for the implementation of change in organizations. In considering the potential consequences of symbolic action, external constraints and dependencies are implicitly held constant. As noted previously, research is required to determine the actual relationship between symbolic action, external constraints, and substantive outcomes.

Mobilization and Motivation

Symbolic action may serve to motivate individuals within the organization and to mobilize persons both within and outside of the organization to take action. The so-called "Hawthorne effect" provides one illustration of this phenomenon. The effect refers to the observation that individuals, when subjected to observation, change, and special treatment may respond with higher levels of performance regardless of the content of the changes implemented. Although there is some question about the scientific validity of the conclusions that were most often drawn from the original Western Electric studies (e.g., Carey, 1967), it does appear that the effect is reasonably robust and general across situations. Change signals that individuals are to be considered and treated differently, regardless of the content of the change. This signal of increased attention and importance may motivate more energetic action on the part of organizational participants.

King (1974) found that the effects of job enrichment as opposed to job enlargement programs on subsequent employee responses had more to do with the expectations surrounding the change than with the content of the specific job redesign per se. This finding is consistent with the argument that it is the symbolism or values associated with the event, rather than the content, that affects responses. It is this fact of the meaning conveyed by change that makes the evaluation of change so difficult—the placebo effect occurs in organizational contexts as well as in medicine.

Participatory decision making and cooptation, more generally, also provide examples of the effects of symbolic actions. One of the consequences of the placing of a representative from a group or organization on the focal organization's board is that this signifies the affiliation symbolically to the world and thus presumed support of the organizations for each other. This mutual identification between the organizations may lead to expectations and labeling effects that serve to reinforce the association between the organizations. Involvement of some constituency in decision making, even if such involvement is more symbolic than real, can have effects on developing commitment to decisions that are reached (Salancik, 1977) and on motivating actions in support of these decisions. Unfortunately, most studies of decision-making participation and of cooptation do not distinguish between the effects achieved through provision of real involvement or through symbolic identification with the decision process. The argument made here is that it is the symbolic involvement, as much as real choice and participation, that can produce commitment and supportive behavior.

Satisfaction of Demands

Symbolic actions may serve to mollify groups that are dissatisfied with the organization, thereby ensuring their continued support of the organization and the lessening of opposition and conflict. To the extent that such results are obtained, a symbolic gesture can be productive in generating real social support for the organization.

Edelman (1964; 1977) has described the creation of administrative agencies and social programs in just these terms. The creation of a regulatory or law-enforcing organization may convince some that action has been taken to monitor and control organizational activities. Thus, the groups that formerly were adversaries of the organization are quieted through the belief in the efficacy of the administrative agencies so created. Complaints about the conduct of lawyers lead to the establishment of bar association committees on judicial ethics with the formal responsibility of disciplining errant lawyers, with similar problems and similar results in the medical profession and in the accounting profession as well. Support for the profession now continues as the problems with professional malpractice are presumably remedied. The fact that few lawyers or doctors, up until very recently, were ever disciplined regardless of the grievousness of their conduct indicates that symbolic action rather than substantive results may suffice to ensure continued political support.

Analogous responses are visible within organizations. Universities establish ombudsmen to handle student complaints, privilege and tenure committees to protect professors from administrative capriciousness, and grievance procedures for students complaining of issues ranging from sexual harassment to unfair grading. In each instance, the aggrieved group is quieted by the appearance of an administrative structure to deal with the problem, regardless of whether anything is done. Business firms establish consumer affairs departments (Fornell, 1976), consumer hotlines, affirmative action offices, offices of public affairs (social responsibility), and thereby provide symbolic evidence that the demands of various interests are now to be dealt with within the organizations. There have been virtually no empirical studies of the effects of such symbolic responses on quieting demands and ensuring continued support or at least quiescence from others; such studies are clearly both possible and desirable.

The firing of managers in professional sports (Gamson and Scotch, 1964) is perhaps the classic example of a ritual activity which has consequences for public perceptions of team responsiveness and concern for performance. An interesting test of the effect of this symbolic response would be to see whether attendance improves upon firing some especially hated coach or manager, and particularly whether such improvement in attendance is greater than might be predicted from team performance after the change. It is more difficult to obtain support with the same organization and individuals that previously failed. A change, particularly at the top, may convey symbolic reaffirmation of improvement which may generate new support.

Implementation

The use of symbolic managerial action in the process of implementing change in organizations has been recognized in an insightful analysis by Peters (1978), in which he argued not only that symbolic administrative behavior was useful in accomplishing change, but that in fact such an approach to organizational change might be more effective than traditional change techniques such as management or organization development, strategic planning, or organizational redesign. Cohen and March (1974), in their analysis of university presidents, derived some rules of action that Peters built from in developing his perspective on implementation. Some of these techniques and their symbolic properties are delineated in Table 1.

The interpretation Peters provided of successful managerial action taken to change organizations is consistent with the arguments developed above. He maintained that ". . . . managing the daily stream of activities might be said to consist of the manipulation of symbols, the creation of patterns of activity, and the staging of occasions for interaction" (1978: 9).

The symbolic actions taken by management, then, can have consequences for the mobilization and motivation of support, for cooling off or placating opposition either inside or external to the organization, and for focusing and organizing activity within the organization to implement change. The focus of management as symbolic behavior, it is important to

Table 1. Symbolic Administrative Action and Its Explanation

Action	*Explanation for Effect*
Spend time on activity that is to be emphasized or defined as important	Time spent is one measure of the importance of a goal, and goals and objectives become the reality defining managerial action; also, time spent conveys to others the importance of the focus of the time.
Change or enhance the setting	A new setting conveys that something new is going on; an enhanced setting will convey the meaning that the activity now occurring is more consequential and important.
Exchange status for substance	Symbolic outcomes may be sufficient to ensure support of a relatively uninvolved group for the proposed action, if the conditions facilitating symbolic action are present.
Interpret history	Events have meaning only through interpretations; interpreting events as consistent with the definition of the problem or the solution can help develop a social consensus around the chosen course of action.
Provide a dominant value expressed in a simple phrase	Language can evoke support or opposition, can serve to organize social consensus, and can provide an explanation and rationalization for activity.

Adapted from Peters (1978)

recognize, does not imply that management is itself of little consequence. Rather, the focus on the symbolic facet of management action can help explain how and why management action is effective. As Peters argued, ". . . symbols are the very stuff of management behavior. Executives, after all, do not synthesize chemicals or operate lift trucks; they deal in symbols" (1978: 10).

METHODS OF MEANING CREATION: LANGUAGE, CEREMONIES, SYMBOLS, AND SETTINGS

If management as symbolic action is to be empirically examined, then the various outcroppings of symbolic administrative behavior will need to be identified so they can be observed and explained. Many administrative actions can have both real immediate effects and symbolic connotations, so this task of examining organizational symbolism is not easy. One potentially useful strategy involves identifying methods of meaning creation, developing hypotheses concerning the conditions of their use, developing hypotheses concerning the conditions under which they will be effective, and then proceeding to see what proportion of the variance in the occurrence or existence of such methods can be explained by the hypothesis. There are many such methods for meaning creation, and the ones considered here should be considered to be representative rather than exhaustive.

Organizational Restructuring: Symbols

Although Peters (1978) argued that redesign was a cumbersome tool for organizational change, organizational restructuring shares many of the same virtues of other change techniques he advocated. There are two approaches to the organizational redesign process. One is a technical approach, and seeks to produce a new organizational structure that is able to meet the problems that have arisen in the organization, perhaps for additional coordination among some subunits, for additional adaptability and responsiveness to market changes, or for some other structural solution to an operating problem. To successfully implement such a redesign, knowledge is required about what levels of interdependence and interaction are necessary, what levels of flexibility and responsiveness are desirable, and what organizational innovations or changes can produce the desired patterns of behavior. Such knowledge is not always available.

A second approach to organizational redesign, however, sees it as a symbolic, attention-focusing process. The very act of restructuring signifies a change in the organization's operations, which may satisfy the demands of clients or customers, owners, or others who were previously unhappy about outcomes being received from the organization. Additionally, the creation of new subunits with new titles permits emphasis to be given to new aspects of the organization's operation. A restructuring which creates a new product-development department, a consumer affairs department, or a public relations department provides visible manifestation to those inside and outside of the organization that the activity presumably within the purview of the newly created department has become more important to the organization.

Pfeffer's (1978) argument about the political aspect of organizational design leads logically to the consideration of the symbolic uses of design, if one accepts Edelman's (1971) argument that politics frequently involves the use of symbolic action. Change and restructuring provides symbolic reassurance that action is being taken. Such restructuring can alter the symbolic value given to different aspects of the organization's operation. Through such symbolic action, it is possible to both motivate and placate various interests in contact with the organization.

Executive Succession: Ceremonies

The occasion of executive succession provides numerous opportunities to manage the creation of meaning within organizations. The fact of involuntary succession, much like organizational redesign, provides symbolic ratification of the intention to change organizational operations, and presumably, the effectiveness of those operations. Scapegoating (Gamson and Scotch, 1964) occurs in organizations other than sports organizations. It is interesting to note how the complaints about organizational illegal political contributions and foreign bribery were readily satisfied by the firing of the chief executives of Gulf Oil and Northrop. In the case of Gulf, it became clear that such activities continued after the departure of Robert Dorsey, indicating that they were not all his responsibility. Nevertheless, although organizations are large, complex systems in which the control of any single individual is undoubtedly limited, demands for change and demands for retribution are typically satisfied by one or a few involuntary successions. This provides symbolic reassurance that the organization as a whole does not tolerate the deviant behavior or poor performance, which is frequently sufficient to placate critics.

The voluntary or involuntary departure of a chief administrator provides the occasion to select a replacement. This act of choosing a successor itself can take on important symbolic meaning with the appointment of search committees and with the expenditure of time and other resources on a search effort. Such expenditures reaffirm the importance of the position to both its potential new occupants and to others in the organization. This creation of the belief that the position is consequential is particularly important when the position incumbent is to be used as a scapegoat for organizational difficulties later on. Such ritualized activities are also particularly necessary when, in fact, the position has little power or effect. The activities to create meaning become more critical when such meaning would not otherwise emerge.

The inauguration of the successor may involve investiture rituals that further ratify the importance of the position and the incumbent. Such inaugurations may range from the pomp and circumstance involved in presidential inaugurations and the investiture of the Pope to parties, lunches, dinners and meetings that announce the choice of a new chief executive in a public or private organization.

Ceremonies of firing and replacement (Gephart, 1978) can help to placate groups from which the organization needs support as well as to signal changes in policies and practices to those who work within the organization. Such ceremonies are an important part of the management and creation of organizational belief systems.

Organization Development: Language

Though not recognized or at least not admitted by its principal practitioners, many of the techniques of organization development operate using symbols and settings in ways quite consistent with the argument developed in this chapter. A complete review of organization development from this perspective is beyond the scope of this chapter but examples can readily be provided.

First, Ouchi and Price (1978) have argued that organizational development is effective when and because it develops a philosophy or culture within the organization. They noted, ". . . a philosophy of management provides a form of control at once all-pervasive and effective because it consists of a basic theory of how the firm should be managed. Any manager who grasps this essential theory can deduce from it the appropriate response to any novel situation" (1978: 42). Thus, Ouchi and Price argued that organizational development should be focused on developing a shared philosophy or culture within the organization, and further implied that development activities tended to be successful only when they were so directed.

But, philosophies and cultures are created by the development of shared systems of meaning and belief, shared organizational paradigms. Thus, the symbolic, ritualized actions that account for the development of shared paradigms within organizations should be isomorphic with major, successful organizational development practices. Such is probably the case.

Many programs of job redesign use many of the symbolic aspects of management we have described. Committees are appointed, which serves to coopt various interests as well as to signify that a change is going to be made. Meetings are held, frequently involving participants who had never been brought together before, and sometimes held at sites away from the company. Such settings and new groups of actors also further signify the occurrence of change. Questionnaires are used to assess individual preferences. As Salancik and Pfeffer (1978) argued, such questionnaires may help to form these very preferences. As important as this priming effect, the questioning process itself provides further symbolic reassurance that changes are being made, and more importantly, that the opinions of employees are significant and will be heeded. Less is known or written about the dramaturgy with which proposed changes are introduced, but clearly the announcement of change, the restructuring of activities, and the promulgation that data from employees were used in formulating the change can serve to further symbolize employee involvement, importance, and organizational reform.

Survey-research-feedback has many of the same elements—the questionnaire which symbolizes the individual's beliefs and preferences are important; the new meetings which bring into being new settings that signify change; and the development of agendas around issues uncovered by the surveys which focus attention on change and implementation. Salancik and Pfeffer's argument about the effects of information saliency as an explanation for the efficacy of these change approaches captures only part of the process. It is not just a cognitive focusing of attention which is critical; it is also the symbolism of the process itself which placates and reassures organizational participants that they are important and potent actors in the organization.

The point is that many organizational activities, ranging from executive succession to organization development practices, can be productively analyzed from the perspective of management as symbolic action. The implication of this point is that understanding organizational language, settings, stories and sagas, ceremonies, and practices can be enhanced by considering the symbolic as well as the more directly behavioral causes and consequences of administrative behavior.

The Design of Physical Space in Organizations: Settings

As Peters (1978) noted in his discussion of the implementation process, skilled managers understand well the importance of physical settings for their symbolic value. The size, location, and configuration of physical space provide the backdrop against which other managerial activity takes place, and thereby influence the interpretation and meaning of that other activity. Although the design of space is important in the management process, there is surprisingly little research on this issue in an organizational context. There has been research on the effects of physical design in classrooms and mental hospitals (Sommer, 1969), but there are few attempts to examine the effect of physical design on business organizations. Steele (1973) has recognized the importance of physical design as an element of organization development efforts. Physical design has real consequences on the amount and content of social interaction which occurs within the organization. And, design has an effect on how organizational participants perceive the organization and their role in it. It is this symbolic use of physical design, rather than the actual effects of design on social interaction patterns, that concerns us here.

In the absence of a well-developed theory of physical settings, as environmental psychology has concerned itself primarily with case analyses and the study of over- and undermanning (Wicker, 1979), examples can be provided to indicate how physical design has been used symbolically and what such effects have been. Perhaps there is no better place to begin to consider the analysis of space than by looking at a map of a university campus. On most campuses, there are territories for the physical and social sciences. This demarcation provides a physical reminder of the political conflicts that exist between these various disciplines. Moreover, on a campus such as at Berkeley, the physical sciences, for the most part, occupy the higher parts of the campus and are in buildings with more commanding views of the bay. The next thing to note about the campus is which departments are in separate buildings, and the location of the buildings on the campus. On most campuses, the business school occupies a separate building. Indeed, at Harvard, the business school is across the river, and the limited amount of contact between the business school and the rest of the campus has led to the river being called the widest in the world. The location of medical schools at separate campuses (as is the case of the University of Illinois and the University of California medical school in San Francisco), the physical separation of the Harvard Business School, and the relative isolation and self-containment of many other professional school buildings conveys to all on the campus symbolically the separation and distinctions between these schools and the rest of the campus. Interestingly, at Berkeley the business school chose some years ago to move into a building with the political science, sociology, and economics departments, to symbolically reaffirm its identification as another social science department.

It may be possible to tell the relative power of departments or institutions by their location and the size and grandeur of their buildings. In San Francisco, the Bank of America built not only one of the taller buildings in the city, but put it on a hill so that its height advantage would be intensified. Thus, in a literal as well as a figurative sense, the Bank of America's world headquarters towers over the other banks in the financial district. The competition among organizations for status takes on physical manifestation in the construction of ever more grand and taller headquarters buildings. The effect of such symbols is nicely illustrated by this discussion of the impact of the building of a new headquarters for McGraw-Hill—a fifty-story structure in Rockefeller Center built at a cost of $84 million:

> The McGraw-Hill building was Fisher's pet project. The shift from the old green building on West Forty-second Street, in Hell's Kitchen, to the Avenue of the Americas next to Exxon was, to Fisher, "moving into the big time." Though the building cost much more than projected, he is convinced it paid off. He recalls that right after McGraw-Hill moved in, while he was prowling around checking things, he encountered a publisher staring out of a window. Says Fisher proudly: "The man turned and said, 'Shel, I'm already thinking bigger than I did last week' " (Holt, 1979: 104).

Internal struggles and disagreements can also take on physical manifestations which serve to keep the cleavages alive through the continual symbolic reminder of the differences. The Berkeley department of Economics was split some years ago by a division between the mathematical economists and those who stressed economic history, development, and more applied, policy-oriented economics. The mathematical economists soon moved to Evans Hall, the home of the computer center, while the others stayed behind in Barrows Hall. Recently, there have been rumors that the whole department will move to Evans, which may provide a clue as to which side won in the ensuing conflict over paradigms.

The use of open offices without the trappings of status that come from different size and location of office space may represent an attempt to remove status distinctions and encourage the free flow of communication among organizational members. Oldham and Brass' (1979) report that the aversive reaction to such a plan may reflect the fact that the open office and its symbol of equality is inconsistent with the decision-making style and hierarchical structure characteristic of most U.S. corporations. Interestingly, the open office arrangement is more common in Japan in which there is more of a consensual, group decision-making style of management, and apparently the problems of acceptance are less.

The rectangular conference table, with the clear demarcation of a head of the table position, provides symbolic reminder as to who is in charge at meetings. Podiums and platforms serve to elevate the speaker using them and to separate the speaker from the audience, another symbolic reminder of status distinctions and social distance.

Although it would be easy to exaggerate the importance of physical space in conveying symbols of power, control, prestige, openness, and so forth, it is important to recognize that the setting in which meetings are held and in which the organization or its subunit works has consequences because of the symbolism of the setting. Peters (1978) told of a new chief executive who, immediately on taking the job, began going around the country to meet with employees at their facilities, a departure from past practice in which the subordinates were summoned to headquarters. The significance was that the message was conveyed that headquarters was interested in learning about the subsidiaries and their operations, and that these operations were important and significant in the organization—significant enough so that the corporate chief executive could take the time and effort to visit them.

The various methods of meaning creation discussed—language, ceremonies, symbols, and settings, are, of course, not mutually exclusive. Indeed, the message and effect is probably greater when the various strategies are used together. It seems evident that there are myriad examples of the use of the kind of symbolic action described, and that the opportunities for examining the causes and consequences of such action are great.

MANAGERIAL SKILLS AND TRAINING

If management involves the taking of symbolic action, then the skills required are political, dramaturgical, and language skills more than analytical or strictly quantitative skills. It should be possible to develop a taxonomy of situations that lend themselves to symbolic action and to find that managers that are judged to be effective in such situations possess more competency in argument, advocacy, and language. It has been frequently noted that the proportion of executives in large corporations who are lawyers is increasing over time. There are several explanations for this effect, including the argument that legal contingencies have become increasingly important to organizations in an increasingly regualted and legislated environment, so that power and control is in the process of shifting to those who can cope with these contingencies (Pfeffer and Salancik, 1978; Ch. 9). A complementary explanation is that environments have become so interconnected, regulated, legislated, and complex that effective managerial action has become more difficult. In this environment, skills of symbolic reassurance and symbolic action are more important in motivating support for the organization and diminishing opposition. The advocacy, language, and dramaturgical skills learned by lawyers are particularly effective in this regard.

It is noteworthy that more and more schools of administration are adding writing and speaking clinics and workshops. One interpretation of this is that other educational organizations such as high schools are doing a less effective job in training these skills than they did in the past, necessitating more remedial action at the college or graduate school level. Another, equally plausible interpretation is that such skills are becoming more important as management is becoming more a symbolic and less a substantively analytical activity. Of course, the two explanations are not mutually contradictory, and both could be true.

The importance of symbolic management activity and the language and advocacy skills that may facilitate such symbolic action can also account for the relative effects of socioeconomic origins on success in different types of business organizations. In a study of stratification in organizations, Pfeffer (1977c) found that socioeconomic origins predicted success more strongly in small rather than large organizations, in staff rather than line positions, and in finance, insurance, and real estate rather than in manufacturing. Pfeffer's argument was that social similarity, presumably indexed by socioeconomic origins, was a more important predictor of success when evaluation on more objective criteria was more difficult and problematic. However, another interpretation can be offered consistent with the reported results. Socioeconomic origins may index verbal skills and facility in using language. Such skills are more likely to be important in staff positions in which advocacy and report presentations are the principal components of work activity. Such skills are also more important in finance, insurance, and real estate—businesses that rely on social contact and in which a basically undifferentiated product or service is being sold, requiring the ability to present and package such a product or service to make it appear distinct. And, language and symbolic skills may be more critical in small organizations with their less formalized and sophisticated performance assessment systems. In the absence of impersonal mechanisms of evaluation, the ability to employ language and symbols to signify success may take on increased value.

It is clearly possible to develop arguments that would predict variance in the importance of symbolic management activity across contexts. Such arguments would imply differential training and skill-building activities, as well as differential predictors of success in such differing environments.

ON UNDERSTANDING THE MANAGEMENT PROCESS

Explanations of management activity have tended to focus on the instrumental, intentional, and behaviorally specific causes and consequences of such activity. The analogous situation is trying to understand the war on poverty by trying to assess those specific actions that have ameliorated the level of poverty and the condition of poor people. Or, a similar example would be focusing on educational reforms in terms of their impact on test scores or behaviors in school settings. The war on poverty had symbolic impact that extended beyond and perhaps was more important than the actual results achieved. Similarly, educational reforms are often repackaging and relabeling undertaken to create the perception of improvement to produce continued funding and support of the educational process. Management is involved in such labeling and the creation of meaning and interpretation as well. Language, symbols, settings, stories, ceremonies, and informational social influence to produce socially constructed realities are as much the tools of managers as are economic analysis, finite mathematics, and theories of leadership and organization design that stress the rational, objective results of managerial action.

Indeed, in contexts in which assessment is difficult, involvement is segmented and incomplete, technology or the connections between actions and results are uncertain, and preferences are ambiguous, the symbolic role of the manager is probably the most important one. If management as symbolic action is a reasonable descriptor of the situation, then it is important to recognize how the very academic literature of organizational behavior and management contributes to the symbol and meaning creation process. This literature provides legitimacy for the position that managerial action is intendedly rational, that there is a science of administration, that leadership can be both learned and important, and that structures can be rationally designed to achieve specific desired results. Whether or not such statements are true or false, the existence of an ideology in the form of presumed science plays a significant part in facilitating the symbolic actions taken in the course of the administrative process.

If we view the literature describing management as an integral part of the material that managers use at least implicitly in their symbolic activities, then the development of arguments emphasizing the social construction of reality, organizations as garbage cans (Cohen, March, and Olsen, 1972), leadership as a language game (Pondy, 1978), organizations as externally constrained (Pfeffer and Salancik, 1978), and loosely coupled (Weick, 1976) involves the production of cynical knowledge (Goldner, Ritti, and Ference, 1977). Cynical knowledge challenges the prevailing view and focuses attention on those components of the administrative process which may be successful only because they are not understood or appreciated by most organizational participants. It is little wonder, then, that such arguments are not well received by practitioners of organization development (Burke, 1979) and others whose very success depends on the ability to engage in symbolic actions which are effective only because the game being played is not well recognized.

The point is not just that organizational analysis can and should proceed on two levels. As noted at the outset of this essay, one theoretical position is that the external constraints and power-dependence relations determine managerial and organizational action, and that the symbolic content of management activity is focused on the rationalization, legitimation, and interpretation of such activity to affect the beliefs and sentiments of other social actors inside and outside the organization. Now, it is being suggested that the effectiveness of this symbolic action is enhanced by the confusion of all involved between substantive outcomes and symbolic results. Clearly, to return to an earlier analogy, the war on poverty was successful in quieting public unrest only to the extent that the symbolic actions of the poverty program were seen as substantive responses to demands (Edelman, 1971). Symbols are effective only to the extent that meaning becomes invested in the symbols.

If it sounds as if management (or politicians more generally) are playing an intentionally deceptive game, this is not the point, in that management and politicians fool themselves as well as others with their symbolic acts. If one sits in a magnificent office in a magnificent structure, surrounded by the various accouterments of power such as limosines, private jets, and large staffs, and engages in activity labeled as management and decision making, one not only convinces others that one is in control and has power over organizations and substantive events, one is also likely to convince oneself. The legitimation and rationalizations serve to convince and structure the meaning of action for *all* concerned in the social system, and certainly this includes the managers and administrators. The government officials in the war on poverty did not take actions to quiet public protest believing that they were making only symbolic responses without any substantive impact—rather, as Edelman (1971) argued, the very symbolic actions provided reassurance both to these officials as well as their constituents that problems could be solved, that attention was being paid to important issues, and that there was the potential to solve and control social problems. The illusion of control affects the managers and administrators as well as their constituents.

This argument explains why there is some ambiguity about ending this essay with the usual prescriptions to do more research on its chosen topic. Such research is manifestly possible. Content analysis (Holsti, 1969), unobtrusive indicators (Webb *et al.*, 1966), the analysis of behavior settings (Wicker, 1979), and other research strategies are possible and can lead to the comparative empirical study of the symbolic aspects of the management process. But such research might, by its very nature, call into question ideologies which are held with almost religious fervor and which legitimate the very position of management and the activities of management scholars. If chief executives rise to their positions because of analytical skill and the ability to prescribe effective action, then their right to draw large salaries and exert influence over tremendous numbers of people and resources appears to be justified. If, however, such positions are attained not because of any real consequences of decisions but because the individuals are able to engage in drama, advocacy, and symbolic action so that meanings and beliefs are produced that attribute potency to them and legitimate the activities of their organizations, then the basis for their positions is much less legitimate given prevailing social values and norms.

The study of organizations, thus, faces an interesting dilemma. To increase the capacity of managers to take effective action it is clearly useful to do research and teaching which elucidates the full range of the management process, including the symbolic content of managerial action. Effective executives, I suspect, already know, at least at an implicit level, much of what is contained in this chapter. The dilemma comes in that pointing out the symbolic aspects of management may make those symbolic activities less effective and may indeed call into question the legitimacy of the administrative activity itself and, by extension, its study and teaching.

ACKNOWLEDGMENTS

The comments of Doug Wholey and Richard Harrison on an earlier version of this manuscript were most helpful and are gratefully acknowledged.

REFERENCES

Adams, J. S. (1965) "Inequity in Social Exchange." In Leonard Berkowitz (ed.), *Advances in Experimental Social Psychology*, Vol. 2. New York: Academic Press.

Aldrich, Howard E. (1971) "Organizational Boundaries and Interorganizational Conflict." *Human Relations*, 24: 279–287.

Asch, Solomon E. (1958) "Effects of Group Pressure upon the Modification and Distortion of Judgments." In E. E. Maccoby, T. M. Newcomb, and E. L. Hartley (eds.), *Readings in Social Psychology*. New York: Holt, Rinehart, and Winston.

Bem, Daryl J. (1972) "Self-Perception Theory." In L. Berkowitz (ed.), *Advances in Experimental Social Psychology*, Vol. 6. New York: Academic Press.

Benson, J. Kenneth (1973) "The Analysis of Bureaucratic-Professional Conflict: Functional Versus Dialectical Approaches." *Sociological Quarterly*, 14: 376–394.

Berger, P., and T. Luckmann (1967) *The Social Construction of Reality*. New York: Doubleday.

Beyer, Janice M. (1978) "Editorial Policies and Practices Among Leading Journals in Four Scientific Fields." *Sociological Quarterly*, 19: 68–88.

Blau, Peter M., and W. Richard Scott (1962) *Formal Organizations*. San Francisco: Chandler Publishing Company.

Bougon, Michel, Karl Weick, and Din Binkhorst (1977) "Cognition in Organization: An Analysis of the Utrecht Jazz Orchestra." *Administrative Science Quarterly*, 22: 606–639.

Brown, Richard Harvey (1978) "Bureaucracy as Praxis: Toward a Political Phenomenology of Formal Organizations." *Administrative Science Quarterly*, 23: 365–382.

Burke, W. Warner (1979) "Review of Leadership: Where Else Can We Go?" *Journal of Applied Behavioral Science*, 15: 121–122.

Carey, Alex (1967) "The Hawthorne Studies: A Radical Criticism." *American Sociological Review*, 32: 403–416.

Child, John (1972) "Organization Structure, Environment, and Performance—The Role of Strategic Choice." *Sociology*, 6: 1–22.

Cohen, Michael D., and James G. March (1974) *Leadership and Ambiguity: The American College President*. New York: McGraw-Hill.

Cohen, Michael D., James G. March, and Johan P. Olsen (1972) "A Garbage Can Model of Organizational Choice." *Administrative Science Quarterly*, 17: 1–25.

Committee on Educational Policy (1974) "Recommendations from the Committee on Educational Policy Regarding the Future of Instruction and Research in Criminology on the Berkeley Campus." Unpublished report, Berkeley, Calif.: University of California.

Cyert, Richard M., and James G. March (1963) *A Behavioral Theory of the Firm*. Englewood Cliffs, N.J.: Prentice-Hall.

Deutsch, Karl W. (1953) *Nationalism and Social Communication*. Cambridge, Mass.: M. I. T. Press.

Dowling, John B. (1978) "Organizational Legitimation: The Management of Meaning." Unpublished Doctoral Dissertation, Palo Alto: Stanford University.

Dowling, John B., and Jeffrey Pfeffer (1975) "Organizational Legitmacy: Social Values and Organizational Behavior." *Pacific Sociological Review*, 18: 122–136.

Downey, H. Kirk, Don H. Hellriegel, and John W. Slocum, Jr. (1975) "Environmental Uncertainty: The Construct and Its Application." *Administrative Science Quarterly*, 20: 613–629.

Downs, Anthony (1957) *An Economic Theory of Democracy*. New York: Harper.

Duncan, Robert B. (1972) "Characteristics of Organizational Environments and Perceived Environmental Uncertainty." *Administrative Science Quarterly*, 17: 313–327.

Edelman, Murray (1964) *The Symbolic Uses of Politics*. Urbana: University of Illinois Press.

——— (1971) *Politics as Symbolic Action: Mass Arousal and Quiescence*. Chicago: Markham.

——— (1977) *Political Language: Words That Succeed and Policies That Fail*. New York: Academic Press.

Etzioni, Amitai (1961) *A Comparative Analysis of Complex Organizations*. Glencoe, Ill.: Free Press.

Festinger, Leon (1954) "A Theory of Social Comparison Processes." *Human Relations*, 7: 117–140.

Fornell, Claes (1976) *Consumer Input for Marketing Decisions: A Study of Corporate Departments for Consumer Affairs*. New York: Praeger.

French, John R. P., Jr. and Bertram Raven (1968) "The Bases of Social Power." In Dorwin Cartwright and Alvin Zander (eds.), *Group Dynamics*, 3rd ed. New York: Harper and Row.

Galbraith, Jay (1973) *Designing Complex Organizations*. Reading, Mass.: Addison-Wesley.

Gamson, William A., and Norman R. Scotch. (1964) "Scapegoating in Baseball." *American Journal of Sociology*, 70: 69–76.

Gephart, Robert P., Jr. (1978) "Status Degradation and Organizational Succession: An Ethnomethodological Approach." *Administrative Science Quarterly*, 23: 553–581.

Gergen, Kenneth J. (1969) *The Psychology of Behavior Exchange*. Reading Mass.: Addison-Wesley.

Goldner, Fred H., R. Richard Ritti, and Thomas P. Ference (1977) "The Production of Cynical Knowledge in Organizations." *American Sociological Review*, 42: 539–551.

Goodman, P., and A. Friedman (1971) "An Explanation of Adam's Theory of Inequity." *Administrative Science Quarterly*, 16: 271–288.

Hackman, J. Richard, and Greg R. Oldham (1975) "Development of the Job Diagnostic Survey." *Journal of Applied Psychology,* 60: 159–170.

Holsti, Ole R. (1969) *Content Analysis for the Social Sciences and Humanities.* Reading, Mass.: Addison-Wesley.

Holt, Donald D. (1979) "The Unlikely Hero of McGraw-Hill." *Fortune,* 99 (May 21, 1979): 97–108.

House, Robert J., and Mary L. Baetz (1979) "Leadership: Some Empirical Generalizations and New Research Directions." In Barry M. Staw (ed.), *Research in Organizational Behavior,* Vol. 1. Greenwich, Conn.: JAI Press.

Jacobs, R. C., and D. T. Campbell (1961) "The Perpetuation of an Arbitrary Tradition Through Successive Generations of a Laboratory Microculture." *Journal of Abnormal and Social Psychology,* 62: 649–658.

Kelley, Harold H. (1971) *Attribution in Social Interaction.* Morristown, N.J.: General Learning Press.

King, Albert S. (1974) "Expectation Effects in Organizational Change." *Administrative Science Quarterly,* 19: 221–230.

Kuhn, Thomas S. (1970) *The Structure of Scientific Revolutions,* 2nd ed. Chicago: University of Chicago Press.

Lawrence, Paul R., and Jay W. Lorsch (1967) *Organization and Environment.* Boston: Division of Research, Graduate School of Business Administration, Harvard University.

Lentz, A., and H. Tschirgi (1963) "The Ethical Content of Annual Reports." *Journal of Business,* 36: 387–393.

Locke, Edwin A. (1968) "Toward a Theory of Task Motivation and Incentives." *Organizational Behavior and Human Performance,* 3: 157–189.

Lodahl, Janice, and Gerald Gordon (1972) "The Structure of Scientific Fields and the Functioning of University Graduate Departments." *American Sociological Review,* 37: 57–72.

——— (1973) "Differences Between Physical and Social Sciences in University Graduate Departments." *Research in Higher Education,* 1: 191–213.

Luthans, Fred, and Robert Kreitner (1975) *Organizational Behavior Modification.* Glenview, Ill.: Scott, Foresman.

March, James G. (1962) "The Business Firm as a Political Coalition." *Journal of Politics,* 24: 662–678.

——— (1978) "Bounded Rationality, Ambiguity, and the Engineering of Choice." *Bell Journal of Economics,* 9: 587–608.

March, James G. and Herbert A. Simon (1958) *Organizations.* New York: John Wiley.

Maslow, Abraham H. (1943) "A Theory of Human Motivation." *Psychological Review,* 50: 370–396.

Meyer, John W., and Brian Rowan (1977) "Institutionalized Organizations: Formal Structure as Myth and Ceremony." *American Journal of Sociology,* 83: 340–363.

Morris, Charles W. (1949) *Signs, Language, and Behavior.* Englewood Cliffs, N. J. : Prentice-Hall.

Nord, Walter (1969) "Beyond the Teaching Machine: The Neglected Area of Operant Conditioning in the Theory and Practice of Management." *Organizational Behavior and Human Performance,* 4: 375–401.

Oldham, Greg R. (1976) "Job Characteristics and Internal Motivation: The Moderating Effect of Interpersonal and Individual Variables." *Human Relations,* 29: 559–569.

Oldham, Greg R., and Daniel J. Brass (1979) "Employee Reactions to an Open-Plan Office: A Naturally Occurring Quasi-Experiment." *Administrative Science Quarterly,* 24: 267–284.

O'Reilly, Charles A., and David Caldwell (1979) "Informational Influence as a Determinant of Perceived Task Characteristics and Job Satisfaction." *Journal of Applied Psychology*, 64: 157–165.

Ouchi, William G., and Raymond, L. Price (1978) "Hierarchies, Clans, and Theory Z: A New Perspective on Organization Development." *Organizational Dynamics*, 7: 25–44.

Parsons, Talcott (1956) "Suggestions for a Sociological Approach to the Theory of Organizations." *Administrative Science Quarterly*, 1: 63–85.

Parsons, Talcott, and Neil J. Smelser (1956) *Economy and Society*, Glencoe, Ill.: Free Press.

Peters, Thomas J. (1978) "Symbols, Patterns, and Settings: An Optimistic Case for Getting Things Done." *Organizational Dynamics*, 7: 3–23.

Pfeffer, Jeffrey (1977a) "The Ambiguity of Leadership." *Academy of Management Review*, 2: 104–112.

——— (1977b) "Power and Resource Allocation in Organizations." In B. M. Staw and G. R. Salancik (eds.), *New Directions in Organizational Behavior*. Chicago: St. Clair Press.

——— (1977c) "Toward an Examination of Stratification in Organizations." *Administrative Science Quarterly*, 22: 553–567.

——— (1978) *Organizational Design*. Arlington Heights, Ill.: AHM Publishing Corporation.

Pfeffer, Jeffrey, Anthony Leong, and Katherine Strehl (1977) "Paradigm Development and Particularism: Journal Publication in Three Scientific Disciplines." Social Forces, 55: 938–951.

Pfeffer, Jeffrey, and Gerald R. Salancik (1974) "Organizational Decision Making as a Political Process: The Case of a University Budget." *Administrative Science Quarterly*, 19: 135–151.

——— (1975) "Determinants of Supervisory Behavior: A Role Set Analysis." *Human Relations*, 28: 139–154.

——— (1978) *The External Control of Organizations: A Resource Dependence Perspective*. New York: Harper and Row.

Pfeffer, Jeffrey, Gerald R. Salancik, and Huseyin Leblebici (1976) "The Effect of Uncertainty on the Use of Social Influence in Organizational Decision Making." *Administrative Science Quarterly*, 21: 227–245.

Pfeffer, Jeffrey, Gerald R. Salancik, and William L. Moore (1979) "Archival Indicators of Paradigm Development of Academic Disciplines." Unpublished ms., School of Business Administration, University of California, Berkeley.

Pondy, Louis R. (1977) "The Other Hand Clapping: An Information-Processing Approach to Organizational Power." In Tove H. Hammer and Samuel B. Bacharach (eds.), *Reward Systems and Power Distributions*. Ithaca, N.Y.: Cornell University School of Industrial and Labor Relations.

——— (1978) "Leadership Is a Language Game." In M. W. McCall, Jr., and M. M. Lombardo (eds.), *Leadership: Where Else Can We Go?* Durham, N.C.: Duke University Press.

Pondy, Louis R., and David M. Boje (1976) "Bringing Mind Back In: Paradigm Development as a Frontier Problem in Organization Theory." Unpublished ms., Department of Business Administration, University of Illinois.

Salancik, Gerald R. (1977) "Commitment and the Control of Organizational Behavior and Belief." In B. M. Staw and G. R. Salancik (eds.), *New Directions in Organizational Behavior*. Chicago: St. Clair Press.

Salancik, Gerald R., and Mary Conway (1975) "Attitude Inferences from Salient and Relevant Cognitive Content About Behavior." *Journal of Personality and Social Psychology*, 32: 829–840.

Salancik, Gerald R., and Jeffrey Pfeffer (1977a) "Constraints on Administrator Discretion:

The Limited Influence of Mayors on City Budgets." *Urban Affairs Quarterly,* 12: 475–498.

——— (1977b) "An Examination of Need-Satisfaction Models of Job Attitudes." *Administrative Science Quarterly,* 22: 427–456.

——— (1978) "A Social Information Processing Approach to Job Attitudes and Task Design." *Administrative Science Quarterly,* 23: 224–253.

Sarason, Irwin G., Ronald E. Smith, and Edward Diener (1975) "Personality Research: Components of Variance Attributable to the Person and the Situation." *Journal of Personality and Social Psychology,* 32: 199–204.

Sherif, M. (1935) "A Study of Some Social Factors in Perception." *Archives of Psychology,* No. 187.

Smith, Peter B. (1973) *Groups Within Organizations.* New York: Harper and Row.

Sommer, Robert (1969) *Personal Space: The Behavioral Basis of Design.* Englewood Cliffs, N.J.: Prentice-Hall.

Staw, Barry M. (1974) "Attitudinal and Behavioral Consequences of Changing a Major Organizational Reward: A Natural Field Experiment." *Journal of Personality and Social Psychology,* 29: 742–751.

Steele, Fred I. (1973) *Physical Settings and Organization Development.* Reading Mass.: Addison-Wesley.

Stouffer, S. A., E. A. Suchman, L. C. Devinney, S. A. Star, and R. M. Williams (1949) *The American Soldier: Adjustment During Army Life,* Vol. 1. Princeton, N.J.: Princeton University Press.

Thompson, James D. (1967) *Organizations in Action.* New York: McGraw-Hill.

Thompson, James D., and Arthur Tuden (1959) "Strategies, Structures, and Processes of Organizational Decision." In J. D. Thompson, P. B. Hammond, R. W. Hawkes, B. H. Junker, and A Tuden (eds.), *Comparative Studies in Administration.* Pittsburgh: University of Pittsburgh Press.

Tosi, Henry, Ramon Aldag, and Ronald Storey (1973) "On the Measurement of the Environment: An Assessment of the Lawrence and Lorsch Environmental Uncertainty Questionnaire." *Administrative Science Quarterly,* 18: 27–36.

Webb, Eugene J., Donald T. Campbell, Richard D. Schwartz, and Lee Sechrest (1966) *Unobtrusive Measures: Nonreactive Research in the Social Sciences.* Chicago: Rand McNally.

Weick, Karl E. (1969) *The Social Psychology of Organizing.* Reading, Mass.: Addison-Wesley.

——— (1976) "Educational Organizations as Loosely Coupled Systems." *Administrative Science Quarterly,* 21: 1–19.

——— (1979) "Cognitive Processes in Organizations." In Barry M. Staw (ed.), *Research in Organizational Behavior,* Vol. 1. Greenwich, Conn.: JAI Press.

White, Sam E., and Terence R. Mitchell (1979) "Job Enrichment Versus Social Cues: A Comparison and Competitive Test." *Journal of Applied Psychology,* 64: 1–9.

Wicker, Allan W. (1979) *An Introduction to Ecological Psychology.* Monterey, Calif.: Brooks/Cole.

Wilkins, Alan Lee (1978) "Organizational Stories as an Expression of Management Philosophy: Implications for Social Control in Organizations." Unpublished doctoral dissertation, Palo Alto, Calif.: Stanford University.

Yoels, William C. (1974) "The Structure of Scientific Fields and the Allocation of Editorships on Scientific Journals: Some Observations on the Politics of Knowledge." *Sociological Quarterly,* 15: 264–276.

Zedeck, Sheldon, and Milton R. Blood (1974) *Foundations of Behavioral Science Research in Organizations.* Monterey, Calif.: Brooks/Cole.

Zucker, Lynne G. (1977) "The Role of Institutionalization in Cultural Persistence." *American Sociological Review,* 42: 726–743.

RATIONALITY AND JUSTIFICATION IN ORGANIZATIONAL LIFE

Barry M. Staw

ABSTRACT

In this essay, rationality and justification are studied as pervasive images of both human and organizational systems. A number of outcroppings of rationality and justification are illustrated at both the individual and organizational levels of analysis, and a cross-level effect is discussed in some detail. However, the overall goal of the essay is pretheoretic. Rather than providing an exact theory or set of hypotheses, the essay addresses the rationality-justification distinction as a central element of organizing from which new hypotheses may be shaped in the future.

INTRODUCTION

In both research and theorizing, the field of organizational behavior has made heavy use of rational models. The individual has been conceived as a rational, goal-seeking entity which processes information and makes decisions in his or her own self-interest (e.g., Vroom, 1964; Porter & Lawler, 1968; Campbell and Pritchard, 1976). The organization has also been conceived as a goal-seeking entity which behaves in ways to protect and expand its domains of interest (e.g., Thompson, 1967; Pfeffer & Salancik, 1978). However, cutting across images of rationality are theories and data on justification processes. Individuals are sometimes conceived as rationalizing as opposed to rational decision makers (e.g., Festinger, 1957; Aronson, 1976). Likewise, organizations have been conceived as vehicles by which ambiguous goals, preferences, and decision plans get put into action and justified (e.g., Cohen, March, & Olson, 1972; March & Olson, 1976). Thus, we have been beset by images of both rationality and justification on each of two levels of analysis.

The goal of this chapter is to dissect and analyze the rationality-justification distinction, but not to solve it. The interrelationship of these two forces is viewed as central to the issues of organizational behavior, yet this essay will not advocate one factor over another or propose a new contingency theory based on these factors. In contrast, this chapter represents a pretheoretic effort to focus attention upon rationality and justification as pervasive elements in organizational life. It is believed these forces are prevalent at multiple levels in organizational systems and influence each other across such levels. Thus, the chapter will first outline and defend the existence of rationality and justification at both the individual and organizational levels of analysis. In the second section of this essay, examples of how these two forces may affect the behavior of both individuals and organizations will be provided. Finally, this chapter will illustrate what is believed to be an important cross-level effect; that is, how organizational rationality can trigger individual forces for justification.

Before advancing further with a task that spans two levels of analysis it is appropriate to admit to certain theoretical preferences and prejudices. In the author's opinion, the parallels between individual and organizational analysis are not by any means a coincidence. Perhaps the similarity stems from the fact that individual scholars working in the organizational field extrapolate from their own cognitive images and metaphors to explain the workings of organizations. Or perhaps large collectivities do, in fact, behave in similar ways to individuals. As suggested by Miller (1978), there may be some principles or laws of behavior which are quite generalizable across levels of analysis. However, probably the simplest and most convincing reason for the existence of cross-level parallels is that organizations are populated by individuals, and thus if there exist any generalizable tendencies within individuals, these tendencies will likely be manifested in organizational actions. Admittedly, organizational actions are not a direct by-product of individual behavior; political maneuvering, coalition formation, and hierarchical systems generally separate the individual from organizational behavior. Yet, if individual administrators do possess strong tendencies for both rationality and justification, many actions undertaken by organizations are likely to exhibit these same general characteristics.

EXISTENCE OF RATIONALITY

Sources of Individual Rationality

At the individual level of analysis, the most common model of rationality has been that of economic decision making. Individuals have been conceived as maximizing their own subjective expected utility (Edwards, 1954). Limits to the ability of man in inputting and processing information have certainly been acknowledged, and so have some limitations to ways data are interpreted into final decisions. Yet the basic conception of individuals as rational, goal-seeking entities has remained relatively intact. We still expect job applicants to choose their most highly rated organization for employment (e.g., Vroom, 1966; Wanous, 1972; Mitchell & Knudsen, 1973; Lawler, Kuleck, Rhode & Sorensen, 1975), and for individuals to perform that behavior which is viewed as subjectively most desirable (Vroom, 1964; Graen, 1969; Campbell & Pritchard, 1976).

A highly elaborate model of the cognitively rational individual is outlined in Figure 1. Several assumptions are implicit in this figure. It is hypothesized that the individual, when faced with a choice to exert a high or low amount of effort on the job, will follow an economic decision-making model. That is, based upon a set of well-articulated expectancies and valences, the individual would be expected to choose that course of action with the greatest subjective utility. For simplicity, only two levels of effort are illustrated in the figure. However, given most individuals' limit to cognitive information processing (cf., Miller, 1956; Simon, 1957; Slovic, 1972), the two-level representation may depart less from empirical reality than Vroom's (1964) or Lawler's (1971) expectancy models (these latter models implicitly assume assessment of "all" levels of effort and performance).

The rational model of individual performance illustrated in Figure 1 could be operationalized by asking individuals to think of the consequences of working at two or more levels of effort. Items could then be designed to assess the likelihood that each type of task behavior would lead to various intrinsic and extrinsic outcomes. The importance or

Figure 1. A Cognitively Rational Model of Task Performance (from Staw 1977a)

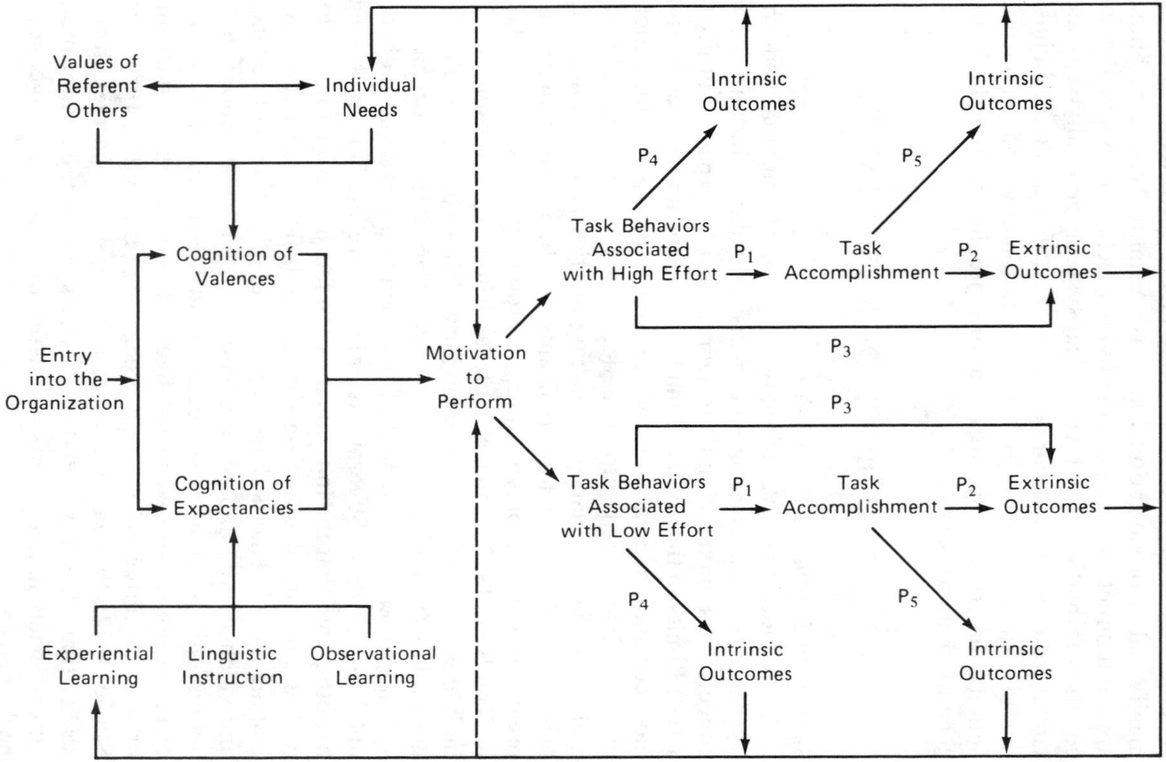

Values of Referent Others
Individual Needs
Entry into the Organization
Cognition of Valences
Cognition of Expectancies
Experiential Learning
Linguistic Instruction
Observational Learning
Motivation to Perform
Task Behaviors Associated with High Effort
Task Accomplishment
Extrinsic Outcomes
Intrinsic Outcomes
Intrinsic Outcomes
P_1
P_2
P_3
P_4
P_5
Task Behaviors Associated with Low Effort
Task Accomplishment
Extrinsic Outcomes
Intrinsic Outcomes
Intrinsic Outcomes
P_1
P_2
P_3
P_4
P_5

relative valence of each of these outcomes could be assessed and a weighted average of expected value could then be computed for both "working hard" and "not so hard." An operationalization of this formulation of "motivation to perform" is presented below:

$$\text{Motivation to Perform} = \left[\begin{array}{l}\text{Expected}\\\text{Value of}\\\text{Working}\\\text{Hard}\end{array}\right] - \left[\begin{array}{l}\text{Expected}\\\text{Value of}\\\text{Working at}\\\text{Leisurely}\\\text{Pace}\end{array}\right],$$

where:

$$\text{Expected Value} = IV_{beh} + P_1\,(IV_{acc}) + \sum_{i=1}^{n}\left[P_1P_2(EV_i)\right] + \sum_{i=1}^{n}\left[P_3EV_i\right]$$

and

IV_{beh} = the intrinsic valence associated with task behavior (i.e., working 5 vs. 12 hours);
IV_{acc} = the intrinsic valence associated with task accomplishment;
EV_i = the extrinsic valences associated with extrinsic rewards;
P_1 = the probability that task behavior will lead to accomplishment;
P_2 = the probability that task accomplishment will lead to extrinsic rewards;
P_3 = the probability that task behavior will lead directly to extrinsic rewards.

By spelling out the cognitively rational model of individual behavior in such detailed form, its implausibility becomes evident. If individuals (even in the two-level of effort case) underwent such computational gymnastics before each action alternative, they would cease to behave at all. Thus, we must acknowledge that much of our behavior has been routinized and is subject to reinforcing cycles (illustrated by broken line in Figure 1). That is, once certain behaviors have been emitted and have been rewarded, they may occur repeatedly without the need for future cognitive decision making. Similarly, individuals frequently utilize behavioral models as guides to their own behavior. They may pattern their behavior after another individual or simply accept culturally prescribed actions without undergoing any active decision making. Such reinforcement and behavioral modeling do not, however, conflict with the basic orientation of individual rationality. They are simply more abbreviated versions of rational goal-seeking than the fully cognitive utility model.

In an earlier paper, this author (Staw, 1977a) proposed that individuals do not merely react to the contingencies of their environment as a cognitive processer of events and outcomes. They are also proactive in the sense that they attempt to control the contingencies of their surroundings. Within the organizational context, control may involve the preservation of expertise, hoarding of essential information, or otherwise making oneself so valuable to the organization that one can dictate the terms of his or her involvement (Martin & Sims, 1956; Pfeffer, 1977). These are obviously the strategies of the highly skilled and centrally located participant who already has a good deal of power. However, for those at the organization's periphery and for those with less-valued skills, other strategies are possible. One method by which a low-power person may improve his situation in the organization is by ingratiation (Wortman & Linsenmeier, 1977). If the individual can manipulate his supervisor's attitudes and opinions, he can improve his share of the resources allocated by the supervisor. Through ingratiation, the individual may receive more than he deserves for a given level of work or at least assure himself of a positive evaluation of his task output. While the ingratiation strategy is highly individualistic, the organization of many low-power individuals into a coalition or union will also yield greater influence within the organization. Unionization of the workplace frequently brings increased worker control over the methods of resource allocation (e.g., weekly wage supplanting a piece-rate system of incentives) and the procedures by which the work is accomplished (e.g., highly restricted work rules replacing employer-designed job descriptions).

The rational individual, as we have described him, is both an adapting and controlling creature. He has the capacity to anticipate, evaluate, and choose that course of action which will satisfy certain needs or valued outcomes. But, he also possesses the capacity to change the very contingencies or "rules of the game" to which he is subjected. This dual nature of man which can be both proactive and reactive is implicity captured in two quotes from White's (1959) work on competence.

> As used here, competence will refer to an organism's capacity to interact with its environment. . . . In the case of man, where so little is provided innately and so much has to be learned through experience, we should expect to find highly advantageous arrangements for securing a steady cumulative learning about the properties of the environment and the extent of possible transactions. Under these circumstances we might expect to find a very powerful drive operating to insure progress toward competence, just as vital goals of nutrition and reproduction are secured by powerful drives (White, p. 297).

> [Human] organisms differ from other things in nature in that they are 'self-governing entities' which are to some extent 'autonomous'. . . . The human being has a characteristic tendency toward self-determination, that is, a tendency to resist external influences and to subordinate the heteronomous forces of the physical and social environment to its own sphere of influence. . . . Of all living creatures it is man who takes the longest strides toward autonomy. This is not because of any unusual

> tendency toward bodily expansion at the expense of the environment. . . . Man as a species has developed a tremendous power of bringing the environment into his service, and each individual member of the species must attain what is really quite an impressive level of competence if he is to take part in the life around him (p. 324).

The image projected by the quotations from White (1959) and our own discussion of rationality should convey the impression that individuals are highly motivated to predict and control their environments. Some specific hypotheses concerning the sequence by which individuals might act to increase predictability and/or control have been elaborated elsewhere (Staw, 1977a). As shown in Figure 2, individuals are postulated, first to attempt control over their environments. However, if control is not possible, then individuals are hypothesized to make their environments more predictable. As proposed, this general sequence is moderated by the individual's expectations of control. Individuals who have had a prior history of self-control are most likely to seek control over the allocation of resources. However, individuals with little history of self-control are predicted to primarily seek predictive power. Finally, if neither prediction nor control is possible, research has shown (Seligman, 1975) that individuals are likely either to become psychologically depressed (learned helplessness) or exit the situation altogether.

Figure 2. Flow Diagram of Upward Control (From Staw, 1977a)

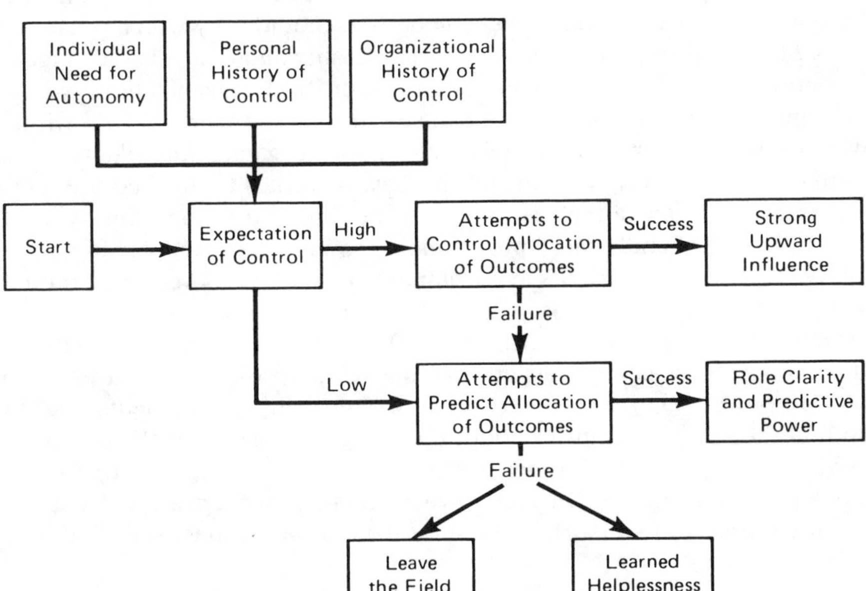

Sources of Organizational Rationality

At the organizational level of analysis there has also been widespread concern with rationality. The managerial literature on organization design and policy (e.g., Lawrence & Lorsch, 1967; Galbraith, 1977; Chandler, 1962) is concerned with fitting the proper organizational structure to varying environmental and task characteristics. The orientation of this body of work is clearly normative, advocating that administrators follow certain design guidelines in increasing the effectiveness of their organizations.

Other more descriptive work on organizational structure (e.g., Blau & Schoenherr, 1971; Pugh, Hickson, Hennings & Turner, 1968) has been directed toward finding verifiable relationships between structural, task, and environmental conditions. However, even the most descriptive research on organizational variables contains the tacit assumption of rationality. It is implicitly assumed in most empirical studies that some functional relationships underlie the observed correlations. Either by natural selection (Hannan & Freeman, 1977) or by conscious administrative decision (Simon, 1957) certain covariations of macrovariables come into being and are maintained over time. Although the soundness of drawing normative implications from descriptive research has been questioned (Argyris, 1972), the underlying theme of rationality is indeed very strong within the empirical literature on design and structure.

In terms of formulating *explicit* hypotheses on the rational behavior of organizations, Thompson's (1967) work is preeminent. Thompson outlined a host of propositions which encompass methods by which organizations make their environments more predictable and controllable. Figure 3 outlines the basic model of an industrial organization within Thompson's framework. As one can see, there is a technical core within which goods or services are produced by an organization. There exist sources of uncertainty in transforming raw materials to finished products and internal organizational structure is designed to reduce this type of uncertainty. Generally more problematic, however, are sources of uncertainty in the organization's environment on both the input and output sides of the system. According to Thompson, organizations reduce environmental uncertainty by various buffering activities such as material stockpiling, forecasting, and contracting. Organizations also attempt to acquire power relative to other forces within their environments, and to do this they may attempt to coopt opposing elements into the organization, form coalitions with other organizations, or seek support from other more powerful entities. In recent years there has been a great deal of empirical research supporting many of these propositions (see Pfeffer & Salancik, 1978).

The Thompsonian view of organizational rationality has dominated the

Figure 3. A Thompsonian View of Industrial Organizations

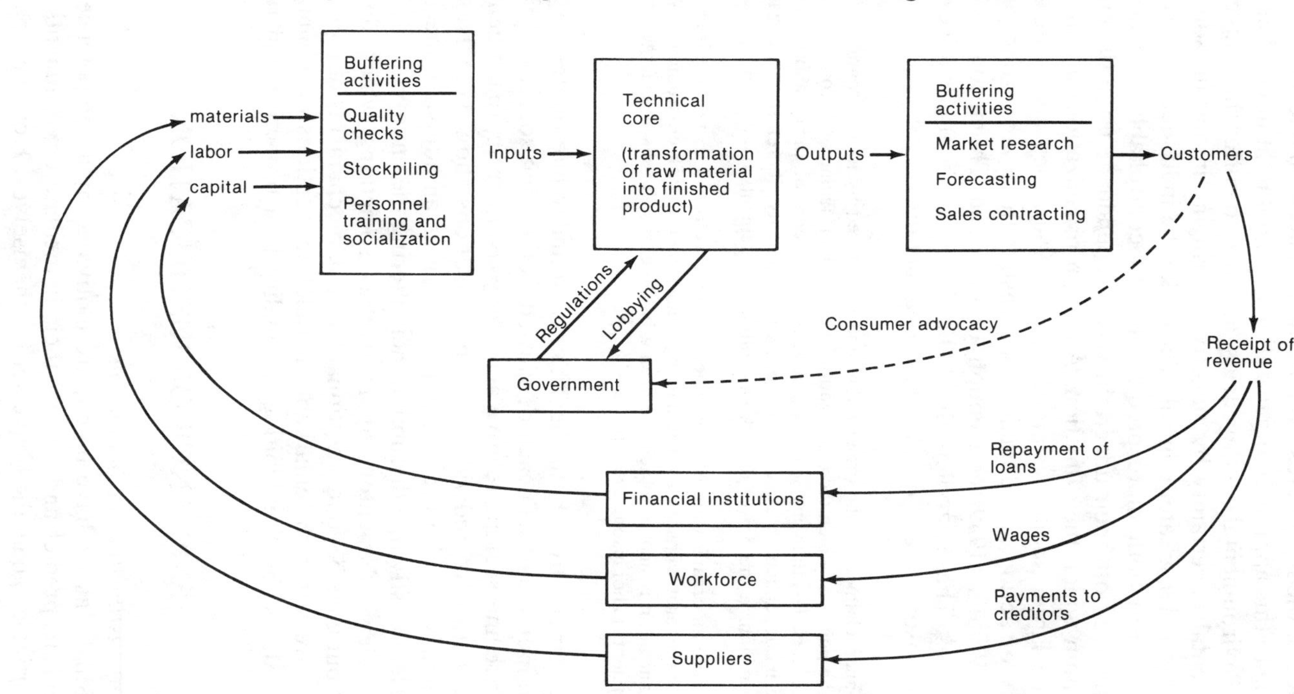

last decade of theory and research at the organizational level of analysis. According to this approach, organizations attempt to fit internal design to task and environmental contingencies, and also to buffer themselves from environmental uncertainty by selectively bringing important sources of uncertainty under greater control. Thus, like the individual who seeks to make his world both more predictable and controllable, organizations seek to reduce both their uncertainty and dependence upon the environments within which they function. Although organizations are integrally tied to the larger social system (Parsons, 1960), they seek to establish autonomy of action and domain. As a result, there are strong parallels between White's (1959) conception of man and Thompson's view of organizations. These parallels should be evident in the following excerpts from Thompson's work on organizational action.

> The domain claimed by the organization and recognized by its environment determines the points at which the organization is dependent, facing both constraints and contingencies. To attain any significant measure of self-control, the organization must manage its dependency. . . . Under norms of rationality, therefore, organizations seek to minimize the power of task-environmental elements over them. . . .
>
> The more an organization is constrained in some sectors of its task environment, the more power it will seek over remaining elements of its task environment. When the organization is unable to achieve such a balance, it will seek to enlarge its task environment. (Thompson, 1967, pp. 37–38.)

As we can see from both the Thompson and White quotes, organizations and individuals can each be viewed as reducing sources of external dependence and seeking relative autonomy. Neither approach denies the adjustive nature of individuals or organizations, however. Thompson deals extensively with organizational design as an adjustive mechanism which is less costly and disruptive than altering the environment. White, likewise, views the autonomy motive as something which does not supplant but goes beyond traditional learning mechanisms of individuals. Thus, we are left with remarkably parallel conceptions of organizations and individuals, both exhibiting rationality in a proactive and reactive sense.

EXISTENCE OF JUSTIFICATION

Sources of Justification in Individuals

Individuals, as we have noted, are motivated by a competence drive. They seek to predict and control their immediate environments and to attain particular goals they have set for themselves. However, paradoxically, the greater are individuals subject to a competence motive, the more they are also susceptible to forces that run counter to rationality. If an individual has a strong need to be correct or accurate, he is also likely to feel the need to justify his decisions—to prove to himself and others that he is indeed competent and rational as a decision maker. Unfortunately, it is precisely the need to demonstrate rationality that can lead to justification processes which run counter to our conception of rational man.

The most extensive body of research relating to self-justification processes are studies originally designed to test the theory of cognitive dissonance. As defined by Festinger (1957), dissonance theory is an extremely simple yet provocative idea. Festinger posited that any two cognitive elements which are inconsistent with each other will lead to a psychologically uncomfortable state of cognitive dissonance. According to Festinger's formulation, cognitive elements are defined broadly as any knowledge, opinion, or belief about oneself or environment. In this form, dissonance theory is almost indistinguishable from other models of cognitive consistency (e.g., Newcomb, 1953; Heider, 1958; Osgood, 1960; Rosenberg, 1960). However, dissonance theory has had a much greater influence on social science theory and research than any other consistency model.

Many reviewers have argued that the disportionate amount of influence of dissonance over other cognitive consistency theories has been due to the highly general nature of Festinger's model or the creativity of the empirical research supporting dissonance theory. In this author's opinion, however, the historical impact of Festinger's theory is at least partly due to the fact that most dissonance studies have implicitly tapped self-justification processes. Dissonance research was given credit for discovering many aspects of human justification and for finding forms of behavior which were more rationalizing than rational. It was these counterintuitive (and seemingly nonrational) findings which largely created the research interest and controversy surrounding dissonance theory.

The most controversial and heavily researched subarea of dissonance theory tests what is known as the "insufficient justification paradigm." The paradigm deals with the consequences of acting in a manner inconsistent with one's beliefs or attitudes in the absence of external justification. According to the theory, dissonance should be aroused by inconsistency between one's attitude toward an activity and knowledge of its enactment. However, as external pressure (e.g., promised reward or threatened punishment) on the individual to perform the activity is decreased, the dissonance aroused by its enactment is increased. The crucial point is that the level of dissonance aroused should be at its maximum if the extrinsic reward or punishment is just barely enough to elicit the behavior; any incentive greater than this minimal amount (being consistent with the behavior) should, theoretically, produce less cognitive dissonance (Festinger, 1957).

In reviewing much of the literature on dissonance theory, Aronson (1968) made a very important point which helps clarify the relation between cognitive dissonance and self-justification processes. Aronson noted that in most dissonance studies, it is not the two inconsistent cognitions about an activity (e.g., "I believe a task is dull," and "I am not getting paid or otherwise compensated for my efforts") that really motivates individuals to change their attitudes. Instead, Aronson noted that it is the inconsistency between behavior or attitudes and one's own self-concept that is dissonance-arousing. If individuals believe they are generally incompetent, discovering that they are undercompensated or have made a behavioral error should not be disturbing and, thus, they would not be motivated to reduce dissonance. However, if individuals possess some degree of self-confidence, being placed into a situation with insufficient rewards should be disturbing. Aronson therefore posits that positive self-concept is an important boundary condition for dissonance theory effects.

We would go beyond Aronson and state that in many dissonance experiments a need for self-justification has been tapped rather than cognitive consistency. Because researchers have typically pitted a dissonance-predicted effect versus self-interest or reinforcement effects, the impact of the theory is due largely to the ability of researchers to find counterhedonic data in a variety of situations. However, a rather parsimonious explanation of most of the dissonance findings is that individuals seek to justify their own actions, decisions, and attitudes so as to protect their self-concepts. If individuals want to demonstrate competence, they will tend to re-evaluate alternatives after a choice in order to "prove" they were right (e.g., Brehm, 1956; Vroom, 1966; Knox & Inkster, 1968). Individuals will also tend to re-evaluate their attitudes toward activities to "prove" that they did not make a mistake in committing themselves to a dull task (Brehm & Cohen, 1959; Freedman, 1963; Weick, 1964; Pallak, Sogin & Van Zante, 1974), boring discussion group (Aronson & Mills, 1959; Gerard & Mathewson, 1966) or in writing an essay against their own position on an issue (Festinger and Carlsmith, 1957; Cohen, 1962; Carlsmith, Collins & Helmreich, 1966; Linder, Cooper, & Jones, 1967).

The case for self-justification becomes even stronger when we examine some of the moderating conditions recently discovered for "dissonance effects." After intensive research using counterattitudinal advocacy as a dissonance-arousing treatment (i.e., writing an essay against one's own position on an issue as in the classic Festinger and Carlsmith procedure) it is now generally agreed that the following conditions are necessary for dissonance to be induced: the essay writing must entail strong negative consequences for the subject, there should be a high degree of choice in writing the essay, and a minimal level or absolutely no external inducement such as money should be involved (Collins & Hoyt, 1972; Calder, Ross & Insko, 1973). What these moderating conditions amount to is that the subject has made a clear-cut mistake in deciding to undertake a negative task without extenuating circumstances or the promise of other rewards. What's more, there is also research that shows that subjects must feel personally responsible for the negative consequences in order to obtain a dissonance effect (Cooper, 1971). That is, the prior decision to undertake the task must not only have been free of duress or outside pressure, but the negative consequences should have been foreseeable at the time of the decision. In short, the subject, despite his general need for competence, is typically induced into behaving irrationally in most dissonance experiments. Therefore, we would interpret most dissonance effects as products of ego-defensiveness. More specifically, we would predict that the need to justify one's actions increases as the irrationality of one's actions are exposed to both self and others.

Prospective and Retrospective Rationality. In moving away from dissonance theory, we have simply affirmed that individuals exhibit certain ego-defensive processes and that ego-defensiveness may often interfere with rationality. Still, if we define rationality in a totally subjective sense, any behavior, including outcroppings of ego-defensiveness, can be viewed as rational. However, we must define rationality in a more limited sense if it is to have any explanatory power. Thus, rationality is usually viewed as decision making approximating economic utility theory or expectancy theory models of behavior. We will refer to this traditional image of man as being *prospectively* rational. Under prospective rationality, the individual will process information and make decisions to attain a high level of outcomes. However, when ego-defensiveness is dominant, individuals will often behave in a *retrospectively* rational manner. They will re-evaluate alternatives and outcomes to make it *appear* that they have acted in a competent or intelligent manner. This type of behavior may be rational in a totally subjective sense, but clinicians would label it as "rationalizing" based on intersubjective criteria or standards used by outside observers of the behavior (Haan, 1977).

Probably the most critical element separating prospective from retrospective rationality is the individual's treatment of *sunk costs.* Under prospective rationality, resources are allocated and decisions entered into when future benefits are greater than future costs. Previous losses or costs, which have been suffered but which are not expected to recur in the future, should not enter into decision calculations. However, under retrospective rationality, there may be motivation to rectify past losses as well as to seek future gain. The individual, in order to appear rational in his decision making, is likely to keep sunk costs as an active part of decision making under retrospective rationality. This desire to recoup sunk costs is probably what underlies much of the behavior that we commonly label as self-justification.

Figure 4 outlines a simple model of some of the determinants of retrospective rationality. As shown in the figure, when action leads to negative consequences ego-defensiveness may occur on the part of individuals. As we have noted, there is evidence showing that the degree of defensiveness is moderated by the amount of personal responsibility for negative consequences. Two previously researched aspects of personal responsibility are *prior choice* and *foreseeability of outcomes* (Cooper, 1971); however, to these variables we have added norms for rationality. If an organization (or any subculture) highly values rationality, individuals are likely to assume greater personal responsibility for negative consequences and therefore suffer greater ego-defensiveness. If ego-defensiveness is indeed high, the individual is predicted to follow one of several retrospectively rational strategies. He may search for exogenerating explanations of the negative consequences to "take himself off the hook." There is a substantial body of research (see Stevens & Jones, 1976) that indeed shows that individuals do engage in self-serving biases. Alternatively, an individual may simply re-evaluate the outcomes he has received and conclude that they are not so bad after all or even "blessings in disguise." However, this is a difficult path to follow when outside observers can easily corroborate outcomes, as in most organizational settings. Finally, the individual can attempt to recoup his losses by committing new resources to the same, negative course of action (Staw, 1976). By throwing good money after bad, individuals sometimes attempt to "prove" that they never really made a mistake after all.

Each of the retrospective strategies shown in Figure 4 are focused upon erasing or alleviating behavioral or decisional error. However, if positive consequences had resulted from one's action, or if negative consequences did not produce ego-defensiveness, then individuals are predicted to follow a more prospectively rational strategy. They will be more likely to search for accurate or plausible explanations of events than to engage in self-serving biases (cf., Fox, 1980). Also, individual commitment to future action is shown to depend on the anticipation of future benefits and costs, rather than on an effort to recoup previous losses.

Internal and External Justification. Most writings on self-justification or dissonance theory have characterized rationalization as a purely internal

Figure 4. Some Determinants of Retrospective and Prospective Rationality

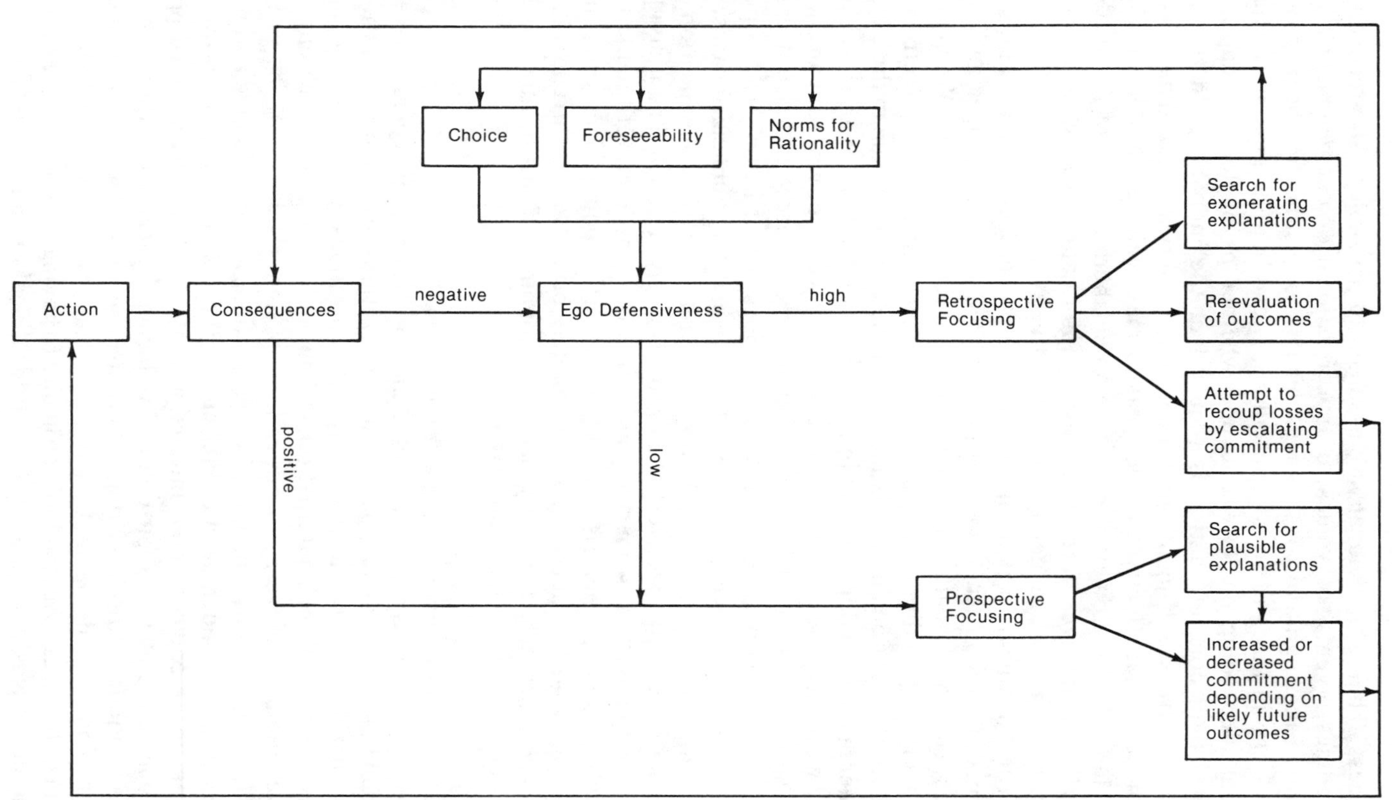

process. That is, individuals are assumed to psychologically reconstruct outcomes, events, or values to appear rational or competent *to themselves*. Like cognitive consistency, this type of justification helps protect one's ego in times of stress and failure. It can be functional or dysfunctional, depending on its extent and whether psychological adaptation rather than concrete action is required of the individual. In times of extreme stress, self-justification may, like a safety valve, reduce tension to the level that effective decision making may again be possible (cf., Janis & Mann, 1977). However, extensive and elaborate forms of justification may, by themselves, forestall necessary information processing and decision making, thus reducing individual effectiveness.

When justification is a largely internal process, individuals attend to events and reconstruct them to protect their own self-images and identities. However, justification may also be directed externally. When faced with an external threat or evaluation, individuals may resort to retrospective forms of rationality or justification. Like Richard Nixon in the case of Watergate or Lyndon Johnson in the case of the Vietnam War, individuals may go to extreme lengths to prove that they were not wrong in an earlier decision. This type of justification is externally directed, since it is designed to prove to others rather than to oneself that he or she is competent. However, as we have seen in these two widely publicized cases, the behaviors individuals can undertake in search of external justification can also be more retrospectively than prospectively rational. The individual may seal himself off from relevant information, misinterpret the facts, or simply take improper risks to save an earlier policy decision. Thus, external as well as internal justification may be viewed as "irrational" by outside observers, especially if the outcroppings of justification lead to further negative consequences.

Sources of Justification in Organizations

In our earlier discussion we noted that the Thompsonian perspective on organizational behavior posits that organizations are intendedly rational (not that they always act rationally). Organizations, from this viewpoint, strive to control their internal operations and external environment, but never totally achieve a closed, rational system (Hall, 1977).

The limitations to rationality in organizations are multifaceted and have been subject to much debate. Pfeffer (1977) has argued that organizations do not make choices about internal allocations of resources based upon rational criteria, but upon political influence. Internal coalitions among organizational actors may thus determine organizational actions as much as internal task demands or environmental exigencies. Hall (1977) has argued that organizations have difficulty behaving rationally since there is little consensus over goal-criteria. Educational organizations, for example, may seek to satisfy mutually inconsistent criteria (e.g., research, teaching, and service), and the process of attempting to reach one of these goals can preclude the attainment of others. Gouldner (1959) and Katz & Kahn (1978) have argued that organizations are natural systems and that organizational actions are relatively unplanned adaptive responses to threats to equilibrium. The open-systems approach stresses the interrelationship of the organization to the environment as elements of the larger social system, rather than the subjugation of the environment *by* the organization as viewed under the "rationality" perspective. Finally, March & Olson (1976) view organizations as rather irrational "garbage cans" into which goals, plans, and actions are paired together. They view organizations as possessing very imperfect sets of goals or utility functions, very limited capacities for communication and information processing, and very poor abilities to resolve conflicts among choice alternatives. From the March and Olson perspective, organizations are fortunate to survive at all, let alone function in a rational manner.

Many of the limitations to rationality can be captured effectively by Thompson & Tuden's (1959) classification of organizational decision making. Using their two-by-two matrix, decisions can be classified by certainty of cause-effect relations and clarity of preferences. According to these authors, when beliefs about cause-effect relations are relatively certain and preferences about desired outcomes are clear, then organizations can approach the rationality of a closed system. However, most organizational decisions lie in the other three cells. Thompson and Tuden have labeled the uncertain cause-effect/clear preferences cell as requiring judgmental decision making, and the certain cause-effect/unclear preferences case as requiring compromising and conflict resolution. Finally, the unclear cause-effect/unclear preferences situation is described as necessitating nothing short of inspiration. This last case brings to mind images of organizations "galumphing" along, not knowing exactly where they want to go or how to get there. Unfortunately, this last case is probably the one that best describes how many complex organizations operate.

Figure 5 attempts to graphically show why organizations are highly limited in rationality. This figure is based partially on the ideas of March & Olson (1976), but is presented in a decision format that is analogous to Figure 1. Organizational actions are shown here to be a product of organizational belief systems and preferences in a manner parallel to individual choice and action. However, organizational beliefs and preferences are not simple variables which can be assumed away or taken as given. Organizational beliefs are a complex product of internal communication, information processing, and storage systems in organizations; while organizational preferences result from complex political processes and coalition formation. We will not attempt in this paper to specify the exact linkages among these variables but must simply state that the process is not at all clear-cut and that blockages can readily occur between these factors. For example, information processing and communication may break down and not accurately affect organizational belief systems. Excess turnover of personnel may cause the loss of a large amount of the informal information on the workings of the organization. Likewise, internal organizational politics may not lead to clear preferences but may instead deadlock on mutually inconsistent goals. Finally, exogenous influences from outside organizations (e.g., consumer and government groups) as well as important changes in the general culture can affect prevailing beliefs and preferences within organizations.

If we do assume that organizations at a given point in time have arrived at some set of beliefs and preferences, this consensus will generally lead to certain organizational actions. However, as March and Olson have noted, even this rather obvious linkage is not at all assured. There may be standard procedures, work rules, or government regulations which may block even the clearest intentions. Thus, consensus that a given action will move the organization toward a valued goal will only lead to organizational behavior in the general case; it does not assure it.

Once organizations emit a particular action (e.g., reduce prices, enlarge the board of directors, revise a social action program) there is also no assurance that it will create the intended response from the organization's environment. Organizational actions are often only one of many influences within a complex environment and such actions must overwhelm exogenous influences from other organizations, institutions, and the general environment. Frequently the organization's actions are not the cause of environmental responses and, as a result, the perception of cause-effect relations can often be more superstition than fact. Indeed, it is almost rare when an organization emits a behavior which leads to an environmental response that is interpretable in a clear-cut way. Most often, organizational action constitutes a highly complex treatment or change which results in barely discernible responses from a complex set of environmental variables. This situation obviously does not lend itself to a highly valid set of causal inferences (Campbell & Stanley, 1966), nor does it provide the feedback on action which most organizations demand.

As a result of all the obstructions in the learning process (shown in Figure 5) it is no wonder that organizations fail to act rationally. Organizations, as depicted here, have difficulty translating beliefs and preferences into actions, and once the actions do take place, organizations find even more difficulty in understanding the causal nature of its environment and building a knowledge base. These imperfections in organizational learning are additionally compounded by internal political processes which may dictate goals and preferences in conflict with even the limited amount of

Figure 5. Organizational Learning as an Obstructed Cycle

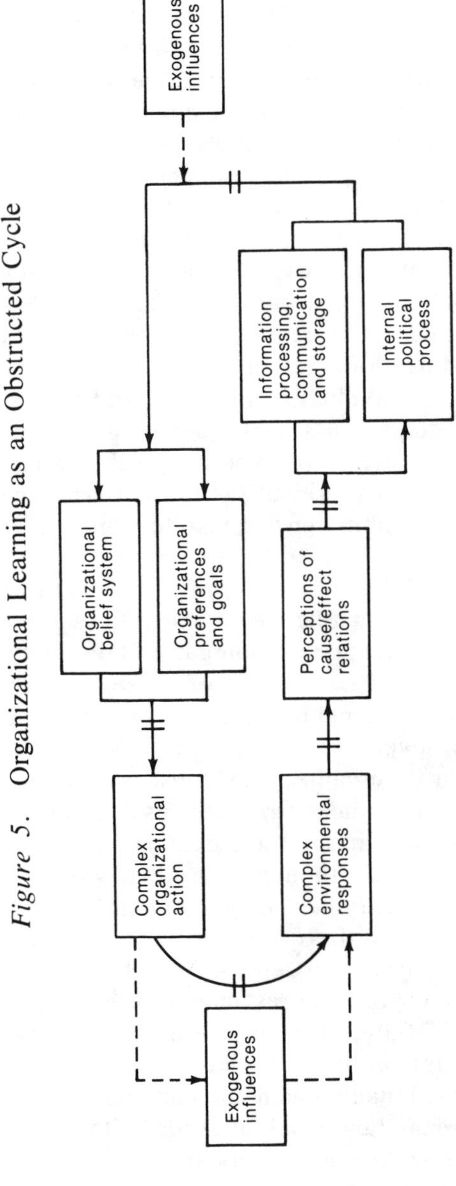

valid knowledge accumulated by a particular organization. This is indeed a bleak picture that we have painted for organizational rationality, and it appears to directly conflict with Thompson's hypotheses on rationality-seeking behavior.

The major point we wish to make is that organizations, like individuals, are *intendedly* rational and operate under norms of rationality. However, organizations, even more than individuals, possess very limited information processing and learning capabilities. Thus, if the parallel still holds, organizations like individuals are often faced with inconsistency between their actions and their expectations of rationality. Just like individuals who are strongly motivated toward rationality but fall short of it, organizations are intentionally rational but do not accomplish their goals. We might therefore predict that organizations will also exhibit signs of rationalization or justification. Earlier, we had posited that the stronger are cultural norms for individual competence and rationality, the more likely it is that individuals will seek to justify their own behavior. In a parallel manner, we will therefore hypothesize that where strong norms for organizational rationality prevail (as in Western society), organizations will be prone to exhibit signs of justification.

Types of Organizational Justification: Internal and External. We can characterize organizational justification in much the same way as we have done with individual justification, dividing it into both internal and external varieties. However, whereas most of existing work on individual rationalization concerns internal justification, exactly the opposite is true for the organizational level of analysis.

Internal justification by organizations consists of relatively uncharted ground. Still, organizations under strong norms of rationality no doubt do exhibit many actions which attempt to create the illusion of rationality for their internal membership, although these behaviors may *not* in fact contribute to effectiveness. For example, standard operating procedures may have been evolved by the organization to deal with old environmental conditions and may now represent nothing more than vestigial characteristics—yet such procedures may still be strictly adhered to. Likewise, a great deal of attention may be paid to making internal rules and regulations consistent although such consistency may not in itself be related to effectiveness. Finally, chain of command and a logically consistent hierarchy system may be publicly defended although actual influence processes in the organization may work quite differently. All of these actions could be classified as outcroppings of internal justification, providing organizational constituents with the illusion of rationality.

We would predict, in line with our reasoning on individual justification, that an organizational failure experience (e.g., low profit or negative review by an outside agency) will increase the drive toward internal justification. That is, poor performance may lead organizations to increase or tighten the internal trappings of rationality such as rule consistency, unity of command, and hierarchical control systems. This hypothesis obviously differs from one that could be derived from an organizational learning theory (Duncan & Weiss, 1978) in which change or adaptation might be predicted to be a product of organizational crises.

In terms of external justification, the analogy between organizations and individuals is quite close. Organizations not only act under norms of rationality, but as Thompson (1967) argues, they also seek to demonstrate such rationality to outside constituents, evaluators, and potential providers of resources. Regardless of whether goals are actually fulfilled or products produced efficiently, organizations seek to demonstrate evidences of rationality. Thus, the organization will place its greatest efforts upon those areas which are most easily measured and quantified. Also, those measures upon which the organization scores well will be most publicized by the organization.

In Thompson's view, organizations act rationally to increase their evaluations or ratings by others on whom they are dependent. This type of behavior could be classified under prospective rationality, since the organization's emphasis may be upon seeking resources and minimizing future dependencies. However, Thompson's hypotheses can also be interpreted as outcroppings of retrospective rationality. Under strict evaluation or scrutiny, organizations may concentrate so heavily on justifying the rationality of past behavior that they fail to act rationally in a prospective sense. Scarce resources may be so heavily allocated to compiling hard data on a program (e.g., number of cases seen by social workers, test scores of entering students, number of new orders filled) that other relevant aspects of performance are omitted. Thus, future opportunities may be lost when attention is unduly concentrated upon rationalizing past performance. Although the Thompsonian strategies for meeting environmental demands are rational from the organization's point of view, some are rational only in the most short-term sense and are more retrospectively than prospectively focused.

THE CONFLUENCE OF RATIONALITY AND JUSTIFICATION IN ORGANIZATIONAL SETTINGS

In this section we will address the issue of how rationality and justification combine in organizational settings. From a simple theoretical perspective these two forces appear in direct conflict with one another. However, we will argue that justification as well as rationality are two central themes of organizational life which are in constant ebb and flow. From the perspective of both individuals and organizations, the merits of rationality are rather obvious and we will not concentrate on them here. Instead, we will argue that some measure of justification can also aid the functioning of both individuals and organizational systems. Although the balance of forces most appropriate for effective functioning is not yet clear, we will emphasize the functional significance of both of these factors.

Some Individual Effects

Individual behavior, even as viewed from the cognitive motivation model of Figure 1, is not complete without justification processes. As shown in the motivation model, action does not simply flow from cognition, but feeds back onto the cognitions of valences and instrumentalities. The individual adjusts his values and probabilities of attainment to the reality around him, and this permeability can constitute a form of justification.

The subjectivity of valued outcomes has already been evidenced by two streams of research. First, research on level of aspiration (e.g., Lewin, Dembo, Festinger, & Sears, 1944; Myers & Fort, 1963; Brickman & Campbell, 1971) shows that individuals generally adjust their aspirations downward when they do not accomplish their goals. Second, research on adaptation level theory (Helson, 1964) has demonstrated that what is viewed as a positive outcome depends greatly upon its comparison level, and that the level of past outcomes provides one important guideline for satisfaction (see Beebe-Center, 1932; Brickman, Coats, & Bulman, 1978). Therefore, persons who must endure physically or psychologically hostile environments usually come to terms with these settings. Through cognitive realignment of affective baselines and aspirations, what appear to outsiders as highly dissatisfying conditions are often not perceived by individuals as so aversive.

In essence, there are almost no worldwide "objective" physical conditions (e.g., temperature, terrain, abundance of raw materials) which lead to positive or negative attitudes of peoples. For example, individuals generally prefer their home regions regardless of how hostile they appear to outsiders (Gould & White, 1974) and migrants to a new geographical area judge its characteristics (e.g., noise, pollution, friendliness) in relation to their previous residences rather than on an absolute standard (Wahlwill & Kohn, 1973). Even "objective" quality of life indicators such as per capita income, life expectancy, and average literacy do not relate strongly to life satisfaction across nations. For instance, Cantril's (1965) thirteen-nation survey showed that, although countries in which individuals were most satisfied appeared to be those in which there had been some recent improvement, the absolute level of a country on objective indicators did not always predict satisfaction. Interestingly, highest levels of satisfaction were scored in countries where there were strong national goals and ideologies (e.g., Cuba and Yugoslavia). Political leadership and ideology may thus provide the justifications and rationale needed by individuals to maintain positive attitudes when objective indicators are still low.

Salancik & Pfeffer (1978) have recently made a similar argument in the case of job attitudes in organizations. Although job characteristics as observed by outsiders do relate to individual satisfaction (Hackman & Oldham, 1976), few of these job characteristics are really objective. Factors such as task variety, significance, and autonomy are frequently the product of individual and social labeling. Therefore, what is a significant and meaningful task may depend greatly on one's definition of the situation, and may be highly subject to cognitive manipulation and realignment (see O'Reilly & Caldwell, in press, for a recent test of this notion).

Although satisfaction appears to be a highly subjective variable, one factor that is central to any tendency of individuals to justify their fates is behavioral commitment. Recent research on commitment (see Zimbardo, Ebbeson & Maslach, 1977; Salancik, 1977) shows that, once individuals are committed to a stream of action, their attitudes will generally become aligned with the behavior. Moreover, the ability of individuals to justify their fates can be heightened when there has been a marked reduction in outcomes. If individuals can easily reverse or change the situation to improve outcomes, this obviously will be the first choice of action for many individuals. However, if the decrease in outcomes in long-lived or irrevocable, readjustment will occur.

The moderating effect of commitment was observed by Staw (1974) in his study of ROTC cadets before and after the draft lottery. Most members of ROTC had joined the military organization to avoid being drafted and were not attracted to the organization by the intrinsic characteristics of ROTC (i.e., drills, summer camp, coursework). However, after the draft lottery occurred some individuals were informed that they were no longer vulnerable to the draft, while others were told that they would almost certainly be drafted if they left ROTC. As expected, most persons who were safe from the draft disenrolled from ROTC since they no longer needed the inducement of a draft deferment. However, a large number of individuals could not easily leave ROTC since they had already signed a binding contract with the Army before the lottery had occurred. Clearly, this group had made a mistake in joining ROTC and did not receive many valued outcomes from the organization after the lottery. They no longer really needed the deferment provided by ROTC and thus they were left only with drills, coursework, and summer camp as organizational outcomes. Yet, because of their binding commitment, this group was not allowed to disenroll. Rather remarkably, these individuals not only maintained their attitudes toward ROTC but actually increased them.

As shown in the ROTC study, the inevitability of a set of outcomes may moderate whether individuals justify their fates or not. When individuals can change their behavior to gain more positive outcomes, they generally will do this, as expected by most rational models in psychology (e.g., expectancy theory, exchange theory, decision theory). However, if individuals are locked into a course of action, they will tend to adjust to the level of outcomes received. Validation of adjustment effects have also been found in the interpersonal attraction area. When individuals are forced to work with another person who is disliked, opinions toward the unattractive person increase if the rater believes the work relationship will be long-lasting (Darley & Bersheid, 1967). No readjustment occurs when the relationship is believed to be temporary.

Self-justification, as evidenced in the ROTC study and the interpersonal attraction literature, does not fit well with a purely rational view of man in which both actions and attitudes are simply determined by the expectancy and receipt of outcomes. However, it is likely that justification is psychologically functional for individuals. Negative attitudes and persistent but futile efforts to avoid aversive outcomes may only lead to psychological stress if the situation is not tractable. In these situations justification is far better than rationality, at least in terms of individual mental health.

The conflict between rationality and justification can be most intense when there are norms for high performance and also a very difficult task to perform. When individuals are confronted with impossible demands, they will tend to lower their aspirations and adjust to lower goals and outcomes. However, there may be strong organizational pressure to persist at what appears to be an insurmountable task. In these cases, self-justification processes may be a less-active force and, as a result, persistence without success can lead to undo stress, depression, or learned helplessness (Seligman, 1975). This problem may especially exist when organizations and individuals do not agree upon what are attainable goals.

The recent upsurge in self-help techniques and career management may also threaten the balance between rationality and justification. The general theme of these efforts is for the individual to take responsibility for his own life and the outcomes produced by that responsibility. Guidelines and exercises are frequently posed for the individual to think of long-term goals and how his present job is or is not instrumental to achieving these goals. Organizations frequently sponsor career management sessions and generally endorse any increase in self-initiated improvement and goal-directedness. Unfortunately, however, career management techniques may actually decrease rather than increase job attitudes. By making careers and long-term goals salient, enormous demands are placed upon the current job one holds. It must not only be pleasant or not too dissatisfying, but also instrumental to important career objectives. Without such pressures for individual rationality, people may instead base satisfaction on more immediate characteristics of the job; and, if the job possesses few positive features, they may still justify it on some very subjective long-term considerations. These long-term factors may, however, be quite unrealistic idealizations of the future—closer to "pipe dreams" than realistic career goals. As Studs Terkel (1974) found in several open-ended interviews, a person performing a basically dissatisfying job may justify it as a temporary shelter or place to bide one's time until the "eventual" satisfying position opens up (e.g., opening own bar, becoming a race car driver, etc.). Obviously, few of these dreams ever materialize and would be discouraged by most realistic career counselors. Yet, these irrational hopes and justifications may actually be what psychologically sustains many individuals in their current lines of work.

Some Organizational Effects

There is literally no empirical research to describe the confluence of rationality and justification on organizations. Yet, we will speculate about some evidences of these cross-cutting forces and attempt to describe the functional interplay of these two factors.

As we have noted, although organizations are intendedly rational their ability to achieve any measure of rationality is quite limited. Only very imperfectly does the organization input and process information, and it has difficulty with even the most primitive learning mechanisms. Thus, we would argue that difficulty in rationally adapting to the environment is most marked for organizations when there is substantial ambiguity on both cause-effect relations and outcome criteria. A university, for example, has difficulty defining what "education" is as an outcome variable, let alone discovering the best way to increase its level. A church has a similar problem with faith, morality, or other outcome criteria by which to measure success, and even a hospital has difficulty defining "health" between the extremes of total malfunctioning and relative survival. In each of these cases, rational learning is made difficult by ambiguity of both purpose and technology.

If we order a variety of organizations along the two dimensions of ambiguity of goals and cause/effect relations, the lowest levels of ambiguity would be associated with a single proprietorship operating within a technologically stable area of the economy. Here the primary methods of production and sales would be known and the chief outcome variable would be clear: economic benefit (i.e., return on investment) for the owner of the business. However, once the private firm grows into a publicly-owned corporation outcome variables become more ambiguous. Although Becker & Gordon (1966) argue that all private corporations have maximization of stockholder wealth as their primary goals, others would disagree. Once a single proprietorship is replaced by professional management, organizational survival and growth often replace return on equity as operating goals (Hall, 1977). Serving consumer interests, providing jobs, contributing to the community tax base, and public responsibility also become more important as corporations grow in size and importance. This multivariate goal structure (Friedlander & Pickle, 1968; Pickle & Friedlander, 1967) leads to ambiguity and uncertainty over what goals to seek or satisfy. In a sense, the larger become private corporations the more like public interest organizations they become.

With most public organizations there are two sources of ambiguity about goals. First, it is not at all clear whose interests a public organization is designed to serve and there is frequently conflict among disparate goals held by each constituent group. In addition, most social service goals (e.g., health, welfare, education) are highly subjective in nature. Each administration has its own operational definition of these terms and changes in health care delivery, social welfare programs and education policy often shift with each change in organizational hierarchy. Finally, as we have noted, most social programs work with a highly ambiguous technology. Instead of hard technical facts, ideas about cause-effect relations are the subject of intuition and custom within many nonprofit organizations—theories of education and child-rearing, for example, run in historical cycles and are based only tangentially on any empirical data.

Against this background of ambiguity, Weick (1977) has developed the notion of enactment in organizations. Organizations, according to Weick, attempt to make sense out of even the most ambiguous environments. However, Weick argues that the terms, constructs, and metaphors by which organizations perceive the events around them can literally *become* the organization's environment. One can best illustrate this enactment notion by carrying it to its extreme. For example, a powerful religious organization has the ability to define religious terms in nearly any way it chooses and, in turn, it can operate upon its own definition of reality. Because outcomes and cause-effect relations are so ambiguous for this type of organization, norms and operating procedures could easily be based on an enacted environment for very long periods of time (this may be why major changes in religious organizations occur so infrequently). In contrast, a highly subjective view of reality does not last long within the competitive private economy. A company with a highly divergent view of its goals and the environment is likely to become economically extinct, with the surviving firms conforming rather well to the more objective rules of the marketplace.

We would argue that for organizations which must operate under highly ambiguous goals and cause-effect relations, justification is of vital importance. Because there is so much uncertainty, it is essential to justify whatever goals are chosen and whatever technology is followed. Under high levels of ambiguity, justification is necessary to both provide purpose for an organization's membership and rationale for parties' external to the organization. In fact, organizations which face a great deal of ambiguity are frequently perceived as more effective when they have developed an elaborate or persuasive set of justifications for their particular goals and technology. For example, the most successful educational organizations are those which have developed the *x* school of thought or approach to education. Likewise, successful governmental units are frequently those which are most eloquent in conveying their own subgoals, philosophy, and procedures. Thus, in many organizational settings justification *can* become the reality; through justification, perceived sources of ambiguity can be explained away or replaced by shared meaning as opposed to economic or technical "facts."

It should be noted that Berlew (1974) has also touched upon the essential role of justification in his discussion of organizational leadership. To Berlew the effective leader is one who clarifies organizational purposes and helps to articulate collective goals. He provides an organizational mission and a path for others to follow. In essence, the leader is one who formulates justifications of goals and technology which are believable and supportable by organizational members. Along these lines, we would predict that the more ambiguous are organizational goals and technology, the more important it is to have a leader who can provide justifications for the organization. This may be why charismatic leaders are frequently demanded by religious and governmental organizations, while less articulate but technically competent managers can successfully fulfill many other executive roles.

A CROSS-LEVEL EFFECT: THE CASE OF ORGANIZATIONAL EVALUATION

An important cross-level effect of rationality and justification can be illustrated with the application of evaluation research techniques in organizations. We will show that evaluation research, as an outcropping of organizational rationality, is very likely to foster individual forces for justification. We will elaborate on this cross-level effect in some depth because of the increasing use of evaluation techniques in organizational settings.

Evaluation activities are representative of the core of rational decision making and can be applied to almost any level of a social system. As originally envisioned by Campbell (1969), evaluation research would aid public officials in allocating scarce resources among a large variety of social programs. The principle was simple. If data from various programs could be collected and analyzed in such a way as to increase its internal validity, public officials would have much greater knowledge of which programs do accomplish societal goals and which do not. Because of the increasing scarcity of public funds and strong cultural norms for rationality, evaluation research has become increasingly popular within the United States (see Riecken & Boruch, 1974; Wortman, 1975).

Recently, Staw (1977b) attempted to extend the principles of evaluation research from societal to organizational decision making. If organizations do operate under norms of rationality, it is strongly in their interest to clarify cause-effect relations. However, gaining greater understanding of the effects of particular organizational actions often requires entirely different modes of data collection, feedback, and analysis than those currently used by organizations. Extrapolating from the principles of evaluation research, organizations would need to systematically experiment with its environment (cf., March, 1971), intentionally trying out many divergent strategies, knowing full well that many of these new alternatives would eventually be dropped from use. In addition, a truly experimenting organization would seek to strengthen causal inference about internal policies through experimental and quasi-experimental design. For example, procedures for personnel selection, job design, pay systems, and work schedules are all variables which could be systematically altered to find the best available method. Currently, only vague knowledge, tradition, and precedent dictate many of the internal actions and policies of organizations.

In its ideal state, evaluation research would be devoted toward improving causal inference and reducing many of the sources of ambiguity which limit rationality in organizations. However, despite all of its potential to increase rationality, the application of evaluation research faces many problems in organizational settings. Many of these problems result from the conflict between organizational rationality and individual justification.

If organizations were to assiduously apply the principles of evaluation research, they would require administrators to experiment sequentially with many policy alternatives, assess each of their effects, and change to new policies when outcomes were not satisfactory. Such an experimenting organization may be difficult to achieve, however, because of individual tendencies of justify their behavior. Contrary to the principles of experimentation, administrators may often hesitate to make major changes in policy following the receipt of negative consequences. As noted earlier, some studies have shown that when people's behavior leads to negative consequences they may, instead of changing behavior, cognitively distort the negative consequences to more positively valued outcomes (e.g., Freedman, 1963; Pallak, Sogin & Van Zante, 1974; Staw, 1974; Weick, 1964). By biasing behavioral outcomes individuals can rationalize their previous actions or psychologically defend themselves against a perceived error in judgment. In addition, it is also possible in many evaluation situations for administrators to go beyond the passive distortion of adverse consequences in an effort to rationalize a behavioral error. When negative consequences are incurred, it is frequently possible for administrators to enlarge the commitment of resources and undergo the risk of additional negative outcomes in order to justify previous behavior or to demonstrate the ultimate rationality of an original course of action.

Using a simulated business decision case, Staw (1976) experimentally tested for the tendency to escalate following the receipt of negative consequences. In his study, business school students were asked to allocate research and development funds to one of two operating divisions of a company. They were then given the results of their initial decisions and asked to make a second allocation of R&D funds. In this study, some subjects also were assigned to a condition in which they did not make the initial allocation decision themselves, but were told that it was made earlier by another financial officer of the firm. The results of the experiment were as follows: (1) there was a main effect of responsibility such that subjects allocated more money when they, rather than another financial officer, had made the initial decision; (2) there was a main effect of consequences such that subjects allocated more money to the declining rather than improving division; and (3) there was a significant interaction of responsibility and consequences. That is, subjects allocated even more money when they were responsible for negative consequences than would be expected by the two main effects acting alone. Personal responsibility for negative consequence, therefore, may lead to the greatest likelihood of escalation behavior.

From these experimental results and observational evidence of some real-world escalations (see, e.g., "Pentagon Papers" for a description of policy making during the Vietnam War), it seems possible that administrators can become trapped by their own previous mistakes. They may, counter to principles of evaluation research, refuse to admit the failure of a policy or procedure and forge ahead in spite of negative consequences.

Internal and External Justification. The conflict we have posed in applying evaluation research has been between organizational demands for rationality and the individual's tendency for self-justification. We have characterized the self-justification effect as one of denial of error and internal rationalization. However, within organizational settings, ego-gratification and the protection of self-esteem (cf., Aronson, 1968, 1976) are often only secondary to simple administrative survival. If a policy or program fails, administrators are often replaced by the next most promising candidate rather than the next best policy alternative! Thus, the administrator may often be forced to make a policy work at almost any cost. The commitment of new and additional resources can, as a result, stem from self-protective actions of the administrator in addition to, or even in lieu of, the need to bolster individual self-esteem.

As we noted in our earlier discussion of individual justification, it is useful to draw the distinction between internal and external forms of justification. Whereas the internal form of justification refers to private monitoring and self-inflicted costs if a decision fails, the external form of justification refers to the public surveillance of one's decisions and the imposition of sanctions by others if errors are detected. Both forms of justification may lead individuals to focus retrospectively on those events and outcomes which might "save" a previous policy and to protect oneself from the exposure of a previous error. However, evaluation research activities within organizations are especially likely to activate forces for external justification. Because evaluation is an external source of control, administrators will frequently go to great length to demonstrate the rationality of the program and services they manage.

An empirical demonstration of the effect of external justification was recently conducted by Fox & Staw (1979). Two face-valid antecedents of external justification were manipulated. It was predicted that both job insecurity and policy resistance would increase administrative inflexibility to change. According to their reasoning, if an administrator is vulnerable to job loss or demotion, he would likely be highly motivated to protect his position in the organization. Thus, one would predict that a highly insecure administrator would be most likely to attempt to save a policy failure by enlarging the commitment of resources. Likewise, one would predict that resistance in the organization to one's policies might also serve to heighten an escalation effect. If an administrator implements a policy that he knows is unpopular within the organization, he may be especially concerned to protect himself against failure. The experimental results confirmed these two hypotheses. The administrator who was both insecure in his job and who faced stiff policy resistance was most likely to escalate his commitment and become locked-in to a course of action.

The situation of high insecurity and high resistance actually represents an operationalization of Campbell's (1969) notion of the "trapped administrator" who has little choice but to forge ahead in his commitment to a losing policy. The trapped administrator is one who stands only to lose if a particular program does not work and who has literally no choice but to remain fully committed to it, even in the face of failure. The trapped administrator is, of course, acting rationally from his own individual perspective. However, this form of rationality is retrospectively rather than prospectively focused. In this case, the issue is not how to maximize future outcomes but to recoup previous losses.

Rationality versus Justification. The notion of the trapped administrator highlights the confluence of rationality and justification. From the organization's point of view, resources should be allocated only to those programs which yield the highest future return. Yet, from the individual administrator's point of view, it is necessary to defend the usefulness of past and current projects so as to justify or demonstrate the rationality of *previous* allocations of resources. Thus, while a truly experimenting organization might wish to use prospective rationality in evaluating the use of resources, each suborganizational unit or administrator may resort to a retrospective form of rationality in their own decision making.

The conflict between rationality and justification can be manifested at multiple levels in an organizational system. Recall that organizations attempt to demonstrate their performance to outside agencies and may become retrospectively focused in order to defend its previous actions. Thus, at the most macroscopic level, one can envisage an experimenting society functioning under prospective rationality, while those individual organizations actually providing the services might still be manifesting strong outcroppings of justification. Likewise, at a much more microscopic level of analysis, the evaluation of individual role performance can involve the same conflict of forces. As Lawler (1971) has noted, the stronger is the evaluation system used for performance appraisal and salary administration, the more defensive are likely to be individuals participating in the program. Therefore, it appears that almost any system which seeks rationality must also suffer some of the costs of justification.

The conflict between rationality and justification seems to exist simply because goals and interests change across each level in an organizational system. Goal seeking and prospective rationality at one level of the system generally translate into self-protecting, retrospective rationality at lower levels. While some authors (e.g., Argyris & Schon, 1978) would characterize this transformation process as a malfunction within an organizational system, we would view it as both inevitable and necessary. Each level in an organizational system faces its own ecology of forces. Thus, whether one views behavior as an outcropping of rationality or justification depends greatly upon one's perspective. From the top of an organizational system, self-protective behaviors emitted by lower levels are frequently viewed as defensive reactions. However, the same behavior may be viewed by its source as highly rational and prospectively focused. This shifting focus of decision making is one reason why organizations can be characterized as loosely coupled systems (Weick, 1976).

Uniformity of purpose and action are difficult to effectuate when perspectives shift throughout an organizational system and when rationality can easily translate into justification across organizational levels. Yet, this loose coupling may be precisely what allows an organization to survive when it faces radically changing conditions. Our point is not to advocate justification over rationality, but again to emphasize the functional interplay of these two forces, even across levels in an organizational system.

CONCLUSION

In this essay we have described forces for rationality and justificaiton at both the individual and organizational levels. In the first section we noted that rationality and justification comprise pervasive images of both human and organizational systems, yet these images often appear to conflict sharply. The second section of this essay dealt with several examples of the confluence of rationality and justification within organizational systems. The purpose of these examples was not simply to review established research areas or to "solve" the conflict between rationality and justification, but to illustrate the functional interrelationship of these two forces. It is this author's contention that the confluence of these two general factors underlie much of what is now known as organizational behavior. By reconsidering this conceptual underpinning, it may thus be possible to generate many new hypotheses and programs of research. Also, because rationality and justification concern central issues of organizing, further research on this issue could help to stem the present trend toward developing greater numbers of mini theories within rather isolated areas of research.

REFERENCES

Appley, M. H. (1971) *Adaptation level theory*. New York: Academic Press.

Argyris, C. (1972) *The applicability of organizational sociology*. London: Cambridge University Press.

——— & Schon, D. A. (1978) *Organizational learning: A theory of action perspective*. Reading, Mass.: Addison Wesley.

Aronson, E. (1968) "Dissonance theory: Progress and problems." In R. Abelson, E. Aronson, W. McGuire, T. Newcomb, M. Rosenberg, & P. Tannebaum (eds.) *Theories of cognitive consistency: A sourcebook*. Chicago: Rand McNally.

Aronson, E. (1976) *The Social Animal* (2nd ed.), San Francisco: W. H. Freeman.

——— & Mills. (1959) "The effect of severity of initiation of liking for a group." *Journal of Abnormal and Social Psychology, 59,* 177–181.

Becker, S. W. & Gordon, G. (1966) "An entrepreneural theory of formal organizations." *Administrative Science Quarterly*, 1966, Vol. 11, No. 3.

Beebe-Center, J. G. (1932) *Pleasantness and unpleasantness*. Princeton, N.J.: Van Nostrand.

Berlew, D. E. (1974) "Leadership and organizational excitement." In D. Kolb, I. Rubin, &

F. McIntyre (eds.) *Organizational psychology: A book of readings*. Englewood Cliffs, New Jersey: Prentice-Hall.

Blau, P. & Schoenherr, R. A. (1971) *The structure of organizations*. New York: Basic Books.

Brehm, J. (1956) "Postdecision changes in the desirability of alternatives." *Journal of Abnormal and Social Psychology, 53,* 384–389.

——— & Cohen, A. R. (1959) "Choice and chance relative deprivation as determinants of cognitive dissonance." *Journal of Abnormal and Social Psychology, 58,* 383–387.

Brickman, P. & Campbell, D. T. (1971) "Hedonic relativism and planning the good society." In M. H. Appley (ed.) *Adaptation-level theory: A symposium*. New York: Academic Press.

———, Coates, D. & Bulman, R. (1978) "Lottery winners and accident victims: Is happiness relative?" *Journal of Personality and Social Psychology, 36,* 917–927.

Calder, B. J., Ross, M., & Insko, C. (1973) "Attitude change and attitude attribution: Effects of incentive, choice, and consequences." *Journal of Personality and Social Psychology, 25,* 84–100.

Campbell, D. T. (1969) "Reforms as experiments." *American Psychologist, 24,* 409–429.

——— & Stanley, J. C. (1966) *Experimental and quasi-experimental designs for research*. Chicago: Rand McNally.

Campbell, J. P. & Pritchard, R. D. (1976) "Motivation theory in industrial and organizational psychology." In M. D. Dunnette (ed.) *Handbook of industrial and organizational psychology*. Chicago: Rand-McNally.

Cantril, H. (1965) *The pattern of human concerns*. New Brunswick, New Jersey: Rutgers University Press.

Carlsmith, J. M., Collins, B. E., & Helmreich, R. L. (1966) "Studies in forced compliance: The effect of pressure for compliance on attitude change produced by face-to-face role playing and anonymous essay writing." *Journal of Personality and Social Psychology,* 1966, *1,* 1–13.

Chandler, A. D. (1962) *Strategy and structure*. Boston: MIT Press.

Child, J. (1973) "Predicting and understanding organization structure." *Administrative Science Quarterly,* 168–185.

Cohen, A. R. (1962) "An experiment on small rewards for discrepant compliance and change." In J. Brehm & A. R. Cohen (eds.) *Explorations in cognitive dissonance*. New York: Wiley, 73–78.

Cohen, M. D., March, J. G., & Olsen, J. P. (1972) "A garbage can model of organizational choice." *Administrative Science Quarterly, 17,* 1–25.

Collins, B. E. & Hoyt, M. F. (1972) "Personal responsibility for consequences: An integration and extension of the forced compliance literature." *Journal of Experimental Social Psychology, 8,* 558–594.

Cooper, J. (1971) "Personal responsibility and dissonance: The role of foreseen consequences." *Journal of Personality and Social Psychology, 8,* 354–363.

Darley, J. & Berscheid, E. (1967) "Increasing liking as the result of the anticipation of personal contact." *Human Relations 20,* 29–40.

Duncan, R. & Weiss, A. (1978) "Organizational learning: Implications for organizational design." In B. Staw (ed.) *Research in Organizational Behavior* (Volume 1). Greenwhich, Conn.: JAI Press.

Edwards, W. (1954) "The theory of decision making." *Psychological Bulletin, 51,* 380–417.

Festinger, L. (1957) *A theory of cognitive dissonance*. Stanford University Press.

——— & Carlsmith, J. M. (1959) "Cognitive consequences of forced compliance." *Journal of Abnormal and Social Psychology, 58,* 203–210.

Fox, F. *Persistence: Effects of Commitment and Justification Processes on Efforts to Succeed with a Course of Action*. Ph.D. dissertation, University of Illinois, 1980.

Fox, F. & Staw, B. M. (1979) "The trapped administrator: The effects of job insecurity and policy resistance upon commitment to a course of action." *Administrative Science Quarterly*, September, 1979.

Freedman, J. (1963) "Attitudinal effects on inadequate justification." *Journal of Personality*, 31, 371–385.

Friedlander, F. & Pickle, H. (1968) "Components of effectiveness in small organizations." *Administrative Science Quarterly*, 13, 289–304.

Galbraith, J. R. (1977) *Organizational design*. Reading, Mass.: Addison-Wesley.

Gerard, H. & Mathewson, G. (1966) "The effects of severity of initiation on liking for a group: A replication." *Journal of Experimental Social Psychology, 2*, 278–287.

Gould, P. & White, R. (1974) *Mental maps*. Middlesex, England: Penguin Books.

Gouldner, A. W. (1959) "Organizational analysis." In R. K. Merton, L. Brown, & L. S. Cothell (eds.) *Sociology today*. New York: Basic Books.

Graen, G. (1969) "Instrumentality theory of work motivation: Some experimental results and suggested modifications." *Journal of Applied Psychology Monograph, 53*, 1–25.

Haan, N. (1977) *Coping and defending: Processes of self-environmental organization*. New York: Academic Press.

Hackman, J. R. & Oldham, G. R. (1976) "Motivation through the design of work: Test of a theory." *Organizational Behavior and Human Performance, 16*, 250–279.

Hall, R. H. (1977) *Organizations: Structure and process*. Englewood Cliffs, New Jersey: Prentice-Hall.

Hannan, M. T. & Freeman, J. H. (1977) "The population ecology of organizations." *American Journal of Sociology, 82*, 929–964.

Heider, F. (1958) *The psychology of interpersonal relations*. New York: Wiley.

Helson, H. (1964) *Adaptation-level Theory: An Experimental and Systematic Approach to Behavior*. New York: Harper & Row.

Janis, I. L. & Mann, L. (1977) *Decision-making: A psychological analysis of conflict, choice, and commitment*. New York: Free Press.

Katz, D. & Kahn, R. (1978) *The social psychology of organizations*. New York: Wiley.

Knox, R. & Inkster, J. (1968) "Postdecision dissonance at post time." *Journal of Personality and Social Psychology, 8*, 319–323.

Lawler, E. E. (1971) *Pay and organizational effectiveness: A psychological view*. New York: McGraw-Hill.

———, Kuleck, W. J., Rhode, J. G., & Sorensen, J. E. (1975) "Job choice and post decision dissonance." *Organizational Behavior and Human Performance, 13*, 133–145.

Lawrence, P. & Lorsch, J. (1967) *Organization and environment*. Boston: Harvard Business School Division of Research.

Lewin, K., Dembo, T., Festinger, L., & Sears, P. (1944) "Level of aspiration." In J. M. Hunt (ed.) *Personality and the behavior disorders*. New York: Ronald.

Linder, D., Cooper, J., & Jones, E. (1967) "Decision freedom as a determinant of the role of incentive magnitude on attitude change." *Journal of Personality and Social Psychology, 6*, 245–254.

March, J. G. & Olsen, J. P. (1976) *Ambiguity and choice in organizations*. Bergen, Norway: Universitelsforlaget.

———. (1971) "The technology of foolishness." *Civilokonamen, 18*, 7–12.

Martin, N. H. & Sims, J. H. (1956) "Power Tactics." *Harvard Business Review*, pp. 25–29.

Miller, G. A. (1956) "The magical number seven, plus or minus two: Some limits on our capacity for processing information." *Psychological Review, 63*, 81–97.

Miller, J. G. (1978) *Living Systems*. New York: McGraw-Hill.

Mitchell, T. R. & Knudsen, B. W. (1973) "Instrumentality theory predictions of students' attitudes towards business and their choice of business as an occupation." *Academy of Management Journal, 16*, 41–52.

Myers, J. L. & Fort, J. G. (1963) "A sequential analysis of gambling behavior." *Journal of General Psychology, 69,* 299–309.

Newcomb, T. M. (1953) "An approach to the study of communicative acts." *Psychological Review, 60,* 393–404.

O'Reilly, C. & Caldwell, D. F. (in press) "Informational influence as a determinant of perceived task characteristics and job satisfaction." *Journal of Applied Psychology.*

Osgood, C. E. (1960) "Cognitive dynamics in human affairs." *Public Opinion Quarterly, 24,* 341–365.

Pallak, M. S., Sogin, S. R., & Van Zante, A. (1974) "Bad decisions: Effects of volition, locus of causality, and negative consequences on attitude change." *Journal of Personality and Social Psychology, 30,* 217–227.

Parsons, T. (1960) *Structure and process in modern society.* New York: The Free Press.

"Pentagon Papers, The" (1971) The *New York Times* (based on investigative reporting of Neil Sheehan). New York: Bantam Books.

Pfeffer, J. (1977) "Power and resource allocation in organizations." In B. Staw & J. Salancik (eds.) *New Directions in Organizational Behavior.* Chicago: St. Clair Press.

——— & Salancik, J. R. (1978) *The external control of organizations: A resource dependence perspective.* New York: Harper and Row.

Pickle, H. & Friedlander, F. (1967) "Seven societal criteria of organizational success." *Personnel Psychology, 20,* 165–178.

Porter, L. W. & Lawler, E. E. (1968) *Managerial Attitudes and Performance.* Homewood, Illinois: Irwin-Dorsey.

Pugh, D., Hickson, D., Hinings, C., & Turner, C. (1968) "The dimensions of organization structures." *Administrative Science Quarterly, 13,* 65–105.

Riecken, H. W. & Boruch, R. F. (1974) *Social experimentation: A method for planning and evaluating social intervention.* New York: Academic Press.

Rosenberg, M. J. (1960) "A structural theory of attitude dynamics." *Public Opinion Quarterly, 24,* 319–340.

Salancik, G. R. (1977) "Commitment and the control of organizational behavior and belief." In B. Staw & G. Salancik (eds.) *New Directions in Organizational Behavior.* Chicago: St. Clair Press.

——— & Pfeffer, J. (1978) "A social information processing approach to job attitudes and task design." *Administrative Science Quarterly,* June 1978.

Seligman, M. E. P. (1975) *Helplessness.* San Francisco: W. H. Freeman.

Simon, H. A. (1957) *Administrative behavior.* New York: Macmillan.

Slovic, P. (1972) "From Shakespeare to Simon: Speculations—and some evidence about man's ability to process information." *Oregon Research Institute Monograph, 12,* No. 2.

Staw, B. M. (1974) Attitudinal and behavioral consequences of changing a major organizational reward: A natural field experiment. *Journal of Personality and Social Psychology, 6,* 742–751.

Staw, B. M. (1976) "Knee-deep in the big muddy: A study of escalating commitment to a chosen course of action." *Organizational Behavior and Human Performance, 16,* 27–44.

——— (1977a) "Motivation in organizations: Toward synthesis and redirection." In B. Staw and J. Salancik (eds.) *New directions in organizational behavior.* Chicago: St. Clair Press.

——— (1977b) "The experimenting organization." In B. Staw (ed.) *Psychological foundations of organizational behavior.* Santa Monica, Cal.: Goodyear Publishing.

Stevens, L. & Jones. E. E. (1976) "Defensive attribution and the Kelley cube." *Journal of Personality and Social Psychology, 34,* 809–820.

Terkel, S. (1974) *Working.* New York: Pantheon Books.

Thompson, J. D. (1967) *Organizations in action.* New York: McGraw-Hill.

——— & Tuden, A. (1959) "Strategies, structures, and processes of organizational decisions." In J. D. Thompson et al. (eds.) *Comparative studies in administration*. Pittsburgh: University of Pittsburgh Press.

Vroom, V. H. (1964) "Work and motivation." New York: John Wiley.

——— (1966) "Organizational choice: A study of pre- and post-decision processes." *Organizational Behavior and Human Performance, 1,* 212–225.

Wanous, J. (1972) "Occupational preferences: Perceptions of value and instrumentality, and objective data." *Journal of Applied Psychology, 56,* 152–155.

Weick, K. E. (1964) "Reduction of cognitive dissonance through task enhancement and effort expenditure." *Journal of Abnormal and Social Psychology, 68,* 533–549.

——— (1976) "Educational organizations as loosely coupled systems." *Administrative Science Quarterly, 21,* 1–19.

——— (1977) "Enactment processes in organizations." In B. Staw & G. Salancik (eds.) *New directions in organizational behavior*. Chicago: St. Clair Press.

White, R. W. (1959) "Motivation reconsidered: The concept of competence." *Psychological Review, 66,* 297–333.

Wohlwill, J. F. & Kohn, I. (1973) "The environment as experienced by the migrant: An adaptation-level view." *Representative Research in Social Psychology, 4,* 135–164.

Wortman, C. B. & Linsenmeier, J. (1977) "Interpersonal attraction and techniques of ingratiation in organizational settings." In B. Staw & J. Salancik (eds.) *New directions in organizational behavior*. Chicago, Illinois: St. Clair Press.

Wortman, P. M. (1975) "Evaluation research: A psychological perspective." *American Psychologist, 30,* 562–575.

Zimbardo, P., Ebbeson, E., & Maslach, C. (1977) *Influencing attitudes and changing behavior*. Reading, Mass.: Addison-Wesley.

THE USE OF INFORMATION IN ORGANIZATIONAL DECISION MAKING:

A MODEL AND SOME PROPOSITIONS

Charles A. O'Reilly, III

ABSTRACT

Organizational decision making is examined in terms of the acquisition and use of information. An argument is made that decision makers may develop, through organizational goals, incentives, and control systems, strong preferences for certain outcomes. Once committed, decision makers are seen as susceptible to biases in both the acquisition and processing of information. Evidence attesting to this propensity to selectively perceive and use information is reviewed. A series of illustrative propositions suggesting when information is likely to be used for decision making is developed.

INTRODUCTION

In the past decade, a number of authors have made a point which is now familiar to most students of organizations: decision making as it occurs in organizations often departs from the traditional rational model (e.g., Cohen, March & Olsen, 1972; Janis & Mann, 1977; Simon, 1978; Staw, 1980). For instance, the question has been raised about the extent to which action is truly purposive and prospective in nature or more random, with rationality emerging retrospectively (Staw, 1980; Weick, 1977). In a provocative set of experiments, Ellen Langer and her colleagues (1978) have demonstrated that what appear to be thoughtful acts may be engaged in mindlessly through the use of scripts or programs. Others have made the case that organizational decision making often reflects a process of power and negotiation rather than a unitary pursuit of goals (Pfeffer, 1981). Still others have questioned the stability of individual or group preferences and called attention to the social, rather than objective, nature of reality and the importance of social and informational influence in changing perceptions and decisions (Berger & Luckmann, 1967; Pfefer & Salancik, 1978).

These and other studies (e.g., Mintzberg, Raisinghami & Theoret, 1976) highlight a gap between our normative theories of decision making and empirical understanding of how decisions are actually made within organizations. On the one hand, we are all familiar with the rational model and its modifications (e.g., Cyert & March, 1963; Lindblom, 1959; March & Simon, 1958; Simon, 1957). On the other hand, we are also familiar with a body of research suggesting that individual and group decisions often depart substantially from the rational ideal (e.g., Allison, 1971; Janis, 1972; Slovic, Fischhoff & Lichtenstein, 1977).

One potential reason for this difference has been suggested by O'Reilly and Anderson (1982). They note that most of the research on decision making has relied on laboratory simulations and focused on individual decision makers. Laboratory conditions typically fail to capture the context in which most organizational decision making occurs. For example, decision makers in the laboratory are usually focused on a limited information set, pursuing a single goal (e.g., profit), and have little or no long-term vested interest in the outcomes of the experiment. In actual organizations almost the opposite is true, with decision makers exposed to large quantities of information, pursuing multiple goals, and highly vested in the consequences of their decisions. Terry Connolly (1977, p. 207) has noted that "the limitation of research based on the individual decision-event model is that the decision maker is considered largely in isolation from the organizational environment which provides his input information, and to which he communicates his output."

If we are to understand organizational decision making, then we must also understand both the processes and the context through which decisions are made; that is, we must understand the circumstances surrounding the decision maker, how information is acquired, how it is processed, and how and why it is transmitted. The distinction between the acquisition and dissemination of information and its use is a critical one which has been largely overlooked. Kenneth Arrow (1973, p. 48) has observed: "Decisions, wherever taken, are a function of information received. . . . In turn, *the acquisition of information must be analyzed, since it is itself the result of decisions*" (emphasis added). While a very large number of laboratory studies of decision making exist, comparatively little attention has been paid to the acquisition of information by decision makers and its use in actual organizational settings.

Given this paucity of research, this paper has three objectives. First, a simplified model of decision making and rationality is developed which highlights the importance of information acquisition in shaping organizational decisions. Second, the effect of contextual factors on decision making is explored. Finally, a diverse body of literature relevant to information acquisition and use by decision makers is reviewed. Propositions relating information to decision making are developed. The purpose of the paper is to link information acquisition and use more closely to decision making as it occurs in organizational contexts.

INFORMATION, RATIONALITY, AND ORGANIZATIONAL DECISION MAKING

An Information Processing Model of Decision Making

Decision making is, simply put, the act of choosing among alternatives. In a typical choice situation, the decision maker is presumed to have a set of values or evaluative criteria, the perception of a problem that requires action, a number of potential alternative solutions, and a calculus for comparing alternatives and estimating the likelihood of attaining certain outcomes given certain alternatives. With perfect rationality, the assumptions underlying the choice process generally include complete information about the alternatives, knowledge of the probabilities associated with different alternative-outcome links, a consistent preference ordering among outcomes, and a selection mechanism that maximizes the value attained by a choice. With bounded rationality, there is a recognition of the limits on both the information available and cognitive processing abilities of the decision maker; that is, the decision maker is intendedly rational but acting with limited computational abilities. In both cases, however, the choice process is one of information assimilation and use, suggesting that an information processing model may be a fruitful way to examine the decision making process.

Consider the simplified model of decision making presented in Figure 1. In this schema, the decision maker is confronted with a problem or situation requiring a choice, generates potential alternative solutions, assesses the probabilities that a given alternative will lead to certain outcomes, and develops a preference ordering among outcomes. In this view, information and the ability to process it are paramount. Information processing is required in all phases, that is, to define the problem, develop alternatives, estimate probabilities, and order outcomes.

The emphasis in this model is *not* that it is a complete or literal representation of the decision making process. A variety of similar models have been proposed (i.e., Cohen, March & Olsen, 1972; Janis & Mann, 1977), and evidence is available which suggests that such models may be oversimplifications (Witte, 1972). Mintzberg, Raisinghami, and Theoret (1976), for example, traced 25 complex organizational decisions and characterize the process as a plurality of subdecisions without a simple sequential relationship such as indicated in Figure 1. Nevertheless, the model in Figure 1 is useful in that it emphasizes the centrality of information and information processing in the decision process. It also suggests a framework for organizing and investigating the limitations and constraints on organizational decision making.

In a typical formulation, decision makers encounter or are presented with problems which require choices. The decision maker then considers a variety of alternatives for solving the problem. Each alternative is examined and some subjective weight or probability estimated that selection of a given alternative will lead to particular outcomes. Typically, the decision maker is not indifferent among the set of outcomes, but has preferences reflected by weights for at least some of the outcomes. Given that information processing limits exist, it may be that the decision maker will not have complete knowledge of the alternatives, probabilities, or outcomes. In general, however, the decision making process is presumed to operate from left to right. Under traditional rationality assumptions it is assumed that in organizations the decision maker will search for unbiased information about the various components in the model, and that the weights attached to various outcomes are determined by organizational goals; that is, the decision maker is attempting to make the choice such that the maximum net benefit accrues to the organization or the agency.

But is this left-to-right progression an accurate description of how decisions are made? Several authors have proposed that, in organizations, problems are seldom clearly defined and alternatives become

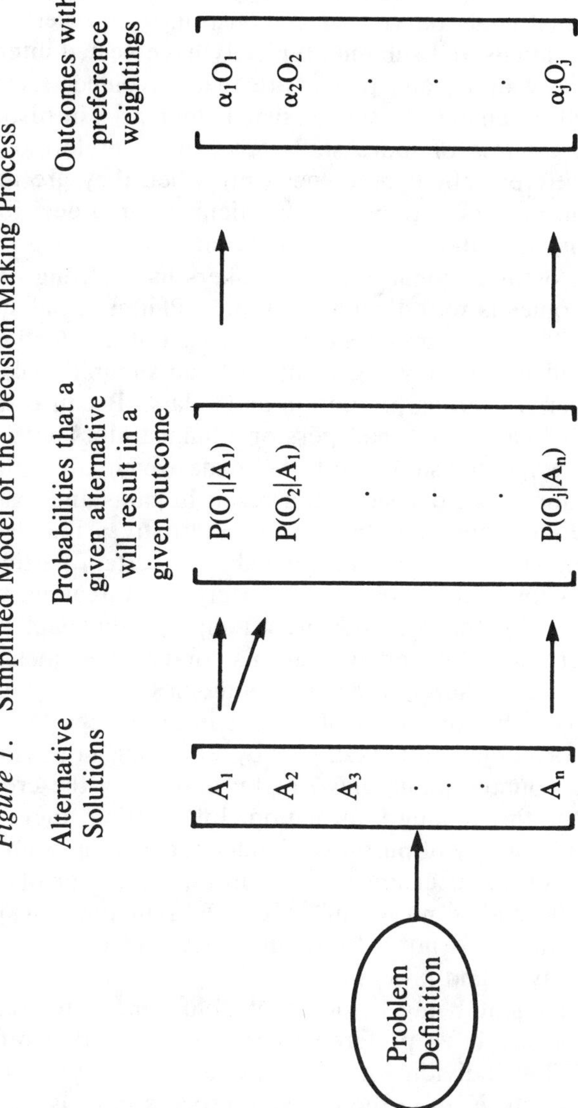

Figure 1. Simplified Model of the Decision Making Process

known only after certain outcomes were preferred (Cohen et al., 1972; Weick, 1977). It may be, in fact, that in organizations the decision making process begins with the preference ordering for outcomes as a set of rather fixed constraints. Simon (1964) suggested this when he proposed that organizational goals be viewed as constraint sets. Certainly in organizations individuals and subunits typically have vested interests. The loss of resources, status, and power are to be avoided. Even the uncertainty caused by change may be resisted. Increases in resources, for example, more funding or more staff, are usually preferred. Decision makers are indifferent about outcomes only when they are unaffected. In fact, decision makers may become participants in a decision making process to insure that they *remain* unaffected.

The fact that organizational decision makers have strong preferences for certain outcomes is well documented (e.g., Pfeffer & Salancik, 1977, 1978; Staw, 1980). These preferences, discussed at greater length later in this paper, reflect not only organizational and subunit goals, but also individual concerns such as promotion and salary. Because these preferences exist, it follows that managers or administrators are unlikely to remain passive when decisions are to be made which affect them. Conflicts may develop when decisions can result in gains and losses to the participants. Under these circumstances, alternatives that lead to undesired outcomes may become unacceptable to certain participants. In addition, as Thompson (1967) observed, uncertainty threatens rationality. Managers, especially those in power, attempt to eliminate potentially disruptive uncertainty. Information, in this context, becomes a political resource. Data which support desired outcomes is sought out, while information which supports opposite views is to be rebutted, either by questioning its accuracy (for example, by obtaining other information that supports a countervailing view) or by impugning the credibility of the source of the threatening information. Information, then, is a commodity used for a variety of purposes. Under some circumstances it may be used as a basis for decision making, in others as corroborative for decisions already made, and in still others for symbolic reasons. Information, in this milieu, is not a fixed substance, but one which may be selectively perceived and processed.

Thus, the argument being made is twofold. First, in organizations participants typically have preferences for outcomes that reflect organizational as well as individual goals. These outcomes act to define a set of constraints which result in the decision process moving from right to left as portrayed in Figure 1. Second, due to the potential for disagreements among participants, the entire decision process may be one of bargaining and negotiation as various actors pursue their interests. In this political process, information becomes a potentially useful or threatening commodity. It is generally not perceived of as "objective." Rather, depending on the nature and importance of the goals sought, decision makers may systematically search for supporting information while ignoring other types.

The perspective on decision making portrayed in Figure 1 provides a framework for examining the effects of context and information on organizational decision makers. The remainder of the paper explores these issues. First, the concept of "rationality" as it applies to organizational decision making and information use is discussed. Second, the impact of the organizational context on the model presented in Figure 1 is considered. Finally, drawing upon a diverse body of research on cognitive information processing and decision making, a number of potential biases in information processing that may affect decision making are explored.

Rationality and the Decision Making Process

As indicated previously, the notion of rationality implied by Figure 1 is not the comprehensive rationality of economic theory in which unbiased decision makers use perfect information to maximize utility according to some completely specified and ordered preference set. Instead, as suggested in Figure 1, decision makers begin with preferences and select actions based on imperfect expectations about the effect of these actions upon future preferences. These actions may include limited and focused information search and the selective perception and processing of information. Thus, "rationality," as used here, does not even refer solely to the notions of bounded rationality, in which choices are made by decision makers who use imperfect information in a satisficing manner to maximize goal attainment, subject to actual rather than perfect knowledge (March & Simon, 1958). Instead, the appropriate calculus for Figure 1 appears to be one which March (1978, p. 592) refers to as "contextual rationality" in which choice behavior is embedded in a complex of other claims on the attention of decision makers and other structures of social and cognitive relations. Organizational decision makers, in this view, are pursuing multiple objectives subject to a variey of pressures and constraints, often with considerable ambiguity surrounding the choice process. Under these circumstances, preferences for outcomes may be the least ambiguous component of the decision process, more certain than the definition of the problem, the range of feasible alternatives, or the probabilities associated with various alternatives. In this situation, it is argued that decision makers are likely to take actions which both reduce their uncertainty and help them achieve desired outcomes (e.g., search for supportive information or selectively interpret signals as favorable to a preferred outcome). Lindblom (1959) offered some support for this when he observed that the selection of goals and the empirical analysis of the needed actions to obtain the goals are not distinct from one another but are closely intertwined. Since ends typically come before means and may be known with greater certainty, it is likely that the search for appropriate means will be highly focused.

Since individual decision makers are known to be limited in their ability to solve problems (Nisbett & Ross, 1980), organizational routines are often established to increase the likelihood that individuals will behave in a traditionally rational way. This focus is on the effectiveness of *procedures* used to make choices, what Simon refers to as "procedural rationality" (1978, p. 8). These routines are established, in light of the limitations suggested by bounded and contextual rationality, to emphasize rational search procedures and, insofar as possible, to insure that decision makers have complete information. This procedural rationality may easily include provisions for information and control systems, carefully prescribed review processes, and even mandated program evaluations. The explicit attempt is to insure that the organizational context promotes comprehensive rationality. These manifestations of procedural rationality may be of considerable symbolic importance (e.g., Meyer & Rowan, 1977; Pfeffer, 1981b), but of limited efficacy if decision makers are only contextually rational.

Such a reformulation of traditional notions of rationality is hardly new. For a number of years, economists, political scientists and others have acknowledged that "perfect rationality" is not an apt description of real-world decision making (e.g., Floden & Weiner, 1978; Simon, 1978). It is worth reemphasizing that in an organizational context, unlike what is implied in the traditional rational model, goals are often ill-specified or lack consensus, information may be incomplete and ambiguous, decision makers may be pursuing multiple or competing objectives and lacking the time and computational abilities necessary to adequately utilize the available information. As Staw (1980, p. 55) has noted, it is not only the lack of computational ability which results in failures of comprehensive rationality, but also "the need to demonstrate rationality that can lead to justification processes which run counter to our conception of rational man." Decision makers, when faced with failure, may engage in activities designed to justify the lack of success and permit continued pursuit of the unsuccessful course of action. It may be, as suggested here, that the decision itself may be driven by the solution rather than the problem.

If it is the case that in organizations decision makers are contextually rational with the decision process in Figure 1 moving from right to left, it is important to consider how preferences are developed as well as how information is used. Evidence suggests that the context in which the decision occurs may affect the choice process, the information available to a decision maker, and the manner in which information is processed cognitively. For instance, occupying a particular organizational role may provide some information but deny other; control systems may make salient certain outcomes and not others; reward systems may increase the value of some actions but punish others, and so on. Figure 2 suggests how context variables such as organizational structure and control systems may limit the information available for decision making as well as modify the processing of this information by making certain outcomes more salient to the decision maker. Acknowledging these constraints, let us now turn our attention to: (1) some of the relevant organizational properties suggested by the notion of contextual rationality, and (2) the cognitive processing limitations associated with the notion of bounded rationality.

The Context of Organizational Decision Making

As suggested earlier, the organizational context in which a decision is taken may affect the acquisition and use of information in decision making. For instance, O'Reilly and Pondy (1979) review how one's location or role in an organization can affect both the set of information available and one's perspective on the problem. A decision made when one is distracted and under time pressures may be different than one made without interruptions and without time constraints (Ebbesen & Kocnecni, 1975; Wright, 1974).

Although a variety of contextual factors may affect organizational decision makers, three are reviewed here: (1) power, (2) goals, and (3) incentives and control systems. A dominating characteristic of organizational life which differentiates it from other contexts is the continual press for uniformity, conformity, and predictability. This is manifested through the establishment of goals for units and individuals, a hierarchy with power to allocate resources for the attainment of specified goals, and the use of incentives and controls to insure coordination and conformity. Each of these three factors can affect information use and decision making.

Organizational Power

To understand the impact of contextual influences on information use, let us first consider the decision maker in an organizational context. As Pfeffer (1981a) has noted, individuals and subunits within organizations may be viewed as actors competing for resources in a political arena. Power, the crucial ingredient in this context, may be envisioned as re-

Figure 2. Contextual and Individual Variables Affecting the Use of Information by Organizational Decision Makers

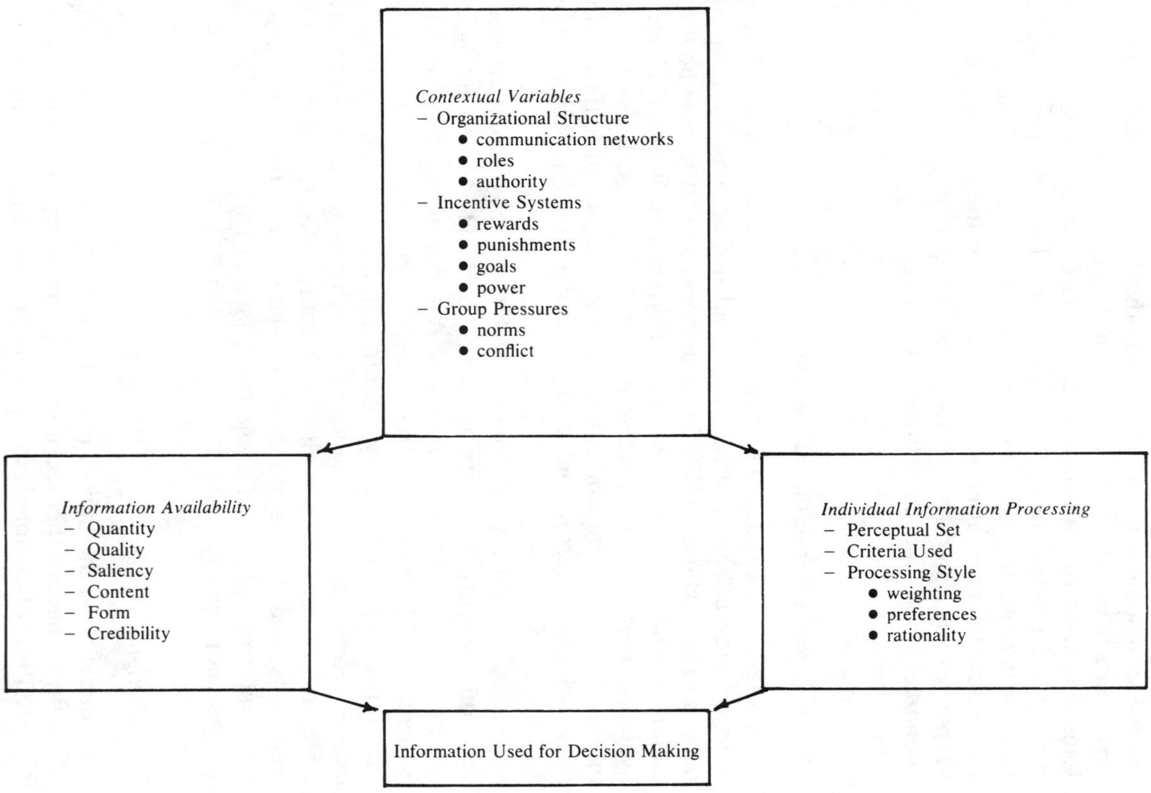

sulting from the ability to control critical contingencies: that is, power stems from the ability to reduce the primary uncertainty which faces the organization. As formulated by Hickson et al. (1971), power may vary according to: (1) how critical the uncertainty is which the subunit can reduce, that is, how central the contingencies are for the overall functioning of the organization; (2) how effective the subunit is in reducing the uncertainty; and (3) how substitutable the function served by the subunit is; that is, how easily can the uncertainty reduction be obtained from other source within the organization. Those who are successful according to these criteria are likely to be powerful. Those who do not act to reduce important uncertainty for the organization, or whose ability to reduce uncertainty is not uniquely held, are unlikely to exert substantial influence with the organizations.

Power has important ramifications for an understanding of the utilization of information for several reasons. First, Pfeffer and Salancik (1978) have shown that power is directly related to the ability to obtain scarce and critical resources, for example budget allocations and staff. Second, Pfeffer and Salancik (1977) have also demonstrated that power may be used to define the criteria used in decision making. More powerful subunits may successfully emphasize those criteria on which they compare favorably. This ability to define or specify evaluative criteria may have direct impacts on subsequent decisions, allowing powerful actors to either specify the basis on which they are to be evaluated and thereby insure their continued success, or by redefining a posteriori the evaluative criteria to invalidate unfavorable findings. Without power, decision makers are likely to find that they lack discretion in selecting the criteria and accepting others' definitions (e.g., Meltsner, 1976), or that they adhere to the more universalistic standards only to have their product labeled as irrelevant or ignored by decision makers.

A final ramification of power which has been noted is the tendency of those in charge to institutionalize their position and to resist changes which might reduce their control. Goldstein et al. (1978) describe how groups often desire evaluation research to satisfy external demands to "do something," but simultaneously are looking for the results to justify established policies and procedures. Decision makers, it seems, are more receptive to research conclusions that fit nicely into established policies. This tendency and ability of powerful units to maintain their position acts to slow down the process of change and may easily contribute to both a desire and an ability on the part of powerful subunits to selectively utilize information depending on their interests.

These findings suggest several propositions with respect to the use of information for decision making:

Proposition 1: Information will be more likely to be used by decision makers when:

a. the originating source is powerful compared to the user.
b. the information is not available from other sources; that is, the control of uncertainty is not substitutable.
c. the information is central to the user's functioning.

Organizational Goals, Incentives, and Control Systems

If, as suggested in Figure 1, the use of information may be a function of the outcomes preferred by a decision maker, it is important to consider how these preferences might develop. In an unconstrained setting, predicting the preferences or tastes of decision makers is problematic. With the exception of some global notions of hedonic preferences or the idea that, *ceteris paribus,* people will choose to be "better off" than "less well off," it is difficult to predict a priori what set of outcomes a given decision maker is likely to value. In organizations, however, the situation is more predictable. Decision makers exist in settings which act to constrain both the range of outcomes that might be preferred in a choice situation and the preferences for particular outcomes within this reduced set. These contextual constraints are typically imposed through a system of goals, control systems, and incentives. Decision makers are usually constrained first by the nature of the job, that is, organizational or subunit goals are imposed along with the responsibility to work toward attaining these goals. To insure that this is accomplished, some form of control system is typically used that allows superiors in the hierarchy to monitor the achievement of subordinate decision makers. Upon discovery of a variance, sanctions can be applied. Thus, the organizational context acts to constrain decision makers to pursue a limited number of goals and to reward or punish them for success or failure.

Without digressing into a lengthy discussion of goals and goal formulation processes (Keeley, 1980; Mohr, 1973), it should be noted that this process involves the translation of often vague, nonoperational, long-term goals into more specific, short-term outcomes. This activity may, as has been empirically demonstrated (e.g., Pfeffer, 1981a), be accomplished through a political process of negotiation, bargaining, cooptation, coalition formation, and the garnering and application of power. The process may also result in the adoption of symbolic and nonoperative goals whose purpose is often to satisfy external audiences and to provide for minimum constraints on organizational actors. Meyer and Rowan's (1977) interpretation of the symbolic nature of the operation of schools is an illustration of these goals. The concern in many public organizations with accountability is a goal perhaps more relevant as a symbolic effort to reassure taxpayers than as an operative goal relevant to effective and efficient organizational functioning.

With respect to evaluation research, Orlans (1973) has noted that enabling legislation is often written in vague terms in order to gain sufficient backing from legislators to insure passage. However, since program goals are not well defined, it is difficult to develop measurable criteria, in spite of the fact that the legislation often mandated an evaluation component. The lack of well-specified goals may encourage the political bargaining over criteria described by Pfeffer and Salancik (1977). Program Head Start legislation, for example, offered no delineation of goal priority or concrete objectives. The result was that evaluation results which showed no impact of the program were often ignored by decision makers as inappropriate or assessing only a part of the program's intent (Gordon & Morse, 1975).

The result of the translation of organizational goals into short-term operative subunit goals, while perhaps an imprecise and ambiguous process, has several important ramifications for an understanding of the use of information by organizational decision makers. First, even when the goals are somewhat ambiguous, objectives act to focus the attention and efforts of those responsible. For instance, Neustadt and Fineberg (1978) describe how jockeying among participants delayed the initiation of the swine flu innoculation program as those responsible argued over ways and means for managing the effort. Second, although the goal may be imprecisely defined, control systems are almost always developed that include measures of objective outcomes. These observable outcome measures act as highly salient foci against which performance may then be assessed. A large and persuasive body of research has documented the motivating effect of simple goal setting (e.g., Latham & Yukl, 1975; Locke, et al., 1981). For example, studies of budgeting (e.g., Wildavsky, 1974), public employees (Blau, 1964), students (Baum & Youngblood, 1975), and homeowners (Erez, 1977) have all demonstrated that merely setting goals can act to direct behavior. Other research has also demonstrated that once an individual becomes committed to an outcome through public actions, he/she tends to continue to pursue the same goal, even if preceding efforts met with failure (e.g., Salancik, 1977; Staw & Ross, 1978). These findings suggest that in an organizational context, decision makers are likely to develop rather explicit preferences for outcomes.

Finally, and most importantly, these preferences are solidified through the operation of organizational control and incentive systems. Decision makers are rewarded for pursuing certain ends and punished for others. The pervasive impact of incentive systems is difficult to underestimate. A *New York Times* article describing the demise of the swine flu program attributed the failure, in part, to "the self-interest of the government health bureaucracy which saw in the swine flu threat the ideal chance to impress the nation with the capabilities of saving money and lives by preventing disease" (Neustadt & Fineberg, 1978, p. 71). Kerr (1975) provides a number of instances in which employees behaved in seemingly contradictory ways, often appearing to do the opposite of the espoused goals. For example, directors of orphanages were found to establish policies that worked against the placement of children in foster homes and acted to keep them in the orphanage; universities routinely establish incentive systems that militate against encouraging high quality teaching; sports teams often reward individual performance when a team-oriented effort is required. Upon analysis, these results were seen not to be contradictory, but to be entirely consistent with the incentive systems; that is, people in organizations typically do those things for which they are rewarded. In Kerr's (1975) example, orphanage directors who succeeded in placing children in foster homes would be "rewarded" by cuts in staff, resources, and prestige among peers. In a direct test of the hypothesis that decision makers would respond to the operative control system, Harrell (1977) demonstrated that subordinate decision makers would follow their superior's lead and make decisions using similar criteria. This effect persisted even when superiors began making decisions that were contrary to official policy.

Obviously the goals of survival and obtaining resources are of critical importance to decision makers. Information which suggests that a decision maker is not effective or efficient is likely to be seen as threatening. Clearly, there may be conflicts between one actor's goal of survival and another's goal of accurate evaluation. The incentives for those with vested interests in a program may be to devise strategies to minimize the collection, dissemination, and use of such unfavorable information, even if such actions go against some "objective" assessment of overall worth.

These findings are applicable in understanding how decision makers develop preferences for outcomes. Subunit goals are made salient and measurable and are rewarded. Control systems provide feedback and sanctions act to focus attention on achieving certain ends. Failure to attain the desired outcomes may result in the loss of important organizational rewards such as promotion, pay, and status, as well as actual punishments such as demotion and termination. As individuals in organizations become more committed and less able to leave the organization, the importance of the outcomes is increased. Since there is seldom complete consensus among individuals and subunits on the goals or outcomes to be sought, the possibility of conflict and competition arises. Under these circumstances, it is possible that one person's gain is another's loss; hence, it is unlikely that decision makers will easily give up preferences for certain outcomes if it means personal loss (Caldwell and O'Reilly, 1982a; Staw, 1980).

Some indirect evidence of these effects may be seen in a review of ninety-three evaluation studies by Gordon and Morse (1975). These authors found that evaluation researchers with some affiliation with the project being evaluated were far more likely to report the project as successful than were nonaffiliated evaluators (52 percent to 14 percent). While not suggesting directly that affiliated evaluators deliberately biased their studies, the results are consistent with the hypothesis that incentives may lead to conscious or unconscious biasing of information.

The set of acceptable or preferred outcomes on which a decision maker is likely to focus is, in part, made salient through the specification of a control system which assesses attainment of the assigned goals, incentive systems that sanction certain actions, and the committing effect of previous behaviors. These factors suggest the following proposition:

Proposition 2: Information will be more likely to be used by decision makers when:

a. It can be used to assess achievement of quantifiable goals.
b. It is fed into a well-articulated and operating control system which includes an effective set of incentives; that is, measured performance can be sanctioned.
c. It does not recommend actions which are incompatible with the existing control system's ability to monitor and sanction.
d. It originates from sources who have a vested interest in the continuation of the project.

INFORMATION ACQUISITION AND USE

As suggested by Figure 1, information plays a central role in the decision making process. Before information can have an impact, however, it must both reach and be processed by the relevant decision makers. In an organizational context this means that the information must not only be available to users but must also be understood, believed, and acted upon. Failure by decision makers either to obtain the information or to process it can result in nonutilization. This suggests the need to examine two separate steps in the dissemination process: (1) how decision makers acquire information, and (2) how information is processed cognitively. A substantial body of research is available which suggests some limitations and biases on organizational decision makers with respect to information acquisition and use (e.g., Einhorn & Hogarth, 1981; Slovic et al., 1977). It is not the purpose of this paper to review this entire literature. Rather, only those factors which may impinge directly upon organizational decision making are discussed. An excellent comprehensive review of many of these limitations is contained in Nisbett and Ross (1980).

Information Acquisition

Accessibility of Information. A large number of laboratory studies of information and decision making have documented the intuitively reasonable conclusion that better-quality information is generally associated with improved decision making performance (e.g., Porat & Haas, 1969; Streufert, 1973). Unfortunately, several authors have also noted that the majority of these studies may be overly structured when compared to the real-world situations they are meant to model (e.g., Connolly, 1977; O'Reilly & Anderson, 1982; Winkler & Murphy, 1973). Thus, while we have support for the importance of information in decision making, we need to examine the process by which decision makers acquire information before concluding that the mere availability of quality information insures improved performance.

When we examine this evidence, doubts about the existence of a simple information-decision making link emerge. Decision makers of many types appear to be noticeably biased in their procurement of information. For example, in a direct test of the impact of accessibility and quality of information on information source use, O'Reilly (1982) found that although decision makers recognized information sources of high quality, they used sources that provided lower quality information but were more accessible. He explains these results in terms of the costs involved in obtaining information from less accessible sources. Given that the decision makers were under time constraints and subject to numerous interruptions, it may have been that they were simply unable to seek out higher quality information when it came from less accessible sources. Similar findings have been reported about the information seeking behavior of physicians (Menzel & Katz, 1955), scientists (Gerstberger & Allen, 1968), policymakers (Clausen, 1973), and managers (Mintzberg, 1973).

This bias towards accessible information is also reflected in managers' strong preferences for oral as opposed to written information (e.g., Dewhirst, 1971) and for information from trustworthy or credible sources (e.g., Beach, Mitchell, Deaton & Prothero, 1978; Caldwell & O'Reilly, 1982b). Research in these areas has shown that managers typically prefer shorter, oral reports to longer written ones. Interestingly, there is also evidence that when obtaining information in this manner, managers may judge the validity of the information, not on the facts of the matter, but on the credibility of the source. This may lead to the acceptance of a piece of information as "true" or "false," depending on how much the recipient trusts the sender. Clausen (1973), for instance, noted that congressmen frequently cast votes on legislation based not on an understanding of the deeper issues but on the advice of a trusted colleague. Upon reflection, this behavior can be seen to be contextually rational. There is no way a congressman or manager can be fully informed on all issues; hence, choice is guided by the actions and advice of others with similar preferences.

The research on source credibility also suggests that it may be that it is the trustworthiness of the source, more than expertise, which determines whether information is believed (O'Reilly & Roberts, 1976). The ramifications of this finding for understanding the utilization of information by decision makers may be important. Oftentimes subunits, by their nature, may be perceived of as not sharing the same objectives as other subunits; that is, they are not trustworthy in source credibility terms. While an information source may be seen as possessing substantial expertise, its preferences may not be similar, and therefore, information emanating from the source may not be trustworthy. This raises the possibility that expert information may be used less by decision makers than information from "safer" sources.

Together, these biases may lead decision makers toward preferences for information from particular channels which may be characterized as accessible and trustworthy, and which provide condensed treatments of complex issues. Information from these sources, as will be suggested later, may be concrete and easily assimilated, but not necessarily detailed or of the highest quality. With respect to information utilization, this suggests the following propositions:

Proposition 3: Information is more likely to be used by decision makers if it is:

a. readily accessible;
b. summarized;
c. presented orally;
d. from a source deemed as credible, that is, trustworthy.

Information Sign. An additional bias noted in studies of information acquisition by decision makers is a tendency to avoid information that may suggest undesirable consequences. Janis and Mann (1977) offer several examples of this behavior, describing how politicians and policy-makers, when faced with unpleasant alternatives, will avoid exploring ominous implications of desired courses of action. Several examples of this sort are available in studies showing that administrators have exhibited tendencies to dismiss negative findings (e.g., Carter, 1971). Goldstein et al. (1978, p. 33) report instances in which evaluation research results were selectively interpreted as offering support for a politically favored position. This willingness to avoid acquiring pejorative information and to seek out or selectively process favorable items has direct ramifications for organizational decision making. As suggested earlier, decision makers often have vested interests in certain outcomes. This may predispose them to seek out information that supports their position. Bear and Hodun (1975), for example, found that subjects were more likely to recall information items that confirmed their position than those that were contradictory. This bias extended to recalling some contradictory items as supportive and even to recalling missing data as confirmatory for a preferred position. In a similar vein, Lord, Ross, and Lepper (1979) demonstrated that subjects would describe evidence that supported their position as "more convincing" than opposing evidence. In an interesting laboratory study, Morlock (1967) demonstrated that it required significantly *less* information for subjects to arrive at a decision favorable to their position than to arrive at a decision against their interests. In an organizational setting, groups of like-minded decision makers may exaggerate these biases toward selective perception and actually act collectively to censor or derogate information in opposition to their desired ends. Janis (1972), labeling this process as "groupthink," provides a number of retrospective accounts in which groups acted to bolster desired opinions and exclude contrary ones. For instance, decision making by President Kennedy's advisory committee during the Bay of Pigs incident was characterized afterwards by the suppression of doubts, creation of feelings of unanimity and invulnerability, and an unwillingness to risk conflict within the group. Johnson (1974) provides a nice example of this tendency to seek unanimity and avoid conflict in a study of group decision making. She hypothesized that executives would make a less desirable but acceptable short-run decision to avoid generating conflict with others in the group. Using 49 businessmen across ten situations she discovered that although subjects could identify the ideal decision for each situation, their overwhelming tendency was to make a suboptimal decision in order to avoid conflict. David (1978) quotes a user of evaluation data as saying, "I look at test scores mainly to confirm my own impression. If they differ, my impression counts" (p. 16). In their retrospective study of decision making during the swine flu program, Neustadt and Fineberg (1978) recount how a memorandum written by a proponent of the innoculation effort converted a 2 percent chance into odds described as a "strong possibility of a pandemic" (p. 19). Nisbett and Ross (1980) conclude that beliefs will tend to sustain themselves despite the total discrediting of the evidence that initially produced the beliefs.

These biases, that is, tendencies to avoid information which suggests undesirable consequences, to seek out supportive information, to require less supportive information to arrive at a favored decision, and a desire to avoid making decisions which will generate conflict, suggest the following proposition.

Proposition 4: Information is more likely to be used by decision makers if the information:

a. is supportive of the outcomes favored by the decision makers.
b. does not lead to conflict among the set of relevant actors.
c. cannot be attacked by those in opposition.

Communication of Information. A final set of potential biases on information acquisition by decision makers in organizational settings is related to the communication of information in organizations. Several authors have noted that communications in organizations may be withheld or distorted (e.g., O'Reilly & Pondy, 1979; Wilensky, 1967). Subordinates have been found to be biased toward passing superiors information which reflects favorably on the subordinate and suppressing unfavorable information. O'Reilly (1978) discovered that subordinates who did not trust their superior were willing to suppress unfavorable information even if they knew that such information was useful to their boss. Manis, Cornell, and Moore (1974) found that subjects required to summarize the main points of a speech concerning the legalization of marijuana to an audience who seemingly favored or opposed legalization, biased their transmission to a position more supportive of listeners' views. This tendency is similar to the mum effect discovered by Rosen and Tesser (1970). Based on several laboratory studies, they discovered that subjects are biased against reporting bad news to others and toward transmitting good news.

Other investigations have shown similar results. For instance, Pettigrew (1972) documented how a single individual, acting as a gatekeeper for information flowing to a policy making group, was able to determine the outcome of a purchasing decision by carefully allowing only certain types of information through to the decision makers. Plott and Levine (1978) demonstrated how, through the arrangement of a meeting's agenda, outcomes could be determined in advance. Lowe and Shaw (1968) provided evidence that departments systematically inflate and bias budget requests to support claims for increased resources. In a slightly different vein, Kaufman (1973) showed how subordinates learned not to pass certain items of information upward in the hierarchy because superiors, upon learning of these, would be required to act in ways contrary to their self-interest. A classic example of this system-induced distortion is provided by McCleary (1977) in a study of how parole officers report violations. He observed that parole officers underreported deviant behavior to their supervisors. As noted by Kaufman (1973), subordinates are often punished for accurate reports. In McCleary's study, this resulted in incidents being reported only when the information sent upward would result in enhancing the subordinate's career.

Numerous other examples are available which attest to the fact that information is often selectively filtered and distorted as it is communicated in organizations (e.g., Allison, 1971; O'Reilly, 1978). Such filtering and distortion appears to come, most often, from individuals or groups who are attempting to either gain desired outcomes, such as increased resources or power, or to avoid losses. Neustadt and Fineberg (1978) report how a memorandum outlining the possible liability of manufacturers of swine flu vaccine was suppressed by staff who wanted the program to proceed. Caldwell and O'Reilly (1982a), in a laboratory study, found that subjects whose initial decision had failed, manipulated information presented to others so as to rationalize their initial decision. A strategy of impression management such as this may include attempts at enhancing the quality of the original decision as well as undermining alternatives (Cialdini & Richardson, 1980). When considered in conjunction with biases toward reliance by decision makers on short, oral reports from trusted sources, the impact of distorted information may be heightened.

Clearly, these biases have important consequences for the transmission and use of information by decision makers. If, as March and Simon (1958, p. 165) note, "inferences are drawn from a body of evidence and the inferences, instead of the evidence itself, are then communicated," the opportunity for subtle distortion is magnified. Findings that have undesirable consequences may be withheld by superior gatekeepers. Direct evidence of this effect is recounted by Coleman (1972) who describes how HEW attempted to minimize the impact of an EEO study, because its findings were inimical to the interests of some other HEW agencies. Here we find decisions being made to suppress or alter information both to minimize conflict and to avoid undesirable outcomes.

It should be noted that not all distortion in organizational communication is necessarily intentional. During transmission from one individual to another there is almost always some degradation of the message. Receivers of information recall certain parts of messages and forget or minimize others. This unintentional distortion, due to differences in cognitive tuning, may be increased when the communication occurs between groups who use different vocabularies, are sensitive to different goals and constituencies, or are using different criteria for determining what is important. Janis (1972), for example, describes how during the period preceding Pearl Harbor, information was not transmitted because senders, unaware of the broader picture, did not perceive certain information to be important. Information providers, whose concerns are often somewhat different than information receivers, may not be fully appreciative of the user's concerns. Again, when coupled with the biases mentioned previously, such as a reliance on accessible and credible information sources, it may be that relevant information will not have the impact expected by a rational observer.

Acknowledging that information may be blocked or altered during communication within organizations suggests the following proposition:

Proposition 5: Information is less likely to be used for decision making when:

a. it is transmitted through several intermediate links in a communication network rather than delivered directly to the relevant decision makers.
b. transmitters of the information are likely to suffer personal or organizational losses from the message.
c. senders and receivers do not trust each other.
d. the information is transmitted to decision makers in another unit or organization.

Information Processing

Until this point, our discussion has focused on biases that may affect the acquisition of information by decision makers in an organizational context. Once the information has been acquired, however, individuals may still fail to process it accurately. A diverse and well-developed body of research is available that documents cognitive information processing limitations (e.g., Nisbett & Ross, 1980; Langer, Blank & Chanowitz, 1978; Petty, Harkins & Williams, 1980; Slovic et al., 1977). Two general categories of this research are relevant to an understanding of the use of information by decision makers: studies of (1) factors which limit one's ability to assimilate information, and (2) processing strategies which may result in inaccurate or misleading inferences.

Cognitive Limits on Information Processing. Early studies of human information processing demonstrated rather unambiguously that only limited amounts of information could be used by decision makers. Simon (1979) has remarked that the scarcest resource of all is man's limited ability to deal with large amounts of information. Miller (1956), in a classic study, demonstrated experimentally that short-term memory is limited in most people to seven "chunks" of information plus or minus two (a "chunk" being the largest single item of information recognized by the processor). An individual's ability to chunk information acts as a direct constraint on the input of data. What is important is that this fundamental physiological limitation appears to act as a constraint for all decision makers. Numerous studies have demonstrated that physicians, stockbrokers, meteorologists, policymakers, and a variety of other "experts" all appear to use only a very limited number of cues in making complex decisions (e.g., Dawes & Corrigan, 1974; Nisbett & Ross, 1980; Slovic et al., 1977).

A universal response to this constraint is for decision makers to develop heuristic procedures that simplify cognitive processing requirements. These heuristics are rules which allow the decision maker to make judgments without fully processing all necessary information (Wright, 1980). These heuristics can, however, produce biases. Langer (1975), for example, has demonstrated that while people are pictured as active information processors, much apparently thoughtful action may be the result of mindless responses, resulting from the invocation of programs of behavior based on a triggering cue, not a thoughtful cognitive decision. In these instances, people may believe that they were thinking but, in fact, were behaving according to well-learned general scripts rather than on the basis of new information. This notion may be likened to a tape "loop" or sequence of responses that is invoked, without thinking, by some often-encountered stimulus. When the stimulus, or decision making situation, is congruent with previous experience, the behavior that results may appear thoughtful, while, in fact, it is a thoughtless response. Langer et al. (1978) demonstrated this with several experiments. For instance, people about to use a public xerox machine were interrupted and asked in several ways to let another person use it first. Either just a request ("Excuse me . . . may I use the xerox machine"), a request plus placebic information ("Excuse me . . . may I use the xerox machine because I have to make copies"), or a request with real information ("Excuse me . . . may I use the xerox machine because I am in a hurry") was used. In the second condition, no real information was presented so the compliance rate should be equivalent to the first request, assuming that subjects actively processed the information. Results of the experiment, however, showed that the compliance rate for the placebic information condition was comparable to the real information group. Langer (1975), in reviewing a number of similar studies, concludes that it is only when individuals encounter novel situations for which no script exists that effortful cognitive processing will occur. Thus, in organizations one response to limits on the cognitive processing abilities of decision makers may be to develop programs of responses which appear to be procedurally rational but, in fact, involve no thinking at all. Under these conditions, incoming information is screened for similarity to previous stimuli. If the signal is categorized as similar, the decision maker can invoke an existing script or response without active processing.

Other research in this area has also shown that variables such as personality, cognitive structure, and demographics are related to information processing abilities (e.g., Schroder, Driver & Streufert, 1967; Taylor & Dunnette, 1974). Buckhout (1974), for example, lists three biases common to perceptions and memory of eyewitnesses: (1) insignificance in the original situation, that is, cues later deemed important which were not closely attended to at the time, (2) the degradation of information in memory over time, and (3) pressures and distractions on the information processor which reduce the amount and accuracy of information used. Each of these limits is potentially important for an understanding of how decision makers may use information. For instance, given that decision makers are able to use relatively limited amounts of information, it becomes problematic to know which items of information of the total quantity available a decision maker will focus on and use. Studies of experts are consistent in finding that experts on the same subject typically use different information in making judgments (e.g., Ostrom & Davis, 1979; Slovic et al., 1977). This suggests that decision makers, when presented with an information set, may interpret and weight the information differentially. Hawkins et al. (1978), for instance, in a drug evaluation study, showed that various actors were weighting information differently according to the evaluation criteria they were using. Other studies have also demonstrated variations in preferences for types of information across decision makers, as well as how stress reduces one's ability to process information (e.g., Nisbett & Ross, 1980; Wright, 1974). Since, as Mintzberg (1973) has shown, managers' work is characteristically fragmented and subject to distractions and time pressures, it is likely that decision makers will be unable to fully assimilate all the information available, and may actually be distracted by irrelevant cues. Troutman and Shanteau (1977), for example, showed that physicians' judgments were often affected by information that was nondiagnostic; that is, it conveyed no relevant information but was nevertheless used by the decision maker as though it were relevant.

Under these conditions, it is likely that users of information may frequently form overall impressions, subject to the biases mentioned previously, and use information accordingly. This interpretation is consistent with studies which show that with the passage of time details are forgotten and the reconstructed meaning is often less ambiguous than originally portrayed and interpreted as offering support for a favored position (e.g., Buckhout, 1974; Ross, 1977; Ross & Sicoly, 1979). Snyder and Uranowitz (1978), for instance, conducted an experiment in which participants read an extensive narrative about a woman. They subsequently received information that she was living either a heterosexual or a lesbian lifestyle. This new information was shown to affect participants' memories. Subjects selectively affirmed or bolstered their interpretations by using only a consistent subset of the information available. Information contained in the original set which is unfavorable or inconsistent is likely to be either forgotten or reinterpreted so as to minimize its negative consequences.

These and other studies of individual limits on cognitive information processing corroborate a reasonable but often neglected fact: memory is a selective and often fallible source of information. The perceptual process of detecting and attending to stimuli is affected by factors such as stress, distractions, and irrelevant or nondiagnostic information. With the passage of time there is also a tendency to reorganize our "memory" into coherent recollections by stripping away contradictory evidence and filling in any gaps with "constructed" facts. These limitations suggest the following propositions.

Proposition 6: Only limited amounts of information from any set are likely to be used for decision making purposes.

Proposition 7: Given the same information set, different decision makers will use different parts in different ways; that is, judges will select and weight information differentially.

Proposition 8: Over time, decision makers will be more likely to interpret favorable information as less ambiguous than originally perceived.

Proposition 9: Over time, decision makers will be more likely to forget unfavorable information or reinterpret such information as either irrelevant (e.g., does not address the "relevant" question) or favorable.

Selective Processing. Aside from these limits, there also exist biases in the manner in which information is cognitively processed by individuals. Three of these biases have direct ramifications for organizational decision making: (1) selective perception, (2) self-serving biases, and (3) a preference for vivid, concrete information. The first relates to the tendency, described in the previous section, for users to "reinterpret" information which has been acquired to fit preconceptions or to allow the user to maintain a consistent set of attitudes and beliefs about a given topic. This consistency bias, injected by the reconstruction of facts, is dramatically increased through the three selective processing mechanisms mentioned previously.

Janis and Mann (1977) offer a number of excellent illustrations of instances in which decision makers either defensively avoided acquiring or processing unfavorable information or bolstered their position through the selective acquisition and interpretation of favorable data. This tendency may be seen in decision makers' willingness to overweight negative information when they desire to make a negative decision (Kanouse & Hanson, 1972). In these circumstances, when a decision maker desires to reject an opposing view, judges have been shown to use whatever negative information is available to say "no." Selection interviewers, when presented with a large number of positive cues and very few negative ones, have been shown to systematically attend to the negative information and use it to reject applicants even though the positive information is far more potent. Miller and Rowe (1967), for example, found that when subjects were required to make assessment decisions, there was a significant tendency to be influenced by negative rather than positive adjectives used to describe a candidate. Other corroborative evidence is available from studies of perception, investment decisions, gamblers, and others (Nisbett & Ross, 1980). When decision makers favor a position, the bias has been shown to operate towards the selection of favorable information as well (e.g., Morlock, 1967). Thus, Snyder and Swann (1978) found in a series of experiments that subjects preferentially searched for information (e.g., in interviews) that would enable them to confirm their hypotheses. This tendency included structuring social interaction in ways that caused targets to provide actual behavioral confirmation for the subjects' hypotheses.

It should be noted that this bias does not necessarily suggest that decision makers truncate their search for information having once obtained data which can be used to support a desired position or oppose an undesired one. The apparent tendency is to selectively seek out information which bolsters one's position and avoid unsupportive information in either acquisition or processing, but not necessarily to avoid searching. In fact, a number of laboratory studies have demonstrated an interesting propensity among decision makers to desire more information than can be effectively used (O'Reilly, 1980). The paradox is that decision makers appear to seek more information than required, even to the point of inducing overload. While the overload may actually impair performance, the additional information has been shown to increase the decision maker's confidence (Oskamp, 1965). The net result may be that decision makers arrive at poorer decisions, but are more confident in their choices.

Thus, it may be that decision makers will selectively seek out information which supports or opposes a position, acquire as much of this information as possible, and be increasingly confident in their decision, although such decisions may be substantially biased. Meltsner (1976), in a book on policy analysts, makes a useful distinction between two categories of information sought by decision makers; that is, information used to *make* decisions and information used to *support* decisions. The latter category is indicative of the type sought by decision makers to justify a position. Meltsner describes at length how it is not uncommon for decision makers to hire outside consulting groups to do evaluation studies, not to be used for decision making purposes but solely to provide credible information which supports a decision that has already been made. This relates directly to the earlier discussion of information as a political resource and suggests the following proposition:

Proposition 10: Information will be more likely to be used when it can be selectively interpreted as either supportive of a desired position of unsupportive on opposing positions.

Self-serving Biases. Aside from propensities to selectively perceive and process information, decision makers have also been shown to consistently engage in what has been labeled "self-serving" biases; that is, researchers have noted that individuals often view themselves more favorably than seems objectively warranted (e.g., Bradley, 1978; Miller & Ross, 1975). Thus, for example, people have been shown to consistently overpredict their gambling successes (Blasovich, Ginsburg & Howe, 1975), production managers overestimate their performance (Kidd & Morgan, 1969), and corporate presidents overpredict their firm's success in meeting competition (Larwood & Whittaker, 1977). Aside from this future-oriented optimism, investigators have also shown that, in retrospect, members of successful groups see themselves as more responsible for their groups than do members of groups that have failed. Ross and Sicoly (1979) found consistent evidence, using samples such as married couples and basketball teams, that individuals typically see their own contribution to success as greater than others. Schlenker and Miller (1977), for instance, found that members of groups that had failed assigned less responsibility for the group's poor performance to themselves than they typically assigned to any other member of the group.

In organizations, such pervasive "self-serving" biases have important ramifications for the acquisition and interpretation of information. These biases become especially important when participants are responsible for previous decisions to allocate resources. Under these conditions, decision makers may be committed to a particular program. Staw and his colleagues (e.g., Staw & Fox, 1977) have demonstrated how commitment to a course of action may result in escalating commitments of resources to failing projects. Staw and Ross (1978), for instance, demonstrated how policymakers who had allocated resources to projects which subsequently failed because of reasons that they should have foreseen, were more likely to devote more resources to the project in succeeding time periods than decision makers who had sponsored successful projects or whose projects had failed for reasons beyond the decision maker's control. This example is similar to foreign policy failures such as the United States' involvement in Vietnam. Staw and Ross quote George Ball (1965), who in the early years of the Vietnam War stated that, "Once we suffer large casualties . . . our involvement will be so great that we cannot—without national humiliation—stop short of achieving our complete objectives."

It may be that the ability of individuals to be overoptimistic about future events predisposes them to commit themselves to courses of action. When cohesive groups are involved, there may be an even greater impetus to choose risky options. Once committed, the selective perception biases described earlier can act to provide information supportive of the original decision. Halberstam (1972) provides numerous illustrations of how Robert McNamara and others engaged in this activity during Vietnam. Gouran (1976) provides similar examples showing that Nixon and his aides persistently discounted the importance of evidence during the Watergate cover-up. Selective perception biases allow the parties involved to choose information, as suggested in Proposition 10, that either supports the aims of the programs or rebuts opposition claims. Self-serving biases may also act to allow for the development of a false consensus or the illusion that their behaviors and choices are common and appropriate while opposing responses are uncommon and not widely supported. These self-serving biases also act to make the decision maker reluctant to abandon a chosen course of action. As long as information is available that can be interpreted as supportive of a given position, the bias on the part of the central actor will be to focus on this corroborative information. As Pfeffer and Salancik (1977) have shown, when ambiguity exists, particularistic criteria can be used by decision makers; that is, unless a widespread consensus exists, it is possible for opposing decision makers to argue for their positions and to selectively use information to support their claims. Given that evaluation is often prescribed precisely because the situation is ambiguous with respect to a given program, it is obviously the case that the selective processing of information will occur. Under these circumstances, individuals are likely to be involved and committed to particular points of view and self-serving biases will be operating. When information and outcomes are ambiguous, the impact of these factors may be heightened.

A final effect of self-serving biases may be seen when decisions result in failure, either for political or substantive reasons. Under these circumstances, self-serving biases may allow involved participants to cognitively reconstruct their involvement and devalue their responsibility for the failure. Selective perception may act to focus on exogenous events which explain the lack of success in terms of others' actions and unforeseeable events. Thus, the operation of self-serving biases suggests the following proposition relevant to an understanding of the use of information.

Proposition 11: Responsibility that results in increased commitment on the part of decision makers increases the likelihood that information will be used when the information can be interpreted as favorable or supportive of the decision maker's position.

Abstract Versus Concrete Information. Evaluation studies are typically conducted in order to assess the extent to which a program meets its goals and is successful compared to other projects, or in order to provide for the feedback of information to improve performance in succeeding time periods. Underlying these reasons is the idea that evaluation information will allow decision makers to derive inferences about causal relationships, for example, between educational interventions and student achievement. An important postulate of this process holds that causal explanations will be influenced by consensus information, that is, information concerning base rates and how a given project fares compared to the base rate. Attribution theory researchers have drawn attention to the substantial amount of evidence which has failed to support the postulated effect of consensus information. For instance, Tversky and Kahneman (1974) have demonstrated this point by asking subjects to judge the probability that a target individual, described in a brief personality sketch, was an engineer, given:

(a) that he was drawn from a population of 70 engineers and 30 lawyers; or
(b) that he was drawn from a population of 70 lawyers and 30 engineers.

Knowledge of the population base rate for occupational categories had no effect whatever on judgments of the probability that the target individual was an engineer. Instead, subjects relied exclusively on the personality sketch and based the decision on the degree to which the description fitted the stereotypic engineer or lawyer. Numerous other examples are available which demonstrate that decision makers, and even scientists familiar with statistics, habitually ignore information about the population and draw recklessly strong inferences about the underlying population from knowledge of a very small sample. Kahneman and Tversky refer to this as the "law of small numbers."

Why do even expert decision makers ignore base rate or consensus information? Kahneman and Tversky speculate that people may not know how to combine base rate information and, therefore, ignore it. Nisbett and Ross (1980) propose that base rate information, by its very nature, is abstract and pallid, and may simply lack the force for subjects to attend to and use. People, it seems, are unmoved by dry, statistical data dear to the hearts of scientists and evaluators. As Bertrand Russell observed, "popular induction depends on the emotional interest of the instances, not upon their number" (1927, p. 269). Individuals respond to vivid, concrete information and ignore abstract data.

Nisbett and Ross (1980) offer several examples of this tendency. Consumers have long ignored medical advice to quit smoking and safety advice to fasten seat belts. Such appeals typically report numbers, such as the probability of being a victim, which are largely ignored. Yet when a highly visible and concrete incident occurs that people can focus on, changes in behavior often occur. In an interesting experiment, Borgida and Nisbett (1977) provided prospective students with course evaluations based on ratings of students who had previously taken the courses. This information had little impact on course choices. In contrast, brief face-to-face comments about the courses had a substantial impact on course choices. Other studies have noted how vivid information that is non-diagnostic and unrelated to the decision to be made, may have an impact on the choice (Troutman & Shanteau, 1977). Thus, information that is concrete and arouses emotional interest appears to have greater impact than information that, while objectively more "accurate," is pallid.

Consider the ramifications of these biases for the use of information by decision makers. A typical report is often a document which relies heavily on the statistical analysis of data and variations from mean levels of performance. The essence of such a report is on base rates and variations from the mean. Complaints by users that information is not helpful, is too dry, relies too much on statistical analysis, or doesn't get at the real problem may, in fact, be symptomatic of decision makers' inability to use abstract information. On the other hand, users of information often focus on a single, concrete, often dramatic, example even though the chosen example may not be representative of the larger picture. Clearly concrete and vivid examples, which are accurate representations of the underlying results, are likely to be accepted and remembered by decision makers more easily than compilations of statistics. Meltsner (1976, p. 234) reports the advice of a chief federal analyst that when writing two-page summaries of reports, it is important to "sprinkle them with juicy punch lines that will catch the reader's interest." Such pragmatic advice reflects the fact that not only are decision makers busy enough not to want to read reports, but they are also more likely to remember, and therefore more likely to use, vivid information. Another analyst reported how half his time was spent in rewrite trying to translate statistical material into a form that would be meaningful to the President and White House staff and agency heads. These observations underscore the bias people have toward concrete information and suggest the following proposition:

Proposition 12: Information is more likely to be used when vivid, concrete illustrations of the conclusions are available.

SUMMARY AND CONCLUSIONS

The treatment of the utilization or nonutilization of information by organizational decision makers began with a simplified model of decision making whose purpose was to highlight the importance and potential impacts of information in the decision process. An argument was made that, in organizational settings, it may be that rather than the decision making process proceeding from a problem to alternatives to a choice which optimizes, organizational decision makers often have strong preferences for certain outcomes. These preferences may direct their information search and processing in ways calculated to maximize the attainment of desired ends. This view recognizes that information is only one commodity which may help or hinder goal attainment. This view also recognizes that some choices are unacceptable to certain decision makers, regardless of the net benefit to the larger collective. Knowledge does not necessarily equate with action.

Given the political process through which goals and objectives are negotiated among groups of organizational participants (e.g., Pfeffer, 1981b), universal agreement on any allocation of resources is unlikely. This lack of consensus makes the process of organizational decision making a political one, often characterized by conflict and disagreement. In order to achieve a semblance of rationality, if only to satisfy constituencies outside the organization, procedures may be established that given the appearance of comprehensive rationality but which, in fact, may be more symbolic than real. Within the bounds of this "procedural rationality" we argued that individual decision makers were "contextually rational,'' that is, attempted to maximize goal attainment, given a set of situational, organizational, and individual constraints. Thus, it may be that the requirement for information and evaluation is a manifestation of the need of procedural rationality, while the actual use of evaluation information is subject to the contextual rationality of relevant decision makers. The fact that other evaluations are conducted for support of previously made decisions may be an example of the contextual rationality of decision makers.

Since the decision making process as illustrated in Figure 1 is an interactive one, and since the argument is that much of the information manipulation stems from the preferred set of outcomes, it is important to consider how these preferences are developed as well as how information is used. We proposed that two primary sets of constraints were relevant. First, in organizational settings decision makers are seldom indifferent to outcomes. Rather, goals are assigned, for example, profit or cost margins, and control systems established to monitor and sanction responsible individuals. Power, or the ability to induce other groups or individuals to behave in prescribed ways, becomes an important consideration for goal attainment. The effect of these variables on decision makers is to make a limited set of outcomes both salient and desirable. These constraints, when coupled with the potential loss of personal rewards such as status, promotion, social approval, and money, act to commit decision makers to certain outcomes.

Once committed, we argued that decision makers were then potentially subject to biases in both the acquisition and processing of information for use in decision making. Evidence was cited which demonstrated that decision makers were biased in their search for information, preferring accessible information that supported their preferences rather than contrary information, even if such information was of higher quality. Further, evidence was also available which documented how commitment to certain desired outcomes was associated with the distortion of information in organizational communication. Hence, it may also be that the information available to unbiased decision makers may, if it has been transmitted through an organizational hierarchy, already contain inaccuracies or distortions.

The information processing of decision makers was also considered as a potential source of nonutilization of information. In pursuing desired outcomes, decision makers were often shown to selectively perceive and interpret information. Importantly, it has also been shown that human information processors do not deal well with dry, statistical data, but prefer more vivid, concrete examples, even though such information may be inaccurate or misleading. These biases may be important since evaluation information is typically quantitative and statistical. It was argued that the combination and general preference for vivid examples biases them away from the use of information unless such information is supportive.

The joint effects of the situational and individual constraints on information use by decision makers is outlined in Figure 2. Context variables such as incentive systems, group norms, and organizational structure may act to affect the information which is available to a decision maker. Context variables may also affect individual preferences for certain types of information as well as the manner in which information is processed cognitively. In turn, these variables may determine how and what information is used by decision makers.

When information and decision making are considered from the perspective developed in this paper, and subject to the constraints presented in Figure 2, several observations about utilization of information are noteworthy. First, information is seldom likely to be regarded by decision makers as objective and nonpartisan. Rather, information is likely to be viewed as useful to some interested parties, threatening to some, and irrelevant to others. The utilization of such information for decision making will probably reflect, not any objective measure of quality, but a number of factors independent of the information set, such as the degree of consensus or conflict among those involved in the decision process, the relative power of the participants, pressures on the primary decision makers, availability of other information, and so on. In some cases, individual characteristics of the decision maker may also determine the utilization/nonutilization. When studies are undertaken, not to provide information for decision, but as a means of increasing confidence in a position or for symbolic reasons, it is unlikely that any direct impact of information will be observable. This does not imply that such information is not useful, only that its function is not directly related to decision making.

Finally, the propositions developed in this paper are clearly tentative and somewhat simplistic and only suggest possible hypotheses which might be tested empirically. Obviously there are a large number of influences on the use of information which have been omitted here. Therefore, what is proposed in this paper is not a well-articulated theory of utilization of information in decision making, but some tentative propositions based on previous research on organizational decision making and information use.

ACKNOWLEDGMENTS

Support for the preparation of this chapter was provided, in part, by the Center for the Study of Evaluation, University of California, Los Angeles. The author wishes to thank W. Gary Wagner, Bill Glick, and Susan Resnick for their helpful comments on earlier drafts of the manuscript.

REFERENCES

Allison, G. *Essence of decision*. Boston: Little-Brown, 1971.

Arrow, K. J. *The limits of organization*. New York: Norton, 1973.

Ball, G. Memo to Lyndon Johnson dated July 1965. As reported in N. Sheehan (Ed.), *Pentagon papers*. New York: Bantam, 1971.

Baum, J., & Youngblood, S. Impact of an organizational control policy on absenteeism, performance and satisfaction. *Journal of Applied Psychology*, 1975, *60*, 688–694.

Beach, L. R., Mitchell, T. R., Deaton, M. D., & Prothero, J. Information relevance, content and source credibility in the revision of opinions. *Organizational Behavior and Human Performance*, 1978, *21*, 1–16.

Bear, G., & Hodun, A. Implicational principles and the cognition of confirmatory, contradictory, incomplete and irrelevant information. *Journal of Personality and Social Psychology*, 1975, *32*, 594–604.

Berger, P. & Luckmann, T. *The social construction of reality*. New York: Doubleday, 1967.

Blasovich, J., Ginsburg, G, & Howe, R. Blackjack and the risky shift II: Monetary stakes. *Journal of Experimental Social Psychology*, 1975, *11*, 224–232.

Blau, P. *Exchange and power in social life*. New York: Wiley, 1964.

Borgida, E. & Nisbett, R. E. The differential impact on abstract vs. concrete information on decisions. *Journal of Applied Social Psychology*, 1977, *7*, 258–271.

Bradley, G. W. Self-serving biases in the attribution process: A re-examination of the fact or fiction question. *Journal of Personality and Social Psychology*, 1978, *36*, 56–71.

Buckhout, R. Eyewitness testimony. *Scientific American*, 1974, *231*, 23–31.

Caldwell, D., & O'Reilly, C. Responses to failure: The effect of choice and responsibility on impression management. *Academy of Management Journal*, 1982a, *25*, 121–136.

Caldwell, D. F., & O'Reilly, C. A. The joint impact of source credibility and message content on decision: An application to personnel selection. Unpublished manuscript. University of California, Berkeley, 1982b.

Carter, R. Client's resistance to negative findings and the latent conservative function of evaluation studies. *American Sociologist*, 1971, *6*, 118–124.

Cialdini, R., & Richardson, K. Two indirect tactics of image management: Basking and blasting. *Journal of Personality and Social Psychology*, 1980, *39*, 406–415.

Clausen, A. *How congressmen decide: A policy focus*. New York: St. Martin's Press, 1973.

Cohen, M., March, J., & Olsen, J. A garbage can model of organizational choice. *Administrative Science Quarterly*, 1972, *17*, 1–25.

Coleman, J. *Policy research in the social sciences*. Morristown, N.J.: General Learning Press, 1972.

Connolly, T. Information processing and decision making in organizations. In B. Staw, & G. Salancik (Eds.), *New Directions in Organizational Behavior*. Chicago: St. Clair, 1977, 205–234.

Cox, G. Managerial style: Implications for the utilization of program evaluation information. *Evaluation Quarterly*, 1977, *1*, 499–507.

Cyert, R., & March, J. *A behavioral theory of the firm*. Englewood Cliffs, N.J.: Prentice-Hall, 1963.

David, J. *Local uses of Title 1 evaluations*. Stanford Research Institute Report EPRC 21, July 1978.

Dawes, R., & Corrigan, B. Linear models in decision making. *Psychological Bulletin,* 1974, *81,* 95–106.

Dewhirst, H. D. Influence of perceived information-sharing norms on communication channel utilization. *Academy of Management Journal,* 1971, *14,* 305–315.

Ebbesen, E., & Kocnecni, V. Decision making and information integration in the courts: The setting of bail. *Journal of Personality and Social Psychology,* 1975, *32,* 805–821.

Einhorn, H., & Hogarth, R. Judgment and decision. In Rosenzweig, M., & Porter, L. (Eds.), *Annual Review of Psychology, 32.* Palo Alto, Ca.: Annual Reviews, 1981.

Erez, M. Feedback: A necessary condition for the goal setting-performance relationship. *Journal of Applied Psychology,* 1977, *62,* 624–627.

Floden, R., & Weiner, S. Rationality to ritual: The multiple roles of evaluation in governmental process. *Policy Sciences,* 1978, *9,* 9–18.

Gerstberger, P., & Allen, T. Criteria used by research and development engineers in the selection of an information source. *Journal of Applied Psychology,* 1968, *52,* 272–279.

Goldstein, M., Marcus, A., & Rausch, N. The nonutilization of evaluation research. *Pacific Sociological Review,* 1978, *21,* 21–44.

Gordon, G., & Morse, E. Evaluation research. *Annual Review of Sociology,* 1975, *2,* 339–361.

Gouran, D. The Watergate cover-up: Its dynamics and its implications. *Communication Monographs,* 1976, *43,* 176–186.

Halberstam, D. *The best and the brightest.* New York: Random House, 1972.

Harrell, A. The decision-making behavior of Air Force officers and the management control process. *Accounting Review,* 1977, *52,* 833–841.

Hawkins, J., Roffman, R., & Osborne, P. Decision m akers' judgments: The influence of role, evaluative criteria and information access. *Evaluation Quarterly,* 1978, *2,* 435–454.

Hickson, D., Hinings, C., Lee, C., Schneck, R., & Pennings, J. A strategic contingencies' theory of intraorganizational power. *Administrative Science Quarterly,* 1971, *16,* 216–229.

Janis, I. *Victims of groupthink.* Boston: Houghton-Mifflin, 1972.

Janis, I., & Mann, I. *Decision making: A psychological analysis of conflict, choice, and commitment.* New York: Free Press, 1977.

Johnson, R. J. Conflict avoidance through acceptable decisions. *Human Relations,* 1974, *27,* 71–82.

Kanouse, D. W., & Hanson, L. R. Negativity in evaluations. In E. E. Jones et al., *Attribution: Perceiving the Causes of Behavior.* Morristown, N.J.: General Learning Press, 1972, 47–62.

Kaufman, H. *Administrative feedback.* Washington, D.C.: Brookings, 1973.

Keeley, M. Organizational analogy: A comparison of organismic and social contract models. *Administrative Science Quarterly,* 1980, *25,* 337–362.

Kerr, S. On the folly of rewarding A, while hoping for B. *Academy of Management Journal,* 1975, *18,* 796–783.

Kidd, J., & Morgan, J. A predictive information system for management. *Operational Research Quarterly,* 1969, *20,* 149–170.

Langer, E. J. The illusion of control. *Journal of Personality and Social Psychology,* 1975, *32,* 311–328.

Langer, E., Blank, A., & Chanowitz, B. The mindlessness of ostensibly thoughtful action: The role of "placebic" information in interpersonal attraction. *Journal of Personality and Social Psychology,* 1978, *36,* 635–642.

Larwood, L., & Whittaker, W. Managerial myopia: Self-serving biases in organizational planning. *Journal of Applied Psychology,* 1977, *62,* 194–198.

Latham, G., & Yukl, G. A review of research on the application of goal setting in organizations. *Academy of Management Journal,* 1975, *18,* 824–845.

Lindblom, C. E. The science of "muddling through." *Public Administration Review,* 1959, *19,* 79–88.

Locke, E., Shaw, K., Saari, L., & Latham, G. Goal setting and task performance: 1969-1980. *Psychological Bulletin,* 1981, *90,* 125–152.

Lord, C., Ross, L., & Lepper, M. Biased assimilation and attitude polarization: The effects of prior theories on subsequently considered evidence. *Journal of Personality and Social Psychology,* 1979, *37,* 2098–2109.

Lowe, E., & Shaw, R. An analysis of managerial biasing: Evidence from a company's budgeting process. *Journal of Management Studies,* 1968, *5,* 304–315.

Manis, M., Cornell, D., & Moore, J. Transmission of attitude-relevant information through a communication chain. *Journal of Personality and Social Psychology,* 1974, *30,* 81–94.

March, J. G. Bounded rationality, ambiguity, and the engineering of choice. *Bell Journal of Economics,* 1978, *9,* 587–608.

March, J., & Simon, H. *Organizations.* New York: Wiley, 1958.

McCleary, R. How parole officers use records. *Social Problems,* 1977, *24,* 576–589.

Meltsner, A. J. *Policy analysts in the bureaucracy.* Berkeley: University of California Press, 1976.

Menzel, H., & Katz, E. Social relations and innovation in the medical profession. *Public Opinion Quarterly,* 1955, *19,* 337–352.

Meyer, J., & Rowan, B. Institutionalized organizations: Formal structure as myth and ceremony. *Americal Journal of Sociology,* 1977, *83,* 340–363.

Miller, G. A. The magical number seven plus or minus two: Some limits on our capacity for processing information. *Psychological Review,* 1956, *64.* 81–97.

Miller, D. T., & Ross, M. Self-serving biases in the attribution of causality: Fact or fiction? *Psychological Bulletin,* 1975, *82,* 213–225.

Miller, J. W., & Rowe, P. M. Influence of favorable and unfavorable information upon assessment decisions. *Journal of Applied Psychology,* 1967, *51,* 432–435.

Mintzberg, H. *The nature of managerial work.* New York: Harper and Row, 1973.

Mintzberg, H., Raisinghani, D., & Theoret, A. The structure of "unstructured" decision processes. *Administrative Science Quarterly,* 1976, *21,* 246–275.

Mohr, L. On organizational goals. *American Political Science Review,* 1973, *66,* 470–481.

Morlock, H. The effect of outcome desirability on information required for decision. *Behavioral Science,* 1967, *12,* 296–300.

Neustadt, R. E., & Fineberg, H. *The swine flu affair: Decision making on a slippery disease.* Washington, D.C.: U.S. Dept. of H.E.W., 1978.

Nisbett, R., & Ross, L. *Human Inference: Strategies and Shortcomings.* Englewood Cliffs, N.J.: Prentice-Hall, 1980.

O'Reilly, C. Individuals and information overload in organizations: Is more necessarily better? *Academy of Management Journal,* 1980, *23,* 684–696.

O'Reilly, C. The intentional distortion of information in organizational communication: A laboratory and field approach. *Human Relations,* 1978, *31,* 173–193.

O'Reilly, C. Variations in decision makers' use of information sources: the impact of quality and accessibility of information. *Academy of Management Journal,* 1982. In press.

O'Reilly, C., & Anderson, J. Organizational communication and decision making: The impact of contextual factors on information acquisition and use in laboratory and field settings. *Management Science,* 1982. In press.

O'Reilly, C., & Pondy, L. Organizational communication. In S. Kerr (Ed.), *Organizational Behavior*. Columbus, Ohio: Grid, 1979.

O'Reilly, C., & Roberts, K. Relationship among components of credibility and communication behaviors in work units. *Journal of Applied Psychology,* 1976, *61,* 99–102.

Orlans, H. *Contracting for knowledge*. San Francisco: Jossey-Bass, 1973.

Oskamp, S. Overconfidence in case study judgements. *Journal of Consulting Psychology,* 1965, *29,* 261–265.

Ostrom, T., & Davis, D. Idiosyncratic weighting of trait information in impression formation. *Journal of Personality and Social Psychology,* 1979, *37,* 2025–2043.

Pettigrew, A. Information control as a power resource. *Sociology,* 1972, *6,* 187–204.

Petty, R., Harkins, S. & Williams, K. The effects of group diffusion of cognitive effort on attitudes: An information-processing view. *Journal of Personality and Social Psychology,* 1980, *38,* 81–92.

Pfeffer, J. Management as symbolic action: The creation and maintenance of organizational paradigms. In B. Staw, & L. Cummings (Eds.), *Research in Organizational Behavior,* Vol. 3, Greenwich, CT: JAI, 1981a, 1–52.

Pfeffer, J. *Power in organizations*. Marshfield, Ma.: Pitman, 1981b.

Pfeffer, J., & Salancik, G. Administrator effectiveness: The effects of advocacy and information on achieving outcomes in an organizational context. *Human Relations,* 1977, *30,* 641–656.

Pfeffer, J., & Salancik, G. *The external control of organizations: A resource dependence perspective*. New York: Harper and Row, 1978.

Plott, C., & Levine, M. A model of agency influence on committee decisions. *American Economic Review,* 1978, *68,* 146–160.

Porat, A., & Haas, J. Information effects on decision making. *Behavioral Science,* 1969, *14,* 98–104.

Rosen, B., & Tesser, A. On reluctance to communicate undesirable information: The MUM effect. *Sociometry,* 1970, *33,* 253–263.

Ross, L. The intuitive psychologist and his shortcomings: Distortions in the attribution process. In L. Berkowitz (Ed.), *Advances in Experimental Social Psychology*. New York: Academic Press, 1977, 173–220.

Ross, M., & Sicoly, F. Egocentric biases in availability and attribution. *Journal of Personality and Social Psychology,* 1979, *37,* 322–336.

Salancik, G. R. Commitment and the control of organizational behavior and belief. In B. M. Staw, & G. R. Salancik (Eds.), *New Directions in Organizational Behavior*. Chicago: St. Clair, 1977, 1–54.

Schlenker, B. R., & Miller, R. S. Egocentrism in groups: Self-serving biases or logical information processing? *Journal of Personality and Social Psychology,* 1977, *35,* 755–764.

Schroder, H., Driver, M., & Streufert, S. *Human information processing*. New York: Holt, Rinehart and Winston, 1967.

Simon, H. *Administrative behavior*. Glencoe, IL.: Free Press, 1957.

Simon, H. On the concept of organizational goal. *Administrative Science Quarterly,* 1964, *9,* 1–22.

Simon, H. Rationality as a process and as product of thought. *American Economic Review,* 1978, *68,* 1–16.

Slovic, P., Fischhoff, B., & Lichtenstein, S. Behavioral decision theory. In M. Rozenzweig, & L. Porter (Eds.), *Annual Review of Psychology,* 1977, *28,* 1–39. Palo Alto, Ca.: Annual Review, Inc.

Snyder, M., & Swann, W. Hypothesis-testing processes in social interaction. *Journal of Personality and Social Psychology,* 1978, *36,* 1202–1212.

Snyder, M., & Uranowitz, S. Reconstructing the past: Some cognitive consequences of person perception. *Journal of Personality and Social Psychology,* 1978, *36,* 941–950.

Staw, B. Rationality and justification in organizational life. In B. Staw, & L. Cummings (Eds.), *Research in Organizational Behavior, 2,* Greenwich, Ct.: JAI, 1980, 45–80.

Staw, B. M., & Fox, F. V. Escalation: Some determinants of commitment to previously chosen course of action. *Human Relations,* 1977, *30,* 431–450.

Staw, B. M., & Ross, J. Commitment to a policy decision: A multi-theoretical perspective. *Administrative Science Quarterly,* 1978, *23,* 40–64.

Streufert, S. C. Effects of information relevance on decision making in complex environments. *Memory and Cognition,* 1973, *1,* 224–228.

Taylor, R., & Dunnette, M. Relative contribution of decision-maker attributes to decision processes. *Organizational Behavior and Human Performance,* 1974, *12,* 286–298.

Thompson, J. D. *Organizations in action.* New York: McGraw-Hill, 1967.

Troutman, C. M., & Shanteau, J. inferences based on nondiagnostic information. *Organizational Behavior and Human Performance,* 1977, *19,* 43–55.

Tversky, A., & Kahneman, D. Judgment under uncertainty: Heuristics and biases. *Science,* 1974, *185,* 1124–1131.

Weick, K. Enactment processes in organizations. In B. Staw, & G. Salancik (Eds.), *New Directions in organizational behavior.* Chicago: St. Clair, 1977, 267–300.

Wildavsky, A. *The politics of the budgetary process.* Boston: Little-Brown, 1974.

Wilensky, H. *Organizational intelligence.* New York: Free Press, 1967.

Winkler, R., & Murphy, A. Experiments in the laboratory and the real world. *Organizational Behavior and Human Performance,* 1973, *10,* 252–270.

Witte, E. Field research on complex decision making processes: the phase theorem. *International Studies of Management and Organization,* 1972, 156–182.

Wright, P. The harassed decision maker: Time pressures, distractions, and the use of evidence. *Journal of Applied Psychology,* 1974, *59,* 555–561.

Wright, W. Cognitive information processing biases: Implications for producers and users of financial information. *Decision Sciences,* 1980, *11,* 284–298.

NEGOTIATOR COGNITION

Max H. Bazerman and John S. Carroll

ABSTRACT

This paper argues that the study of the cognitions of negotiators offers a new and important direction in the study of negotiation. This paper outlines various directions that the study of negotiator cognition might follow. We examine the existing literature on behavioral decision theory effects in the negotiation domain, propose that additional biases occur in the negotiation context because of a tendency to ignore the cognitions of others, and outline the unexplored potential of the social cognition area to further inform the negotiation literature. Together, these perspectives of negotiator cognition offer a view of the negotiation process that is in sharp contrast with the rationalistic expectations that are common in economic models of negotiation.

Negotiation is a process by which two or more interdependent parties who do not have identical preferences across decision alternatives make joint decisions (Pruitt, 1981, 1983; Kelley & Thibaut, 1980). Despite the obvious prevalence and importance of negotiation, substantial evidence exists that negotiators frequently fail to attain readily available and mutually beneficial outcomes, and that these inefficiencies in the negotiation process reduce society's available resources, productivity, and creative opportunities, and increase society's conflict and self-destructiveness (Pruitt & Rubin, 1986; Raiffa, 1982). For example, in the labor–management domain, failures of negotiation lead to costly strikes, decreased harmony in the workplace, and threats to the survival of the organization and the jobs of organizational members (Walton & McKersie, 1965; Kochan, 1980). The dangers of negotiation failures in the international sphere include inefficient economic trade, war, and threats to our survival.

Although the preceding definition places negotiation within the domain of decision making, there is little work in the negotiation literature that has examined negotiation from the perspective of behavioral decision theory or cognition in general. In this paper we examine the capacities and limitations of human cognition in dealing with the complex cognitive task of negotiation, a perspective that we believe offers a new direction in the negotiation literature (Bazerman & Neale, 1983).

Past research in the area of negotiation has focused on three major topics: (1) economic models of how people would make decisions in negotiation tasks if they were fully rational (Nash, 1950; Raiffa, 1982); (2) structural (situational) determinants of negotiated outcomes, such as differential information or payoffs (Kochan, 1980) or the effects of other surrounding characteristics (e.g., the form of third-party intervention that will be used if the negotiators reach impasse); and (3) individual differences among negotiators, such as competitiveness (Rubin & Brown, 1975). Unfortunately, there has been little interaction among these perspectives. The lack of interaction is attributable to the varying disciplinary backgrounds of the researchers from the three domains of inquiry and the lack of a common conceptual focus for discussion. The economic models were developed by economists, the structural determinants approach developed out of industrial relations, and the personality approach was developed in psychology.

We believe interaction among these approaches is possible within a framework that views negotiation as a decision-making process. The preceding approaches focus on *inputs* to the negotiation process in the structure of the issues, the setting, and the types of negotiators, and *outputs* in relation to a normative outcome. Figure 1 provides a simplified schematic portrayal of the negotiation process as portrayed in economic models (Panel A) and in those models specifying the negotiation task and the types of negotiators as inputs determining the negotiation outcomes (Panel

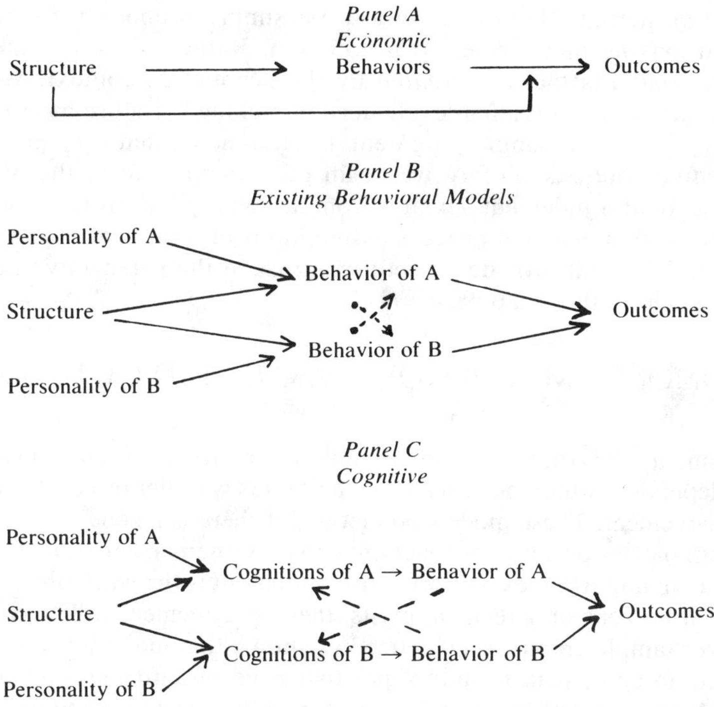

Figure 1. Negotiation Models

B). The dotted arrows in Panel B refer to possible sequences of behavior by negotiators who affect each other's subsequent behaviors.

Neither of these approaches examines intervening decision processes. We believe that a conceptual focus on the *intervening decision processes* in negotiation will offer new insights and provide a common ground for linking the alternative approaches that currently dominate the negotiation literature. A decision-making approach to negotiation views each party to the negotiation as a decision maker. The behaviors of each party are seen as choices based on judgments about the negotiation situation. Each party is thus considering information about the situation, analyzing each other's behavior, predicting future events, and assessing possible consequences. The actual consequences received by each party are then a function of everyone's behaviors and the contingencies of the negotiation context. As portrayed in Panel C of Figure 1, the impacts of personality, expertise, and features of the situation are mediated by the judgments negotiators make during the negotiation process. The dotted arrows leading from one person's behavior to the other's cognitions again refer to possible sequences of interaction over time during negotiation.

Our cognitive perspective of negotiation focuses on the decisions of the negotiation actors. However, we are not simply proposing a model of decision making that applies to negotiation. Rather, we are examining cognitive patterns that are *created* by the negotiation context. We will examine what the individual-level decision-making literature has to offer. But, we will also examine judgmental deficiencies that are specific to competitive contexts. Before we begin the examination of the ways in which negotiator judgment deviates from rationality, this introduction overviews the outcome and process assumptions of a rational model of negotiation. This will provide a useful contrast to the perspective that we later develop in this chapter.

ECONOMIC MODELS OF NEGOTIATED OUTCOMES

Economic models of negotiation assume rationality and focus on two primary dependent-outcome variables. The *first* is whether or not the parties reach agreement. These models predict that if there is a zone of agreement that both parties prefer over reaching impasse, then an agreement will be reached (an important exception to this statement is the work of Crawford [1979]). If no zone of agreement exists, then no agreement will be reached. However, ample empirical evidence has shown that individuals often fail to reach an agreement despite a positive zone of agreement (cf. Pruitt, 1981). A great deal of research has examined the structural and individual difference variables that affect settlement in cases in which a positive zone of agreement is defined to exist (cf. Pruitt & Rubin, 1986; Rubin & Brown, 1975). However, negotiation research has not provided a process explanation of why negotiators fail to reach agreement despite a positive zone of agreement.

The *second* outcome variable receiving attention in negotiation research is the degree to which the agreement reached by the parties is efficient. An agreement is said to be efficient, or *pareto optimal,* when there is no alternative joint resolution available that would be preferable to both parties. Economic models argue that negotiators will maximize their utility and that the resolution between two negotiators will be *pareto optimal* (Zuethen, 1930; Nash, 1950; Cross, 1969; Farber, 1980, 1981). This sounds great, because efficient agreements tend to maximize joint benefit (Walton & McKersie, 1965), provide resolution of conflict when both sides have high aspirations, strengthen the relationship between parties, and contribute to the welfare of the broader community (Pruitt, 1983). Unfortunately, negotiators often reach inefficient outcomes. Part of the explanation for this disturbing fact is that negotiators face conflicting demands in seeking successful negotiations. What social psychologists call mixed-motive games are considered to pit cooperation against competition (Kelley & Thibaut, 1980). The behaviors that are optimal for gaining concessions from the opponent are likely to be suboptimal for creating joint gains, and the behaviors that are optimal for creating joint gains are likely to be suboptimal for obtaining concessions from the opponent. However, this statement of internal conflict concerning the motives of the negotiator does not explain the decisions of the negotiator that lead to inefficient outcomes.

If economic models of negotiation provided accurate descriptions of the decision processes of negotiators, there would be no need to write this chapter. The cognitive processes of negotiators would be accounted for in the rationalistic descriptions of economic models. However, there are theoretical and empirical reasons to believe that actual negotiator behavior does not exhibit the rationality of economic models. First, and most generally, behavioral decision research shows that individuals deviate from rationality in systematic and predictable ways (Kahneman Slovic, & Tversky, 1982; Hogarth, 1980; Nisbett & Ross, 1980). Second, and more specifically, recent research demonstrates that *negotiators* deviate from the economic model of negotiator rationality in a number of systematic ways that reduce outcomes to the parties and to society in general (Neale & Bazerman, 1985; Bazerman, 1983). However, the work of Bazerman and Neale has drawn almost exclusively from the behavioral decision theory literature, which represents only one segment of what we know about how people actually make decisions. This chapter attempts to map out a broader definition of the area of negotiator cognition that has theoretical, empirical, and applied relevance.

AN OUTLINE OF DECISION PROCESSES IN NEGOTIATING

The decision-making or problem-solving process in negotiation can be usefully separated into a set of stages (Huber, 1980; Hogarth, 1980; March & Simon, 1958), without implying that the process necessarily takes a simple linear form (Mintzberg, Raisinghani, & Theoret, 1976). It will be useful to keep this framework in mind as we discuss negotiator cognitions, and we will return to this framework at the end of the chapter to integrate the themes that will be developed throughout the paper. The first stage is the recognition that there is a problem to solve (something to negotiate), and acceptance of responsibility for solving it (see Corbin, 1980, for a discussion of decision avoidance strategies). The first stage can be more actively construed as problem finding, although most problems seem to find people rather than vice versa. The second stage is the structuring or formulation of the problem. This stage involves the classification of problem type, the exploration of the problem, the recognition of possible consequences, and so forth. The third stage consists of gathering relevant information about conflict, your alternatives to negotiation, the other parties' alternatives to negotiation, your interests, the opponents' interests, etc. With this information available, you are ready for the fourth stage—information evaluation. Which pieces of information are directly relevant to the negotiation? What are the implications of this information? Finally, the fifth stage consists of strategy evaluation. This stage consists of using the information acquired to develop a coherent strategy for interacting with the opponent.

These stages help to structure the concept of negotiation as decision behavior, but this analysis is neutral regarding the presumed rationality of the negotiator. A *rational* view of negotiation would expect that negotiators follow each of these steps in an optimal fashion, for example, identifying all alternatives and all outcomes, gathering all relevant information, and combining it optimally. In contrast, the behavioral literature suggests that negotiators behave in a more selective, abbreviated, and even biased manner. Each stage in the decision process is prone to oversimplifications and errors, some of which are common to decision making and cognition in general, others of which are unique to the negotiation setting. The simplifications and cognitive errors that occur in negotiation are the central concern of this chapter.

The remainder of the chapter is organized in four sections. First, we examine the behavioral decision theory research of Neale and Bazerman. This is the most well-developed area in this chapter, because it is the only area of the chapter that is based on published empirical work on the cognitive processes of negotiators. Second, we develop the argument that the negotiation context produces additional sources of deviations from rationality that would not be observed in an individual decision context. Specifically, we argue that individuals have a systematic tendency to ignore important and easily available information about the decision processes of opponent negotiators. This section is based on a few pieces of completed research, but is presented in the form of a theoretical integration that is only now emerging from our ongoing research. Third, we will delve into the social cognition literature to explore other conceptualizations of judgment that have the power to inform the field of negotiation. Finally, the fourth section reconsiders the steps of the decision process of negotiation (outlined earlier) in light of the evidence of systematic deviations from rationality in negotiation that are presented throughout the chapter.

BEHAVIORAL DECISION THEORY IN NEGOTIATION

Most of the existing research dealing with the cognitions of negotiators has derived from behavioral decision theory, which is the major alternative to neoclassical economics for describing individual decision processes (Kahneman & Tversky, 1979; Kahneman et al., 1982; March & Simon, 1958; Simon, 1947). Specifically, behavioral decision research has identified a number of systematic ways in which judgment deviates from rationality. This section will overview some of the behavioral decision theory effects that have been observed in negotiations, evaluate the contribution that this area of research can make to the study of negotiation, and offer suggestions for future research.

Overconfidence

Negotiators are *overconfident* in evaluating their likelihood of achieving successful negotiations (Bazerman & Neale, 1982). Overconfidence has been demonstrated in a broad range of judgments (Einhorn & Hogarth, 1978, 1981; Fischhoff, 1981). In the negotiation context, overconfidence can lead to at least two related effects. First, in a simple two-party bargaining context, overconfidence could inhibit an agreement, despite the existence of a positive bargaining zone. If both sides expect the other party to eventually yield, they will not be the first to yield. Second, overconfidence could lead parties to use third parties unnecessarily, because each party overestimates the likelihood that the third party will favor their position.

In a careful economic analysis of the use of a third party, Farber (1981) shows that overconfidence provides a sufficient theoretical explanation for why negotiators fail to reach agreements and then use arbitrators, despite the fact that the arbitrator imposes costs on both parties and does not typically increase the joint benefit obtained by the parties. Farber shows that overconfident negotiators will not settle for the middle ground that an objective third party is likely to choose. Because each party expects the third party to see the world closer to their own eyes, neither party will accept the compromise that lies between their positions, even when this point represents a good actual estimate of the eventual decision of the third party (which will not always be the case—see Bazerman, 1985; Farber & Bazerman, 1986).

Neale and Bazerman (1983) show empirically that negotiators do tend to be overconfident. After submitting decisions to arbitration, Neale and Bazerman found that negotiators estimate a 68% likelihood, on average, that the arbitrator will select their final offer. Objectively, with two parties, only 50% of the offers actually can be selected. If negotiators were more realistic, and thereby less confident in their fallible assessment of the likely behavior of the third party (or any other alternative to a negotiated settlement), they would tend to be more concessionary in order to reach negotiated settlements.

Escalation in Neogtiation

A second well-researched judgmental distortion is the tendency of negotiators to nonrationally *escalate* their commitment to a previously selected course of action (Staw & Ross, 1987; Brockner & Rubin, 1985; Teger, 1980). At an individual level, it has been shown that individuals will tend to continue a previously chosen course of action in order to justify *cognitively* a past decision (Staw, 1976, 1981). Empirical research shows that individuals will stay in such disputed contexts well beyond the quitting point that would be dictated by a rational analysis of the situation (Teger, 1980; Brockner & Rubin, 1985). This logic has also been used to explain the Vietnam war (Staw, 1976), the Falklands crisis (Bazerman & Neale, 1983), and numerous other well-known failures of negotiation. Both sides escalate their commitment in order to justify their current stance in the conflict and to avoid admitting past mistakes.

Bazerman (1986) offers four causes of escalation that are relevant to the negotiation situation. First, once a negotiator makes an initial commitment to a position, *perception* is biased toward information that is supportive of the initial position. Second, a negotiator's *judgment* will be biased toward justifying the earlier position. One good example of this is when we our *overconfident* in the viability of our position (as discussed in the previous subsection). Third, negotiators often escalate in order to *"save face"* with their constituency. Negotiators often go against their constituencies' best interests in order to look "strong" to that same constituency. These three explanations of escalation apply to all types of escalatory situations. However, the *competitive context* of the negotiation situation adds a fourth cause of escalation: Negotiators are often uncertain about the future actions of the opponent negotiator. Rather than thinking through the possibilities, negotiators leave their predictions open so they can later justify their position in retrospect. The unfortunate result can be seen in the famous "dollar auction" (Shubik, 1971; Teger, 1980), where individuals bid more than a dollar for a dollar because of their uncertainty about the opponent's future behavior (see p. 261 of this paper or Teger [1980] for details).

Salience of Information in Negotiation

A third deficiency that biases negotiator cognition is concerned with the *saliency* of information. Tversky and Kahneman (1973) suggest that more salient information has more impact on an individual's decision process (Nisbett & Ross, 1980), perhaps because salient events are more *available* in memory.

In a laboratory study of bargaining behavior, Neale (1984) found that varying the saliency of negotiation-related costs and arbitration-related costs (while holding objective costs constant) altered both the process and outcome of negotiation. When negotiation costs (i.e., perceived costs of a negotiated settlement) were made particularly salient to the negotiators, they were less concessionary and more likely to declare impasse. However, when arbitration costs (i.e., perceived costs of an arbitrated settlement) were made particularly salient to the negotiators, they were more concessionary and less likely to declare impasse. Obviously, in other negotiation settings, the salience of negotiation- and arbitration-related costs can be generalized to the costs of negotiation versus the costs of "walking away" from the negotiation.

The Framing of Negotiations

Kahneman and Tversky's (1979) "prospect theory" holds that outcomes are evaluated as gains or losses from an imputed reference point (part of the "frame" of the problem), and that most individuals are risk averse for potential gains, but risk seeking for potential losses. Bazerman, Magliozzi, and Neale (1985) extend the framing effect to negotiators by arguing that negotiators framing outcomes as gains or profits would be more concessionary in order to obtain the sure (risk-averse) outcome available in a negotiated settlement. In contrast, they argue that negotiators framing outcomes as losses or costs would show comparatively risk-seeking behavior by holding out and risking an impasse in order to attempt to obtain a better agreement through concessions by the opponent.

Bazerman et al. (1985) examine the impact of framing on buyers and sellers in a free market simulation. They instructed positively framed negotiators to *maximize* net profit and negatively framed negotiators to *minimize* expenses to be subtracted from gross profit. They found that positively framed negotiators completed more agreements (due to their desire for certain outcomes) than did their negatively framed counterparts. In addition, positively framed negotiators obtained significantly more profitability across multiple transactions in a fixed amount of time than did negatively framed negotiators. These results challenge economic models of decision making, which argue that the frame of the problem should not affect negotiator behavior.

The framing effect has important, yet untested, implications for negotiator and mediator tactical behavior. How negotiators phrase options is a factor that matters. For example, negotiators should always make it salient to the opponent that they are in a potentially risky situation where a sure gain is possible through a negotiated settlement. Similarly, mediators, whose goal is a mutually acceptable compromise, should strive to have both parties view the situation in a positive frame and to be aware that an impasse is a risky proposition. Empirical testing is needed to confirm the power of framing as a tactical behavior by negotiators and mediators.

The Mythical Fixed Pie of Negotiations

Integrative agreements are nonobvious solutions to conflict that reconcile the parties' interests and yield higher joint benefit than a simple compromise could create. Skill building in helping negotiators find integrative agreements is the most central concern of the rapidly proliferating field of negotiation (Kochan & Bazerman, 1986). A key element in this training is the recognition that individuals enter into negotiations assuming that they are in direct competition with the opponent negotiator. This frequently false assumption—the mythical fixed pie of negotiations—may be the most common barrier to the creation of mutually beneficial agreements.

The existence of a mythical fixed pie can be a result of the simplification of a complex cognitive task. In order to cope with complex problems, individuals make simplifying assumptions to make the problem cognitively manageable (Simon, 1957; Newell & Simon, 1972). In negotiation, folklore and many of our past experiences tell us that we are in competition with the other negotiator and thus directs us to attend to the distributive or competitive aspects of negotiation. Once it becomes part of our cognitive repertoire, the habitual tendency to make that assumption can be difficult to break.

The importance of the mythical fixed pie and the benefits of overcoming it can be seen in Pruitt and Rubin's (1986) depiction of the Camp David talks:

> When Egypt and Israel sat down to negotiate at Camp David in October 1978, it appeared that they had before them an intractable conflict. Egypt demanded the immediate return of the entire Sinai Peninsula; Israel, which had occupied the Sinai since the 1967 Middle East was, refused to return an inch of this land. Efforts to reach agreement, including the proposal of a compromise in which each nation would retain half of the Sinai, proved completely unacceptable to both sides. (p. 1)

Neither side found the proposal of splitting the Sinai acceptable. This is a classic case in which agreement could not be reached until the fixed-pie assumption was broken. Israel cared about the security that the land offered, whereas Egypt was primarily interested in sovereignty over the land. With the fixed-pie assumption broken, the two parties were able to agree that Israel would return the Sinai in exchange for assurances of a demilitarized zone and new Israeli air bases.

Bazerman (1983) used the mythical fixed-pie argument to analyze the housing market in 1979 and 1980. When interest rates first shot above 12% in 1979, the housing market came to a dead stop. Sellers continued to expect the value of their property to increase as it had in the past. Buyers, however, could not afford the monthly payments on the houses that they aspired to own. Viewing this as a distributive problem, the fixed-pie assumption led to the conclusion that transactions would not occur until seller resistance points decreased, buyer aspirations decreased, and/or interest rates came down. None of these changes emerged. However, once the industry began to view the problem integratively, some relief was provided. Sellers wanted a price that showed profit. Buyers wanted to hold monthly payments down. The integrative and efficient solutions were the wide variety of creative financing plans that emerged after the mythical fixed pie was broken.

In a more controlled laboratory setting, Bazerman et al. (1985) found that in a novel integrative bargaining task requiring both cooperation and competition, it is the competitive aspect that first becomes salient—resulting in a win–lose orientation and a distributive approach to bargaining. Bazerman et al. (1985) and others (McAlister, Bazerman, & Fader, 1986; Neale & Bazerman, 1985) also found that experience allows negotiators to break this fixed-pie assumption and learn to integrate. Although it is reasonable to assume that experienced negotiators are skilled at finding integrative agreements in their own area of expertise, Neale and Northcraft (in press) provide evidence that experienced negotiators have limited ability to translate their expertise at finding integrative agreements from one domain to another.

Opportunities for Negotiator-Bias Research

We have provided evidence that deficiencies in judgment hinder the processes and outcomes of negotiated activity. We believe that this work identifies a new direction for negotiation research that can provide an important unifying thread to the negotiation literature. A cognitive approach that provides a process-level understanding of negotiation has the potential to get economists, psychologists, industrial relations experts, and organizational behaviorists all talking about the same negotiation problems. Economists need to reconsider their assumptions about rationality in negotiation, and behavioral scientists need a more rigorous approach to examine how their structural and individual-difference variables affect behavior.

Research on negotiator cognitions could also unify the separate approaches of prescriptive and descriptive models. The prescriptive camp focuses on how a rational negotiator should behave when confronting an equally rational opponent (whom many of us would argue does not exist). Unfortunately, the rational course of action suggested by these models is not necessarily the optimal strategy against real (nonrational) others. The descriptive camp provides more realistic findings, but lacks prescriptions for practitioners. Recently, the prescriptive camp moved to an important middle ground in Raiffa's (1982) seminal book in which he argues for an asymmetrically prescriptive/descriptive approach that prescribes the optimal course of action, given the best description of the opponent.

Our approach to negotiator cognitions complements this middle ground by arguing that descriptions of negotiator behavior should be grounded in a framework that allows for the identification of specific deviations from rationality, the diagnosis of situations in which biases are most prevalent, and techniques for eventually providing training and other remedies. This would allow human intuition to move closer to rationality. There are many unexplored opportunities for important research in the future. We see growing evidence of a negotiation literature that provides valuable *prescriptions* based on reasonable *descriptions* of the opponent's behavior and the focal negotiator's cognitions.

The previous discussion of negotiator errors or biases is an extension of the biases and errors studied in behavioral decision theory (Kahneman et al., 1982; Nisbett & Ross, 1980; Pitz & Sachs, 1984). In addition, we believe that negotiators make many of their most serious errors when they improperly model the behavior of other actors, by ignoring their actions or assuming the others will continue behaving the same way despite changes in the negotiator's own behavior. The next section will extend what we know about decision biases by examining a new set of biases that are introduced when an individual is faced with competing others. Thus, while the last section examines how the behavioral-decision literature could inform our understanding of negotiation, the next section examines how a consideration of competitive others allows us to identify new biases in judgment.

IGNORING THE ACTIVE DECISION PROCESSES OF COMPETITIVE OTHERS

Many researchers have argued that negotiators must consider the planned strategy of the other party (Walton & McKersie, 1965; Rubin, 1980). Siegal and Fouraker (1960) state that successful negotiation depends on considering how the opponent will assess possible outcomes. Kelley and Thibaut (1980) argue that relationships achieve mutually satisfactory sets of outcomes by recognizing the mutual benefits of certain joint activities or joint sets of activities (trading). Despite the clear importance of analyzing the cognitive strategy of an opponent negotiator, virtually no research has examined the ability of negotiators to follow this prescription. Although the importance of understanding the cognitions of the opponent negotiator is well specified by negotiation theorists, we argue that a fundamental (and correctable) impediment in negotiation processes is the failure of negotiators to cognitively consider the intended decisions of the opponent negotiator. In this section, we present the basic argument for believing that negotiators fail to consider adequately the cognitions of opponent negotiators and carefully examine recent empirical research that uses protocol analyses to directly test this argument.

The Basic Argument

Samuelson and Bazerman (1985) show that negotiators under an information disadvantage deviate from normative behavior by (passively) ignoring the information available to the opponent and, consequently, fall prey to the "winner's curse"—they consistently (and voluntarily) enter into loss-making purchases. In one of Samuelson and Bazerman's studies, subjects are given an opportunity to make one bid (take it or leave it) for the acquisition of a company. As potential acquirers, subjects know only that the company is equally likely to be worth any value between $0 and $100 and that, whatever its value, it is worth 50% more to the acquirer than to the target owner. The target owner knows the exact value and will accept any bid at or above that value. What should the acquirer bid? (The problem as presented to the subjects is presented in Appendix 1.)

The pattern of responses is provided in Table 1. The most common response was in the $50–$75 range. Samuelson and Bazerman suggest

Table 1. The Distribution of Price Offers in the "Acquiring a Company" Problem

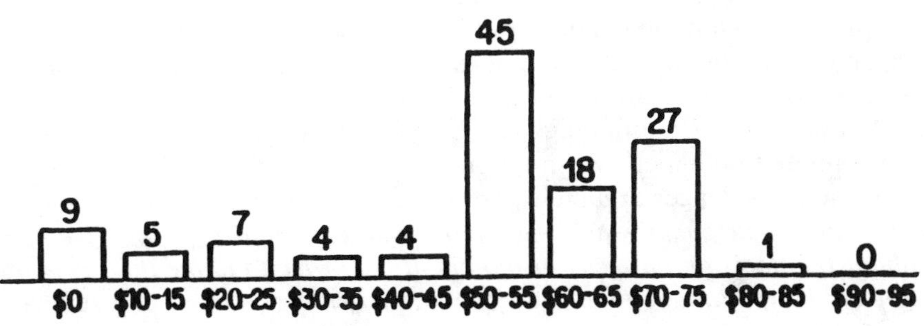

Source: Samuelson and Bazerman (1985)

(but do not provide direct evidence) that subjects arrive at this response by the following logic:

> The value of the firm is uncertain, but its expected value to me is $75/share. In addition, the expected value of the firm to the target is $50/share. Thus, I can make a reasonable expected profit by offering some price slightly in excess of $50/share. (p. 112)

This logic would be rational if the target was also uninformed about the value of the firm and only had the distributional information available to the acquirer. However, the fact that the target has significantly more information that the acquirer has important implications: An informed target will only accept offers if they are profitable, which leads to an expected loss (the "winner's curse") for any offer above $0. This is illustrated by the following normative logic for the acquirer considering an offer of $60/share:

> Suppose that I make an offer of $60/share. If it is accepted, the firm must be worth between 0 and $60/share. Since all values are equally likely, the average value of the firm to the target when my offer is accepted is $30/share. Since the firm is worth 50% more to me than to the target, the expected value of the firm to me is then $45/share. My profit has the expected value of $45–$60, or −$15/share. (Samuelson & Bazerman, 1985, p. 110)

It is not hard to generalize the reasoning for this problem into the conclusion that, when an offer is accepted, the acquirer can expect to obtain a company worth 25% less than the price the acquirer pays. Thus, the acquirer's best offer is $0/share, or no offer. This problem is paradoxical in that although the company is worth more to the acquirer in all cases, it is never rational for the acquirer to make an offer.

Samuelson and Bazerman's data show similar results even when subjects were paid for good performance and when a subject population with unusually high analytical capability (M.I.T. Sloan School of Management master's students) was used. They conclude that individuals cope with the complex cognitive task involved in competitive decisions by making simplifying assumptions about the behavior of the other party, resulting in the (unintentional) exclusion of the contingency that the opponent has access to key information and thus selectively accepts offers.

At one level, these findings can be taken as evidence of a systematic bias unique to competitive situations under asymmetric information. We propose the stronger argument, however, that *individuals in competitive situations make simplifying assumptions that deviate from normative logic about the decision patterns of opponents in order to make the task cognitively more manageable*. This systematic pattern is indirectly reflected in several other studies.

Supporting Evidence

Neale and Bazerman (1983) found that negotiators with greater perspective-taking ability (as assessed with an individual difference measure) would be more likely to consider the perspective of the opponent in negotiation, and thereby achieve greater success. A simple questionnaire measure of the general tendency to consider the opponent's viewpoint and values (Davis' perspective-taking scale, 1981) was highly predictive of concession rate and negotiator success in an integrative, five-issue, labor–management simulated (interactive) negotiation.

Perrow's (1984) description of marine accidents also reflects our view of the decision processes of competitors. Figure 2 provides one example of a ship accident presented by Perrow. Perrow explains this accident in terms of the inability of complex systems to take into consideration all of the possible combinations of things that can go wrong. We propose an alternative (and complementary) explanation based on our argument that individuals tend to ignore the cognitions of competitive others. Each captain appears *passively* to make the simplifying and false assumption that the other ship will continue its current direction and head straight. However, when both parties think in the same active but naive mode—crunch! Both parties failed to consider that the other party might decide to make further adjustments.

Finally, consider the dollar auction (Shubik, 1971; Teger, 1980), which we briefly mentioned in an earlier section of this paper: A dollar is auctioned to the highest bidder, who pays the bid and receives the dollar, *but* the second highest bidder also pays his or her bid and receives nothing. The common result is an escalating pattern in which individuals bid far in excess of a dollar, which has been explained by arguing that individuals nonrationally escalate their commitment to *justify* their earlier bids—and to save the loss from quitting and coming in second (Rubin, 1980). We agree with this explanation of the tendency of individuals to stay in the auction. However, we now argue that it is at least as important to explain why individuals voluntarily enter into an auction that favors the auctioneer at the expense of the bidders. Our explanation is that individuals see the potential for profit early in the auction, and *fail to consider what the auction will look like to other bidders*. If the bidder considered that the auction will look desirable to many bidders, it is easy to see the benefits of staying out of the auction.

Measuring Cognitive Processes

The evidence presented in the preceding sections in support of the argument that individuals ignore the cognitions of competitive others has

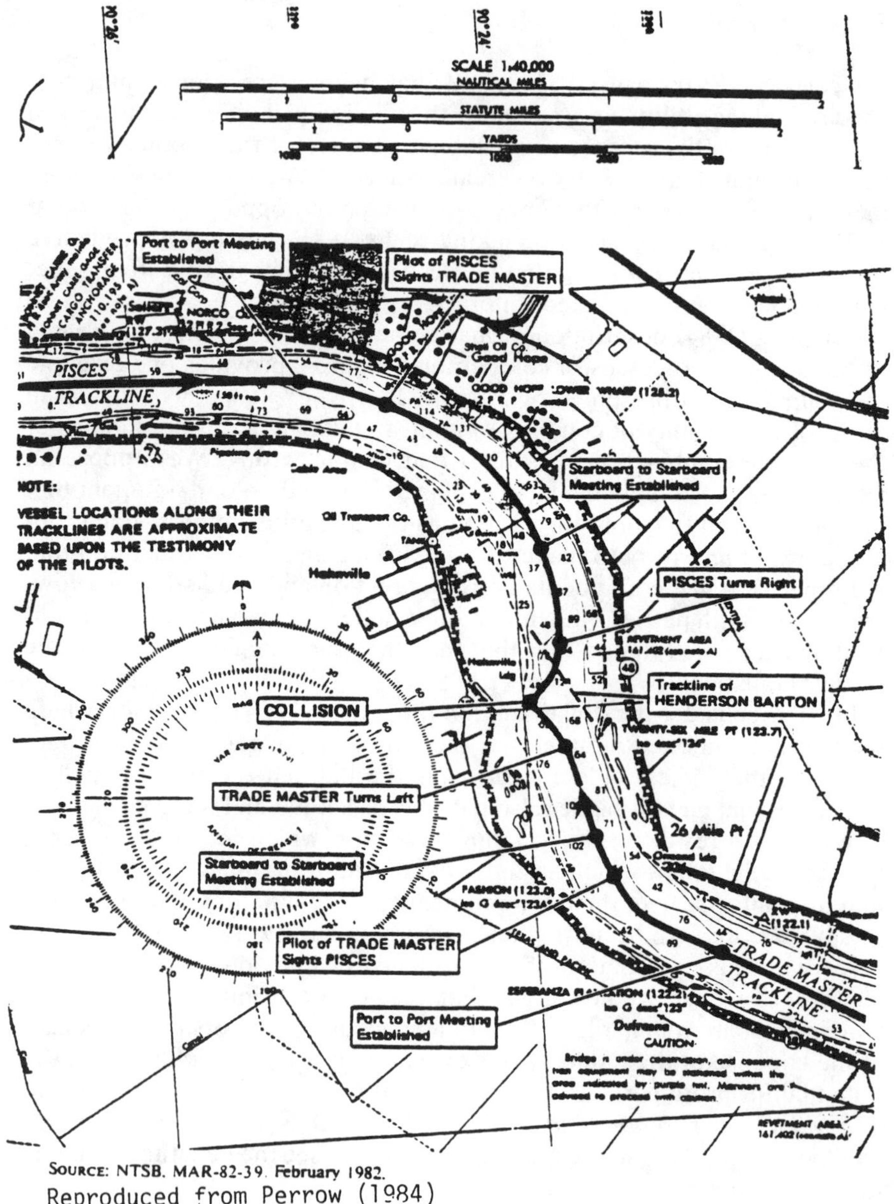

SOURCE: NTSB. MAR-82-39. February 1982.
Reproduced from Perrow (1984)

Figure 2. Tracklines of Pisces and Trade Master

relied on inferences of decision process based on decision outcomes. No explicit attempts were made to measure the hypothesized cognitive patterns. The failure of subjects to achieve optimal performance was labeled "inefficient" or biased and attributed to the use of a suboptimal strategy. Thus, the existence of inferior strategies has always been *inferred* rather than observed. Recently, Carroll, Bazerman, and Maury (1986) have attempted to verify the inferred cognitive deficiencies in a problem conceptually identical to Samuelson and Bazerman's "Acquiring a Company" problem.

Carroll et al. asked subjects to respond to the task of deciding what to offer (as a potential buyer) for a used car that has a value known only to the seller of between $0 and $1,000 (buyer only knows that all values are equally likely) and is worth 50% more to the buyer. The instructions to the subjects clarified that they were to make a "take-it-or-leave-it" offer. If accepted, the price would be used to calculate the buyer's profit (loss). If not accepted, no transaction would take place. Notice that this problem has all of the same properties as the "Acquiring a Company" problem (the "Used Car" problem is presented in Appendix 2).

Table 2 classifies the 75 subjects into four categories based on their offers: $0, the right answer (8 responses); $500–750, the answer produced by the naive logic that the car is worth about $500 on average (39 responses); $1–499, a conservative but incorrect offer (12 responses); and offers over $750, a liberal and incorrect offer (16 responses). This distribution is very similar to the distribution obtained by Samuelson and Bazerman in the "Acquiring a Company" problem. The distribution obtained

Table 2. Percentage of Subjects Making Offers for a Used Car Who Exhibited Selected Categories of Verbal Protocol Statements

	Offer Group			
Protocol Category	*A: $0*	*B: $1–499*	*C: $500–750*	*D: $751–1500*
Protocol distinguishing A versus B, C, D				
Generalized hypothetical	88	17	13	0
False objectives	6	50	40	56
Realize don't have to buy	94	17	14	12
Protocols distinguishing C versus B, D				
Fixed value for car	0	46	24	53
Guess median value	31	12	40	12
Protocols distinguishing B versus D				
Offer buyer's value	0	4	28	25
Realize can lose money	88	38	26	6
N	8	12	39	16

Note: Disagreement between coders yielded a code of .5.

confirms a number of observations. First, normative logic continues to be counterintuitive in the context of an additional problem. Second, the naive reasoning again appears to be the most common. Third, a significant number of subjects respond with offers that follow neither naive normative reasoning.

The major purpose of this study was to assess the cognitive processes by which subjects solved the problem, and thereby to provide more direct evidence for the hypothesized failure of normative logic. In short, is the reasoning used in the Samuelson and Bazerman study correct in explaining the deviant cognitions of subjects who responded between $500 and $750? What characterizes the cognitions of subjects who offered $0? And, what explains the offers that follow neither naive nor normative logic?

Specifically, this study employed verbal protocols as a "process tracing technique" (Newell & Simon, 1972; Payne, Braunstein, & Carroll, 1978) to examine the cognitions underlying the pattern of results previously demonstrated in Samuelson and Bazerman (1985). Verbal protocols were collected by instructing subjects as follows:

> Speak all of your thoughts out loud and we will tape record them. Everything that goes through your head is equally important, even if you said it once before. Say everything, even if you are just rereading a sentence.

If subjects had difficulty speaking their thoughts or simply forget to do so, the experimenter prompted them with neutral phrases such as "Tell me what you are thinking" or "Say anything that comes into your mind."

Unlike introspections, the verbal protocol procedure does not ask subjects to speculate on what they are doing but merely to verbalize as much of the content of their thoughts as possible. This is used as a partial record of thought processes. Although verbal protocols have been criticized as inaccurate and disruptive of ongoing processes (Nisbett & Wilson, 1977), the consensus among psychologists has been strongly supportive for protocols collected concurrently with task performance (Ericcson & Simon, 1980; Smith & Miller, 1978). Verbal protocols are particularly useful when coupled with other types of measures and a strong design (Einhorn, Kleinmuntz, & Kleinmuntz, 1980; Payne et al, 1978). Verbal protocols have proven useful in both laboratory settings (e.g., Ericcson & Simon, 1980; Payne et al., 1978), and in such real-world settings as stock portfolio selection (Clarkson, 1962), consumer purchasing (Payne & Ragsdale, 1978), and medical diagnosis (Johnson, Hassebrook, Duran, & Moller, 1982).

The verbal protocols were coded by breaking them up into phrases each representing a single thought or idea, and then coding these phrases into one of 16 categories. Five of these categories represented thoughts that were characteristic of our expected decision processes for naive subjects (e.g., the subject assumed a fixed value for the car), 6 categories represented thoughts that were characteristic of our expected normative decision processes (e.g., the subject explained the contingent behavior of the seller in a generalized manner), and 5 categories represented thoughts that were neutral in reference to the naive vs. normative distinction (e.g., the subject repeated that the car was worth 1.5 times as much to the buyer as to the seller).

Subjects who made incorrect offers differed dramatically from those who made the correct offer of $0. Table 2 gives the three protocol codes that most strongly differentiated between the $0 offer category and the other three categories, and were significant in a multiple discriminant analysis using the 16 codes to predict offer category. For each category of subject, Table 2 lists the percentage of those subjects who verbalized a thought in each of the three listed codes. *For example, 87.5% (7 out of 8) of the subjects who offered $0 developed a generalized argument that articulated the likely contingent behavior of the seller.* Only 7 of the remaining 67 incorrect subjects (10.4%) exhibited this protocol. An example of a generalized hypothetical is illustrated in the following quote from one of the subjects who offered $0:

> 3/2 the actual value minus my offer is my gain, now I want to maximize that. Somehow I need to relate my offer to the actual value of the car, I don't know the value, so I have to come up with an offer. Let's say I offer 500, then my gain is 250 if the car is 500 at maximum. If it is worth 0, at worst, my gain is −500. So my expected benefit is linear between those two, halfway between −500 and 250. . . . This looks like I lose all the time. If I offer 1,000, I can make 500 or lose 1,000, in which case I lose bigger. The more I offer, the more I lose. So from that I think I will offer him $0 for his car. (Carroll et al., 1986, p. 17)

Large differences occurred in the other two protocol categories listed in Table 2. Correct subjects tended to make statements that emphasized that they did not have to buy the car, realizing that they only wanted the car at a profit. This was not true for nonoptimal bidding subjects. Subjects in the nonoptimalcategories often made statements reflective of false objectives for the task (e.g., "I want to make sure that I get the car"), whereas correct subjects did not verbalize such false objectives.

Table 2 also lists the results for four protocol categories that strongly discriminate among the three types of incorrect answers. The middle-range offers emerge from subjects who assume a value for the car or guess a median-range value. For example, one subject reasoned in the following way:

> I'd say it's equally possible that its worth between 0 and 1,000, so in the average case, it's worth 500 to the dealer which means on the average is worth 750 to me. So I have to offer him, on the average, at least 500 for him to sell it and on the average, any offer under 750 is worthwhile to me. And, I'd say its worth 50% more

> to me . . . out of that 250, I'd go 150/100 split so I'd say 650. (Carroll et al., 1986, p. 17)

Although the mid-range value was a common assumption or best guess, we also observed that assuming a fixed value for the car explained many of the subjects who offerred between \$1–499 or \$751–1,000. The following example shows such a result:

> The car is very old, so I don't think it would be worth more than 200 or 300 so I would probably offer him \$150 . . . it says here I could use the car, so I'd offer him 200. (Carroll et al., 1986, p. 18)

Although this subject is not following the valuation basis provided in the instructions, his assumption of a value was moderately common on both the high and low ends. In addition, high offers were associated with offering the *buyer's* value for the car instead of one closer to the seller's value, and low offers were associated with realizing that the buyer can lose money.

Carroll et al.'s (1986) results lend general support to the hypothesized process explanation provided by Samuelson and Bazerman (1985), and provide direct evidence of the cognitive patterns of the subjects. They show that correct subjects do go through some approximation of the normative logic that has been suggested. That is, they develop a reasoning pattern that articulates the impact of the contingent behavior of the opponent. Interestingly, Carroll et al. show that nonoptimal subjects typically simplify their task by assuming some value for the car (and presumably for the company in the Samuelson and Bazerman task). This provides a cognitive explanation for subjects who could not be categorized as either naive or normative subjects in the Samuelson and Bazerman study. It seems that subjects simply bring into the experiment some past knowledge to make an assumption of value other than the midpoint. The integrating theme, however, is that *once subjects assume a best estimate* (based on information internal or external to the task), *it simplifies the task for them, they use that assumed value, and never develop the appropriate normative logic*.

In this section we argue that individuals commonly ignore the cognitions of a competitive other, and we provide a cognitive explanation for this tendency. Although we have illustrated this tendency in a fairly simplistic environment, we would expect this tendency to generalize to complex negotiations. In our tasks, the subjects had the potential to deal cognitively with the information requirements. In fact, when presented with the normative logic after completing the task, subjects often were disgusted by their offers—"it was so obvious." In complex negotiations, the cognitive demands are far more severe (more options exist, more factors need to be considered, more pressure exists, etc.), leading to greater use of cognitive simplifications, and the greater likelihood of assuming some knowledge such as the value of the commodity for sale.

Nevertheless, future research should specifically focus on negotiators' tendency to ignore the cognitions of competitive others in more complex and realistic settings. In addition, we need research designed to train subjects to eliminate these biases. Recently, a colleague in the economics department presented the "Acquiring a Company" problem to his analytically trained 2nd-year master's students who had been taught how to include relevant information about the opponent in their decision processes, and less than one-third got the correct answer. Clearly, something more than prescriptive training is needed.

The first two sections of this chapter explore cognitive deficiencies for which we have evidence in the negotiation context. However, the social-cognition literature has developed many additional insights that may be relevant to negotiation. The next section is more exploratory and considers some relevant areas for inquiry that have yet to be touched by empirical negotiation research. In the subsequent and final section of the chapter, we provide a framework to incorporate and integrate the ideas we have presented.

SOCIAL COGNITION AND NEGOTIATION

The previous sections of the chapter deal with the identification of specific biases that affect *specific* judgments required in a negotiation task. However, the ideas in these sections do not provide a comprehensive approach for describing the complete cognitive process required by the negotiation task, and no such model exists in the negotiation literature. The lack of a comprehensive description of decision making in a realistically complete decision task is also a limitation of the behavioral decision-theory literature (Pennington & Hastie, 1985). We believe that the social–cognitive psychology literature can provide the basis for developing a more complete model of the cognitive processes involved in negotiation.

Social cognition examines the complex cognitive strategies that individuals use to make sense of their social world. Social cognition integrates work in cognitive psychology on memory, attention, and problem solving with the concerns of social psychologists regarding less structured social problems (Carroll & Payne, 1976; Fiske & Taylor, 1984; Nisbett & Ross, 1980). Because the task of negotiation is by definition social, the area of social cognition is an obvious place to look to gain additional insights concerning negotiator cognition.

The guiding principles of social cognition research concern information processing capabilities and limitations, heuristics and strategies, and errors and biases. In this sense it is very compatible with the behavior decision theory literature. These limitations of attention, memory, speed, and effort produce a natural reliance on shortcut methods that generally produce satisfactory, but not necessarily optimal, results. Social cognition theories portray people as using their past experience, organized into knowledge structures, to understand and respond to the world around them (Pennington & Hastie, 1985). Social cognition research studies the nature, origins, and use of these knowledge structures, including stereotypes, categories, norms, roles, implicit theories, schemas, prototypes, scripts, heuristics, and attributions (Fiske & Taylor, 1984). We use our knowledge base to make some educated guesses, asking ourselves "What kind of situation is this?" and "What kind of people are these?" instead of analyzing the elements *de novo* from first principles. Thus, we tend to appreciate the power of analogy, such as when Afghanistan is called a "Vietnam" for the Soviets. It seems much easier to reason comparatively from representative cases based on our existing knowledge structures than to reason absolutely.

We describe negotiators as trying to make rational decisions. However, they are affected by their existing knowledge structures and biased by the effects documented in earlier sections of this chapter. We portray negotiator cognition as an act of imagination by which the negotiator cognitively constructs a reality about the negotiation situation. The negotiator uses past knowledge to understand the current situation and to make predictions about what will happen in the future. The negotiator constructs a mental model of the situation, including explanations of the behaviors of individuals in the situation. Within this model, the negotiator acts like the director of a play, imagining various scenarios and instructing the actors to play their roles in character. These mental simulations are played out in the imagination and outcomes are recorded. This produces a distribution of outcomes of various subjective likelihood based on their availability (Einhorn & Hogarth, 1985). The reflective aspects of this process are not unlike a chess game in which the moves and responses are first imagined, and then enacted against the real opponents. The central question then becomes, how do negotiators create these mental models and manipulate them? Where do they get the bits of information used to build the models and "run" them?

The social cognition literature offers a variety of knowledge structures concerned with organizing different types of concepts. Many different terms have been used to describe knowledge structures and their theoretical representations. We use terms informally and sometimes interchangeably to alert the reader to relevant aspects of the literature, without commitment to a single approach. Our examination of negotiator cognition gives specific attention to the way behavior is guided by our "implicit theories" of situations, people, and causality. In addition, we will examine the confirmatory way in which implicit theories are applied.

In previous sections of the chapter, we illustrate the conceptual arguments through the existing empirical research in negotiation. However, there is no empirical evidence concerning knowledge structures in the negotiation context. As an alternative form of illustration, we focus the discussion with an example to which we refer throughout the remainder of the section. Consider the following:

> As dean of a major management school, you are faced with a common, yet troubling, situation. You have heard informally that one of your promising untenured associate professors has received a very attractive offer from another school. You had assumed that she was fairly compensated. However, her competitive offer is rumored to be at a prestigious competitor, with tenure, a 40% pay increase, and a number of other attractive features. You would like to keep this individual, but not at any cost. How do you proceed?

The social cognition area raises a number of questions that help organize our understanding of the cognitions of the dean and the professor in this situation. What situations are activated in the dean's mind to interpret the current situation? What person schemas are activated in the dean's mind about the characteristics of this faculty member? How does the dean explain *why* this situation was created? And, how will the dean collect information to develop a response? Parallel questions exist concerning the cognitive processes of the professor. These questions raise important issues concerning both parties' decision processes, and outline the subsections that follow.

Implicit Theories of Situations

Abelson (1976) coined the term *script* to refer to a temporally connected set of events with certain specified features, variables, and default values. For example, the negotiations involved in "car buying" can be described by a sequence of events: entering the showroom, meeting a salesperson, viewing cars, focusing on one car, test driving, assessing any trade-in allowance, haggling over price, settling on a price, and signing contracts. This script is not a rigid set of events but is bounded and structured. There are subscripts or "tracks" such as whether a trade-in is possible. If the buyer provides a low offer, the salesperson may enter a track where the offer is taken to the sales manager, whereupon the salesperson comes back and says that he could not convince the sales manager to accept such a low amount, followed by more haggling. The script concept provides an incisive way to discuss the information people know about norms and roles (buyer, seller, sales manager) and how this information is formed and used (Schank & Abelson, 1977).

The use of scripts or "event schemas" (Hastie, 1981) creates an easily understandable social world for both parties in a negotiation. Experienced car buyers can understand a car dealership quite readily, despite variation in the make of car, the number of salespeople present, the title of the sales manager, etc. These surface variations are incidental or are tracks (e.g., Toyota dealerships) within the more general script.

The fact that some dealerships do not fit within the typical script matches our experiences: it can be very disconcerting, humorous, embarassing, and difficult to cope with events that are not easily coded. How does the salesperson respond when the buyer "violates" the script by refusing to tell the salesperson a price at which he or she is willing to buy the car? Sometimes, a track is activated and the sales manager comes out to discuss the car directly with the buyer. At other times, a "script" violation can cause negotiations to reach an impasse. For example, when a buyer who has only bought American cars enters a Toyota dealership to negotiate price on a bottom-of-the-line Tercel, the refusal of the salesperson to consider a lower price can cause an awkwardness that leads to an impasse—even when the buyer cannot do better elsewhere.

Abelson makes the interesting suggestion that social behavior depends on the selection of a particular script to represent the situation and the taking of a participant role within the script. The encoding of a situation as one script rather than another has substantial influence on which aspects of the situation are seen as important, which are recalled, what behaviors and events are expected, and what alternative actions are easily available or imaginable. For example, in recalling the details of a specific dealership, taking a mental tour with the goal in mind of buying a car makes it easy to remember certain features of cars. Retaking the tour with the goal of becoming a car salesperson changes what is recalled. Changing scripts can allow a decision maker (negotiator) to recall details not easily recalled under an alternative script (Anderson & Pichert, 1978).

If we presume an essential similarity of social and nonsocial scripts, there are some interesting lessons regarding expertise or variations in knowledge structures with experience (e.g., Chase & Simon, 1973, on chess experts). Johnson (1980) argues that expert decision makers (across domains) have far greater ability to match existing schemata to particular situations than do novices. Experts in social situations, such as experienced negotiators, probably develop an extensive set of scripts for their respective situations. Any seasoned negotiator can tell you some version(s) of the Bathroom Script, in which a difficult bargaining session is resolved during a "spontaneous" discussion in the bathroom. Neale and Northcraft (in press) argue that expert negotiators have a greater ability to recognize the opportunity to develop joint gains (to find integrative agreements) than do nonexperts. An untested explanation for this result is that expert negotiators have available useful scripts (or tracks within scripts) that are activated when the opportunity for joint gain may be present.

In the problem cited earlier, rather than analyzing his problem with the recruited professor as a unique and new problem, the dean may activate a readily available script. For example, the "bidding war" script suggests that this competing offer is only the first bid by the competitor, that the process necessary to keep this faculty member will be complex, and that keeping this faculty member may destroy the internal pay structure that the dean has worked so hard to create. In contrast, the "losing all of our good junior faculty" script suggests that losing this faculty member may lead to losing others, that rumors will begin to spread about faculty jumping ship, and a lower reputation for the school. Obviously, most good deans would think of both of these scripts (and others). However, the salience of each of these may be a critical determinant of the dean's response. Thus, as the professor and other interested parties discuss the situation with the dean, they can affect his decision processes not only by their arguments directly, but also by the scripts that they activate in his mind.

The scripts involved in a negotiation come from at least two actors. The professor's behavior will be governed by the scripts that are activated in her mind. Because the dean is confronted with similar situations more often than is the professor, he is likely to have more scripts available in memory. In addition, the dean's experience is likely to have increased the sophistication of his scripts. Nevertheless, the professor is still likely to have scripts available in memory, but they may be less developed and they may be based on vicarious learning (learning through the experiences of colleagues who have received outside offers) (Gioia & Manz, 1985). Does she have a "competing offer" script or a "they will think I am holding them hostage" script in her mind? The difference in scripts are likely to affect how she approaches the dean and how she more generally formulates the choice to stay or leave.

It is easy to see that expert negotiators attempt to elicit selected scripts in the mind of the opponent negotiator. For example, a car salesperson will frequently try to activate an "I need to buy the car now" script by suggesting "By the time you finish your comparison shopping, the car you want will probably be gone." Similarly, our dean may try to activate certain scripts through such statements as, "We fully expect to have a behavioral lab by late next year." Although these examples deal with activation by negotiators, it is easy to generalize the logic to see how mediators could effectively use a knowledge of script processing to increase the likelihood of two parties reaching agreement. Activating different scripts would lead to different behaviors and negotiated outcomes. The language used by mediators, the points made by negotiators that are acknowledged by the mediator, and the general way in which the mediation is structured are all likely to affect which scripts are salient in the minds of the negotiators. The connection of scripts to negotiation is waiting for further conceptual development and empirical research.

Implicit Theories of People

The competent social animal not only has available a repertoire of schemata or social scripts representing situations, but also a catalog of actors or personality types. The terms *person schema* or *prototype* refer to our organized knowledge of other people. These include the same sort of knowledge long referred to as stereotypes, but extend from the earlier use in describing ethnic or gender groupings to describing any recognizable "type" or social category. These categories are called prototypes when they are arranged around an exemplar, that is, a real or imaginary person who typifies the category (Rosch, 1978). Person schemas refer more generally to a list of attributes or "central tendencies" (Hastie, 1981) associated with the category, such as an extrovert, librarian, or elderly person, of which some features are not specified (Fiske & Taylor, 1984).

The concept of person schema is very similar to classification typologies used by researchers and practitioners. Cantor, Smith, French, and Mezzich (1980) argue that expert decision makers categorize people into "fuzzy categories" by comparing the similarity of individuals to the prototypical individual of each category. Individuals that fit closely are assessed rapidly and confidently; individuals that do not fit as well take longer and produce uncertainty. Consistent with this argument, Lurigio and Carroll (1985) found that experienced probation officers organized their knowledge of probationers into person schemas such as the Burglar and the Gang Member. Cases that fit a schema were processed more consistently, faster, and more confidently than those that did not fit, and this effect did not occur for clerical staff who lacked these schemas. Comparisons of experienced and less experienced probation officers with clerical staff showed that person schemas develop through experience. New schemas are added and enriched with experience, and some commonsensical schemas are dropped as they fail to be useful.

Person schemas contain a lot of information about traits, preferences, and goals that enable the perceiver to understand exhibited behavior, predict future behavior, and develop appropriate responses. Schemas allow for a rapid understanding of even incomplete or "fuzzy" information. This "filling in" of incomplete information is important. For example, someone who fits the Burglar schema but does not have the expected long record may be seen as a Burglar who has *rarely been caught*.

Just as the dean did not evaluate the situation as a unique and new problem, so he may not identify the faculty member as a unique individual. Rather, the Star prototype suggests that the faculty member is superb, greatly in demand, and a highly visible source of prestige for the university. However, the Stars are constantly in demand, and can be demanding, costly, and unpredictable. In the mind of the dean, the Star may often take a role in the "bidding war" script, or the "manipulation" script in which the faculty member does not have a sincere desire to leave, but has cultivated this offer or even just the rumor of an offer, in order to coerce raises and promotion from her university. It is obvious that the dean's response will be affected by which person schema is activated. More generally, we argue that the manner in which a dean differentially treats (negotiates with) different professors in the absence of external offers can be partially explained by the match between a specific professor and alternative person schemas in the dean's memory.

Again, the professor's person schemas concerning deans are likely to be far less developed than the dean's person schemas concerning professors. However, she is still likely to have some alternative prototypes available. Does the dean activate a Tough but Fair, a Responder to Competition, or a Demander of Loyalty schema? These person schemas may be generalizations from previous academic positions (if she held many previous academic positions), other work experiences, the discussions of colleagues, or some more abstract construction of managerial types. Regardless of the source, the person schema activated is likely to have an important effect on the professor's behaviors and choice.

An expert negotiator can be described as an individual who can readily assess the opponent negotiator and predict the way different "types" of opponents will respond under varying circumstances. This argument is part of negotiation folklore, but lacks empirical support. The concept of person schema provides a mechanism to operationalize this ability that expert negotiators are thought to possess.

Future research should examine to what extent and under what circumstances the number and sophistication of person schemas predicts the success of a negotiator. Factors such as limited time, the uniqueness of the situation, and variety of person types possible would be good candidates as determinants of when person schema sophistication will be most important. Could person schemas incapacitate an expert negotiator when an opponent negotiator is falsely matched to a person schema, resulting in poor negotiation strategies? Finally we raise the issue of whether or not third parties can use the knowledge of the parties' implicit theories to identify an appropriate strategy for moving toward resolution, particularly when one (or both) negotiator's false stereotypes are at the core of the conflict. These questions are clearly related to our earlier discussion on the ability of negotiators to include an understanding of an opponent negotiator in their cognitive strategies.

Implicit Theories of Causality

Our understanding of the events around us is based on our natural tendency to see the world in *causal* terms. Magic, religion, and science are human enterprises that provide explanations for important events (Malinowski, 1948). We tend to believe that events have causes and to seek a *sufficient explanation* for these events. People, as practical philosophers, need to feel that events are understandable and predictable (Heider, 1958; Langer, 1975), and that they have enough understanding to make an appropriate response (Jones & Thibaut, 1958).

Attribution theorists argue that our attributions of the causes of events that surround us affect our evaluations of the actors involved, predictions for future events, and choices of our own behavior. Although the motivation for having implicit theories of causality sounds logical, and highly rational descriptions of attribution processes have been offered (Jones & Davis, 1965; Kelley, 1967), attribution theory is a description, not a prescription, of cognition (Ross, 1977). People tend to make characteristic errors when they attribute causality, such as the "fundamental attribution error" of assuming that other people's actions reflect their inner dispositions, giving too little attention to the power of situations to call forth behavior. Thus, observers of speakers who were assigned to give a speech either favoring or opposing an issue judged the speakers to have attitudes consistent with their speeches even though the observers knew the speakers had been *assigned* to their positions (Jones, 1979). Observers of students assigned to either make up questions or to respond to the questions judged the questioners to be more *generally* knowlegeable than the respondents (the respondents themselves perceived the questioners to be more knowledgeable) (Ross, Amabile, & Steinmetz, 1977).

As noted in an earlier section of this chapter, Siegal and Fouraker (1960) identify the importance of understanding the opponent in developing an effective negotiation strategy. Attribution theory would suggest, for example, that the dean, in the problem cited previously, can focus on questions such as "Why did the other university make this offer" and "Why has the faculty member let this be known in this manner"? The dean is likely to generate some hypotheses about these events, and to check them against evidence such as the manner in which the event occurred, the past histories of the key actors, and the comparison to other similar actors (Kelley, 1973; Carroll, Galegher, & Weiner, 1982). This information is predicted to affect his attributions of the causes of the current situation, which in turn affects his feelings about the professor, his predictions about future events, and his response to the current situation.

The extremity of the offer suggests the degree to which the other university is serious about hiring the professor. The past behavior of the university is clearly relevant: do they grab other faculty, do they make big offers, what sort of resources and salary structure do they have, what has been the relations between the two universities? In short, what kind of competitor are they? Consensus information is important; that is, what seems to be the "market price" of this person or type of person? Naturally, such comparisons depend on who is categorized as an appropriate comparison; if the dean only considers this faculty member average, the market price is very different than if the person is unique and therefore has a very high or indeterminate price.

Causes are also inferred from the professor's behavior. The manner in which she conveys the offer, her past history of salary negotiations, and her past responses to offers (including the one that brought her to this job), allow an inference of her motives in this situation. The interesting part of attribution theory is that any behavior on the part of the professor can be attributed to have different meaning under different circumstances. Thus, the simple presentation of the offer with an air of openness can be seen as "soft," as an attempt to generate negotiations, as a "ploy," as an expression of uncertainty, and so forth, depending on the dean's assessment of the situation. It makes a great deal of difference if this is the third time this faculty member has generated an offer, or if this is the third time the other university has tried to poach our faculty, or if the dean has just been "held hostage" by a different faculty member.

Accurate understanding of the *causes* of the opponent's behavior is central to identifying appropriate responses in the negotiation arena. However, negotiators may fall victim to systematic biases in assessing the causes of events. For example, the fundamental attribution error can be generalized to posit that negotiators will hold opponent negotiators responsible for their actions more than is appropriate from a more rational assessment of the situation. That is, they will not realize the full extent to which the opponent's behavior is situationally determined. One false attribution can cause the unraveling of what would otherwise have been a successful negotiation for both sides. Effective negotiators are likely to be those who can most accurately assess the true causes of their opponent's behavior and also manage the attributions that the other party will make of their own behavior.

The dean example provides a vivid illustration of the importance to negotiation of attribution theory. The cognitions by which negotiators explain the causality of their opponent's actions should be central to our understanding the process of negotiation. Unfortunately, we have no empirical evidence in the negotiation context to support the arguments made about our implicit theories of causality.

The False Confirmation of Our Implicit Theories

The implicit theories we have reviewed share the concept of a knowledge-driven, "top-down" process; they are more inference than perception, more hypothesis testing than induction. Our understanding of the world around us, carried in event schemas, person schemas, causal theories, and other knowledge structures, are used to make rapid evaluations and categorizations (snap judgments) (Schneider, Hastorf, & Ellsworth, 1979) or to generate hypotheses that guide information acquisition. One problem is that our hypothesis testing through information acquisition and evaluation may tend to be confirmation biased.

People tend to seek information whose presence would confirm the hypothesis or implicit theory; they rarely think to seek disconfirming information. However, disconfirming information is often the more powerful, whether in formal research (Popper, 1959) or in informal assessment, but this concept is difficult for people to grasp cognitively (Hovland & Weiss, 1951). For example, to discover whether Jack is an extrovert, people ask questions such as "What would you do to liven up a party?" (Snyder & Swann, 1976). These questions give respondents an opportunity to display evidence of extroversion, and thus tend to confirm that quality.

Further, even when presented with mixed information that could confirm or disconfirm an hypothesis, the information can be interpreted as confirmation. Lord, Ross, and Lepper (1979) found that people who start with a hypothesis interpret research opposing their hypothesis as irrelevant or methodologically flawed. Thus, presented with a series of studies offering results favorable to different sides of an issues, supporters on each side can feel that the research supports their side and that the evidence against them is of low quality.

Confirmatory biases can often produce self-fulfilling prophesies. In other words, not only do our confirmatory strategies tend to mislead us about the nature of the world, but because we act on our assumptions we may *change* the nature of the world to conform to our hypotheses (i.e., we become right but for the wrong reasons) (Darley & Fazio, 1980; Jones, 1977).

The results of reliance on confirmatory biases over time is a failure to learn from experience and overconfidence in our fallible judgment (Einhorn, 1980). These fallacious or confounded confirmations tend to produce feedback that reinforces our confidence in our opinions, our judgment, and the processes by which we test our understanding. Thus, people fail to learn the falsehood of their beliefs and fail to question the validity of the processes by which they test their beliefs. The function of research methods courses, is to provide a fair and unbiased way of testing beliefs, and this is also the reason they are so difficult to teach. Unfortunately, these biases can never be completely removed, even in expert researchers.

The tendency to look for confirmatory evidence makes our activation of implicit theories particularly crucial. Once a negotiator attributes the causes for a particular behavior (e.g., the dean concludes that the faculty member is greedy), it becomes very difficult to get the negotiator to reformulate his or her implicit theories. For example, if the dean concludes that the faculty member really wants to leave, makes a token counteroffer, and the faculty member leaves, then he has been "proven" correct. However, had the dean made a decent counteroffer, the faculty member might have stayed, but this feedback is unavailable in the dean's constructed world. Thus, deans who act positively by believing they can get faculty or keep faculty, and who suggest they know better than the faculty member himself or herself what that person really needs, may end up getting more than their share. The authors are aware of two such situations where a dean's refusal to take no for an answer led to the return of highly contested faculty after one-year leaves. In each of these situations, it is easy to envision the dean enacting an alternative knowledge structure to confirm the fact that the faculty member has been lost (in fact, this is probably the common knowledge structure once a faculty member leaves and accepts permanent employment elsewhere). Had these pessimistic knowledge structures been activated, the deans would not have pursued the faculty members, and the faculty members would have been lost.

Presumably, experienced negotiators may have learned to seek disconfirming evidence or to seek multiple schemas and theories for any situation, to avoid falling prey to the obvious when it is wrong. However, it is also possible that experienced negotiators are so pleased with their schemas that they stop learning new lessons.

Overall, we see our implicit theories as necessary tools for the negotiator. However, they are fallible. To the extent that our discussion of social cognition could lead to new, interesting, and researchable questions about negotiation, then the budding area of negotiator cognition should be encouraged to bloom.

TOWARD INTEGRATION

We have attempted to present some recent empirical findings and emerging themes in the study of negotiator cognition. At this point, it would be ideal to unfold a grand theory that provides an underlying logic for all the pieces presented. Unfortunately, we have no such theory. At this point in the development of our thoughts, our strategy for integrating the themes in this chapter is to compare the evidence presented concerning negotiator judgment against the decision stages specified in the beginning of the chapter (problem recognition, problem structuring, information gathering, information evaluation, and strategy evaluation). We close this chapter with an integrative framework that views negotiators as engaged in this sort of decision process, but influenced at each stage by the various cognitive processes specified in this chapter. As we discuss each stage, we give examples of cognitive processes that are relevant for describing how a negotiator might deal with that component of the decision process.

Problem Recognition

In the case of the dean, it appears that problem recognition occurred at the point when information filtered to the dean about the professor's offer. The solution to this problem may involve negotiation, in the sense that the dean tries to ascertain what would keep the professor and to make some countermoves, whereas the professor is trying to figure out how to get the best deal from this situation. Of course, the dean could entirely avoid recognizing these events as a "problem" by claiming that the professor is already being cared for by the system and the "problem" is the professor's alone, namely, which alternative to select. Most deans recognize the problem as one requiring negotiation and their acceptance of responsibility. The best deans recognize problems before they become crises: The dean in our hypothetical problem could have been aware of the professor's needs and even of the efforts by other universities to fill vacancies and, therefore, he could have been prepared for such action or made it difficult to move the professor (promises of a lighter teaching load next year, and so forth). Preemptive moves can be a successful strategy, as when companies use "shark repellents" to discourage takeover bids. In some cases, these maneuvers may even prevent the faculty member from considering the possibility of moving (refusing the invitation to come look at the other university).

In our example, this stage in the negotiation process is the least cognitively problematic. Most good deans would easily recognize that a problem exists. However, we can identify some situations where deans have not fully recognized a problem, as a result of overconfidence ("Why would she ever leave our school?") or a variety of false implicit theories (the "manipulator" script). Once the manipulator script is activated, the dean may quickly dismiss the problem, because he believes the offer exists not because the professor has a sincere desire to leave, but because she is creating the opportunity to manipulate the dean. Many opportunities may be lost when the opportunity to negotiate is ignored because of the lack of recognition of the conflict or of the feasibility of negotiation.

Problem Structuring

The first part of any consideration of this situation is to provide a structure, frame, or script for the problem. The structure will identify the outcomes, key actors, alternative actions, and major issues, contingencies, and uncertainties. From this viewpoint, identifying alternative actions involves an act of imagination to translate into the current situation the behaviors suggested by past experience (e.g., select a role in a script), or to construct a new course of action built out of the bits and pieces of past knowledge.

The dean in our example could structure this problem narrowly in terms of the salient features: a faculty member has a good offer. If we really want to keep her then we must come back with a better offer or an offer good enough to keep her. The dean views the problem as negotiating with the faculty member, perhaps over a "fixed pie" of resources. However, the problem can be framed in more complex ways that consider other interested parties, other values, and consequences over longer time periods. The problem could be seen as a type of bidding script in which universities compete for the services of the faculty member. In this situation the faculty member is represented as passively choosing the best offer. More complex scripts recognize the impact on other faculty at the university and the signals they will receive regarding the treatment of faculty in general or this kind of faculty member (represented by eminence, field, research style, or whatever); the impact on other universities and their readiness to "raid" us for faculty; the impact on future salaries and recruiting, and so forth.

How the dean structures this situation depends on the availability of such frames or scripts—which ones occur to the dean? Experienced, sophisticated, or politically savvy deans may have available more scripts and more complex or abstract ones. More intelligent or cognitively complex deans may be able to handle the ramifications of scripts involving more interested parties, more conflicting values, and trade-offs over longer time periods. Socially sensitive deans or those with better role-taking skills may be better able to perceive the relevance of this situation for other parties. Particularly astute deans may view the problem not as finding the right script, but as using *multiple* frames or scripts to gain insights and evaluate more options and contingencies.

Once the broad outline of the problem is set, the dean must think about the particular details within the picture. Knowledge of the situation, persons, and causality must be brought to bear. What are the possible behaviors of the interested parties? What are their interests and how are those interests affected by various scenarios? What are the likely determinants of whether the professor is receptive to a counteroffer? Why did the offer come in? What aspects of the dean's world knowledge are wrong and must be updated? What are the various contingencies among the responses of the interested parties? What can the dean do to play out this multiperson chess match to get the most favorable result? What options is the dean constrained from using? It is because of the numerous uncertain and interrelated questions that attempts to import viewpoints, diagnoses, strategies, and other hints from knowledge structures are so important.

Information Gathering

Once the dean structures the problem, he must identify and gather additional information about the other party, the environment, and the preferences of interested parties. The "rational" negotiator will have access to all relevant information. However, the actor in the literatures we have examined in this chapter will collect information that is biased by a large number of influences, including the way in which the problem is structured, as well as the process of information gathering itself. What information is salient to the dean? What assumptions does the dean make about the nature of the conflict? How does the dean collect information concerning whether the negotiation is zero-sum or whether joint benefits are available? Does the dean collect information that is available by considering the cognitions of the professor? Substantial evidence suggests that most negotiators ignore this normatively relevant information. Our implicit theories and confirmation biases are likely to be particularly critical at this stage. These implicit theories guide the information that we seek. Overconfidence in our understanding and our skills may result in too little information being gathered. Ample evidence suggests that a perfect set of information is unlikely to be gathered by most negotiators.

Information gathering itself can be structured as a problem to be solved, which calls forth a nested set of stages similar to those we are discussing for the larger problem. For example, the dean may consider and evaluate alternate mechanisms for obtaining key information about the professor and the competition, such as frank discussions, tapping his "network" of friends and ex-students for information, designating another faculty member to inquire as subtly as possible about the professor's thoughts, designing a test of the professor's loyalty, or whatever. However, these strategies are based on the creativity and breadth of experience of the dean, conditioned on the implicit theories that operate to suggest both what is happening and what needs to be known. Similarly, the professor may be engaged in feeling out both the dean and the depth of interest at the other school.

Information Evaluation

The rational negotiator will fully understand the information obtained. However, actual negotiators do not possess a perfect understanding of the information that they obtain. Just as our implicit theories affect the information that we obtain, these theories also affect the way in which we evaluate the obtained information. Inferences, diagnoses, and predictions are drawn from our assessment of the situation and checked against available information. Virtually all aspects of this process are subjective, with interpretations and pattern matching conditioned on the salience, subjective structuring, selectivity, and fit of the given information in the context of our knowledge structures. For example, suppose that the dean calls in the professor for a frank discussion, and reveals that he has heard of the offer and wishes to know what the faculty member is thinking at present, to which the professor replies that she is thinking over everything and does not yet know what to think. If the dean has activated the "manipulator" script, he is likely to evaluate such ambiguous information about the professor in a different manner from how he would have evaluated the same information under the "bidding war" script.

Strategy Evaluation

Once the information is gathered and evaluated, the rational negotiator identifies the strategy that maximizes his or her expected utility. We believe this process is not so rational, but is affected by the imagination and experience of the negotiators, as expressed through the knowledge structures that are activated, the strategies they develop, and the various decision biases we have discussed. Framing outcomes as gains (an expensive person can be replaced by a younger, more energetic, and cheaper faculty member) or as losses (what will it cost the school to keep/lose the professor?) influences strategy. The dean may be overconfident the professor will stay because of the outstanding quality of the school. Of course, the professor's evaluation may not be perfectly correlated with the dean's. If a conflict emerges, each side may escalate their commitment to a position that is no longer in their best interests. Despite what would constitute a rational strategy evaluation, once two negotiators make commitments to their positions, both parties may maintain these positions nonrationally and forego opportunities for mutually beneficial agreements.

CONCLUSION

The introduction to this chapter offered a five-step model of the decision-making process of negotiators. When it was introduced, we suggested that a rational actor would perform each of the steps in an optimal manner. However, the evidence presented throughout this chapter argues that individuals are not well described by a rational-actor model. Rather, individuals strive toward rationality, but are limited because of simplifications and biases that they bring to the negotiation context. This chapter outlines many of the specific simplifications and biases that affect negotiators, and has shown how they limit rationality in each of the steps in the negotiation process.

Past research on negotiation has typically been concerned with normative models and the descriptive study of situational and personality determinants of negotiation effectiveness. Yet, researchers realize that negotiation is a *decision-making* process in which multiple parties jointly make decisions to resolve conflicting issues (Pruitt, 1981). This chapter seeks to bring the study of negotiator judgment to the forefront of negotiation research. We argue in this chapter that *a great deal of the sub-optimality that can be observed in negotiation is the result of deviations from rationality in the judgmental processes of negotiators*. Research should continue to study the ways in which negotiator behavior systematically deviates from normative models. It is argued that judgmental imperfections reduce the outcomes that negotiators receive from competitive situations, reduce the joint profitability to the two parties in a dispute, and decrease the ability of competing parties to reach mutually beneficial agreements.

Finally, this chapter reiterates the importance of descriptive research in the study of negotiators. Recent books on negotiation emphasize the role of normative frameworks (Fisher & Ury, 1981; Raiffa, 1982). In contrast, we argue that it is beneficial to examine how negotiators actually make decisions, allowing for training that responds to deficiencies in existing thought processes. Lewin (1947) argues that it is necessary to "unfreeze" an individual before one can expect any changes to take place. Our strategy recommends that negotiation training realize that the normative recommendations for training negotiators may not be effective in influencing individuals, if unfreezing does not take place first. Our cognitive perspective on negotiation has the potential to confront people with their own limitations as the first step toward improving their negotiation abilities.

APPENDIX 1

Acquiring a Company

In the following exercise you will represent Company A (the acquiror), which is currently considering acquiring Company T (the target) by means of a tender offer. You plan to tender in cash for 100% of Company T's shares but are unsure how high a price to offer. The main complication is this: the value of Company T depends directly on the outcome of a major oil exploration project it is currently undertaking. Indeed, the very viability of Company T depends on the exploration outcome. If the project fails, the company under current management will be worth nothing—$0/share. But if the project succeeds, the value of the company under current management could be as high as $100/share. All share values between $0 and $100 are considered equally likely. By all estimates, the company will be worth considerably more in the hands of Company A than under current management. In fact, whatever the ultimate value under current management, *the company will be worth 50% more under the management of Company A than under Company T.* If the project fails, the company is worth $0/share under either management. If the exploration project generates a $50/share value under current management, the value under Company A is $75/share. Similarly, a $100/share value under Company T implies a $150/share value under Company A, and so on.

The board of directors of Company A has asked you to determine the price they should offer for Company T's share. This offer must be made *now, before* the outcome of the drilling project is known. From all indications, Company T would be happy to be acquired by Company A, *provided it is at a profitable price.* Moreover, Company T wishes to avoid, at all cost, the potential of a takeover bid by any other firm. You expect Company T to delay a decision on your bid until the results of the project are in, then accept or reject your offer before the news of the drilling results reaches the press.

Thus, *you (Company A) will not know the results of the exploration project when submitting your price offer, but Company T will know the results when deciding whether or not to accept your offer. In addition, Company T is expected to accept any offer by Company A that is greater than the (per share) value of the company under current management.*

As the representative of Company A, you are deliberating over price offers in the range $0/share (this is tantamount to making no offer at all) to $150/share. What price offer per share would you tender for Company T's stock?

My tender price is $______ per share

APPENDIX 2

Acquiring a Used Car

In the following exercise, you are asked to make an offer on a '72 Pontiac from a dealer at John's used car lot. The dealer will accept or reject your offer and that will end negotiations. Your objective is to make the offer that will maximize your own expected benefit whether or not you buy the car.

The value of the car is directly proportional to the mileage on it. Because the dealer could have rolled back the odometer, you have no way of knowing the true mileage. However, the dealer does know it.

In the worst case, the car is worthless to the dealer. In the best case it is worth $1,000 to him. Given the range of possible mileages, all values between $0 and $1,000 are equally likely.

Since you can make good use of the car, it is worth more to you than to the dealer. In fact, it is worth 50% more to you. At worst the car is worth $0 to both you and the dealer. If it is worth $500 to him it is worth $750 to you. Similarly, if it is worth $1,000 to him it is worth $1,500 to you.

You have to determine a price to offer for the car without knowing its true value. The dealer can accept your offer and you will get the car at the price offered, or he can reject it. If he rejects your offer, no further negotiation will take place and you will not buy the car. You should assume that the dealer will only accept profitable offers.

Thus, you do not know the value of the car when making your offer, whereas the dealer does when deciding whether to accept or reject your offer. In addition, the dealer will accept any offer that is greater or equal to the value of the car to him.

You are deliberating between price offers in the range of $0 (this is the same as making no offer) to $1,500. What price offer do you make?

My offer for the car is $______

Source: NTSB. MAR-82-39. February 1982.
Reproduced from Perrow (1984)

ACKNOWLEDGMENTS

The authors thank Bob Bies, Larry Cummings, Reid Hastie, Marvin Manheim, Maggie Neale, Barry Staw, and Leigh Thompson for comments on previous drafts of the manuscript. This research was funded by a grant awarded to the two authors by the National Science Foundation.

REFERENCES

Abelson, R.P. (1976). Script processing, attitude formation and decision making. In J.S. Carroll & J.W. Payne (Eds.), *Cognition and social behavior* (pp. 33–46). Hillsdale, NJ: Erlbaum.

Anderson, R.C., & Pichert, J.W. (1978). Recall of previously unrecallable information following a shift in perspective. *Journal of Verbal Learning and Verbal Behavior, 17*, 1–12.

Bazerman, M.H. (1983). Negotiator judgment: A critical look at the rationality assumption. *American Behavioral Scientist, 27*, 211–228.

Bazerman, M.H. (1985). Norms of distributive justice in interest arbitration. *Industrial and Labor Relations Review*, *38*, 558–570.

Bazerman, M.H. (1986). *Judgment in managerial decision making*. New York: Wiley.

Bazerman, M.H., Magliozzi, T., & Neale, M.A. (1985). The acquisition of an integrative response in a competitive market. *Organizational Behavior and Human Performance*, *34*, 294–313.

Bazerman, M.H., & Neale, M.A. (1982). Improving negotiation effectiveness under final offer arbitration: The role of selection and training. *Journal of Applied Psychology*, *67*, 543–548.

Bazerman, M.H., & Neale, M.A. (1983). Heuristics in negotiation: Limitations to dispute resolution effectiveness. In M.H. Bazerman & R.J. Lewicki (Eds.), *Negotiation in organizations* (pp. 51–67). Beverly Hills, CA: Sage.

Brockner, J., & Rubin, J.Z. (1985). *The social psychology of entrapment in escalating conflicts*. New York: Springer-Verlag.

Cantor, N., & Smith, E.E., French, R., & Mezzich, J. (1980). Psychiatric diagnoses as prototype categorization. *Journal of Abnormal Psychology*. *89*, 181–193.

Carroll, J.S., Bazerman, M.H., Maury, R. (1986). *Negotiator cognition: A descriptive approach to negotiators' understanding of their opponents*. MIT working paper. Cambridge, MA: Massachusetts Institute of Technology.

Carroll, J.S., Galegher, J., & Wiener, R.L. (1982). Dimensional and categorical attributions in expert parole decisions. *Basic and Applied Social Psychology*, *3*, 187–201.

Carroll, J.S., & Payne, J.W. (1976). The psychology of the parole decision-making process: A joint application of attribution theory and information-processing psychology. In J.S. Carroll & J.W. Payne (Eds.), *Cognition and social behavior* (pp. 13–32). Hillsdale, NJ: Erlbaum.

Chase, W.G., & Simon, H.A. (1973). Perception in chess. *Cognitive Psychology*, *4*, 55–81.

Clarkson, G. (1962). *Portfolio selection: A simulation of trust investment*. Englewood Cliffs, NJ: Prentice-Hall.

Corbin, R.M. (1980). Decisions that might not get made. In T.S. Wallsten (Ed.), *Cognitive processes in choice and decision behavior* (pp. 47–68). Hillsdale, NJ: Erlbaum.

Crawford, V. (1979). On compulsory arbitration schemes. *Journal of Political Economy*, *87*, 131–159.

Cross, J. (1969). *The economics of bargaining*. New York: Basic Books.

Darley, J.M., & Fazio, R.H. (1980). Expectancy confirmation processes arising in the social interaction sequence. *American Psychologist*, *35*, 867–881.

Davis, M. (1981). A multidimensional approach to individual differences in empathy. *JSAS Catalogue of Selected Documents in Psychology*, *10*, 85.

Einhorn, H.J. (1980). Learning from experience and suboptimal rules in decision making. In T. Wallsten (Ed.), *Cognitive processes in choice and decision behavior* (pp. 1–20). Hillsdale, NJ: Erlbaum.

Einhorn, H.J., & Hogarth, R.M. (1978). Confidence in judgment: Persistence of the illusion of validity. *Psychological Review*, *85*, 395–416.

Einhorn, H.J., & Hogarth, R.M. (1981). Behavioral decision theory: Processes of judgment and choice. *Annual Review of Psychology*, *32*, 53–88.

Einhorn, H.J., & Hogarth, R.M. (1985). Ambiguity and uncertainty in probablistic inference. *Psychological Review*, *92*, 433–461.

Einhorn, H.J., Kleinmuntz, D.N., & Kleinmuntz, B. (1979). Linear regression and process-tracing models of judgment. *Psychological Review*, *86*, 465–485.

Ericsson, K.A., & Simon, H.A. (1980). Verbal reports as data. *Psychological Review*, *84*, 231–259.

Farber, H.S. (1980). An analysis of final-offer arbitration. *Journal of Conflict Resolution*, *5*, 683–705.

Farber, H.S. (1981). Splitting-the-difference in interest arbitration. *Industrial and Labor Relations Review, 35,* 70–77.

Farber, H.S., & Bazerman, M.H. (1986). The general basis of arbitrator behavior: An empirical analysis of conventional and final offer arbitration. *Econometrica, 54,* 819–844.

Fischhoff, B. (1981). Debiasing. In D. Kahneman, P. Slovic, & A. Tversky (Eds.), *Judgment under certainty: Heuristics and Biases* (pp. 422–444). New York: Cambridge University Press.

Fisher, R., & Ury, W. (1981). *Getting to yes.* Boston: Houghton Mifflin.

Fiske, S.T., & Taylor, S.E. (1984). *Social cognition.* Reading, MA: Addison-Wesley.

Gioia, D.A., & Manz, C.C. (1985). Linking cognition and behavior: A script processing interpretation of vicarious learning. *Academy of Management Review, 10,* 527–539.

Hastie, R. (1981). Schematic principles in human memory. In E.T. Higgins, P. Herman, & M. Zanna (Eds.), *Social cognition: The Ontario symposium on personality and social psychology* (pp. 39–88). Hillsdale, NJ: Erlbaum.

Heider, F. (1958). *The psychology of interpersonal relations.* New York: Wiley.

Hogarth, R.M. (1980). *Judgment and choice: The psychology of decision.* New York: Wiley.

Hovland, C.I., & Weiss, W. (1951). The influence of source credibility on communication effectiveness. *Public Opinion Quarterly, 15,* 635–650.

Huber, G.P. (1980). *Managerial decision making.* Glenview, IL: Scott, Foresman.

Johnson, E.J. (1980). *Expertise in admissions judgments.* Unpublished doctoral dissertation, Carnegie-Mellon University, Pittsburgh, PA.

Johnson, P.E., Hassebrock, F., Duran, A.S., & Moller, J.H. (1982). Multimethod study of clinical judgment. *Organization Behavior and Human Performance, 30,* 201–230.

Jones, E.E. (1979). The rocky road from acts to disposition. *American Psychologist, 34,* 107–117.

Jones, E.E., & Davis, K.E. (1965). From acts to dispositions: The attribution process in person perception. In L. Berkowitz (Ed.), *Advances in experimental social psychology: Vol. 2* (pp. 219–266). Orlando, FL: Academic Press.

Jones, E.E., & Thibaut, J.W. (1958). Interaction goals as bases of inference in interpersonal perception. In R. Tagiuri and L. Petrullo (Eds.), *Person perception and interpersonal behavior* (pp. 151–178). Stanford, CA: Stanford University Press.

Jones, R.A. (1977). *Self-fulfilling prophecies.* Hillsdale, NJ: Erlbaum.

Kahneman, D., Slovic, P., & Tversky, A. (1982). *Judgment under uncertainty: Heuristics and biases.* New York: Cambridge University Press.

Kahneman, D., & Tversky, A. (1979). Prospect theory: An analysis of decision under risk. *Econometrica, 47,* 263–291.

Kelley, H.H. (1967). Attribution theory in social psychology. In D. Levine (Ed.), *Nebraska symposium on motivation* (pp. 192–238). Lincoln: University of Nebraska Press.

Kelley, H.H. (1973). The process of causal attribution. *American Psychologist, 38,* 107–128.

Kelley, H.H., & Thibaut, J.W. (1980). *Interpersonal relations: A theory of interdependence.* New York: Wiley.

Kochan, T. (1980). Collective bargaining and organizational behavior research. In B. Staw, & L. Cummings (Eds.), *Research in Organizational Behavior: Vol. 2* (pp. 129–176). Greenwich, CT: JAI Press.

Kochan, T.A., & Bazerman, M.H. (1986). Macro determinants of the future of the study of negotiations in organizations. In R.J. Lewicki, B.H. Sheppard, and M.H. Bazerman (Eds.), *Research in Negotiation in Organizations: Vol. 1* (pp. 287–309). Greenwich, CT: JAI Press.

Langer, E.J. (1975). The illusion of control. *Journal of Personality and Social Psychology, 32,* 311–328.

Lewin, K. (1947). Group decision and social change. In T.M. Newcomb and E.L. Hartley

(Eds.), *Readings in social psychology* (pp. 459–473). New York: Holt, Rinehart and Winston.

Lord, C.G., Ross, L., & Lepper, M.R. (1979). Biased assimilation and attitude polarization: The effects of prior theories on subsequently considered evidence. *Journal of Personality and Social Psychology, 37,* 2098–2109.

Lurigio, A.J., & Carroll, J.S. (1985). Probation officers' schemata of offenders: Content, development, and impact on treatment decisions. *Journal of Personality and Social Psychology, 48,* 1112–1126.

Malinowski, B. (1948). *Magic, science and religion and other essays.* Garden City, NY: Doubleday.

March, J.G., & Simon, H.A. (1958). *Organizations.* New York: Wiley.

McAlister, L., Bazerman, M.H., & Fader, P. (1986). Power and goal setting in channel negotiations. *Journal of Marketing Research, 23,* 228–236.

Mintzberg, H., Raisinghani, D., & Theoret, A. (1976). The structure of "unstructured" decision processes. *Administrative Science Quarterly, 21,* 246–275.

Nash, J. (1950). The bargaining problem. *Econometrica, 18,* 128–140.

Neale, M.A. (1984). The effect of negotiation and arbitration cost salience on bargainer behavior: The role of arbitrator and constituency in negotiator judgment. *Organizational Behavior and Human Performance, 34,* 97–111.

Neale, M.A., & Bazerman, M.H. (1983). The effect of perspective-taking ability under alternate forms of arbitration on the negotiation process. *Industrial and Labor Relations Review, 36,* 378–388.

Neale, M.A., & Bazerman, M.H. (1985). The effect of framing on conflict and negotiator overconfidence. *Academy of Management Journal, 28,* 34–49.

Neale, M.A., & Northcraft, G. (in press). Experts, amateurs, and refrigerators: Comparing expert and amateur negotiators in a novel task. *Organizational Behavior and Human Decision Processes.*

Newell, A., & Simon, H.A. (1972). *Human problem solving.* Englewood Cliffs, NJ: Prentice-Hall.

Nisbett, R.E., & Ross, L. (1980). *Human inference: Strategies and shortcomings of social judgment.* Englewood Nisbett, R.E., & Wilson, T.D. (1977). Telling more than we can know: Verbal reports on mental processes. *Psychological Review, 84,* 231–259.

Nisbett, R.E., & Wilson, T.D. (1977). Telling more than we can know: Verbal reports on mental processes. *Psychological Review,* 84, 231–259.

Payne, J.W., Braunstein, M.L., & Carroll, J.S. (1978). Exploring predecisional behavior: An alternative approach to decision research. *Organizational Behavior and Human Performance, 22,* 17–34.

Payne, J.W., & Ragsdale, E.K.E. (1978). Verbal protocols and direct observation of supermarket shopping behavior and some findings and discussion of methods. In H.K. Hunt (Ed.), *Advances in consumer research: Vol. V* (571–577), Ann Arbor, Michigan: Association for Consumer Behavior.

Pennington, N., & Hastie, R. (1985). *Causal reasoning in decision making.* University of Chicago working paper. Chicago: University of Chicago.

Perrow, C. (1984). *Normal accidents.* New York: Basic Books.

Pitz, G.F., & Sachs, N.J. (1984). Judgment and decision: Theory and application. *Annual Review of Psychology, 35,* 139–163.

Popper, K.R. (1959). *The logic of scientific discovery.* London: Hutchinson.

Pruitt, D.G. (1981). *Negotiation behavior.* Orlando, FL: Academic Press.

Pruitt, D.G. (1983). Integrative agreements: Nature and antecedents. In M.H. Bazerman & R.J. Lewicki (Eds.), *Negotiating in organizations* (pp. 35–50). Beverly Hills, CA: Sage.

Pruitt, D., & Rubin, J.Z. (1986). *Social conflict: Escalation, impasse, and resolution.* Reading, MA: Addision-Wesley.

Raiffa, H. (1982). *The art and science of negotiation*. Cambridge, MA: Harvard University Press.

Rosch, E. (1978). Principles of categorization. In E. Rosch, & B.B. Lloyd (Eds.), *Cognition and categorization* (pp. 27–48). Hillsdale, NJ: Erlbaum.

Ross, L.D. (1977). The intuitive psychologist and his shortcomings: Distortions in the attribution process. In L. Berkowitz (Ed.), *Advances in experimental social psychology: Vol. 10* (pp. 173–221). Orlando, FL: Academic Press.

Ross, L.D., Amabile, T.M., & Steinmetz, J.L. (1977). Social roles, social control, and biases in social-perception processes. *Journal of Personality and Social Psychology, 35*, 485–494.

Rubin, J. (1980). Experimental research on third party intervention in conflict: Toward some generalizations. *Psychological Bulletin, 87*, 379–391.

Rubin, J., & Brown, B. (1975). *The social psychology of bargaining and negotiation*. Orlando, FL: Academic Press.

Samuelson, W.F., & Bazerman, M.H. (1985). Negotiating under the winner's curse. In V. Smith (Ed.), *Research in experimental economics: Vol. 3* (pp. 105–137). Greenwich, CT: JAI Press.

Schank, R.C., & Abelson, R.P. (1977). *Scripts, plans, goals, and understanding: An inquiry into human knowledge structures*. Hillsdale, NJ: Erlbaum.

Schneider, D.J., Hastorf, A.H., & Ellsworth, P.C. (1979). *Person perception*. Reading, MA: Addison-Wesley.

Shubik, M. (1971). The dollar auction game: A paradox in noncooperative behavior and escalation. *Journal of Conflict Resolution, 15*, 109–111.

Siegal, S., & Fouraker, L.E. (1960). *Bargaining and group decision making: Experiments in bilateral monopoly*. New York: McGraw-Hill.

Simon, H.A. (1947). *Administrative behavior*. New York: Free Press.

Simon, H.A. (1957). *Models of man*. New York: Wiley.

Smith, E.R., & Miller, F.D. (1978). Limits on perception of cognitive processes: A reply to Nisbett and Wilson. *psychological Review, 85*, 355–362.

Snyder, M., & Swann, W.B. Jr. (1976). When actions reflect attitudes: The politics of impression management. *Journal of Personality and Social Psychology, 34*, 1034–1042.

Staw, B.M. (1976). Knee-deep in the big muddy: A study of escalating commitment to a chosen course of action. *Organizational Behavior and Human Performance, 16*, 27–44.

Staw, B.M. (1981). The escalation of commitment to a course of action. *Academy of Management Review, 6*, 577–587.

Staw, B.M., & Ross, J. (1987). Behavior in escalation situations: Antecedents, prototypes, and solutions. In L.L. Cummings & B.M. Staw (Eds.), *Research in Organizational Behavior: Vol. 9* (pp. 39–78). Greenwich, CT: JAI Press, Inc.

Teger, A.I. (1980). *Too much invested to quit: The psychology of the escalation of conflict*. New York: Pergamon Press.

Tversky, A., & Kahneman, D. (1973). Availability: A heuristic for judging frequency and probability. *Cognitive Psychology, 5*, 207–232.

Walton, R.E., & McKersie, R.B. (1965). *A behavioral theory of labor negotiations: An analysis of a social interaction system*. New York: McGraw-Hill.

Zeuthen, F. (1930). *Problems of monopoly and economic welfare*. London: George Routledge & Sons.

ACCOUNTABILITY:
THE NEGLECTED SOCIAL CONTEXT OF JUDGMENT AND CHOICE

Philip E. Tetlock

ABSTRACT

The last decade has witnessed a dramatic increase in experimental studies of the cognitive processes underlying judgment and choice behavior. Although this cognitive research program has certainly increased our understanding of how people make up their minds in laboratory settings, the research program has virtually ignored the social and organizational context of judgment and choice. The information processor image of human nature underlying the cognitive research program provides at best an incomplete picture of how people think in the social and organizational settings in which they live and work. A pervasive feature of natural decision environments—but not of laboratory experiments on cognitive processes—is the fact that people are potentially accountable for the judgments and decisions they express. A need exists for a complementary research program—premised on a view of the person as politician—that focuses on the wide variety of strategies people develop for coping with demands for accountability in everyday life. Empirical and theoretical implications of the proposed politician research program are sketched.

Few fields of psychological research have expanded as rapidly as laboratory studies of judgment and decision-making. In the last ten years, there has been an explosion of interest in the basic cognitive strategies people use to interpret events and to choose among alternative courses of action. The enormity of the research effort is reflected in the size of the bibliographies of recent reviews of the literature. Since 1973, there have been well over 1000 experimental studies of social cognition and causal attribution (Hastie, 1983; Kelley & Michela, 1979; Nisbett & Ross, 1980; Taylor & Fiske, 1978). There has been a comparable growth of work in behavioral and psychological decision theory(Abelson &Levi, in press; Einhorn & Hogarth, 1981; Kahneman, Tversky & Slovic, 1982; Slovic, Fischhoff, & Lichtenstein, 1977).

Laboratory studies of cognitive processes do not, however, represent the only possible approach to the study of judgment and choice behavior. One can explore these topics from the perspective of a variety of different disciplines and levels of analysis. For instance, many social psychologists have focused on the impact of interpersonal and small group processes on decision-making (Bales, 1970; Janis, 1982; Moscovici, 1981; Shaw, 1980). Most important decisions are not, after all, the product of isolated information processors; they are the product of intensive interactions among members of groups. Working at a still higher level of analysis, many investigators in organizational behavior, political science and economics have preferred a bird's eye social system perspective on decision-making. Both individuals and small groups of individuals are constrained by the norms, procedures, and resources of the institutions in which they live and work (Allison, 1971; March & Simon, 1958; Katz & Kahn, 1978; Lindblom, 1959). Investigators in this tradition often view experimental studies with skepticism; they feel we need to study decision-making "in vivo"—in the actual institutional settings in which it occurs.

One's choice of level of analysis has profound consequences for how one conceptualizes decision-making. Using a metaphor drawn from general systems theory, Hogarth (in press) has compared the different levels of analysis to looking through a microscope at various levels of magnification. At the most intense level of magnification—such as provided by laboratory experiments of cognitive processes—one can see the phenomenon in detail. The price of the ability to see detail is, however, the inability to see the phenomenon within a broader systems context. At less intense levels of magnification—such as provided by field studies of organizational decision-making—one gains the ability to see context, but only at the cost of not seeing subsystem detail. Not surprisingly, communication across levels of analysis is both difficult and rare. What excites the attention of investigators at one level of analysis may well be invisible to investigators at other levels. One can study decision-making at a purely cognitive level of analysis without ever referring to research on group dynamics, role theory or bureaucratic politics. Conversely, one can study bargaining, coalition formation and incrementalism in organizations without ever referring to cognitive research on knowledge structures or judgmental heuristics.

My most general goal in this chapter is to encourage communication across levels of analysis. Despite substantial advances in cognitive and social psychology, group dynamics and organizational behavior, the linkages among these traditions are still primitive. A major challenge still confronting decision theorists is the creation of conceptual frameworks which bridge the traditionally separate cognitive, small group and institutional levels of analysis (cf. George, 1980a; Holsti & George, 1975; Staw, Sandelands, & Dutton, 1981).

I have divided the chapter into two sections. The first section provides a broad overview of experimental research on cognitive processes underlying judgment and choice behavior. Drawing on the writings of the philosopher of science Imré Lakatos (1970), I use the concept of "research program" as a framework for organizing my discussion of this literature. Little doubt exists that the cognitive research program has stimulated significant theoretical and empirical advances in our understanding of human thought. These successes of the research program should not, however, blind us to its limitations. "Contextualist" critics have made a strong case for reducing the reliance on highly controlled laboratory experimentation and in favor of studying information processing in more ecologically representative situations. The search for completely context-free laws of information processing may often (although *not always*) be misguided.

In the second section, I advance a social psychological version of the contextualist critique. The "isolated information processor" image of human nature underlying the cognitive research program is too restrictive as a basis for a comprehensive theory of judgment and decision-making. People typically make up their minds in rule-governed social and organizational settings in which they feel personally accountable or responsible for the stands they take. We need an alternative research program that builds upon the cognitive tradition by placing the information processor in social context. The guiding metaphor I suggest for this alternative research program is that of the politician whose primary goal is to maintain the positive regard of important constituencies to whom he or she feels accountable. A major empirical goal of the politician research program is the identification of the cognitive, social, and political strategies that people use for coping with demands for accountability from significant others in their lives.

THE CURRENT STATE OF THE COGNITIVE RESEARCH PROGRAM

Implicit or explicit assumptions about human nature underlie virtually all empirical work in psychological and social science. These assumptions profoundly influence how we design, execute, and interpret research (cf. Deutsch & Krauss, 1965; Kendler, 1981; Shaw & Costanzo, 1982).

Imré Lakatos (1970) has advanced an insightful analysis of how underlying assumptions influence the conduct of scientific research. According to Lakatos, the most natural unit for describing scientific progress is not the isolated hypothesis or even theory, but rather the research program. Research programs can extend over decades (even centuries) and inspire an enormous number of hypotheses and empirical studies. Underlying all of the activity inspired by a research program is, however, a "hard core" of basic, unmodifiable assumptions about the subject matter. This hard core gives coherence, impetus, and direction to the research program. It specifies the ground rules for theory formulation and empirical work. The primary objective of the scientific community is to develop and test theories compatible with the hard core. And the defining characteristic of a mature research program is the emergence of consensus among investigators on the most effective theoretical and methodological strategies for achieving that objective (cf. Kuhn, 1970; Royce, 1976).

Viewed in the above light, the dominant research program on judgment and decision-making has clearly been the cognitive or information processing approach. The hard core of this now well-established program consists of two central philosophical ideas that have a long and distinguished history in psychology (a history that can be directly traced to Descartes and Kant) (Russell, 1945). The first is mentalism: a belief in the primacy of the cognitive structures and processes of the knowing subject. Our knowledge of the world is not direct, but mediated through these cognitive structures and processes. The second is individualism: a belief in the primacy of the thinking and reasoning processes of the *individual* knower. Thought and action are seen as products of the cognitive operations of the individual thinker, rather than as products of the social, organizational and technological settings in which the individual is embedded. Together, the mentalist and individualist elements of the hard core define the natural unit of analysis for the cognitive research program: the information processor in experimental isolation from the social world he or she normally inhabits (cf. Sampson, 1981).

The hard core assumptions of the research program are not directly testable; they have the status of "ontological axioms" (Lakatos, 1970). However, the assumptions are not empirically inconsequential. The hard core provides the conceptual starting point for most psychological theory and research on judgment and decision-making. The hard core directs investigators to develop theories that take for granted the adequacy of the isolated information processor image of human nature. The central questions for empirical inquiry become: What type of information processor is the average person? How well does the average person perform the information processing tasks widely regarded as crucial for arriving at valid causal interpretations of events (e.g., estimating the degree of covariation among events, recalling evidence accurately, generating alternative hypotheses, testing these hypotheses in an unbiased fashion, adjusting prior beliefs in response to new evidence)? How well does the average person perform the information processing tasks widely regarded as crucial for making optimal or utility-maximizing decisions (considering the full range of options, accurately estimating the likelihood of occurrence of possible consequences of these options, assessing in an unbiased way the positive or negative value of each consequence, confronting difficult value trade-offs)?

A staggering body of research has addressed these challenging issues. The vast majority of this work consists of well-controlled laboratory experiments in which researchers systematically manipulate independent variables that they believe to be important determinants of judgment and choice behavior. The rationale for the heavy reliance on experimentation has been clear-cut: researchers have sought to identify basic psychological principles underlying judgment and choice behavior (e.g., information processing heuristics, knowledge structures). The laboratory experiment appears to provide the ideal means of studying these basic processes in pure or isolated form (cf. Hogarth's, in press, microscope analogy). Assuming that a small number of basic processes exist, and that they do not interact with the laboratory setting, it makes eminent sense to capitalize on the well-known internal validity advantages of experiments for testing and refining basic-process theories (Aronson & Carlsmith, 1969).

The current chapter is not the appropriate place to review the experimental literature on judgment and choice. This literature has been thoroughly reviewed elsewhere (Abelson & Levi, in press; Einhorn & Hogarth, 1981, Kelley & Michela, 1979; Nisbett & Ross, 1980; Payne, 1982; Slovic, Fischhoff & Lichtenstein, 1977). It is worth noting, however, that a sense of progress and guarded optimism does exist within much, if not all, of the research program. Many feel that the program is advancing satisfactorily. The most frequently mentioned sign of progress is the growing consensus on the nature of the human information processor. It is increasingly common to see people characterized as fallible information processors who are susceptible to a depressing number of errors and biases. People apparently do not think as normative models say they should think (e.g., Bayes' theorem for adjusting opinions in response to new evidence, expected utility theory for choosing among multi-attribute options). In summarizing the relevant evidence, some reviewers have gone so far as to describe people as cognitive misers (Taylor, 1980) or lazy organisms (McGuire, in press) who avoid mental procedures that require sustained attention, comprehension, or computing power. People, it is maintained, seek inferential shortcuts or heuristics (e.g., availability) which permit them to make up their minds quickly, easily, and with excessive confidence in the correctness of their decisions. People are also characterized as predominantly theory-driven (as opposed to data-driven) information processors who accept belief-supportive information uncritically, but are slow to acknowledge disconfirmatory evidence (Nisbett & Ross, 1980). Sometimes, people even see belief-supportive evidence where it simply does not exist (Chapman & Chapman, 1969). In brief, far from being maximizers—relentlessly searching for the best possible solutions to the problems confronting them—people seem to be chronic satisficers, frequently unwilling or unable to perform the demanding cognitive tasks that normative models specify as essential to good decision-making.

The sense of progress in the research community is not, however, universal. A number of writers have begun to question the fruitfulness of an exclusively laboratory-based research program on information processors who have been isolated from the everyday environments in which they normally function. The grounds for the rising skepticism are many and varied, including: (1) methodological concerns for external validity; (2) mounting empirical evidence of the context-specificity of laboratory findings; (3) philosophical (functionalist) arguments on the need to understand the information processing environments with which people must deal on a daily basis.

Methodological concerns. We know little about the generality or robustness of most experimental findings reported in the literature (Borgida & Howard-Pitney, 1983; Ebbesen & Konecni, 1980; George, 1980; Jenkins, 1981; Katz & Kahn, 1978; O'Reilly & Anderson, 1982; Tetlock, 1983b). Laboratory experiments differ in multifarious ways from decision-making episodes in everyday life: the types of tasks presented to subjects, how the tasks are presented to subjects, subjects' goals in performing the tasks and the importance of the tasks. It is only prudent to ask whether these many differences make a difference—whether major dissimilarities exist between how people process and analyze information in the laboratory and in less artificial settings (cf. Brunswik, 1956).

Context specificity of findings. The concerns for external validity are greatly aggravated by the mounting evidence from experimental work of the context-specificity of many findings. Information processing in judgment and decision-making, as in other areas of cognitive psychology (Jenkins, 1981), appears to be highly contingent on the demands of the task. In their authoritative review of work on behavioral decision theory, Einhorn and Hogarth (1981) declared:

> The most important empirical results in the period under review have shown the sensitivity of judgment and choice to seemingly minor variations in tasks.

They also explicitly warned us to be cautious in accepting broad-brush portraits of the human information processor such as the cognitive miser, portraits that, they suggested, "are often painted to be interesting rather than complete." Ebbesen and Konecni (1980) and Payne (1982) have been even more skeptical. These writers suggested that the dominant conception of decision-making as controlled by a few basic cognitive processes which can be discovered via artificial tasks is seriously flawed; people generate different decision rules and processes to deal with each particular task.

Ecological and functionalist arguments. Partly in response to the mounting evidence on the context-specific nature of experimental findings and partly in response to functionalist arguments on the need to understand the environments that information processors must understand in order to survive, many prominent cognitive psychologists have begun to have second thoughts about the hard core underpinnings of the research program. It is not unusual now to see appeals for a significant redirection of effort within the research program—a shift away from the study of information processing in "artificial laboratory settings" and toward the study of information processing in more ecologically representative situations. Neisser (1976), for example, argued that the revolution in computer technology and simulation has spurred the development of an excessively intrapsychic cognitive psychology that is concerned only with modeling inside-the-head data processing rules.

> We have been lavishing too much attention on hypothetical models of the mind and not enough on analyzing the environment that the mind has been shaped to meet.

Many writers have echoed this theme (e.g., Bronfenbrenner, 1977; Gibson, 1966; Jenkins, 1981). For instance, Jenkins (1981) strongly urged investigators to adopt a "contextualist" model of human information processing. According to Jenkins, the search for *the* information processing rules which people *always* use to interpret events and make choices is misguided. The appropriate question is not, "What kind of machine is the human information processor?", but rather, "What kinds of machines do people become when confronted with various types of tasks in various types of environments?" (See also Ebbesen & Konecni, 1980; Payne, 1982). Shaw and Bransford (1977, p. 6) have stated the general case for a reassessment of the objectives of the cognitive research program forcefully:

> the nature of humans is inextricably intertwined with the nature of the world in which they live, move, and have their being . . . the ecological approach germinates in the minds of theorists who come to the stark realization that humans, as must all living things that survive, depend on their natural and cultural environments for knowledge as well as victuals. For such theorists it is impossible to accept any longer models of man whose only virtue is that they were contrived to function efficiently in artificial (laboratory) contexts.

These contextualist critiques challenge one of the basic elements of the hard core of the cognitive research program: the usefulness of studying individual information processors in isolation from the world in which they normally function. The research implications of the critiques are also not difficult to discern. We must pay much more systematic attention to the everyday environments in which people think and act. Laboratory experiments may reveal only a very restricted range of the cognitive strategies that people employ in less artificial and contrived situations. The primary objective of research should be a functionalist one: careful, systematic description of how people cope with the diverse decision problems they face in their natural habitats.

Who is Right?

In closing this section, it is appropriate to ask who is right: the defenders or critics of the cognitive research program? My position is that each side possesses, in Rapoport's (1964) phrase, a "region of validity." It is not self-contradictory to believe both that the cognitive research program has made important contributions to our understanding of judgment and choice behavior and that the contextualist critics have identified serious limitations to the cognitive research program. Defenders of the research program may well be correct in insisting that some highly abstract, context-free laws of information processing do, indeed, exist. Contextualist critics may well be correct in insisting that the research program provides us with a very incomplete picture of how people think and leads us to underestimate the situation-specificity of information processing. Available evidence suggests that the truth does, in fact, lie somewhere between the two positions. Different components of judgment and choice processes appear to be under *varying degrees* of personal control (Abelson & Levi, in press; Atkinson & Shiffrin, 1968; Schneider & Shiffrin, 1977). Especially relevant here is the distinction between structural and control processes. Structural processes are assumed to be "wired into" the organism and very difficult to change. Examples include the well-known limits on short-term memory holding capacity and basic laws of perception and attention (e.g., a fundamental assumption of Kahneman & Tversky's, 1979, prospect theory is that our perceptual systems are designed to detect changes in the status quo, not absolute magnitudes, and that we encode the outcomes of decisions as gains or losses relative to some neutral reference point). By contrast, control processes are assumed to be much more modifiable and subject to conscious direction. Examples include decision-makers' ability to monitor and determine the number of options, consequences, and values they consider in the deliberation process and the temporal sequence in which they consider these factors (e.g., Svenson, 1979, on breadth-first versus depth-first search strategies). Obviously, it is an empirical issue whether any given finding is rooted mainly in structural or control processes. People may be cognitive misers due to built-in structural limitations, highly context-specific control processes or (most likely) some combination of structural and control processes (Abelson & Levi, in press; Payne, 1982).

The important point here is not the exact mix of structural and control processes in producing a given effect, but rather that the contextualist critiques (except in their most radical form—Sampson, 1981) do not automatically negate the value of all empirical work inspired by the cognitive research program. For certain purposes, it is useful to focus on the isolated individual information processor. The critiques do, however, help to put the research program in perspective by underscoring its limitations and blind-spots. In so doing, the critiques serve a crucial knowledge-advancing function. They point to ways of formulating theories and doing research outside of the dominant cognitive research program. It is in this spirit that in the next section of this chapter I propose an alternative "social contextualist" research program—an alternative that is intended to complement rather than negate the cognitive research program.

AN ALTERNATIVE TO THE COGNITIVE RESEARCH PROGRAM: THE DECISION-MAKER AS POLITICIAN

Investigators should not allow the impressive achievements of the cognitive research program to blind them to insights that can be gained by exploring alternative images of human nature and functioning in the world, Feyerabend (1970) stated the general argument (against limiting empirical work to dominant research programs) persuasively in his response to the question, "How can one be a good empiricist?"

> A good empiricist will not rest content with the theory that is in the center of scientific attention and with those tests of the theory that can be carried out in a direct manner. Knowing that the most fundamental and the most general criticism is criticism produced with the help of alternatives, he will try to invent such alternatives. It is, of course, impossible at once to produce a theory that is formally comparable to the main point of view and that leads to equally many predictions. His first step will therefore be the formulation of fairly general assumptions which are not yet directly connected with observations; this means that his first step will be the invention of a new metaphysics (Author: a new hard core). This metaphyics must then be elaborated (p. 338).

The Politician Research Program and Its Hard Core

On what image of human nature (metaphysics) should the alternative research program be built? My nomination is that of the person as politician. In its pursuit of highly abstract, context-free laws of information processing, the cognitive research program has ignored the social and organizational environments in which people make the overwhelming majority of decisions. Subjects in laboratory studies of cognitive processes rarely feel accountable or responsible for the positions they take. Subjects function in a social vacuum (or as close an approximation to a social vacuum as can be achieved) in which they do not need to worry about the interpersonal consequences of their conduct (How will others react if I do this? How effectively can I justify my views to others if challenged?). Such issues are simply seen as irrelevant to the explanatory goals of the cognitive research program.

The politician research program begins where the cognitive research program leaves off. The starting point for analysis is the information processor—with whatever general cognitive limitations and biases he or she possesses—in an environment structured by the complex social and organizational systems to which the individual belongs. Whereas the central objective of the cognitive research program is to identify fundamental or invariant laws of human information processing, the central objective of the politician research program is to identify the behavioral strategies that people have developed for coping with fundamental or invariant features of natural decision environments (features likely to be present at least to some degree in all social and organizational settings).

Like the cognitive research program, the politician research program rests on two hard core assumptions concerning its subject matter. Given the crucial role that hard core assumptions play in guiding empirical work (especially in the early stages of a research program—Royce, 1976), these assumptions deserve to be spelled out in detail. The first assumption deals with the nature of the real-world decision settings in which people make up their minds; the second, with the goals and motives that drive the decision-making process.

Accountability of conduct as a universal feature of natural decision environments. Attribution theorists have long noted that in everyday life people are presumed to be agents of their actions, i.e., they are responsible for what they do (cf. Heider, 1944). It makes sense to ask people for the reasons underlying their actions because it is assumed that people possess the "power" of monitoring and controlling their conduct in accord with self-generated plans of action (an assumption that, incidentally, is no longer controversial in social and personality psychology—Bandura, 1977; Carver, 1979; Gergen, 1971; Schlenker, 1980, 1982; Semin & Manstead, 1983; Suls, 1981; Wicklund, 1980). Shotter (1981) made this critical point in the following way:

> in our ordinary, everyday, common-sense view of people as autonomous, we assume people know how to make their actions conform to something in their common-sense, and furthermore, we also assume that they are able, potentially at least, to report upon, or to account for, how they made themselves so conform. In a moral world, self-regulation and accountability are inextricably interlinked (p. 279).

The accountability of conduct is an inevitable sociocultural adaptation to the problem of how to organize and coordinate the interrelationships among individuals who are capable of monitoring and controlling their own actions (Semin & Manstead, 1983). From this perspective, accountability is a necessary part of the solution to the classic Hobbesian riddle of how society is possible (cf. Scott & Lyman, 1968). Organized social life cannot exist without some degree of regularity. This regularity is provided by shared rules, norms, and social practices (Weick, 1979). Accountability is a critical rule and norm enforcement mechanism: the social psychological link between individual decision-makers on the one hand and the social systems to which they belong on the other. The fact that people are accountable for their decisions is an implicit or explicit constraint upon all consequential acts they undertake (If I do this, how will others react?). Failure to behave in ways for which one can construct acceptable accounts leads to varying degrees of censure—depending, of course, on the gravity of the offense and the norms of the organization (cf. Pfeffer, 1981; Schlenker, 1980; Scott & Lyman, 1968; Tetlock, in press).

An important qualification should, however, be added to the above analysis. Although a powerful case can be made for the trans-historical and cross-cultural invariance of accountability (Semin & Manstead, 1983), the specific norms, values and ideologies to which people are held accountable differ dramatically from one situation to the next. The sociologist C. Wright Mills (1940) noted that when people leave groups and join new ones, they must learn new "vocabularies of motives"—in other words, new rules for generating socially acceptable explanations of behavior. These vocabularies of motives vary in content and structure as a function of a variety of social contextual factors, ranging from the macro to the micro (Beyer, 1981; Haberstroh & Gerwin, 1972). "Macro-contextual" factors refer to "cultural system" ideologies and values (e.g., science, Protestantism, capitalism, Marxism) and societal ideologies and values (e.g., nationalism). "Micro-contextual" factors include ideologies and values that characterize distinctive organizations within societies (e.g., IBM, Antioch College) and roles within organizations (e.g., occupants of boundary roles such as union negotiators who must be responsive to the expectancies of conflicting constituencies). An important empirical task within the politician research program is systematic ethnographic work designed to describe the normative beliefs and values (vocabularies of motives) that define the standards of accountability in particular decision-making settings (cf. Pepitone, 1976). The emerging body of research on organizational culture represents a step in this direction (Martin, 1982; Martin et al., 1983).

People as approval- and status-seekers. There are many reasons why people seek the approval and respect of those to whom they are accountable, including both symbolic psychological and tangible material rewards and punishments. Theories of impression management and self-esteem maintenance have emphasized symbolic motives (e.g., Baumeister, 1982; Blumer, 1969; Greenwald, 1980; Schlenker, 1980; Stryker & Gottlieb, 1981). Especially important here are:

1. The motivation to protect and enhance one's social image or identity. One of the most influential motivational assumptions in social science is that people seek the approval and respect of others as ends-in-themselves. In the words of the cultural anthropologist Linton (1945, p. 9):

> The need for eliciting favorable responses from others is an almost constant component of personality. Indeed it is not too much to say there is very little organized human behavior which is not directed towards its satisfaction in at least some degree (cf. Hogan, 1982; Parsons, 1951; Schlenker, 1980).

Zetterberg (1957, p. 189) proposed that "The maximization of favorable attitudes from others [is] the counterpart in sociological theory to the maximization of profit in economic theory." A warehouse of findings in experimental social psychology attests to the influentiality of the approval- and status-seeker view of human nature, including work on ingratiation (Jones & Wortman, 1973; Wortman & Linsenmeier, 1977), conformity (Hare, 1976; Paulus, 1980), and strategic attitude shifts (Cialdini, Petty, & Cacioppo, 1981).

2. The motivation to protect and enhance one's self-image. This assumption has an equally venerable status in social and personality psy-

chology (Allport, 1937; Greenwald, 1980; Sherif & Cantril, 1947). From this perspective, people do not seek the approval and respect of others as ends-in-themselves, but rather as means of bolstering their confidence in their own internalized estimates of self-worth on important dimensions of evaluation (e.g., intelligent, conscientious, likable, mature). A substantial literature exists in social psychology on the "ego-defensive" behavioral tactics that people use to disassociate themselves from negative outcomes and to associate themselves with positive outcomes (Greenwald & Ronis, 1978; Schlenker, 1980; Tetlock & Levi, 1982).

3. Social exchange theorists (e.g., Blau, 1964) have emphasized a third source of motivation for maintaining the approval and respect of others: the desire to gain control of desirable material resources (e.g., promotions, office space, budget allocations, authority over staff). Researchers in organizational behavior have tended to be most sensitive to this motivational dimension of human nature: decision-makers in organizational settings can be fruitfully viewed as actors in competition for scarce resources within a rule-governed political contest for power (Pfeffer & Salancik, 1978). Much of what people in organizations do can be understood as tactical maneuvers designed to "legitimize" their claims to scarce resources (Pfeffer, 1981).

Any complete analysis of the decision-maker as politician should take all three of the previously mentioned sources of motivation into account. Unfortunately, we do not have a good understanding of the relative importance of these motives or of the conditions under which one versus another becomes dominant. Attempts to disentangle motives will, moreover, prove frustrating. In most situations, the three motives are closely intertwined; for example, creating favorable impressions on others will not only enhance one's social-image, but also one's self-image (as advocates of the looking-glass self hypothesis would argue—Shrauger & Schoenemann, 1979) and one's material standing in the world (one's social image largely determines one's interpersonal "market value"—Blau, 1964). Conversely, improvements in one's material standing will tend to enhance both one's self- and social-image (as observers of "conspicuous consumption" have long been aware—James, 1910; Veblen, 1899).

Strategies for Coping with Accountability

To summarize, the politician research program rests on two hard core assumptions: the first posits that the accountability of conduct is a universal problem of social life with which people must deal; the second posits that people are generally motivated to maintain the approval and respect of those to whom they are accountable. These hard core postulates direct empirical work in radically different directions from the cognitive research program. The central question becomes: What type of politician is the average person? What judgment and decision-making strategies do people use to cope with demands for accountability from the various constituencies in their lives? What are the basic "types" or "dimensions" of accountability relationships? What are the consequences of these relationships? How do personality and situational variables affect coping responses to accountability?

The politician research program obviously raises many unanswered questions—certainly far more than can be addressed in this chapter. The major point I wish to make in the following sections is that the effects of accountability are likely to be highly variable. There are as many different types of accountability as there are distinct types of relationships among people (Stryker & Gottlieb, 1981). Furthermore, there are good reasons for suspecting that different types of accountability have markedly different effects on judgment and choice behavior. Accountability can be highly oppressive as in groupthink (Janis, 1982) when members of policy-making groups exert great normative pressure on each other to arrive at unanimous recommendations. Accountability can be highly threatening as in situations in which decision-makers feel their jobs and reputations hinge on their ability to justify past actions to superiors (Fox & Straw, 1979). Accountability can even be conducive to complex and self-reflective information processing as in situations in which people know in advance that they will be called upon to explain their stands on controversial issues to unknown others (Tetlock, 1983a). The common theme running through these examples is, of course, the fact that people need to justify their judgments and decisions to others. However, people generate dramatically different strategies for coping with this problem depending on the nature of the accountability relationship (who is accountable to whom and under what ground rules?) as well as cognitive and motivational predispositions of the individual decision-maker (e.g., cognitive style, interpersonal needs, self-esteem, security of position).

In the following discussion, I propose that the cognitive miser image of the information processor provides a useful initial basis for predicting how people cope with accountability predicaments. All other things being equal, people prefer "least effort" solutions: They simply adopt positions likely to gain the favor of those to whom they feel accountable (a coping strategy that I have called the acceptability heuristic). Unfortunately for cognitive misers, the solutions to accountability predicaments are not always straightforward. In some situations, it is not at all obvious what the most acceptable response option is. Demands for accountability in these contexts appear to motivate cognitive work: *Vigilant information processing is necessary to identify the most defensible policy*. In other situations, people have already irrevocably committed themselves to a course of action. Accountability here may motivate people to devote considerable cognitive effort not so much to identifying optimal future courses of action as to developing cogent rationalizations for past courses of action.

The Acceptability Heuristic: The Cognitive Miser in Social Context

The simplest way of coping with accountability is by making decisions that one is reasonably confident will be acceptable to others. This coping strategy is obviously compatible with a view of people as cognitive misers who avoid mental calculations that require sustained attention, effort or computing power. Often the most socially acceptable option is obvious, likely to come to mind quickly and likely to be bolstered by supportive arguments readily available in the environment (especially true in groupthink situations). The acceptability heuristic allows one to avoid much "unnecessary" cognitive work (analyzing the pros and cons of alternative courses of action, interpreting complex, often contradictory, patterns of environmental information, making difficult value trade-offs). All one needs to do is to adopt the salient "acceptable" option.

Evidence from both laboratory and field studies indicates that people frequently do adopt this straightforward tactic. They choose the most clearly defensible course of action open to them. For instance, several experiments on negotiation behavior have found that negotiators who expect to justify bargaining outcomes to the groups they represent have much more difficulty arriving at mutually beneficial compromise agreements than do negotiators not under such pressure (Benton, 1972; Gruder & Rosen, 1971; Klimoski, 1971; Lamm & Kogan, 1970; Pruitt, 1981). The most plausible explanation for these findings is that accountability to constituents (who presumably favor tough negotiation stands) induces concern for appearing strong by refusing to make concessions. People respond by employing competitive bargaining tactics that, while obstacles to resolving conflicts of interest, are quite effective in protecting their images in the eyes of constituents. Experimental work on ingratiation also reveals the willingness of people to tailor their opinions to those of others—especially high status others (Jones & Wortman, 1973; Wortman & Linsenmeier, 1977). People view opinion conformity as a reliable means of gaining approval and respect, and available evidence suggests that they are generally correct. Although limiting conditions exist (one should avoid appearing too sycophantic—Jones, Stires, Shaver, & Harris, 1968), we generally evaluate others more positively to the degree they express attitudes similar to our own. We see similar others as more likable and intelligent than dissimilar others (Byrne, Nelson, & Reeves, 1966) as well as more deserving of promotion (Baskett, 1973).

Adelberg and Batson (1978) conducted an interesting experiment that demonstrated some of the dysfunctional consequences of reliance on the acceptability heuristic in a particular type of organization: social welfare agencies. They hypothesized that accountability would impair effective helping whenever agency resources were inadequate to assist everyone in need and difficult choices were necessary. Accountability would do so by distracting help-givers away from problems they were supposed to be addressing and focusing their attention on the need to justify what they were doing. Accountable help-givers would be more likely to avoid hard-to-justify, but necessary decisions on which applicants for aid (in this case, student loans) would receive assistance. The results supported this prediction. Accountable subjects made a much higher proportion of wasteful decisions (giving ineffectively small amounts of money to large numbers of students).

The acceptability heuristic is not limited to laboratory experiments; it also operates in high-level policy-making settings. The political necessity of defending one's conduct is an important constraint on how policy-makers choose among the options confronting them. As C. Wright Mills (1940) argued:

> Often anticipations of appropriate conduct will control conduct. ("If I did this, what could I say? What would they say?") Decisions may be, wholly or in part, delimited by answers to such queries.

The political scientists Snyder, Bruck, and Sapin (1962) took a similar stand in their pioneering analysis of the foreign policy-making process:

> The decision to perform or not to perform a given act may be taken on the basis of available answers to the question "what will be said?"

Consistent with these positions, historical case studies of important governmental decisions abound with references to policy-makers assessing possible lines of defense (accounts) against critics and opponents (Anderson, 1981; Bennett, 1980; Graber, 1976). For instance, after Egypt nationalized the Suez Canal in 1956, British leaders tried to avoid open collusion with Israel because they thought it could not be justified to their constituents. The British therefore delayed the Franco-British invasion until after the initial Israeli strike into Egypt when they thought (erroneously) that they could assume the role of peacemaker. In Goldman's (1970) words: "The British searched for an acceptable justification. Having found one, actions were modified accordingly." Similarly, Kennedy rejected direct American participation in the 1961 Bay of Pigs invasion because he felt it would be "very awkward" to justify after he had pledged abstinence from such a conflict. This decision meant that air cover for the invasion would be inadequate and would contribute to the failure of the mission. These examples illustrate what Snyder et al. (1962, p. 183) called "the continual interaction between considerations of what to do, and what to say. . . . Statecraft, from this point of view, is the art of combining the desirable and the justifiable."[1]

In a similar vein, Pfeffer (1981) stressed the importance of "justifiability" of policy options in managerial decision-making. He argued that the primary task of managers "is making what is going on in the organization meaningful and sensible to the organizational participants, and furthermore, developing a social consensus and social definition around the activities being undertaken" (p. 21). A critical determinant of managerial success is the ability to convince both internal (within-organization) and external observers that the operations of the organization are consonant with prevailing social values and the larger social system. Management involves more than labeling and making sense of the world—it requires developing social support for the labels and policies that management endorses.

Over time, policy-makers' search for courses of action that can be readily justified to important constituencies may become "scripted" (Abelson, 1981) or ritualized (Starbuck, 1983), thus requiring even less cognitive effort. For instance, Meyer and Rowan (1977) argued that the formal structures of many organizations in postindustrial society reflect the "justificatory myths" of their institutional environments, not the "rational demands" of their work activities as Weber's (1930) classic analysis of bureaucracy suggests. One way in which organizational decision-makers demonstrate to significant others that they are acting on collectively valued purposes in a proper manner is by designing a formal structure for the organization that conforms to the normative expectancies of those significant others. Meyer and Rowan (1977, pp. 349–350) wrote:

> Vocabularies of (organizational) structure which are isomorphic with institutional rules provide prudent, rational, and legitimate accounts. Organizations described in legitimated vocabularies are assumed to be oriented to collectively defined, and often collectively mandated, ends. The myths of personnel services, for example, not only account for the rationality of employment practices but also indicate that personnel services are valuable to an organization. Employees, applicants, managers, trustees, and governmental agencies are predisposed to trust the hiring practices of organizations that follow legitimated procedures—such as equal opportunity programs, or personality testing—and they are more willing to participate in or fund such organizations. On the other hand, organizations that omit environmentally legitimated elements of structure or create unique structures that lack acceptable, legitimated accounts for their activities . . . are more vulnerable to claims that they are negligent,

irrational or unnecessary. Claims of this kind, whether made by internal participants, external constituents, or the government, can cause organizations to incur real costs.

In overview, the acceptability heuristic complements and fleshes out the cognitive miser characterization of the decision-maker. The most salient consideration in many decisions is the justifiability of policy options to others. The cognitive research program tells us that people often use a very small number of items of information in making up their minds; the politician research program tells us that decision-makers' estimates of the probable reactions of those to whom they are accountable will be prominent among the few items of information considered. The cognitive research program appears to focus primarily on process (how people think), the politician research program, primarily on content (what people think). Although this may seem to be a natural division of labor, the distinction is far from airtight. Demands for accountability not only effect *what* people think; demands for accountability also affect *how* people think.

Motivating Cognitive Misers to be Thoughtful

The acceptability heuristic is a cognitively economical and socially adaptive strategy for making decisions in many experimental and real-life contexts. The usefulness of this heuristic is, however, limited to settings in which one can discern relatively quickly the expectations of the constituencies to whom one is accountable. The question arises: How do people cope with accountability in normatively ambiguous situations in which it is not obvious what the most socially acceptable response is?

Available evidence indicates that under these conditions accountability can be a potent inducement to getting people to abandon their cognitively miserly ways. Accountability to others of unknown views has been found in a number of studies to "motivate" people to become more vigilant, complex, and self-critical information processors (Chaiken, 1980; Cvetkovich, 1978; Hagafors & Brehmer, 1983; McAllister, Mitchell, & Beach, 1979; Rozelle & Baxter, 1981; Tetlock, 1983a, 1983b). Below I briefly review the research evidence indicating what accountability to unknown others can lead to:

1. the utilization of more cognitively complex judgment and decision strategies;
2. greater awareness among decision-makers of their own cognitive processes;
3. less theory-driven and more data-driven processing of evidence in forming impressions.

Inducing complex information processing. A study by Tetlock (1983a) provides the most direct evidence that people cope with accountability in normatively ambiguous situations (i.e., when the policy preferences of others are unknown) very differently from the way they cope with accountability in normatively unambiguous situations (i.e., when the policy preferences of others are obvious). He hypothesized that when people know the views of those to whom they are accountable, they rely on the acceptability heuristic and simply shift their views toward those of others in the situation ("strategic attitude shifts"). By contrast, when people do not know the views of the individual to whom they are accountable, they need to think through the issue much more carefully in order to arrive at a defensible position. Accountability to unknown others motivates people to consider arguments and evidence on both sides of issues in order to prepare themselves for a wide variety of possible critical reactions to their views. To test these hypotheses, Tetlock asked experimental subjects to report their positions on controversial policy issues (capital punishment, defense spending, affirmative action) under one of four conditions: expecting the positions they took to be confidential or expecting to justify the positions they took to an individual with liberal, conservative, or unknown views. In addition, he asked subjects to report their thoughts (confidentiality always guaranteed) on each issue *prior to* committing themselves to an attitudinal position. These thought protocols were then subjected to detailed content and structural analysis designed to assess the complexity of subjects' thinking on the issues (How many aspects or dimensions of each issue did they distinguish? Did they interpret issues in dichotomous, good-bad terms or did they recognize positive and negative features of stands on both sides of the issues?).

The data indicated that subjects coped with pressures to justify their opinions on controversial policy issues in two qualitatively distinct ways: strategically shifting their public positions on the issues (thus making the task of justification easier) and thinking about issues in more complex, multidimensional ways (thus preparing themselves for the various arguments that could be raised against their positions). Subjects relied on strategic attitude shifts (the acceptability heuristic) when they felt accountable to an individual with well-defined liberal or conservative views. Not surprisingly, subjects accountable to a liberal expressed more liberal views; subjects accountable to a conservative expressed more conservative views. Accountability to an individual with well-defined views had no impact on the complexity of subjects' thinking on the policy issues. The reverse pattern of findings emerged among subjects who felt accountable to an individual with unknown views. Here accountability had no effect on the liberalism-conservatism of the policy stands taken, but had a pronounced effect on the complexity of subjects' thinking on the policy issues. Subjects displayed much more tolerance for cognitive inconsistency (recognizing good features of rejected policies and bad features of accepted policies) and much more recognition of the need to confront difficult value trade-offs (e.g., the need to deter crime and protect the lives of the innocent, the need to remedy past racial injustices without creating new ones). Subjects accountable to an individual with unknown views appeared to engage in "preemptive self-criticism." They attempted to anticipate the counterarguments that potential critics could raise to their positions. Tetlock proposed that this cognitive reaction could be viewed as an adaptive strategy on the part of decision-makers for protecting both their self-esteem and social images. Expecting to justify one's views to an unknown individual raised the possibility of failure: The other person might have found serious flaws in the positions taken. In order to reduce the likelihood of such an esteem-threatening and embarrassing event, subjects sought to demonstrate their awareness of alternative perspectives on the issues to be discussed. ("You can see I am no fool. I may believe this, but I understand the arguments on the other side.")

Several other studies—in which subjects have felt accountable to an individual with unknown or, at least, difficult-to-guess policy preferences—have reported effects similar to those reported in the Tetlock research. For instance, McAllister, Mitchell and Beach (1979) performed a series of business simulation experiments in which subjects were asked to recommend strategies for solving financial problems facing corporations. McAllister et al. manipulated three independent variables designed to affect subjects' willingness to employ cognitively complex strategies for choosing among courses of action. The decisions subjects had to make were either *significant* or *insignificant* (in terms of potential financial impact on the company) and *reversible* or *irreversible*. In addition, decision-makers either *were* or *were not* personally accountable for the stands they took. As predicted, subjects employed more analytic and complex judgment strategies the more accountable they felt for their decisions and the more important and less reversible they perceived the decisions to be.

Chaiken (1980) reported evidence on the power of accountability to motivate cognitive work in attitude change situations. She performed two experiments to test the hypothesis that subjects who believed they would have to justify their opinions would process persuasive arguments on those topics more "systematically" than subjects who did not expect to justify their opinions. Accountable subjects, she argued, would actively try to comprehend and evaluate the arguments contained in persuasive messages whereas unaccountable subjects would rely on "lazier" strategies of assessing the validity of messages such as source evaluation (Does the speaker appear honest? smart? likable?) The results supported these predictions. Accountable subjects were unaffected by an experimental manipulation of the likableness of the sources of the persuasive messages they read (the messages were on technical topics so that source likableness could not be plausibly construed as informationally relevant). Accountable subjects were, however, strongly affected by an experimental manipulation of the number of arguments contained in the messages. Unaccountable subjects showed the opposite pattern of results. They were strongly influenced by the likableness of the message sources but uninfluenced by the number of arguments contained in the messages. In short, the data pointed to two different methods of dealing with incoming information: one method required no more than superficial, top-of-the-head reactions to the communicator, the other required thoughtful analysis of message content. The social context determined which mode of information processing was activated.

Inducing awareness of the cognitive strategies one uses to make decisions. A number of experimental psychologists have argued that people lack awareness of their own cognitive processes. The cues that people think are important determinants of their judgments are often not the same cues that statistical analyses of experimental data reveal to be important (cf. Nisbett & Wilson, 1977). Although the "awareness issue" is by no means resolved within the cognitive research program (Ericsson & Simon, 1980), I will comment here on the role that social context plays in determining the "degree of awareness" people display into their own cognitive processes.

Cvetkovich (1978) reported two experiments that explored the ability of subjects to report accurately on the strategies they used in making gambling decisions on a "duplex-bet" task that Slovic (1967) developed. The game consisted of 27 gambles. For each gamble, the experimenter presented information on the probability of winning (.2, .6, or .8), the amount of the win ($1, $2, or $4), the probability of losing (.2, .6, or .8) and the amount of the loss ($1, $2, or $4). Since the occurrence of win and loss values was determined independently and no relationships existed between each of the four task dimensions (uncorrelated cue structure), it was possible to win and not lose, both to win and to lose, to lose and not win, and neither to win nor to lose. After subjects completed the 27 gambles, they reported the decision strategy they used. The experimenter asked them to distribute 100 points among the four task dimensions according to how important they thought each was as a determinant of their decisions. Cvetkovich then compared these subjective importance weights to "objective" importance weights derived from multiple regression analysis of each person's betting decisions on each of the four task dimensions across the 27 gambles. The comparison revealed that subjects who felt accountable for their betting decisions reported subjective weights that were significantly closer to the objective weights than subjects who did not feel accountable. These findings suggest that when people are made "self-conscious" via an accountability manipulation, they shift to analytic, effort-demanding cognitive strategies that increase their awareness of the determinants of their decisions.

Hagafors and Brehmer (1983) found compatible results in a "multiple-cue probability learning task." They presented subjects with a medical diagnosis problem in which the task was to predict the level of a disease (the outcome variable) from the amount of two substances in the bodies of the patients (the cue variables). Both cues were linearly related to the outcome and uncorrelated with each other. The researchers manipulated three independent variables: low or high outcome predictability ($R = .60$ vs. $R = .98$), presence or absence of feedback to subjects on the accuracy of their judgments, and presence or absence of accountability. A complex, but interpretable, interaction emerged. Accountable subjects had much more consistent patterns of cue utilization (judgment policies) than unaccountable subjects, but only under conditions of low outcome predictability and no accuracy feedback. These findings were consistent with the authors' hypothesis that accountability would induce people to process information more "analytically" in ambiguous problem environments (environments that are obviously common in daily life). Anticipating the need to offer coherent explanations for the judgments they expressed, accountable subjects paid more careful attention to the rules they used in generating predictions and applied these rules in a more consistent manner.

Inducing responsiveness to evidence. The prevailing view of the person within the cognitive research program is that of a theory-driven information processor who relies heavily on existing knowledge structures in interpreting new information. A good deal of evidence buttresses this conception. Work on belief perseverance and primacy effects in judgment indicates that people are sometimes extremely slow in revising their initial impressions of events, even in the face of information that directly contradicts those initial impressions (e.g., Jones & Goethals, 1971; Nisbett & Ross, 1980).

Belief perseverance is not, however, an immutable law of human information processing. Tetlock (1983b) found that accountability can—under certain conditions—be extremely effective in preventing first impressions from dominating final judgments. He presented subjects with a long list of evidential arguments from a murder trial: half of the arguments cast doubt on the defendant's guilt and half suggested that the defendant was indeed guilty. He also varied the order in which subjects received the evidence: an exonerating/incriminating, an incriminating/exonerating, or a randomly alternating order of presentation. Subjects who did not expect to justify their judgments of the defendant's guilt showed a substantial primacy effect: Early-presented information had a significantly greater impact on subjective probability ratings of guilt than later-presented information. Subjects who expected to justify their judgments of the defendant's guilt before viewing the evidence were, however, immune to the primacy effect: Order of presentation made no difference. Accountability did not, moreover, eliminate the primacy effect by merely affecting the types of judgments subjects were willing to express (e.g., accountability did not turn people into "fence-sitters" who were unwilling to commit themselves to any position). Two lines of evidence argued strongly against such a response bias artifact. First, accountability per se was not sufficient to eliminate the primacy effect. Tetlock found that subjects who realized they were accountable *only after* exposure to the evidence displayed primacy effects comparable in magnitude to those of unaccountable subjects. Only accountability prior to exposure to the evidence destroyed the primacy effect. Second, subjects who realized they had to justify their views prior to exposure to the evidence recalled significantly more case information than subjects who felt unaccountable or accountable only after exposure to the evidence. A response bias interpretation cannot explain these effects on memory. Taken as a whole, the data strongly suggest that preexposure accountability induced people to become more thorough and vigilant information processors—willing to revise initial impressions of the case in response to changing evidence.

Rozelle and Baxter (1981) reported evidence consistent with the position that accountability can encourage data-driven and discourage theory-driven information processing. They noted that previous work on person perception had shown that characteristics of the perceiver are frequently more important determinants of the descriptions offered of stimulus persons than are characteristics of the stimulus persons being judged. Perceivers tend to offer undifferentiated descriptions of stimulus persons (a given perceiver tends to see different stimulus persons as similar to each other) as well as idiosyncratic descriptions of stimulus persons (little overlap exists in the descriptions that different perceivers offer of the same stimulus person). This pattern is exactly what one would expect if people were theory-driven information-processors who rely on their own implicit theories of personality and give little weight to actual properties of the persons being judged (cf. Bourne, 1977).

The earlier work was conducted in settings in which people did not believe their judgments would have important consequences for either themselves or others. Rozelle and Baxter explored the impact of two (conceptually interrelated) social context variables on the person perception process: whether perceivers felt their decisions would be important (i.e., their decisions would influence applicants' admission to graduate school) and whether perceivers believed they would later have to justify their decisions to a faculty review committee. Under conditions of high decision importance and high accountability, they found a reversal of the typical finding of undifferentiated and idiosyncratic descriptions of stimulus persons. These perceptual patterns emerged: (a) differentiated perceiver descriptions of different stimulus persons (low within-judge-overlap of descriptive characteristics assigned to others); (b) substantial agreement among judges in the descriptions offered of the same stimulus person. In brief, accountability appeared to sensitize perceivers to "what was actually out there."

The theoretical significance of the above findings should not be understated. The findings directly support contingency models of judgment and decision-making which challenge the universality of the cognitive miser portrait of how people think (Beach & Mitchell, 1978; Jenkins, 1981; Payne, 1982). Contingency models emphasize the capacity of people to adopt different strategies and styles of information processing in response to changing circumstances. As Beach and Mitchell (1978) stated, people "decide how to decide." In any given situation, people may choose—consciously or unconsciously—from a wide variety of possible strategies for making up their minds—strategies that range from the highly analytic (maximization of expected utility) to the highly intuitive (repeating previous responses, acting on impulse, flipping a coin). Two considerations are of paramount importance in this "meta-decision-making" task: (1) the amount of time and cognitive effort required to use a strategy (which, as cognitive misers, people seek to minimize); (2) the likelihood that the strategy will lead to the identification of an optimal response (which people naturally seek to maximize). From a contingency theory perspective, accountability can increase decision-makers' willingness to employ cognitively demanding strategies in two basic ways: by decreasing the perceived likelihood that less demanding strategies such as the acceptability heuristic will lead to the identification of the optimal response and by increasing the importance of identifying the optimal response. The available evidence suggests that both processes are operating.

The practical implications of the findings should also not be understated. As Weick (1979) noted:

> It is not evident that cognitive organizational theory is best served by yet one more documentation of the phenomenon of simplification. What we need instead is to cultivate sensitivity to thinking practices that complicate rather than simplify the world.

Accountability does—under certain conditions—cultivate sensitivity to complex thinking practices. A promising direction for empirical work is the assessment of the effectiveness of different organizational norms of accountability in promoting complex thought (cf. George, 1980a; Tetlock, 1983c). Alexander George's (1980a) multiple advocacy proposals for the design of organizational systems of accountability are particularly worthy of investigation. The central goal of multiple advocacy is to make "good use" of inevitable intraorganizational conflict by creating a normative framework for *structured, balanced* debate (mutual accountability) among policy advocates drawn from different parts of the organization. One of the crucial ingredients that George specified for the success of multiple adovcacy is the willingness of top leadership to avoid partisan engagement in this debate process (i.e., the views of top leadership—to whom all participants in the debate are ultimately accountable—should be unknown).

The Rationalization Heuristic: The Cognitive Miser on the Defensive

The previous section focused on situations in which the desire to maintain the approval and respect of others encouraged complex, vigilant information processing. In all of these situations, people had no basis for confidently inferring the policy preferences of those to whom they were accountable, thus greatly reducing the usefulness of the low-effort acceptability heuristic. Another critical ingredient was also present. People realized that they would need to explain their conduct to others before they had committed themselves to a course of action. Predecisional accountability—combined with normative ambiguity—promoted what Staw (1980) has termed "prospective rationality." Under these conditions, people devoted substantial cognitive effort to identifying the most defensible response options.

Other combinations of circumstances can trigger very different coping responses. For instance, imagine a situation in which people are accountable not for decisions they have yet to make, but for decisions they have already made. Imagine, moreover, that these decisions have led to questionable or undesirable consequences (lower profits, bad publicity, employee dissatisfaction, etc.,). Under these conditions, the same basic motive—the desire to maintain the approval and respect of those to whom one is accountable—is likely to lead not to "prospective rationality" but rather to "retrospective rationality"—a defensive search for ways of rationalizing past conduct. The primary concern of decision-makers is likely to be with portraying earlier actions in the best possible light (as sensible, rational, moral. . .).

A growing body of research exists in social psychology on the "accounting tactics" people use to extricate themselves from such image-threatening predicaments (Schlenker, 1980, 1982; Scott & Lyman, 1968; Semin & Manstead, 1983; Tedeschi & Reiss, 1981; Tetlock, 1981, in press). These tactics take many forms. The simplest—but often most implausible—defense is that of innocence. Individuals maintain that the image-threatening event did not occur ("I did not make the decision to invest in that firm, X did"). When simple denials of association with the undesirable act do not seem likely to work, however, people turn to more sophisticated lines of defense. The best known of these are justifications and excuses. Justifications are accounting tactics in which individuals accept responsibility for their conduct, but deny that the act in question provides grounds for attributing negative traits or characteristics to them. Examples of justifications abound. People can argue, for example, that the apparently harmful consequences of their actions are really not that harmful (e.g., "We may be losing money now, but things are going to turn around." "Our business practices are no more unethical than those of our competitors.") Unlike justifications, excuses are accounting tactics in which individuals acknowledge that their past decisions were somehow bad, wrong or inappropriate, but try to minimize their responsibility for them. Excuses invoke mitigating circumstances (e.g., "The FBI entrapped our executives into the price-fixing scam"; "Even the best financial analysts could not have foreseen the economic events which produced last year's record losses"). Social psychological research on these accounting tactics is reviewed in Semin and Manstead (1983), Schlenker (1980), Tetlock (in press) and Weary and Arkin (1981).

For our purposes, the key point is that people have invented an impressive array of accounting tactics for minimizing damage to their social images in embarrassing predicaments. A major effect of accountability—especially for poor decisions that people have already made—may simply be to focus people's attention on identifying the best available accounting tactic (a type of retrospective political rationality). Schlenker (1980) has actually developed a formal expectancy-value analysis of this account-selection process. People, he proposed, choose accounting tactics that maximize their "reward-cost ratios" in the situation. Reward-cost ratios are a function of both the desirability of the identity one claims through one's account and the likelihood of the account being accepted (believed) by important constituencies or audiences. For instance, consider a manager called upon to account for the poor sales performance of his district. The most self-flattering accounts are ones that cast no aspersions on his character or competence (e.g., overwhelming foreign competition, deep economic recession). Unfortunately for him, the most self-flattering accounts often lack plausibility or credibility. To protect his social image (not to mention his job), he needs to find the optimal combination of plausibility and self-enhancement in the account he offers. According to Schlenker, the expected value (EV) of any given account can be computed using the following formula:

EV = probability (image claimed via account accepted) × (desirability of claim being accepted) + probability (image claimed via account rejected) × (undesirability of consequences of rejection)

This analysis suggests that people devote considerable cognitive effort to identifying the best possible accounts for themselves in image-threatening situations. This analysis also suggests that the types of accounts people ultimately offer depend on a number of specific features of the social context in which they find themselves. People will offer self-flattering (blame-denying) accounts if they perceive little danger that others will reject these accounts. This tends to be true to the degree: (1) self-flattering accounts are highly plausible (cogent justifications or excuses exist); (2) decision-makers believe that those to whom they are accountable are highly sympathetic. People will become increasingly self-critical to the degree they believe that others will not honor or accept self-flattering accounts (i.e., the opposites of the above two propositions hold true). Schlenker (1980) has reviewed considerable evidence consistent with these hypotheses.

It is tempting to downplay the practical importance of post-decisional accounting tactics. The image-saving maneuvers in which people engage might be dismissed as inconsequential for future policy. The work of Staw suggests that this is not true. Postdecisional accounting goes beyond mere verbal rationalizations. The need to justify policies that have worked out badly can place great pressure on decision-makers to increase their behavioral commitments to these failing policies (a prediction that follows from both cognitive dissonance and impression management theories—Schlenker, 1980; Wicklund & Brehm, 1976).

In a series of business simulation experiments, Staw has clearly documented this point. Pressures to account for poor past decisions can reinforce decision-makers' commitments to these earlier lines of action, increasing the rigidity and inflexibility of the policy-making process. For instance, Staw (1976) experimentally studied the tendency for decision-makers to escalate commitments to a policy following the receipt of disappointing feedback on the policy's effectiveness. One group of business school students (the personally responsible group) was instructed to allocate research and development funds to one of two operating divisions of a company. They were then given the results of their initial decisions (successful or unsuccessful) and asked to make a second allocation decision. Another group of students (the not personally responsible group) received the same information, but did not make the initial allocation decision themselves (this decision had supposedly been made earlier by a financial officer of the firm). The results revealed a significant interaction between the success-failure and personal responsibility manipulations. Subjects allocated the most money to the failing division of the company when they felt personally responsible for having directed funds to that division in the initial allocation decision. These findings are consistent with the hypothesis that subjects sought to justify an ineffective course of action by escalating their commitment to it.

Staw's earlier work—inspired by cognitive dissonance theory—treated justification as an intra-individual process (people are concerned with protecting their self-images as competent and rational beings). A later simulation experiment by Fox and Staw (1979) explicitly focused on the impact of social-political pressures for accountability on the decision process. In this simulation, subjects were placed in an administrative situation in which they possessed high or low job security and in which they believed that the Board of Directors (to whom they were accountable) was receptive or unreceptive to the policies they had been pursuing. Fox and Staw hypothesized that decision-makers would feel the greatest need to engage in justificatory escalation of their commitment to a failing policy when decision-makers were most vulnerable (low job security and a skeptical Board of Directors). The results supported these hypotheses. Decision-makers who were worried about keeping their jobs and fending off high-level critics within the organization were most likely to escalate their commitment to their initial decision and most inflexible in their defenses of the positions they took.

There are reasons to suppose, then, that post-decisional accountability—far from encouraging complex, self-critical thinking practices—actually exacerbates many of the judgmental biases and defects of the cognitive miser. Demands for accountability may sometimes motivate people to "bolster" previous decisions, to be overconfident in the correctness of those decisions, to "over-assimilate" new evidence, and to deny difficult value trade-offs, particularly when the trade-offs require acknowledging flaws in past decisions and judgments (cf. Festinger, 1964; Kiesler, 1971).

Hybrid Responses to Accountability

The discussion up to this point has identified a variety of ways in which people cope with accountability, including mindless endorsement of organizational rituals, myths, and mind-sets, thoughtful and vigilant analysis of available evidence and response options, and the rigid defense of previously chosen courses of action. The antecedent conditions hypothesized to activate each of these coping strategies are not however likely to appear in pure form, but rather in varying degrees and combinations in any given situation. The coping strategies are thus not as mutually exclusive as presented here. In many situations the views of those to whom one is accountable may be neither perfectly obvious not completely unknown. We may have suspicions (held with varying degrees of confidence) about what others want to hear. We may also be accountable not to one but to many individuals whose views may be either harmonious or in conflict. These forms of accountability will probably trigger multiple coping responses, including both a search for a "least common denominator" acceptable policy and vigilant information processing to anticipate possible objections to that policy. In other situations, we may be called upon to account both for actions we have already performed and for decisions we have yet to make. The views of those to whom we are accountable may be only partly known. Again, multiple coping responses will probably be activated: for instance, a search for a policy acceptable to key constituencies in conjunction with vigilant information processing and the development of rationalizations for earlier decisions that render those decisions consistent with the new policy.

We should also not fall into the trap of only emphasizing situational determinants of how people cope with accountability. Cognitive stylistic and motivational differences among decision-makers may influence responses to accountability. Personality variables such as social anxiety, public self-consciousness and need for approval are likely predictors of how motivated people will be to gain the approval and respect of those to whom they are accountable (cf. Buss, 1980). Cognitive style variables such as dogmatism, integrative complexity and need for cognition are likely predictors of coping response "thresholds" (e.g., of when decision-makers engage in flexible, self-critical information processing as opposed to rigid bolstering of preferred options). A comprehensive theoretical analysis of how people deal with accountability will undoubtedly have to incorporate individual difference as well as situational and contextual variables.

CONCLUDING THOUGHTS

The major theme of this chapter can be stated simply: experimental cognitive research on judgment and decision-making has adopted a misleadingly narrow focus on its subject matter and needs to be broadened to take into consideration the impact of social and organizational context. Enormous room exists for an expansion of theoretical and empirical work on the role of contextual variables—in particular, accountability—in shaping what and how people think. People are, in a fundamental sense, politicians who need to achieve and maintain the good will of the constituencies to whom they are accountable. The strategies people develop for coping with this ubiquitous problem of social existence merit much more systematic attention than has thus far been accorded them.

The politician research program proposed here does not map neatly into any of the traditional levels of analysis: the individual, the small group of the organizational level. The unit of study is the *individual in relation to the social and organizational systems to which he or she belongs*. The program as such is an eclectic interdisciplinary creation. It possesses the conceptual flexibility to incorporate insights drawn from research on basic cognitive processes, interpersonal behavior in small groups and organizational structure and functioning. The program borrows, qualifies, and elaborates upon the cognitive miser image of the thinker that prevails in experimental cognitive/social psychology. The program adopts the approval- and status-seeker image of human nature that has been so influential in role theory, symbolic interactionism and impression management theory. The program draws on sociological and anthropological theory on the necessary conditions for social order in positing accountability to be a universal feature of natural decision environments. Taken together, these disparate conceptual themes define a distinctive approach to the study of judgment and choice.

The politician research program is also not tightly linked to any particular empirical methodology (in contrast to the cognitive research program, which is closely tied to laboratory experimentation). The theoretical eclecticism of the program demands a corresponding commitment to methodological eclecticism in research. Controlled laboratory experimentation can play a key role by clarifying situational determinants of the strategies people adopt for coping with accountability. Investigators can isolate the effects of independent variables (e.g., pre- versus post-decisional accountability, knowledge of the views of those to whom one is accountable), systematically assess interactions between independent variables, and test detailed models of the processes mediating relationships between independent and dependent variables. But laboratory experimentation by itself is inadequate. Other methodologies are equally crucial. Self-report personality questionnaires and interviews are needed to assess individual differences in propensities to adopt coping strategies and the possible interactive effects of personality and situational variables. Field experiments are needed to assess the generality and robustness of laboratory findings as well as the effects of normative interventions such as multiple advocacy on organizational decision processes. Comparative (cross-sectional and historical) ethnographic studies of organizational culture are needed to document and organize the diverse forms that "accountability relationships" take and the styles of decision-making associated with these relationships. To state an often-violated dictum, one's choice of methodology should be tailored to the theoretical problem at hand. The politician research program poses problems that cross many disciplinary boundaries and that require a plurality of methodologies.

ACKNOWLEDGMENTS

I appreciate the helpful comments of Barry Staw, Larry Cummings and Sharon MacLane on an earlier version of the chapter. The writing of this chapter was facilitated by NIMH Grant R03 MH35907. Correspondence concerning this chapter should be sent to Philip E. Tetlock, Department of Psychology, University of California, Berkeley CA 94720.

NOTES

1. Practitioners of foreign policy echo this theme. Henry Kissinger states of American foreign policy: "The acid test of a policy is its ability to obtain domestic support. This has two aspects: the problem of legitimizing a policy within the governmental apparatus . . . and that of harmonizing it with the national experience" (quoted in George, 1980b).

REFERENCES

Abelson, R. P. Psychological status of the script concept. *American Psychologist*, 1981, *36*, 715–729.

Abelson, R. P., & Levi, A. Decision-making and decision theory. In E. Aronson & G. Lindzey (Eds.), *Handbook of social psychology* (3rd Ed.). Reading, MA: Addison-Wesley, in press.

Adelberg, S. & Batson, C. D. Accountability and helping: When needs exceed resources. *Journal of Personality and Social Psychology*, 1978, *36*, 343–350.

Allison, G. T. *Essence of decision*. Boston: Little, Brown, 1971.

Allport, G. W. *Personality: A psychological interpretation*. NY: Holt, 1937.

Anderson, P. A. Justifications and precedents as constraints in foreign policy decision-making. *American Journal of Political Science*, 1981, *25*, 738–761.

Aronson, E., & Carlsmith, J. M. Experimentation in social psychology. In E. Aronson & G. Lindzey (Eds.), *Handbook of social psychology* (Vol. 2; 2nd Ed.). Reading, MA: Addison-Wesley, 1969.

Atkinson, R. C., & Shiffrin, R. M. Human memory: A proposed system and its control processes. In K. W. Spence & J. T. Spence (Eds.), *The psychology of learning and motivation: Advances in theory and research* (Vol. 2). New York: Academic Press, 1968.

Bales, R. F. *Personality and interpersonal behavior*. NY: Holt, Reinhart & Winston, 1970.

Bandura, A. Self-efficacy: Toward a unifying theory of behavioral change. *Psychological Review*, 1977, *84*, 191–215.

Baskett, G. D. Interview decisions as determined by competency and attitude similarity. *Journal of Applied Psychology*, 1973, *57*, 343–345.

Baumeister, R. F. A self-presentational view of social phenomena. *Psychological Bulletin*, 1982, *91*, 3–26.

Beach, L. R. & Mitchell, T. R. A contingency model for the selection of decision strategies. *Academy of Management Review*, 1978, *3*, 439–448.

Bennett, W. L. The paradox in public discourse: A framework for the analysis of political accounts. *Journal of Politics*, 1980, *42*, 792–817.

Benton, A. A. Accountability and negotiations between group representatives. *Proceedings of the 80th annual meeting of the American Psychological Association*, 1972, *7*, 227–228.

Beyer, J. M. Ideologies, values, and decision making in organizations. In P. C. Nystrom and W. H. Starbuck (Eds.), *Handbook of organizational design*. Oxford: Oxford University Press, 1981.

Blau, P. *Exchange and power in social life*. NY: Wiley, 1964.

Blumer, H. *Symbolic interactionism: Perspective and method*. Englewood Cliffs, NJ: Prentice-Hall, 1969.

Borgida, E., & Howard-Pitney, B. Personal involvement and the robustness of perceptual salience effects. *Journal of Personality and Social Psychology*, 1983, *45*, 560–570.

Bourne, E. Can we describe an individual's personality? Agreement on stereotype versus individual attributes. *Journal of Personality and Social Psychology*, 1977, *35*, 863–872.

Bronfenbrenner, U. Toward an experimental ecology of human development. *American Psychologist*, 1977, *80*, 307–336.

Brunswik, E. *Perception and the representative design of psychological experiments*. Berkeley, CA: University of California Press, 1956.

Buss, A. H. *Self-consciousness and social anxiety*. San Francisco: Freeman, 1980.

Byrne, D., Nelson, D., & Reeves, K. Effects of consensual validation and invalidation on attraction as a function of verifiability. *Journal of Experimental Social Psychology*, 1966, *2*, 98–107.

Carver, C. S. A cybernetic model of self-attention processes. *Journal of Personality and Social Psychology*, 1979, *37*, 1251–1281.

Chaiken, S. Heuristic versus systematic information processing and the use of source versus message cues in persuasion. *Journal of Personality and Social Psychology*, 1980, *39*, 752–766.

Chapman, L. J. & Chapman, J. P. Illusory correlation as an obstacle to the use of valid diagnostic signs. *Psychological Bulletin*, 1969, *74*, 271–280.

Cialdini, R. B., Petty, R. E., & Cacioppo, J. T. Attitude and attitude change. *Annual Review of Psychology*, 1981, *32*, 357–404.

Cvetkovich, G. Cognitive accommodation, language, and social responsibility. *Social Psychology*, 1978, *41*, 149–155.

Deutsch, M. & Krauss, R. *Theories in social psychology*. New York: Basic Books, Ebbesen, E. B. & Konecni, V. J. On the external validity of decision-making research: What do we know about decisions in the real world? In T. Wallston (Ed.), *Cognitive processes in choice and behavior*. Hillsdale, NJ: Erlbaum, 1980.

Einhorn, H. & Hogarth, R. M. Behavioral decision theory. *Annual Review of Psychology*, 1981, *31*, 53–88.

Ericsson, K. A., & Simon, H. A. Verbal reports as data. *Psychological Review*, 1980, *87*, 169–176.

Fauconnet, P. *La responsibilite*, (2nd ed.) Paris: Alcan, 1928.

Festinger, L. (Ed.), *Conflict, decision, and dissonance*. Stanford, CA: Stanford University Press, 1964.

Feyerabend, P. K. How to be a good empiricist—A plea for tolerance in matters epistemological. In B. A. Brody (Ed.), *Readings in the philosophy of science*. Englewood Cliffs, NJ: Prentice-Hall, 1970.

Fox, F. & Staw, B. M. The trapped administrator: The effects of job insecurity and policy resistance upon commitment to a course of action. *Administrative Science Quarterly*, 1979, *24*, 449–471.

George, A. L. *Presidential decision-making in foreign policy: The effective use of information and advice.* Boulder, CO: Westview Press, 1980. (a)

George, A. L. Domestic constraints on regime change in U.S. foreign policy: The need for policy legitimacy. In O. R. Holsti, R. M. Siverson, & A. L. George (Eds.), *Change in the international system.* Boulder, CO: Westview Press, 1980. (b)

Gergen, K. J. *The concept of self.* New York: Holt, Rinehart, and Winston, 1971.

Gibson, J. J. *The senses considered as perceptual systems.* Boston: Houghton-Mifflin, 1966.

Goldmann, K. *International norms and war between states.* Stockholm: Laromedsforlagen, 1971.

Graber, D. *Verbal behavior and politics.* Urbana, IL: University of Illinois Press, 1976.

Greenwald, A. G. The totalitarian ego: Fabrication and revision of personal history. *American Psychologist*, 1980, *35*, 603–618.

Greenwald, A. G. & Ronis, D. L. Twenty years of cognitive dissonance: Case study of the evolution of a theory. *Psychological Review*, 1978, *85*, 53–57.

Gruder, C. L. & Rosen, N. Effects of intragroup relations on intergroup bargaining. *International Journal of Group Tensions*, 1971, *1*, 301–317.

Hagafors, R. & Brehmer, B. Does having to justify one's decisions change the nature of the judgment process? *Organizational Behavior and Human Performance*, 1983, *31*, 223–232.

Haberstroh, C. J. & Gerwin, D. Climate factors and the decision process. *General Systems*, 1972, *17*, 129–141.

Hare, A. P. *Handbook of small group research* (2nd ed.). NY: Free Press, 1976.

Hastie, R. Social inference. *Annual review of psychology*, 1983, *34*, 161–188.

Heider, F. Social perception and phenomenal causality. *Psychological Review*, 1944, *51*, 358–374.

Hogan, R. A socioanalytic theory of personality. In M. M. Page (Ed.), *Nebraska symposium on motivation.* Lincoln, NE: University of Nebraska Press, 1982.

Hogarth, R. M. Why bother with experiments? *Journal of Accounting Research*, in press.

Holsti, O. R. & George, A. L. The effects of stress on the performance of foreign policymakers. In C. P. Cotter (Ed.), *Political science annual* (Vol. 6). Indianapolis, IN: Bobbs-Merrill, 1975.

James, W. *Psychology: The briefer course.* NY: Henry Holt and Co., 1910.

Janis, I. L. *Groupthink.* Boston, MA: Houghton-Mifflin (2nd Ed.), 1982.

Jenkins, J. Can we have a fruitful cognitive psychology? In J. H. Flowers (Ed.), *Nebraska symposium on motivation.* Lincoln, Nebraska: University of Nebraska Press, 1981.

Jones, E. E., & Goethals, G. Order effects in impression formation. In E. E. Jones et al. (Eds.), *Attribution: Perceiving the causes of behavior.* Morristown, NJ: General Learning Press, 1971.

Jones, E. E., Stires, L. K., Shaver, K. G., & Harris, V. A. Evaluation of an ingratiator by target persons and bystanders. *Journal of Personality*, 1968, *36*, 385–400.

Jones, E. E. & Wortman, C. *Ingratiation: An attributional approach.* Morristown, NJ: General Learning Press, 1973.

Kahneman, D. & Tversky, A. Prospect theory: An analysis of decision under risk. *Econometrica*, 1979, *47*, 263–291.

Kahneman, D., Tversky, A., & Slovic, P. *Judgment under uncertainty.* Cambridge: Cambridge University Press, 1982.

Katz, D. & Kahn, R. L. *The social psychology of organizations* (2nd ed.) New York: Wiley, 1978.

Kelley, H. H., & Michela, J. Attribution theory and research. *Annual review of psychology*, 1979, *31*, 457–501.

Kendler, H. H. *Psychology: A science in conflict.* NY: Oxford University Press, 1981.

Kiesler, C. A. *The psychology of commitment*. NY: Academic Press, 1971.

Klimoski, R. J. The effects of intragroup forces on intergroup conflict resolution. *Organizational Behavior and Human Performance*, 1971, *8*. 363–383.

Kuhn, T. *The structure of scientific revolutions*. Princeton, NJ: Princeton University Press, 1970.

Lakatos, I. Falsification and the methodology of scientific research programs. In I. Lakatos & A. Musgrave (Eds.), *Criticism and the growth of knowledge*. Cambridge, MA: Cambridge University Press, 1970.

Lamm, H. & Kogan, N. Risk-taking in the context of inter-group negotiation. *Journal of Experimental Social Psychology*, 1970, *6*, 351–363.

Lindblom, C. E. The science of "muddling through." *Public Administration Review*, 1959, *19*, 79–88.

Linton, R. *The cultural background of personality*. NY: Appleton-Century Co., 1945.

March, J. & Simon, H. *Organizations*. New York: Wiley, 1958.

Martin, J. Stories and scripts in organizational settings. In A. Hastorf & A. Isen (Eds.), *Cognitive social psychology*. New York: Elsevier-Holland, 1982.

Martin, J., Feldman, M., Hatch, M. J., & Sitkin, S. The uniqueness paradox in organizational stories. *Administrative Science Quarterly*, 1983, *28*, 438–453.

McAllister, P. W., Mitchell, T. R., & Beach, L. R. The contingency model for the selection of decision strategies: An empirical test of the effects of significance, accountability, and reversibility. *Organizational Behavior and Human Performance*, 1979, *24*, 228–244.

McGuire, W. J. Attitudes and attitude change. In G. Lindzey & E. Aronson (Eds.), *Handbook of social psychology* (Vol. 3, 3rd ed.) Reading, MA: Addison-Wesley, in press.

Meyer, J. W. & Rowan, B. Institutionalized organizations: Formal structure as myth and ceremony. *American Journal of Sociology*, 1977, *83*, 340–363.

Mills, C. W. Situated identities and vocabularies of motives. *American Sociological Review*, 1940, *5*, 904–913.

Moscovici, S. Toward a theory of conversion behavior. In L. Berkowitz (Ed.), *Advances in experimental social psychology* (Volume 13). New York: Academic Press, 1980.

Neisser, U. *Cognition and reality*. San Francisco: Freeman, 1976.

Nisbett, R. E. & Ross, L. *Human inference: Strategies and shortcomings of social judgment*. New York: Appleton-Century-Crofts, 1980.

Nisbett, R. E. & Wilson, T. Telling more than we can know: Verbal reports on mental processes. *Psychological Review*, 1977, *84*, 231–259.

O'Reilly, C. & Anderson, J. Organizational communication and decision-making: The impact of contextual factors on information acquisition and use in laboratory and field settings. *Management Science*, 1982.

Parsons, T. *The social system*. New York: The Free Press, 1951.

Paulus, P. B. *Psychology of group influence*. Hillsdale, NJ: Erlbaum, 1980.

Payne, J. Contingent decision behavior. *Psychological Bulletin*, 1982, *92*, 382–402.

Pepitone, A. Toward a normative and biocultural social psychology. *Journal of Personality and Social Psychology*, 1976, *34*, 641–653.

Pfeffer, J. Management as symbolic action: The creation and maintenance of organizational paradigms. In L. Cummings & B. M. Staw (Eds.), *Research in organizational behavior* (Volume 3). Greenwich, CT: JAI Press, 1981.

Pfeffer, J. & Salancik, G. R. *The external control of organizations: A resource dependence perspective*. New York: Harper and Row, 1978.

Pruitt, D. *Negotiation behavior*. NY: Academic Press, 1981.

Rapoport, A. *Fights, games, and debates*. Ann Arbor, MI: University of Michgan Press, 1964.

Royce, J. R. Psychology is multi-methodological, variate, epistemic, world-view, systemic, paradigmatic, theoretic and disciplinary. In W. J. Arnold (Ed.), *Nebraska symposium on motivation*. Lincoln, NE: University of Nebraska Press, 1976.

Rozelle, R. M. & Baxter, J. C. Influence of role pressures on the perceiver: Judgments of videotaped interviews varying judge accountability and responsibility. *Journal of Applied Psychology*, 1981, *66*, 437–441.

Russell, B. *A history of western philosophy*. NY: Simon & Shuster, 1945.

Sampson, E. E. Cognitive psychology as ideology. *American Psychologist*, 1981, *36*, 730–743.

Schlenker, B. R. *Impression management: The self-concept, social identity, and interpersonal relations*. Belmont, CA: Brooks-Cole, 1980.

Schlenker, B. R. Translating actions into attitudes: An identity-analytic approach to the explanation of social conduct. In L. Berkowitz (Ed.), *Advances in experimental social psychology* (Vol. 15). NY: Academic Press, 1982.

Schneider, W., & Shiffrin, R. M. Controlled and automatic human information processing: I. Detection, search and attention. *Psychological Review*, 1977, *84*, 1–66.

Scott, M., & Lyman, S. Accounts. *American Sociological Review*, 1968, *33*, 46–62.

Semin, G. R., & Manstead, A. S. R. *The accountability of conduct: A social psychological analysis*. London: Academic Press, 1983.

Shaw, M. E. *Group dynamics: The psychology of small group behavior* (2nd ed.). NY: McGraw-Hill, 1980.

Shaw, M. & Costanzo, P. *Theories of social psychology* (2nd ed.). NY: McGraw-Hill, 1982.

Shaw, R., & Bransford, J. D. *Perceiving, acting, and knowing: Toward an ecological psychology*. Hillsdale, NJ: Erlbaum, 1977.

Sherif, M., & Cantril, H. *The psychology of ego-involvements*. NY: Wiley, 1947.

Shotter, J. Vico, moral worlds, accountability, and personhood. In P. Heelas & A. Lock (Eds.), *Indigenous psychologies: The anthropology of the self*. London: Academic Press, 1981.

Shrauger, J. S., & Schoeneman, T. J. Symbolic interactionist view of self-concept: Through the looking glass darkly. *Psychological Bulletin*, 1979, *86*, 549–573.

Slovic, P. The relative influence of probabilities and pay-offs upon risk of a gamble. *Psychonomic Science*, 1967, *9*, 223–224.

Slovic, P., Fischhoff, B., & Lichtenstein, S. Behavioral decision theory. *Annual review of psychology*, 1977, *28*, 1–39.

Snyder, R. C., Bruck, H. W., & Sapin, B. (Eds.), *Foreign policy decision-making*. NY: Free Press, 1962.

Starbuck, W. H. Organizations as action generators. *American Sociological Review*, 1983, *48*, 91–102.

Staw, B. M. Knee-deep in the big muddy: A study of escalating commitment to a chosen course of action. *Organizational Behavior and Human Performance*, 1976, *16*, 27–44.

Staw, B. M. Rationality and justification in organizational life. In B. M. Staw and L. Cummings (Eds.), *Research in organizational behavior* (Vol. 2). Greenwich,CT: JAI Press, 1980.

Staw, B. M., Sandelands, L. E., & Dutton, J. E. Threat-rigidity effects in organizational behavior: A multilevel analysis. *Administrative Science Quarterly*, 1981, *26*, 501–524.

Stryker, S., & Gottlieb, A. Attribution theory and symbolic interactionism: A comparison. In J. H. Harvey, W. Ickes, & R. F. Kidd (Eds.), *New directions in attribution theory* (Vol. 3). Hillsdale, NJ: Erlbaum, 1981.

Suls, J. *Psychological perspectives on the self* (Vol. 1). Hillsdale, NJ: Erlbaum, 1980.

Svenson, O. Process descriptions of decision making. *Organizational Behavior and Human Performance*, 1979, *23*, 86–112.

Taylor, S. E. The interface of cognitive and social psychology. In J. H. Harvey (Ed.), *Cognition, social behavior, and the environment*. Hillsdale, NJ: Erlbaum, 1980.

Taylor, S. E., & Fiske, S. T. Salience, attention, and attribution: Top of the head phenomena. In L. Berkowitz (Ed.), *Advances in experimental social psychology* (Vol. 11). NY: Academic Press, 1978.

Tedeschi, J. T., & Reiss, M. Predicaments and verbal tactics of impression management. In C. Antaki (Ed.), *Ordinary language explanations of social behavior*. London: Academic Press, 1981.

Tetlock, P. E. The influence of self-presentation goals on attributional reports. *Social Psychology Quarterly*, 1981, *41*, 300–311.

Tetlock, P. E. Accountability and the complexity of thought. *Journal of Personality and Social Psychology*, 1983, *45*, 74–83. (a)

Tetlock, P. E. Accountability and the perseverance of first impressions. *Social Psychology Quarterly*, 1983, *46*, 285–292. (b)

Tetlock, P. E. Policy-makers' images of international conflict. *Journal of Social Issues*, 1983, *39*, 67–86.

Tetlock, P. E. Toward an intuitive politician model of attribution processes. In B. R. Schlenker (Ed.), *The self in social life*. NY: McGraw-Hill, in press.

Tetlock, P. E., & Levi, A. Attribution bias: On the inconclusiveness of the cognition-motivation debate. *Journal of Experimental Social Psychology*, 1982, *18*, 68–88.

Veblen, T. *The theory of the leisure class*. NY: MacMillan, 1899.

Weary, G., & Arkin, R. M. Attributional self-presentation. In J. H. Harvey, W. Ickes, & R. F. Kidd (Eds.), *New directions in attribution research* (Vol. 3). Hillsdale, NJ: Erblaum, 1981.

Weber, M. *The Protestant's ethic and the spirit of capitalism*. NY: Scribner's, 1930.

Weick, K. E. Cognitive processes in organizations. In B. M. Staw (Ed.), *Research in organizational behavior*. Greenwich, CT: JAI Press, 1979.

Wicklund, R. A. Objective self-awareness. In P. B. Paulus (Ed.), *Psychology of group influence*. Hillsdale, NJ: Erlbaum, 1980.

Wicklund, R. A., & Brehm, J. W. *Perspectives on cognitive dissonance*. Hillsdale, NJ: Erlbaum, 1976.

Wortman, C. B., & Linsenmeier, J.A. W. Interpersonal attraction and techniques of ingratiation in organizational settings. In B. M. Staw & G. Salancik (Eds.), *New directions in organizational behavior*. Chicago, IL: St. Clair's Press, 1977.

Zetterberg, H. L. Compliant actions. *Acta Sociologica*, 1957, *2*, 188–192.

AN ATTRIBUTIONAL MODEL OF LEADERSHIP AND THE POOR PERFORMING SUBORDINATE: DEVELOPMENT AND VALIDATION

Terence R. Mitchell, Stephen G. Green and Robert E. Wood

ABSTRACT

A theory is presented that attempts to understand how leaders respond to poor-performing subordinates. It is suggested that the leader first attempts to diagnose the cause of the poor performance. This diagnosis takes the form of an attribution. The second stage involves the choice of a response. The attribution (perceived cause) combines with other factors such as norms and organizational policies and results in a response by the leader. A review of the different variables influencing both the diagnosis phase and response phase is presented.

The second part of the paper reviews the empirical work that we have completed testing the model. This research covers both phases and has been conducted in laboratory and field settings. A summary of the findings is presented as well as a discussion of the practical and theoretical implications of the findings. The paper concludes with an analysis of how the model fits into the current body of literature on leadership theory and attribution theory.

One of the most time-consuming and emotionally trying tasks of a supervisor or manager is dealing with subordinates who are performing poorly. Few of us like being punitive or the bearer of critical or negative feedback. Yet, the supervisor's role demands that such problems be dealt with and that his or her response be effective. The leader is responsible for the performance of his or her subordinates and poor performance cannot be tolerated.

While the comments above highlight the practical nature of this problem, unfortunately there has been very little empirical research on this topic. While a considerable amount has been written on the topic of performance appraisal in general, the focus of this literature is on formal evaluations summarizing performance over a period of time. There is a distinct emphasis on the appraisal instrument used and the methodological treatment of the observations.

The purpose of the present paper is to take a different approach. We wish to examine (1) what constitutes poor performance, (2) the extent to which supervisors or managers try to diagnose the causes of the poor performance, (3) the nature of that diagnosis, (4) what they do about it, and (5) the effectiveness of their response. The literature that we will draw on comes from many sources. For example, some of Miner's work (Miner, 1973; Miner and Brewer, 1976) has been helpful for the definitional task, while attribution theory (Kelley, 1967) has addressed many of the diagnostic issues. In the following sections we will review this background research, present an attributional model of how leaders deal with poor performing subordinates,[1] report on some data that tests the model, and discuss the implications of the findings.

THE FORMATION OF LEADER ATTRIBUTIONS

The attributional perspective on leader-member interactions argues that one major aspect of leadership is information processing. The leader "collects" information about a subordinate's behavior and then forms causal attributions. That is, the leader tries to figure out what caused the behavior, and based upon that information, a response to the poor performance is selected. Thus, attributions are seen as mediating the leader's responses to the stimulus behavior of the subordinate. A rough description of this view of leader-member interactions could be depicted by a two-step process: Subordinate Behavior $\xrightarrow{1}$ Leader Attributions $\xrightarrow{2}$ Leader Behavior (Green and Mitchell, 1979). In the following sections, we will explore step 1 by reviewing the work of Kelley (1967) concerning the processes by which attributions come to be formed. Also, we will examine some variations in the basic information processing model Kelley proposes. Finally, we will review some of the literature which has explored the relationship between attributions and subsequent behavior of the leader (step 2).

Diagnostic Procedures: Generation of Attributions

There are a great variety of information cues a leader might attend to and process in forming attributions about poor performance. The theorizing of Kelley (1967, 1972a, 1973) suggests that there are three primary informational dimensions which a leader might use. Those dimensions are what he terms distinctiveness, consistency, and consensus. For any particular subordinate behavior, the leader tries to determine if the behavior was *distinctive* in response to a particular entity (task), i.e., did the behavior occur on this task but not on other tasks. Similarly, the leader uses information concerning the extent to which the member has behaved this way in other situations or contexts or at other times. That is, how consistent is this action with other actions (*consistency*)? Finally, the leader estimates the extent to which other members or subordinates also behave the same way; is the behavior unique to this particular member (*low consensus*) or common to many members (*high consensus*)?

In processing this information, the leader would be expected to apply a naive covariation analysis to the three sources of information in order to determine if causality for the behavior should be attributed to the subordinate (a person attribution), to some specific causative agent in the situation (an entity attribution), or to some unique interaction of causative factors surrounding that particular event (a context attribution). Kelley (1967, 1972a, 1973) typically represents this process as a three-dimensional cube where the sides represent persons, entities, and contexts (see Kelley, 1973, for a more complete discussion).

Perhaps an example would clarify the attributional model proposed. Suppose you are a physician, and you have asked a nurse to administer some medication to one of your patients. You check back later in the day, and you find that the medication was not given. Upon further discussions with the nurse, the supervisor, and other involved parties, you discover that (1) this nurse has failed to administer the proper medication on other occasions (low distinctiveness), and (2) this nurse has had difficulty on other tasks such as charting or patient care (high consistency), and (3) none of the other nurses have failed to carry out a physician's order in the last three months (low consensus). The nurse has performed poorly on this task before, he or she has performed poorly on other tasks, and no one else seems to have this difficulty. In this case, context or entity attributions are unlikely. The physician will most probably make a person attribution—the cause of the poor performance was some characteristic or trait of that particular nurse (e.g., lack of effort or ability).

Although Kelley's covariation model represents the basic information processing which a leader might use in forming attributions, it is not likely that leaders go through that process every time they form an attribution. They may lack both the time and the motivation to make the multiple observations which are required (Kelley, 1973). Instead, leaders may employ what amounts to an information-processing shortcut—causal schemata. A causal schema is a simplified set of rules to judge cause and effect, a conception of the way two or more causal factors interact in relation to a particular effect (Kelley, 1972b). These schemata may be derived from experience or from cultural norms about the causal structure of the world (Kelley, 1972b).

One causal schema which is particularly pertinent to the leader-member interaction describes causal explanations for success and failure at achievement-related tasks (Weiner, Frieze, Kukla, Reed, Nest, and Rosenbaum, 1972). Weiner *et al.* (1972), propose that individuals utilize four main agents for explaining and predicting outcomes of achievement-related tasks. The four causal elements are ability, effort, task difficulty, and luck, and are seen as representing two major dimensions: stability and locus of control (see Table 1). Two of the factors, ability and effort, represent an internal locus of control. The person is seen as being responsible for the action, and in Kelley's terms a person attribution is likely. Task difficulty and luck are externally controlled and would correspond more closely with Kelley's context and entity attributions. Recently, however, Weiner and his associates (1974) have reported problems with their original categories. The classification of ability as stable and effort as unstable is not so clear. For example, lack of effort may be unstable (i.e., due to fatigue); or it may be construed as a stable property such as laziness. In response to this ambiguity, Rosenbaum (1972) has proposed a third dimension in Weiner's original categorization, an intentionality dimension. Within his new classification scheme, Rosenbaum allows for both ability and effort to vary along the stability dimension. Also Frieze (1976) used open-ended questions to ascertain people's naturally generated causes for success and failure. She suggests that while Weiner's categories accounted for most of the attributions that two additional factors, mood and other people, were also important. It should

Table 1. Classification Scheme for the Perceived Determinants of Achievement Behavior

	Locus of Control	
Stability	*Internal*	*External*
Stable	Ability	Task Difficulty
Unstable	Effort	Luck

therefore be noted that, while we will focus on Weiner's four categories in our later research, the situation is still relatively unclear about the exhaustiveness and completeness of this system.

Both schemata suggest that leaders will use a fairly simple system of categorization to diagnose the causes of poor performance and that some fairly fundamental judgments regarding the subordinate will be made. Does the subordinate have sufficient ability? Is the subordinate's performance due to lack of motivation? What sort of tasks is this subordinate capable of handling? These questions also point out the significance Weiner *et al.* (1972) and Rosenbaum's (1971) schemata hold for the understanding of leader-member interactions. A member whose successes are seen as due to ability and effort could be expected to have a very different relationship or exchange with the leader (Jacobs, 1971; Dansereau, Graen, and Haga, 1975; Graen, 1976) than a member whose successes were attributed to luck or an easy task.

Variations in the Information Processing Model

There are a great many patterns of information possible, and not all of them lead to clear attributional interpretations (Kelly, 1973). To the extent that these patterns do not offer clear interpretations, they will be a source of uncertainty for the leader when interacting with subordinates. Furthermore, evidence suggests that the attributional process presented by Kelley is complicated by issues of multiple causation, tendencies to not use all of the informational dimensions equally, and actor-observer differences in information processing. Each of these variations to the basic model will be briefly discussed.

First, let us examine the use of different types of information available to the attributor. Of the three types of information one might use in forming attributions, it appears that consensus information may have the weakest effects on attribution (see, for example, Nisbett and Borgida, 1975; McArthur, 1976; Nisbett, Borgida, Crandall, and Reid, 1976). Many factors (i.e., order of presentation of consensus data) seem to moderate the use of consensus information, and its role in attributional processes remains an issue of debate (Ruble and Feldman, 1976; Feldman, Higgins, Karvalac, and Ruble, 1976; Wells and Harvey, 1977; Hansen and Lowe, 1976; Hansen and Donoghue, 1977). One explanation for the apparent weakness of consensus data is that people tend to use "self-based consensus" as opposed to "sample-based consensus" (Hansen and Lowe, 1976; Hansen and Donoghue, 1977). With self-based consensus, people judge another's performance by comparing it to how they, themselves, would have performed in the situation; in using sample-based consensus, people judge another's performance by comparing it to how a sample of the population has performed in the situation. If the use of self-based consensus is common, it would suggest that leaders judge subordinates by their own personal standards and ignore the standards one might infer from observing all of one's subordinates.

The second issue which complicates the attributional process is the possibility of the leader seeing multiple causes for the same event. Multiple causation may be the result of several simultaneously occurring causal factors or may arise through causal chains, i.e., an immediate cause is seen as the result of a previous event (Brickman, Ryan, and Wortman, 1975). A subordinate may miss a deadline due to lack of effort, but that lack of effort might have been caused by (1) a sick child keeping the employee awake all night or (2) a party for a friend—keeping the employee awake all night. As one can see, the nature of prior causes can dramatically affect a leader's reaction to his or her subordinate. In general, the perception of multiple causes results in a discounting effect where the role of any given cause is discounted if other plausible causes are also present (Kelley, 1973; Ajzen and Fishbein, 1978; Fischoff and Lichtenstein, 1978).

Furthermore, if multiple causes are embedded in a schema, the nature of that schema can affect the types of information a leader feels he or she has available to him or her. For example, if a leader is using a multiple sufficient schema, a number of causes are seen as sufficient to produce an effect, e.g., success at an easy task could be caused by ability *or* effort. In this case, a leader observing success in the presence of effort by the subordinate is unsure about ability attributions. On the other hand, a multiple necessary schema can be in effect (e.g., both effort and ability are needed for success). Now, the leader observing success in the presence of effort by the subordinate feels more certain that ability is also present. Similarly, causal chains complicate the process when attributions drawn from immediate causes may be drastically changed by introducing a contradictory prior cause (Brickman, Ryan, and Wortman, 1975).

Whether one is dealing with multiple causation due to simultaneously occurring causes or to causal chains, it seems that the uncertainty of the leader will be greater in these more complex informational systems. The more uncertainty in the leader's causal analysis, the less likely he or she is to use extreme responses with that subordinate. Also, in the face of multiple possible causes, it seems likely that the leader will provide the member with other opportunities, or tests, to attempt to gather more information and reduce his or her uncertainty about why the subordinate performed in such a way.

The third and final variation to the basic information-processing model presented by Kelley (1967, 1972a, 1973) has been characterized as the Actor-Observer phenomenon (Jones and Nisbett, 1972; Jones, 1979). This phenomenon is essentially represented as the tendency of observers (our leaders) to explain other's (our member) behaviors in dispositional terms or as internally caused, whereas actors (our members) attribute their own behavior to situational or external factors. There are a number of explanations of this phenomenon (Monson and Snyder, 1977); the most plausible, however, is that the actor and the observer process different sources of information. The environment is the central focus of the actor, while the actor is the central focus of the observer. More specifically, we, as actors, are aware of and focus on the environment surrounding us. People observing us do not have direct access to our awareness or perceptions. Instead, they focus on what we do. As a result, observers are likely to report that other people's behavior is caused by something about them as persons—internal dispositional characteristics such as effort or ability. This tendency to see internal causes for subordinate behavior may cause the leader to choose inappropriate responses when dealing with poor performance. Also, the actor-observer discrepancy between the leader's explanation for a behavior and the subordinate's explanation for that same behavior may be a source of leader-member conflict.

As one can see, the variations to the basic information processing model of attribution create considerable complexity in understanding how attributions might come to be formed by a leader. It seems relatively clear, however, that the attributional process frequently occurs, and it is important for understanding a leader's behavior. The second step of the process portrays these attributions as affecting leader behavior. The next section examines some of the possible relationships between attributions and leader behavior.

Attributions and Behavior

If leaders do employ an attributional process of information search, logical causal analysis, and logical problem solving behavior, as we believe they do, that process will have some implication for their behavior. Previous research has indicated that the leader's attributions about the causes of a member's behavior can be central to several types of leader behaviors such as (1) rewarding and punishing member performance, (2) closeness of supervision, (3) expectancies about the member's future performance, and (4) aspirations the leader might hold for the member. The relationship of these behaviors and judgments to attributional processes will be briefly discussed below.

The perceived causes of a subordinate's performance have been shown to have clear implications for how a leader rewards or punishes that performance. Regardless of ability, causal attributions to effort appear to be primary determinants of how performance is evaluated and the nature of subsequent rewards or punishments (Weiner and Kukla, 1970; Omelich, 1974). When success is seen as accompanied by effort, it is most rewarded; when failure is seen as due to a lack of effort, it is most severely punished. On the other hand, where the causal explanation for a member's performance was an external cause (e.g., task difficulty or luck), the leader is not likely to reward or punish performance. In general, we would suspect that internal attributions will result in the leader focusing his or her response on trying to change the subordinate. Effort attributions might result in punitive actions such as reprimands or docking of pay, while ability attributions might result in training. On the other hand, external attributions should prompt the leader to focus change efforts on the situation. If the task is too difficult (or not difficult enough), then task redesign or job enrichment may be in order. Bad luck attributions should result in sympathy, support, and encouragement to try again.

The closeness of supervision used by a leader is also affected by attributional processes. Kruglanski (1970) and Strickland (1958) have shown that when a leader attributed a worker's earlier performance to the surveillance of the leader, the leader was more likely to continue close supervision. On the other hand, when the leader attributed that performance to the worker's own efforts, the leader's supervision was less close.

Just as overt leader behavior is affected by attributions, so, too, are expectations about future performance. When forming expectations, the stability of the causal explanation seems to be a crucial factor (Weiner *et al.*, 1972). If a subordinate's performance is attributed to stable factors (e.g., ability or task difficulty), the leader is likely to expect a similar level of performance in the future (Weiner, Nierenberg, and Goodstein, 1976; Frieze and Weiner, 1971; Green, 1978; McMahan, 1973). Expectancies about future performance based on unstable causes (e.g., effort), however, are more problematic and not as predictive of expectations (Weiner and Kukla, 1970).

Finally, Weiner's work on achievement motivation argues that the attributional process is an integral part of subsequent achievement-related expectations. Although Weiner's work has focused on how individuals guide their own behavior, his conclusions are relevant for analyzing a leader's aspirations for his subordinates. The essence of Weiner's work indicates that the more a leader attributes a subordinate's successes to internal factors (e.g., ability) and failures to external factors (e.g., luck), the higher the leader's aspirations should be for that subordinate's future performance. Given higher aspirations, the leader should also provide more achievement-related opportunities for that subordinate.

At this point, we have described the process by which leader attributions may be formed, some complicating variations in those information processes, and the impact of attributions upon leader behavior. In general, it would appear that three critical questions about the leader's attributions guide his or her behavior: 1) Is the cause of poor performance internal or external? If it is seen as internal the supervisor is more likely to focus his or her actions on the member and try to change some aspect of him or her. If the cause is external, actions are likely to be focused on changing situational factors. 2) To what extent does the member have control over the causative agent? The more control the subordinate is seen to have, the more responsible he or she is seen to be for performance. High perceived control will likely result in both more rewarding and more punishing behavior by the leader, depending upon the quality of the performance. 3) Is the causative agent likely to continue to be in effect in the future? The more an agent is seen as stable, likely to persist, the more the leader will expect future performance to be consistent with present performance. The opportunities provided to a member by a leader are expected to be directly affected by his or her answer to this question.

Also intruding upon the attributional process are social, situational, and normative factors that may affect both the subordinate behavior → leader attribution step and the leader attribution → leader behavior step. More specifically, while attributional processes are helpful in understanding how leaders respond to poor performance, they are not the complete story. A number of other factors are related to both the diagnostic and response phases of the process. Including these factors provides both a broader and more realistic analysis.

MODERATORS OF THE ATTRIBUTIONAL PROCESS

The following discussion briefly presents some of the more salient moderators which have implications for the leader's attributions in a leader-member interaction. Self-serving attributions, the leader-member relationship, individual characteristics, and leader expectations are all seen as moderating the subordinate behavior → leader attribution link. Perceptions of responsibility, the effects of the subordinate's behavior, accounts, and the tendency to focus change on the subordinate are all seen as moderating the leader attribution → leader behavior link. Both sets of moderaters tend to confound the logical information processing predictions outlined earlier in the paper.

Self-Serving Attributions by the Leader

An extensive literature stresses that attributional processes often are moderated by self-serving or ego-biasing motives (see Miller and Ross, 1975; Bradley, 1978, for reviews).[2] This phenomenon takes many forms, but one of the most common positions is that people readily take responsibility for positive behavioral outcomes but deny responsibility for negative behavioral outcomes. In work organizations, it seems likely that the leader's attributions could fall prey to this particular type of bias. Leaders may attribute causation to themselves for successful ventures and attribute failures to external causes, perhaps their subordinates. Or when faced with a poor-performing subordinate, the leader is more likely to see the cause as something internal to the subordinate (for which the leader cannot be blamed) than something about the task (which might be seen by some as an indication of poor supervision). When one combines the actor-observer differences with the self-serving biases, it seems that leaders are likely to make mistakes in the direction of attributing subordinate poor performance to internal causes.

Relationship of Leader and Member

Research on factors such as empathy (Regan and Totten, 1975; Storms, 1973), similarity (Banks, 1976), and liking (Regan, Straus, and Fazio, 1974) indicates that the probability of the leader making attributions similar to the member's self-attributions is increased when these factors are present. Essentially any factor which makes the leader psychologically closer to the member should increase the tendency for the leader to make selflike attributions regarding the member (Banks, 1976). On the other hand, anything that increases the psychological distance between leader and member will reduce this tendency and increase the likelihood of leader attributions being discrepant from the member's causal explanations of his or her own behavior. For example, it appears that the more powerful the leader is relative to the member (i.e., the more rewards and punishments the leader has at his or her disposal) the more likely he or she is to make attributions different from what one would expect the member to offer as causal explanations (Kipnis, 1972; McFillen, 1978). In these latter cases, leaders with power were more punitive and made more internal attributions when dealing with poor performance than were leaders with less power.[3]

Personal Characteristics

As in most perceptual processes, attributions are affected by characteristics of the perceptual object. A number of studies indicate that characteristics, such as race and sex, affect causal explanations usually to the detriment of those individuals who have suffered other forms of stereotyping and prejudice. For example, leaders (male and female) are likely to attribute female successes more to external causes and attribute their failures more to internal causes than they do for their male counterparts (see, for example, Garland and Price, 1977; Deaux and Emswiller, 1974; Feldman-Summers and Kiesler, 1974). One can only assume that many other characteristics, such as level in the organization and type of job, also are likely to distort the leader's causal explanations of the leader's behavior (Rosen and Jerdee, 1974).

Leader Expectations

When a leader expects a member to succeed or fail, and the member does, the leader is likely to give the member credit for his/her performance and to attribute it to dispositional causes (e.g., ability and effort). On the other hand, when a member's performance is inconsistent with the leader's expectations, the leader is likely to attribute that performance to external factors, such as task difficulty (Feather, 1969, 1971). Inconsistencies also may lead to uncertainty in the leader about his/her causal view, especially if several disconfirming events occur. This situation might well lead to the leader testing the member by presenting other tasks or opportunities for the member so the leader could gather covariation information and assess the "validity" of his or her attribution. This process also might lead in turn to a change in leader expectations.

Leader's Perception of Responsibility

Another crucial judgment which accompanies attributions is that of responsibility, referring principally to an evaluation of moral accountability (Shaver, 1975; Elig and Frieze, 1975). For example, a subordinate may be seen as responsible for some stable internal characteristics (e.g., a trait such as rudeness) but not responsible for other characteristics (e.g., a lack of an ability). The judgment of responsibility is not seen as moderating the formation of attributions so much as it is seen as moderating the leader's response to an attribution. Clearly, the more an outcome is seen as caused by some aspect of the subordinate and the subordinate is judged to be responsible for that outcome, i.e., it was in his or her control, the more likely the leader is to take some action toward that subordinate. Also, the judgment of responsibility should moderate the quality of the leader's response. Actions for which the subordinate is seen as responsible are likely to be more rewarded or more punished (Weiner and Kukla, 1970).

The Effects of Behavior

Suppose a subordinate shows a lack of effort on the same task on two separate occasions. Perhaps on both occasions the worker had a sick child and the leader should objectively make similar attributions and similar responses. Nevertheless, on the first occasion, the lack of effort has little impact on the overall work going on in the group. On the second occasion, a critical deadline is missed because of the lack of effort. The same behavior was seen (i.e., poor performance). The same attribution was made (an internal cause for which responsibility was low), but the response by the leader is likely to be different. It is much more likely that a reprimand or some other punitive action will be used for the situation where the effect of the behavior was more important (Shaver, 1975; Rosen and Jerdee, 1974; Walster, 1966).

What we are saying is that the effect of a behavior is important as well as the behavior itself. It can be argued that in many cases the behavior-outcome information is seen as an inseparable unit. The leader, therefore, is likely to temper his or her response with an analysis of the effects of the action. Unfortunately, this may result in leaders overlooking behaviors that should be corrected until it is too late and something severe happens.

Accounts

Another factor that may moderate both the behavior-attribution and the attribution-response links is the subordinate's explanation of the event, his or her "account" (Scott and Lyman, 1968; Goffman, 1971). Accounts may take various forms, e.g., excuses, justifications, apologies, and can change the meaning that a leader otherwise might attach to an event. Thus, a situation which could be seen as offensive and requiring punishment can be transformed into something more acceptable (Goffman, 1971).

The degree to which an account is able to neutralize negative attributions and responses of the leader depends on the information base of the leader and the acceptability of the accounts. A leader who feels that he or she has unclear or insufficient information for the required judgment will be more influenced by accounts. Similarly, an account that is considered believable, sincere and adequate for the circumstances is more likely to be accepted by the leader (Blumstein *et al.*, 1974).

By offering accounts, the subordinate may get the leader to disassociate the evaluation of the poor performance from an evaluation of his or her moral character and potential for future performance. Therefore, we would expect that acceptable accounts will lead to less punitive responses by the leader and may even serve to offset the leader's tendency to use internal attributions.

Ease of Change

Finally, although not substantiated in the literature, from informal observations of leaders it appears that they believe that it is somehow easier for other people to change their behavior than it is to change the environment. What this suggests is that when there is high uncertainty about an attribution or that two very plausible causes exist, a leader is more likely to choose a response directed at changing the subordinate rather than changing the task or the situation.

Our suppositions about the cause of this bias are twofold. First, by dealing with the subordinate the responsibility for corrective action shifts to the subordinate. Changing the environment remains the responsibility of the supervisor. Second, it is somehow easier (requires less thought and time) to say to a subordinate "work harder" than it is to try to figure out how the task or situation should be changed. The conclusion is that when errors are made they are likely to be in the form of trying to change the subordinate's behavior rather than changing the task or situation.

Summary of Moderators

In summary, we now see that during both steps of the leader attributional model a number of factors other than the classical attributional factors (e.g., Kelley or Weiner's work) may moderate the informational processes. Some of these moderators such as individual characteristics seem likely to alter or distort the causal explanation the leader believes. Other moderators such as the effects of the subordinate's behavior seem likely to alter the leader's behavior so it does not follow directly from prior attributions. In either case, it is clear that factors outside of the classical information processing models have real implications for the extent to which attributions affect leader behavior toward the member.

BOUNDARY CONDITIONS IN LEADER ATTRIBUTIONS

We see the attributional processes of the leader as an ongoing phenomenon, constantly shaping the leader's views of his or her subordinates and constantly changing as new information is processed. There are conditions, however, which might attenuate the mediating effects of attributions. Three major boundary conditions would seem to constrain the attributional effects: restrictions on leader behaviors, supplanting attribution processes with organizational policies, and the development of personal policy decision rules. These boundary conditions are seen as affecting both the formation and use of attributions as well as the possible link between attributions and leader behavior.

On some occasions, the leader is confronted with contextual factors which reduce the leader's freedom in choosing a response. Thus, even though the leader's naive causal analyses say the subordinate failed due to a lack of effort and should be terminated, social norms, pressure from a superior, or a host of other factors might prevent the leader from so responding. This reasoning does not allow us, however, to say the leader's attribution had no effect. Even though the most apparently contingent response was not affected by the leader's attributions, it may be that other responses will be. An interesting question is raised by this dilemma. What do leaders do when their causal analyses conflict with contextual constraints? We suspect that these causal beliefs are maintained and are manifested at other times, in other ways.

Organizational policy may act as a contextual constraint on leader behavior as noted above. It also may supplant the leader's causal analysis. In some cases, or in certain job domains, the leader may not ask why but simply say, "If the subordinate does this, policy dictates I do that." If three days' work are missed in a week, the subordinate is fired. This obviously bureaucratic response does not seem likely to be very effective if used exclusively. All leaders, however, may have aspects of their job where they allow organizational policy to guide their behavior.

Finally, one must allow for the possibility of the leader developing his or her own personal policies which preclude the necessity of looking for causal analyses—or they may be the result of prior attributional processes. Past attributional analyses may have led the leader to be fairly certain what the cause of certain behaviors is likely to be. Therefore, rather than engage in redundant information processing, the leader takes action based upon a policy which will be right most of the time. On the other hand, past causal analyses may have never yielded a clear causal explanation due to factors such as incomplete information or multiple causation. In this case, the leader reduces uncertainty by making a decision rule and abandoning attributional analyses as fruitless.

Two examples might help. Perhaps you have observed over the years that one or two of the tasks which you ask your subordinates to do is particularly difficulty and unpleasant. When you find that a new group member is absent on the day when he or she is supposed to perform that task, you don't bother to try to figure out why—you are fairly sure of the reason. On the other hand, in some cases it is very difficult to determine the cause of an event. Teachers dealing with an undergraduate student who fails a test in a 10-week quarter system often don't have the time or information to make accurate assessments of causation. They may, therefore, develop a policy such as letting each student drop their lowest quiz grade or providing one make-up opportunity for everyone. These policies essentially bypass the attributional process.

There are probably some other factors which constrain the usefulness of the attributional analysis of the leader-member interaction. Those discussed above were salient to us from our own experience. The challenge is to identify the conditions under which the leader's attributional processes are active and then examine their relationship to leader behavior.

A MODEL

Given the previous review, we are now able to present a tentative model of the attributional process in the leadership setting (see Figure 1). As one can see, the original depiction of subordinate behavior → leader attribu-

Figure 1. Basic Attributional Model

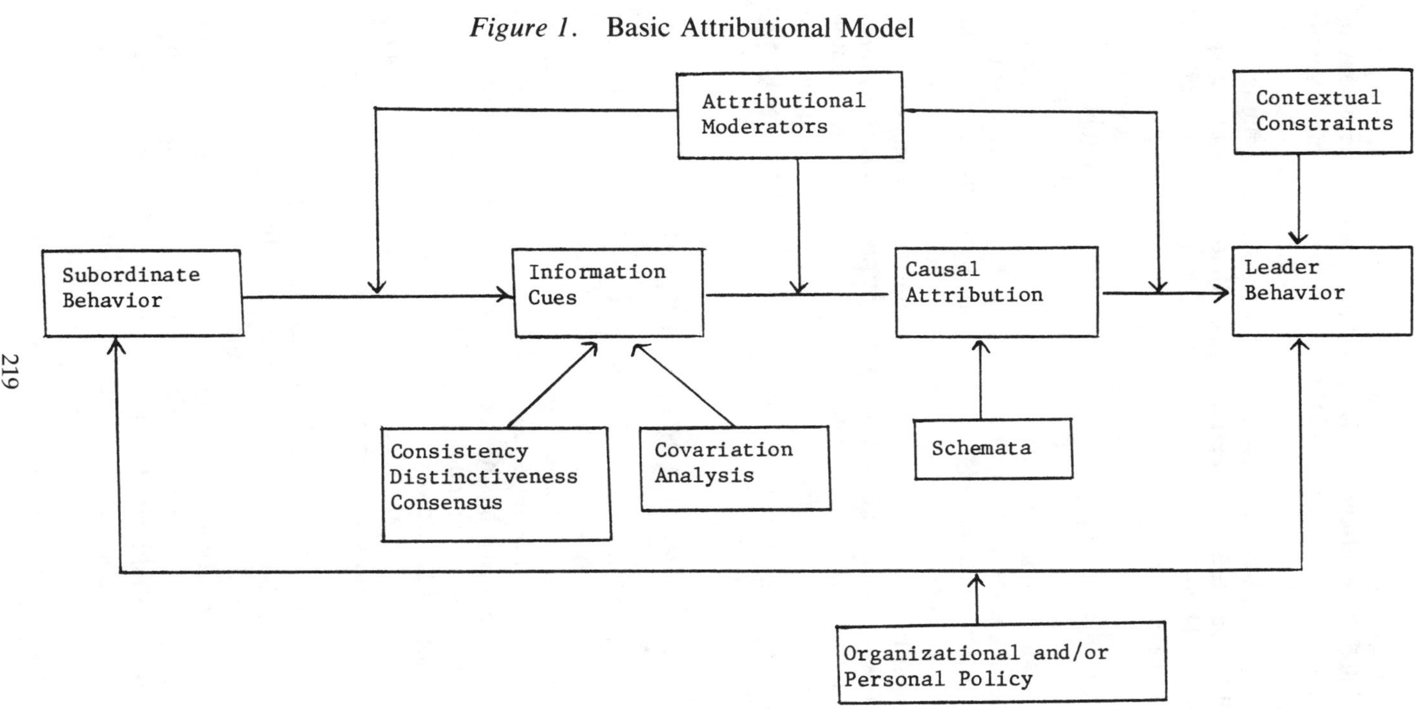

tion → leader behavior model was accurate but too simplified. In summary, the mediating effects of attributions upon leader behavior are viewed as being set in motion by the occurrence of some stimulus behavior (e.g., tardy, a missed deadline, disruptive behavior, absenteeism) by the subordinates. The leader then "collects" informational cues, which facilitate a causal understanding of that event. Three types of information are likely to be used by the leader: consistency, distinctiveness, and consensus. These cues are then processed through a covariation analysis and/or some causal schema which the leader has developed. This information processing results in an attribution being made. Using this causal attribution, the leader chooses a response which reflects the leader's naive understanding of what caused the member's behavior. All through this process moderators may affect both the subordinate behavior → leader attribution link and the leader attribution → leader behavior link. Finally, boundary conditions are acknowledged as potentially affecting the process in several ways. They may constrain the leader's behavior so that it does not seem to follow his or her attributions ("contextual constraints") or they may circumvent the attributional process completely ("organizational and/or personal policy"). In the following sections we present some research which tests some of the general propositions stated in the model.

RESEARCH SUPPORT

The model described above is both rich and complex. Numerous hypotheses can be generated from it, and over the past two years we have attempted to test some of these hypotheses. But before we describe this research we feel that it is important to point out how our research efforts differ from the work that has been completed already. More specifically, we see our efforts as being much more than just an attempt to generalize social psychological laboratory findings to an organizational setting. We feel that the setting itself, the focus of the research and our ultimate goals differ quite significantly from previous work and these differences are discussed below.

In terms of the setting, the organizational context differs in some major ways from the typical laboratory environment. In most lab studies the cues about an event are relatively unambiguous and there is little backlog or competing information with which to contend. A supervisor, on the other hand, may be faced with reports from the subordinate, from other supervisors or peers and with his or her own information about the event. The veracity of the source, the motivation of the different sources and the variability of this information makes this situation more complex than the typical social psychological study.

A second issue related to the setting is that there may be constraints, norms and expectations about the actions which are available and appropriate for the supervisor. Therefore, a number of factors may intervene between intention (or the prediction made from an attribution) and the response. This issue is typically of little relevance for social psychological studies.

The focus of the research is also somewhat different. Most of the relevant social psychology work has emphasized actors attributions about their achievement-related actions. Our research is different in two major ways. First, we are interested almost exclusively in the observer's point of view. The perspective of the subordinate has been of minor importance. Second, we are interested in behavior. We want to know not only the attribution, but what the leader does about it. This emphasis on action has played a minor role in most of the social psychological research.

Finally, we see our goals as different from the previous work. Part of a supervisor's task is to both evaluate and increase the performance of their subordinates. Our eventual goal is to develop techniques that allow a supervisor to make performance judgments more accurately and through this increased accuracy provide more effective feedback to subordinates. Thus we want to not only demonstrate that errors occur, but we ultimately wish to figure out ways to reduce those errors.

With these distinctions in mind, we turn to a review of our research. Some of these studies have not been published elsewhere while others have appeared in more detailed forms. But pulling them all together is important to get a complete view of the current support for the model.

Definition of Poor Performance (Green, 1979)

One of our first problems was to try to integrate the more practical, descriptive definitions of poor performance as elaborated on by Miner (1963) and Miner and Brewer (1976) with the more theoretical orientation suggested by Weiner *et al.* (1972). More specifically, Weiner's work, you will recall, suggests that performance is seen as caused by four factors: effort, ability, task difficulty, and luck. These four factors represent the four combinations of the two underlying dimensions of locus of control (internal/external) and stability (stable/unstable).

Miner (1963), on the other hand, provides a taxonomy of strategic factors that are seen as reasons for why people fail on the job. Combining the factors represented in a series of studies by Miner (1963, 1965, 1975) and by Steinmetz (1969) led us to the list of causes presented in Table 2. While it was relatively clear to us that some of these factors would fit nicely into the Weiner-type analysis, it was not clear that this would be true for all of the factors or that practicing managers also would view these factors as varying along such dimensions.

Table 2. Definitions of Possible Causes of Ineffective Performance

1. *Insufficient intellectual ability*—a lack of ability to understand, learn, or express oneself well, e.g., low IQ or low verbal ability.
2. *Insufficient job knowledge*—a lack of adequate information about job duties and/or job requirements or a lack of experience with a particular type of job, e.g., being unaware of a company policy or production technique.
3. *Counterproductive emotional states*—emotional states which interfere with or prevent satisfactory performance on the job, e.g., severe anxiety or depression.
4. *Use of drugs or alcohol*—being under the influence of, or the aftereffect of, drugs or alcohol, e.g., drunk, under influence of amphetamines, or hungover.
5. *Alcoholism or drug addiction*—having a dependency on the drug as well as being under its influence or the influence of its aftereffects, e.g., amphetamine addiction or alcoholism.
6. *Low work standards*—a worker defining success in terms of very low personal standards and/or experiencing satisfaction at low levels of performance, e.g., a worker being content to be the least productive employee.
7. *Low work motivation*—a generally demonstrated lack of interest in the job and/or a general lack of effort on the job, e.g., the "lazy" or "uninvolved" worker.
8. *Physical limitations*—insufficient, personal physical capacities for a particular job, e.g., a person may be too short, too weak, blind, uncoordinated.
9. *Family crises*—unusual family situations which interfere with or prevent satisfactory job performance, e.g., divorce, sickness or death in family.
10. *Predominance of family considerations over work demands*—a noncrisis family situation in which the worker is more responsive to family demands than to job demands, e.g., taking job time for child care, refusing to travel because of family commitments.
11. *Negative work group influences*—informal work group influences which are counterproductive for the organization, e.g., group norms to restrict output or a group ostracizing a worker and negatively affecting his/her work.
12. *Counterproductive work environment*—environment factors which interfere with or prevent satisfactory job performance, e.g., excessive heat or cold for a particular worker or excessive noise level.
13. *Inadequate communications to the worker concerning performance*—the organization does not clearly communicate expectations about job performance and/or does not give feedback about deficiencies which need correcting, e.g., failing to make clear when a worker is to be at work or a supervisor failing to tell a worker he/she is breaking a work rule.
14. *Conflict of personal values and job requirements*—the worker's personal values, derived from family and culture, prevent or interfere with the worker performing satisfactorily, e.g., religious values proscribe a worker from working overtime on Saturday.

Method. Sixty-four managers participated in the research. They were asked to read the 14 causes of ineffective performance and rate all possible nonredundant pairs on a 5-point similarity scale. For example, they were asked, "How similar do you feel insufficient intellectual ability as a possible cause of ineffective performance is to insufficient job knowledge?" These data were used as input for multidimensional scaling (MDS) and hierarchical cluster analysis. Each subject also rated all 14 causes on 4 separate scales representing 4 dimensions: locus of control (internal/external); stability (stable/unstable); legitimacy (acceptable/unacceptable); frequency (frequent/infrequent). These latter ratings helped to confirm the meaning of the clusters and underlying dimensions suggested by the MDS.

Results. The cluster analysis suggested 5 main clusters with two of the 14 causes (insufficient intellectual ability and physical limitations) not appearing in any cluster. The 5 clusters were labeled (1) personal role/job role conflict (included items 9—family crisis, 10—predominance of family considerations over work demands, and 14—conflict of personal values and job requirements); (2) personal pathology (included items 3—counterproductive emotional states, 4—use of drugs or alcohol, 5—alcoholism or drug addiction); (3) negative work context (including items 11—negative work group influences, 12—counterproductive work environment); (4) low role orientation (including items 6—low work standards, 7—low work motivation); and (5) low job role knowledge (including items 2—insufficient job knowledge and 13—inadequate communications to the worker concerning performance).

Using both the MDS and clustering techniques suggested a three-dimensional space provided the best fit, and two of the dimensions were

Figure 2. Dimensions I and II

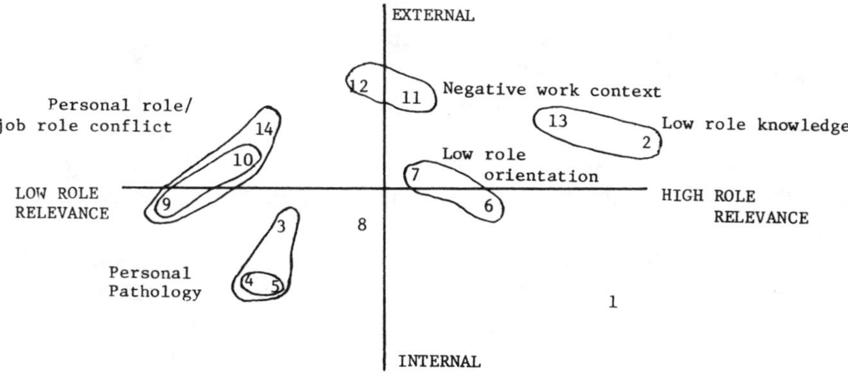

readily identifiable. Figure 2 shows this solution and the fit of the clusters in this space. One dimension was clearly an internal/external distinction, while the other dimension seemed to reflect factors that were specifically relevant or not relevant for the job at hand. A stability distinction failed to appear.

Finally, 4 composites were found for each cluster by summing the 4 attribute-ratings scores (i.e., locus of control, stability, legitimacy, and frequency) for each cause within a cluster resulting in a locus of control, stability, legitimacy and frequency score for each cluster. Statistical comparisons suggest that the managers did view the five sources of poor performance as differing in terms of Weiner's dimensions, the legitimacy of the causal category, and how frequently they encountered that particular source of poor performance. For example, low role orientation was seen as more internal than the other clusters except personal pathology and one of the least legitimate causes of poor performance. Conversely, low role knowledge was seen as external and much more legitimate as a cause of poor performance.

Some correspondence between Miner's work and Weiner's analysis of causes of poor performance is evident. The internal/external distinction is very clearly salient to practicing managers while the stability dimension is not (similar results have been reported by Orvis, Kelley, and Butler, 1976). Furthermore, the apparent relationship between internality and legitimacy suggests that some of the attributional model predictions concerning internality and a manager's punishing behavior are likely to be supported in the field. More generally speaking, the findings provide some heuristic information. The information on clusters, the role-relevance dimension and the frequency of causes should be useful in directing future research questions on managing poor performers.

Demonstration of Self-Serving Bias by Subordinates (Soulier, 1978)

Numerous studies have illustrated that people attribute their successes to themselves (e.g., their effort or ability) and their failures to external causes (e.g., bad luck, an impossible task). However, few of these studies have attempted to test this proposition with tasks that were representative of actual jobs or in settings where the workers received feedback over a series of trials. The following study was designed to look at worker attributions when faced with success or failure feedback over a series of trials.

Method. Two hundred and forty accounting students participated as subjects. They worked on a set of financial decisions concerned with determining which of several variances (a discrepancy between expected costs and actual costs), as shown in a budgetary report, should be investigated. They believed their decisions were to be evaluated using a predetermined normative model requiring no personal judgments by the experimenter. Each subject participated in two trials and received one of four feedback conditions: success-success; success-failure; failure-success; failure-failure. At the end of each trial the subjects indicated the degree to which their performance could be attributed to (1) decision-making ability, (2) intrinsic motivation, (3) task difficulty, and (4) luck.

Results. Table 3 presents the means for the four attribution measures for both trials. In general, people who went from success to failure saw ability as relatively less important, while people who went from failure to success saw ability and effort as relatively more important and task difficulty as relatively less important. Looking at the data just for the first trial suggests similar conclusions. Success people have higher scores than failure people on ability and motivation causes, while the reverse is true for task difficulty. We were not able to interpret the findings for the data reflecting luck as a cause.

In summary, these data suggest that people who fail are more likely to see the cause of that failure as due to task difficulty than people who succeed. People who succeed are more likely to attribute their success to ability and effort than people who fail. Also, when one goes from success to failure or failure to success, they change their attributions in the direction of a self-serving bias. In the series of studies reported in the next section we will show that supervisors tend to have an opposite view: When faced with a poor-performing subordinate, they are likely to attribute that performance to the internal dispositional characteristics of the subordinate.

Tests of the Model's Propositions (Mitchell and Wood, 1979)

Three studies have been conducted in a similar fashion with similar subjects in an attempt to test some of the model's central hypotheses. Of major importance were such questions as (1) does information about past work history influence attributions, (2) are attributions related to responses, (3) does the seriousness of the outcome affect the attributions and responses, (4) will apologies diminish the severity of response, (5) does perceived responsibility influence the response, and (6) do supervisors in general use internal attributions for subordinate poor performance?

The three experiments utilized the same background procedures. The first stage of the research involved interviews designed to gather critical incidents of poor performance by nurses in a hospital setting. The second stage involved supervisors reading, making attributions, and indicating how they would respond to some of these incidents. Information about the nurses' work history (distinctiveness, consistency, consensus), likely attributions, apologies, responsibility, and the consequences of the poor

Table 3. Means of Causal Attributions Between Success/Failure Feedback Conditions for Both Trials

Attributions		Feedback Condition											
		Success/Success			*Success/Failure*			*Failure/Success*			*Failure/Failure*		
	Trial	*1st*	*2nd*	*p*	*1st*	*2nd*	*p*	*1st*	*2nd*	*p*	*1st*	*2nd*	*p*
Internal	Decision-Making Ability	4.43	4.49		4.40	3.78	**	3.38	4.15	***	3.62	3.31	
	Intrinsic Motivation	4.00	4.35		3.80	3.81		3.55	4.08	**	3.37	3.81	*
External	Task Difficulty	4.32	4.02		4.45	4.47		4.73	3.85	****	4.82	4.82	
	Luck	4.58	4.46		4.27	3.68	***	3.80	4.36	****	3.72	3.40	*

Comparison of means with one-tailed t-test

* $p < .05$
** $p < .01$
*** $p < .005$
**** $p < .0005$

performance were manipulated within these cases to create different experimental conditions.

In stage one, the Directors of Nursing of seven hospitals in the Seattle area were contacted, informed of the research, and agreed to participate. In-depth interviews gave us critical incidents of poor performance, as well as information about possible causes of the poor performance (attributions) and possible responses to poor performance. The incidents served as our stimulus materials, and the information about potential causes and responses helped us to develop realistic scales on which supervisors could respond. More detail about these procedures is available elsewhere (Mitchell and Wood, 1979).

Method *(Experiment 1)*. The first experiment utilized six episodes of poor performance. Based on consistency, consensus, and distinctiveness, three levels of work history for the nurse in question were used (good work history, no work history, and poor work history), as well as two levels of outcome severity (severe, not severe). These manipulations produced a 3 × 2 design with each case representing one cell. Each participant responded to six cases, which represented all six conditions, by giving attributions and responses.

Twenty-three nursing supervisors from one of the hospitals participated in the study. Six cases were used involving poor performance on the hospital ward. For example, one episode dealt with the administration of too much of a dangerous drug, while another dealt with the failure of a nurse to put up the side railing on a patient's bed. The cases were one or two paragraphs long.

Each case provided a work history for the nurse in question. She was described as having done well on other tasks, done well on this task in the past, and her colleagues had also had difficulty with this task (a good work history—high distinctiveness, low consistency, high consensus), or she was described as having done poorly on other tasks, she had made similar mistakes before, and her peers seldom made this error (a poor work history). A third condition had no work history.

The seriousness of the outcome was provided as information within the case. For example, when the wrong drug was administered, the patient suffered either mild discomfort or a cardiac arrest. There were six different cases and six different experimental conditions. The cases and conditions were counterbalanced so that for each case the manipulations appeared approximately an equal number of times.

There were three types of measures: Manipulation checks, attributions, and responses. The manipulation checks asked about the seriousness of the outcome and the degree to which the nurse in question was generally a good performer. The attribution questions provided eight possible causes for the nurses' performance. Four of these were internal (e.g., the nurse was not putting enough effort into her work), and four were external (e.g., the nurse was working on a continually busy ward without support staff). The supervisors responded to each attribution on a "very likely cause" to "very unlikely cause" 7-point scale. The four internal items were summed to form an internal composite and the four external items formed an external composite. In addition, a summary question was asked that inquired, "In general, how important do you feel the nurse's personal characteristics (such as ability, attitudes, mood, and so on) were as possible causes of her behaving the way she did?" Participants responded on an "extremely important" to "extremely unimportant" 7-point scale. A second summary question asked about the degree to which the supervisor felt the characteristics of the situation (e.g., busy ward) were as causes of the behavior.

The response questions provided ten different actions ranging from "take no action at all" to "immediate termination." Some of these actions were directed at the nurse such as verbally reprimand the nurse, and some were directed at the task such as reschedule the work load. Some were positive in nature (e.g., provide counseling) and some were negative (e.g., termination). Participants indicated their response on a seven-point "very appropriate" to "very inappropriate" scale. Again, summary questions were used which asked, "To what extent do you feel this incident demands that you direct your response at the nurse and attempt to change something about her (her job attitude, level of effort, etc.)," and a second question asked, "To what extent would you want to change something about the situation." Seven-point scales ranging from "not at all" to "to a great extent" were used on both questions.

Results *(Experiment 1)*. An analysis of the manipulation checks showed that the mean rating for the good work history ($\bar{X} = 6.00$) condition was significantly higher ($t = 16.0$, $p < .001$) than that for the poor work history ($\bar{X} = 1.86$). Comparison of the mean ratings for the serious ($\bar{X} = 6.94$) and non-serious ($\bar{X} = 3.80$) conditions was also significant ($t = 10.7$, $p < .001$) and in the expected direction.

Two hypotheses were tested for the causal attributions questions: (1) that work history, in terms of distinctiveness, consistency, and consensus, would have a main effect on a subject's internal attributions of causality; (2) that seriousness of outcome would have a main effect on subjects' internal attributions of causality.

A 2×3 analysis of variance was run, with the dependent variable being the subjects' overall rating of the nurse as a cause of the incident (the summary question). These results are shown in Table 4. Poor work history led to the nurse's being rated higher as a possible cause of the incident being evaluated, $F(2,22) = 28.06$, $p < .001$. Also, as hypothesized, a more serious outcome resulted in a higher rating for the nurse as a

Table 4. Subjects' Ratings of the Nurse in Each Incident as a Possible Cause of the Poor Performance (Study 1)

	Work History		
Outcome	*Good*	*Not Available*	*Poor*
Non-Serious	3.34	4.57	6.18
Serious	4.14	5.65	6.36

Note: Higher values indicate a higher rating of the nurse as a possible cause, i.e., more internal attribution.

possible cause of the incident of poor performance, $F(1,22) = 9.00$, $p < .01$. The interaction was not significant. The summary question asking about the degree to which the environment was seen as a cause produced a main effect for work history [$F(2,22)$ $F = 16.05$, $p < .001$]. A poor work history led to the environment being rated lower as a possible cause of the incident being evaluated. The main effect for seriousness of outcome and the interaction were both not significant. We should add that a more detailed analysis of the internal and external attribution composites produced essentially the same results.

It was also hypothesized that both the work history of the nurse and seriousness of the outcome would influence the supervisor's ratings of the appropriateness of directing a response at the nurse. In addition, it was felt that these two factors would also influence the severity of the response.

A 2 × 3 analysis of variance, with the summary question regarding the appropriateness of directing a response at the nurse as the dependent variable, provided support for the first hypothesis. These results are shown in Table 5. Poor work history resulted in higher ratings of a response directed at the nurse, $F(2,22) = 10.72$, $p < .001$. Seriousness of outcome also had a main effect on choice of response, $F(1,22) = 7.75$, $p < .01$, while the interaction was not significant.

Analyses were also conducted on the specific responses. When they were divided up into responses directed at the nurse or at the job, and

Table 5. Subjects' Ratings of the Appropriateness of Directing a Response at the Nurse Described in the Incident (Study 1)

	Work History		
Outcome	*Good*	*Not Available*	*Poor*
Nonserious	4.74	5.36	6.50
Serious	5.61	6.48	6.59

when the three most negative personal responses were looked at (i.e., termination, written and verbal reprimand), the results were essentially the same. A severe outcome resulted in more personal and severe punishment than did a poor work history.

A third hypothesis suggested that internal attributions would be related to responses directed at the subordinate. To test the hypothesis, we correlated the summary attribution questions with summary response questions. The more the supervisor felt that the nurse was the cause of the incident, the more she considered it appropriate to direct her response at the nurse ($r = .55$, $p < .01$). Also, the more the supervisor felt that the situation was responsible, the more she considered it appropriate to direct her response at the situation ($r = .64$, $p < .01$).

Our last hypothesis suggested that there would be a general bias on the part of the supervisors toward using internal attributions and internal responses. To test this hypothesis, we again used the summary questions. The mean difference between the internal attribution question and external attribution question was significant ($t = 3.63$, $p < .001$) and in the predicted direction. Over all conditions the nurse was more likely to be seen as the cause ($X = 5.07$) of the incident than the situation ($X = 4.41$). The results for the two summary response questions were similar. The t value was 10.89, ($p < .001$) and the means were 5.87 for the internal response question and 3.76 for the external response.

Method *(Experiment 2).* Twenty-three nurse supervisors from a different hospital where the respondents and the procedures were the same as in the first experiment, except that four cases were used instead of six. A 2×2 design was used with one factor being the seriousness of outcome (severe or not severe). The second factor was some "additional information" supplied directly to the respondent about an appropriate attribution (internal or external). The additional information variable was provided by adding a section which supplied the respondent with an attribution. For example, the internal attribution information for one of the episodes was, "From your discussions with Nurse Connally and some other nurses on the ward, you believe that the failure to tape down the catheter was due to a lack of effort on Nurse Connally's part. She had not spent sufficient time or thought on her duties at the time of the incident. This lack of attention to detail had caused an error on a somewhat simple task at a time when the ward was not very busy."

The severity of outcome was manipulated the same way as in Experiment 1. As before, the manipulations and cases were counterbalanced so that each combination appeared approximately an equal number of times.

There were two manipulation checks and the attributional questions used in Experiment 1 were dropped, because the attribution was directly manipulated. The response questions were the same as in Experiment 1, with ten separate behaviors and two summary items.

Results *(Experiment 2)*. The manipulations appeared successful. The mean rating of seriousness for the serious consequences condition was 6.64, while it was 4.14 for the nonserious condition ($t = 7.09$, $p < .001$). The mean rating of the nurse as a cause was 6.28 in the internal attribution condition and 3.31 in the external condition ($t = 9.84$, $p < .001$). The mean rating of the situation as cause in the internal condition was 2.20 and 5.67 in the external condition ($t = 11.10$, $p < .001$).

We had hypothesized that the internality of the attribution and the seriousness of the outcome would affect both the response and the seriousness of the response. A 2 × 2 analysis of variance supported these hypotheses for the subjects' ratings of the appropriateness of directing a response at the nurse (see Table 6). An internal attribution resulted in the response being directed at the nurse, $F(1,22) = 62.88$, $p < .001$, as did a serious outcome, $F(1,22) = 5.25$, $p < .03$.

The summary question for the degree to which the response should be directed at the situation produced a main effect for the attribution [$F(1,22) = 122.58$, $p < .001$] but not for the outcome seriousness or the interaction. An external attribution resulted in the response being directed at the situation ($\bar{X} = 5.20$) more than an internal attribution ($X = 1.70$). As before, when the ten specific responses were first broken down into the internal responses and the external responses, similar results appeared.

While attributions were manipulated in study 2 but not study 1, it was still possible to test whether internal attributions were related to internal responses and external attributions to external responses. Two of the manipulation check items asked to what extent the supervisor thought the nurse was the cause or the situation was the cause of the incident. These two items were correlated with the summary response questions.

The results supported the hypothesis. The more the supervisor saw the nurse as the cause the more her response was directed at the nurse (r =

Table 6. Summated Ratings of the Appropriateness of Directing a Response at the Nurse (Study 2)

	Attribution	
Outcome	*External*	*Internal*
Nonserious	3.50	6.72
Serious	4.63	6.68

.70, $p < .01$). The more the supervisor saw the cause as external, the more her response was directed at external factors ($r = .71$, $p < .01$).

Finally, to test for the general bias towards personal responses we used the summary response questions only since no attributions were made in study 2. Across all conditions, the mean appropriateness of an internal personal response was 5.36 and for an external response was 3.57 ($t = 4.46$, $p < .001$). These results suggest that internal responses were preferred over external ones regardless of the conditions surrounding the incident.

Method *(Experiment 3).* The third experiment used four incidents of poor performance. Presented along with the case was some additional information that included or did not include an apology and included or did not include a recognition of responsibility. These manipulations resulted in a 2 × 2 design with each case representing one cell. Each respondent read all four cases and indicated their preferred response.

Forty-three nurse supervisors from one of the hospitals participated in the study and the procedures were the same as in the previous two studies. The dependent variables were the manipulation checks, the preferred response and three new variables; 1) the expectation that a similar failure would happen again; 2) the supervisor's confidence in the nurse's ability to perform in critical situations; and 3) the extent to which the supervisor should closely supervise the nurse in the future. These last three variables were measured on seven point scales with "not at all" and "to a great extent" serving as anchors.

Results *(Experiment 3).* The manipulations checks indicated that the procedures had been successful. The nurse was rated as more responsible in the responsible condition than in the nonresponsible condition ($T = 2.39$, $p < .01$). Also, the nurse was seen as more sorry in the apology condition than in the no-apology condition ($T = 10.21$, $p < .001$).

We again used as our dependent variable the summary question as to the degree to which a response should be directed at the nurse [i.e., "To what extent do you feel this incident demands that you direct your response at the nurse and attempt to change something about her (her job attitude, level of effort etc.)"]. A 2 × 2 analysis of variance resulted in a main effect for the responsible factor [$F(1,41) = 40.4$, $p < .001$] and for the apology factor [$F(1,41) = 40.4$, $p < .001$]. The results are presented in Table 7. As you can see, the supervisor was more likely to direct a response at the nurse when she did not apologize compared to when she did apologize and she was more likely to direct her response at the nurse when she thought the nurse was responsible for the incident than when she thought she was not responsible.

More detailed analyses of these results are available elsewhere (Wood, 1980). However, we should probably mention two additional results.

Table 7. Subjects' Ratings of the Appropriateness of Directing a Response at the Nurse (Study 3)

		Apology	
		Apology	*No Apology*
Responsibility	Responsible	5.62	6.36
	Not Responsible	4.02	5.91

First, more detailed analyses of the specific responses confirms the above findings. Second, there were main effects for the apology and responsibility factors on the three new dependent variables. When the supervisor believed the nurse was not sorry and responsible for the incident she had lower future expectations, less confidence in her ability and supervised her more closely. These findings are as predicted by the model.

Effort and Ability as Performance Cues (Knowlton, 1979)

Since supervisors seem to, in general, use internal attributions more than external ones to explain subordinate failures, we decided to investigate the internal attributions more thoroughly. Given the existing literature, we expected effort attributions to result in more extreme performance evaluations on the part of the supervisor than ability attributions (Weiner and Kukla, 1970; Omelich, 1974). Therefore, we set up a study where supervisors would be given information about the effort or ability of their subordinates, and we measured the supervisors' responses.

Method. Forty groups were run. The supervisor (naive subject) worked with three subordinates (confederates) on a coding task requiring some data to be added and transferred from existing data sheets. In each group the supervisor was faced with two average performers (defined in terms of the number of sheets completed) and one good performer or one poor performer. Certain informational cues were manipulated so that the leader would attribute the good/poor performance to effort or ability. The combinations of this information resulted in the following design (ten leaders in each condition):

		Effort Cue	*Ability Cue*	*Condition*
Performance of Key Subordinate	Good	High	Average	1
		Average	High	2
	Poor	Low	Average	3
		Average	Low	4

The ability cue was manipulated by the use of Wonderlic Personnel Test scores. All four subjects took the test, and the leader was given the scores for the three subordinates. The key subordinate was either the same (for the average ability conditions) as the other two subordinates or substantially higher or lower (for the high or low ability cue). Effort was manipulated through behavioral cues. The key subordinate either worked at the same pace (for the average effort conditions) as the other two subordinates are worked substantially harder/less hard than the other two subordinates. After the one-hour session was over the supervisor rated the three subordinates on a number of measures including manipulations checks, various aspects of performance, and an overall evaluation of performance.

Results. The manipulations checks were generally supportive, although some difficulties arose (see Knowlton, 1979, for more details). The overall assessment of performance (a summed composite of 6, 7-point scales) supported our hypothesis. The rating of the good performer with high effort was 39.9, and this score was 36.5 for the good performer with high ability. The poor performer with low effort was rated lower than the poor performer with low ability (13.7 to 21.1). A 2 × 2 analysis of variance shows a significant main effect for performance, but more importantly a significant interaction for these means [$F(1,36) = 28.34$, $p < .001$]. These data suggest quite strongly that even when *actual* performance is exactly the same, *rated* performance will differ as a function of the attribution made by the supervisor.

Organizational Policy and Attributions (Green and Liden, 1979)

As the model stated, often attributional processes are embedded in organizational contexts which may alter them. One final study examined the relative influence of organizational policies and attributions upon supervisor's responses to poor performance.

Method. Sixty-nine pairs of students were the subjects. Each pair had a randomly selected supervisor and subordinate, and a role description was given to each person that described an incident which was to be discussed (a missed production deadline). These descriptions were exactly the same except for two critical dimensions: The reason for the poor performance and the company policy for dealing with such an incident (the latter being given to the supervisor). The reason given for the subordinate's missing the deadline was either that necessary materials had been somewhat late arriving from another department (external) or that the employee extended his or her lunch hour 45 minutes to talk with a friend (internal). Company policy in dealing with a missed production deadline was either to issue a verbal warning stating that pay would be docked if a deadline was missed again (mild penalty) or to dock one day's pay (severe penalty). This resulted in a 2 × 2 × 2 design crossing role (supervisor/subordinate) by causality (internal/external) by policy (mild/severe).

Before the end of a 20-minute session, the supervisor made his or her decision as to what action to take and conveyed that decision to the subordinate. These responses were guided by a list of possible actions given to each supervisor which included the company policy as well as other alternatives differing in severity. The open-ended responses were rated by independent judges on three dimensions: (1) the degree to which the response focuses on internal or external factors, (2) the severity of the supervisor's action, and (3) the extent to which the supervisor's action followed company policy. A separate manipulation-check question asked the extent to which the subordinate was responsible for the poor performance.

Results. The manipulation check was significant and in the predicted direction. All participants indicated that the subordinate's responsibility was greater in the internal condition than in the external condition [$F(1,130) = 307.79$, $p < .001$].

The responses seemed to fit our hypotheses. As expected, the supervisor was seen as focusing the response more on the subordinate in the internal condition than in the external condition [$F(1,130) = 78.00$, $p < .001$]. Also, the supervisor's response was more severe; that is, more punitive and involving more change to the subordinate's job in the internal condition than the external condition [$F(1,130) = 31.7$, $p < .001$]. For the above two dependent variables, there were no main effects or interactions due to role or policy.

The third dependent variable, adherence to policy, resulted in two main effects and one interaction. Company policy was more likely to be followed in the internal condition than in the external condition [$F(1,130) = 39.50$ $p < .001$], and when the policy was mild rather than severe [$F(1,130) = 20.20$, $p < .001$]. The interaction was marginally significant [$F(1,130) = 2.90$, $p < .09$]. These data suggested that policy was most likely to be followed in the internal/mild conditions and least likely to be followed in the external/severe conditions.

SUMMARY OF THE RESULTS

The above research program was carried out in different settings using different methodologies, types of subjects, and instruments. A number of the findings are summarized below.

1. The definitions of causes of poor performance generated from descriptions of practice (e.g., Miner's work) seem to correspond fairly well

with the theoretical typology suggested by Weiner and his colleagues. Of primary importance is the distinction between internal and external causes.

2. Subordinates tend to see their poor performance as externally caused, while supervisors see it as internally caused.

3. When supervisors have internal attributions for the poor performance of subordinates, they are more likely to be punitive and direct their response at the subordinate than when they have external attributions.

4. A poor work history, as reflected by consistency, consensus, and distinctiveness information, is likely to result in internal attributions and a personal punitive response by the supervisor.

5. When the outcome of the performance failure is serious, the supervisor is more likely to have internal attributions and utilize personal punitive responses than when the outcome is not serious.

6. When a subordinate apologizes or denies responsibility (gives an external explanation), the supervisor is less likely to be severe or personally punitive than when there is no apology.

7. Given the same performance, a supervisor will make more extreme evaluations based on an effort attribution than an ability attribution.

8. Organizational policy seems to interact with attributions in guiding supervisory action and is most likely to be followed when the policy guidelines correspond with the attributions of the supervisor.

While many of these findings need to be replicated, and there are many more aspects of the model to be tested, our initial feeling is that there is substantial evidence that this type of attributional process occurs and is important for supervisor-subordinate interactions.

DISCUSSION

We have been quite encouraged by our results to date. Nevertheless, in the development of any theory, there are new perspectives and changes that occur as a result of reflection and the analysis of data. Also, in presenting these ideas in a variety of forums (e.g., symposia, journals), a number of issues have come up over and over again. Therefore, a few clarifying comments are probably in order.

First, and perhaps most important to point out, is that we do not see attributions as the only or even necessarily the most important determinant of the leader's behavior. While attributions are clearly important, they appear to be only one item of information which is used by the leader. Also, when attributions are used they seem to be formed only partially by the use of the classical cues suggested by Kelley (i.e., consensus, consistency, and distinctiveness).

We visualize the leader as combining the attribution with a number of other factors. One distinction, which has been important for our theoretical thinking, is between informational cues of the classical type based on previous work history and those cues supplied by the immediate circumstances surrounding the event. In this latter category we would include such things as accounts, the seriousness of the outcome, and the seriousness of the act itself. These cues are clearly important for predicting the leader's behavior and may be congruent or incongruent with an attribution generated from consistency, consensus, and distinctiveness data.

Another distinction, which we have found helpful, is between informational cues dealing with the poor-performance incident itself (all of the cues above) and various types of social or normative cues. Social pressure to be "considerate" or to be "hard-nosed," company norms or explicit policy, and other social factors fit into this latter category. Thus, we see our model as distinctly broader in focus than just an attributional analysis.

These distinctions along with our empirical results have some implications for attributional theory, research and practice. As we mentioned earlier, the organizational context seems to be more complex and therefore requires a somewhat more complex theory. This complexity occurs in two ways. First, with the multiple cues, attributions become only one of a set of informational cues. Second, with an emphasis on behavior, there are two links instead of one. Our results tended to show some lack of clarity with respect to where and when attributions and other cues entered into the process. Any direct and simple application of attributional theory or research procedures to more natural settings is not likely to do well without attention to these factors. In particular, more theory and research is needed on the attribution-behavior link.

Another issue has to do with the general question of leadership bias. We have suggested that where errors occur they seem to result in leaders seeing their subordinates as more responsible for their poor performance than perhaps they actually are. The key part of this phrase is "where errors occur." We are *not* suggesting that subordinates are never or even infrequently the cause of poor performance. In many cases the subordinate is clearly at fault, and an internal attribution and severe response is not only appropriate, it will probably get the best results.

The question then becomes one of reducing errors when they occur. Our findings show that given exactly the same factual performance (in the form of a case or actual data), leader's judgments and responses are influenced by attributions, immediate cues, social norms, and company policies. We would suggest that perhaps the best way to reduce these errors is to train supervisors to recognize their biases, to systematically explore possible external causes of poor performance, to focus their response on behaviors, not outcomes, and to utilize consistency, consensus, and distinctiveness data effectively. One of our long-term goals is to empirically test the effectiveness of such a training program.

Finally, we would like to place our model in perspective with respect to the rest of the leadership field. Over the past twenty years, the general approach to leadership has been to focus on the results of a leader's behavior. The general question posed has been what kind of behavior will result in good performance in a specific situation. Fiedler's contingency model (Fiedler, 1967) and House's path-goal model (House, 1977) are the best examples of this tradition.

However, in recent years the focus has begun to shift from an analysis of the consequences of leader behavior to the causes of leader behavior. A recent review of the leadership area (Mitchell, 1979) indicated that a number of researchers have emphasized a more interactionist or exchange-type analysis of leadership (Graen, 1976; Hollander, 1978; Hunt and Osborn, 1978). Leadership is seen as a two-way process. The important point is that these authors have placed the causes of leader behavior on an equal footing with its consequences. We also see our attributional model as focusing on the causes of leader behavior in the short run. However, as we have mentioned before, ultimately we wish to show that training leaders to understand the causes of their behavior will reduce bias and errors. This reduction will, in turn, lead to a more effective response which will, of course, be measured in terms of the effects of the leader's behavior. Thus, we see our model as an integral part of the general shift in orientation in the leadership field. The next few years should help to determine the utility of such an approach; initially we are optimistic about its promise.

ACKNOWLEDGMENT

Part of the research discussed in this paper was supported by the Army Research Institute Contract No. MDA 903-79-C-0543 and the National Science Foundation Grant No. DAR 79-09792 (Terence R. Mitchell and Lee Roy Beach, Principal Investigators).

NOTES

1. The attributional model presented here draws on a previous theoretical article by Green and Mitchell (1979) which proposes a general attributional model of leader-member interactions.

2. The role of ego-biasing motives in attributional processes is far from resolved. Some authors question their existence as anything other than misunderstood information processes (Miller and Ross, 1975).

3. The effects of power differentiation on the attributions and behavior of leaders is not extensively researched. Kipnis's (1972) and McFillen's (1978) findings only partially support one another. Further research is required to understand the relationship of power to leader-member interactions.

REFERENCES

Ajzen, I., and Fishbein, M. (1978) "Use and Misuse and Bayes' Theorem in Causal Attribution: Don't Attribute It to Ajzen and Fishbein Either," *Psychological Bulletin,* 85: 244–246.

Banks, W. C. (1976) "The Effects of Perceived Similarity upon the Use of Reward and Punishment," *Journal of Experimental Social Psychology,* 12: 131–138.

Blumstein, P. W., Carssow, K. G., Hall, J., Hawkins, B., Hoffman, R., Ishem, E., Maurer, C. P., Spens, D., Taylor, J., and Zimmerman, D. L. (1974) "The Honoring of Accounts," *American Sociological Review,* 39: 551–566.

Bradley, G. W. (1978) "Self-serving Biases in the Attribution Process: A Re-examination of the Fact or Fiction Question," *Journal of Personality and Social Psychology,* 36(1): 56–71.

Brickman, P., Ryan, K., and Wortman, C. (1975) "Causal Chains: Attributions of Responsibility as a Function of Immediate and Prior Causes," *Journal of Personality and Social Psychology,* 32: 1060–1067.

Dansereau, F., Graen, G., and Haga, W. J. (1975) "A Vertical Dyad Linkage Approach to Leadership in Formal Organizations," *Organizational Behavior and Human Performance,* 13: 46–78.

Deaux, K., and Emswiller, T. (1974) "Explanations of Successful Performance on Sex-linked Tasks: What Is Skill for the Male Is Luck for the Female," *Journal of Personality and Social Psychology,* 29: 80–85.

Elig, T. W., and Frieze, I. H. (1975) "A Multi-dimensional Scheme for Coding and Interpreting Perceived Causality for Success and Failure Events: The Coding Scheme of Perceived Causality (CSPC)," JSAS Catalog of *Selected Documents in Psychology,* 5: 313.

Feather, N. T. (1969) "Attribution of Responsibility and Valence of Success and Failure in Relation to Initial Confidence and Task Performance," *Journal of Personality and Social Psychology,* 13(2): 129–144.

Feather, N. T., and Simon, J. G. (1971) "Causal Attributions for Success and Failure in Relation to Expectations of Success Based upon Selective or Manipulative Control," *Journal of Personality,* 39: 527–541.

Feldman, N. S., Higgins, E. T., Karvolac, M., and Ruble, D. N. (1976) "Use of Consensus Information in Causal Attributions as a Function of Temporal Presentation and Availability of Direct Information," *Journal of Personality and Social Psychology,* 34(4): 694–698.

Feldman-Summers, S., and Kiesler, S. (1974) "Those Who Are Number Two Try Harder: The Effect of Sex on Attributions of Causality," *Journal of Personality and Social Psychology,* 30(6): 846–855.

Fiedler, F. E. (1967) *A Theory of Leadership Effectiveness.* New York: McGraw Hill.

Fischhoff, B., and Lichtenstein, S. (1978) "Don't Attribute This to Reverend Bayes," *Psychological Bulletin,* 85: 239–243.

Frieze, I., and Weiner, B. (1971) "Cue Utilization and Attribution Judgments for Success and Failure," *Journal of Personality and Social Psychology,* 39: 591–605.

Garland, H., and Price, K. (1977) "Attitudes Toward Women in Management and Attributions for Their Success and Failure in a Managerial Position," *Journal of Applied Psychology,* 62(1): 29–33.

Goffman, E. (1971) *Relations in Public.* New York: Doubleday.

Graen, G. (1976) "Role Making Processes Within Complex Organizations." In M. Dunnette (ed.)., *Handbook of Industrial and Organizational Psychology.* Chicago: Rand McNally.

Green, S. G. (1978) "Aptitude Test Scores, Past Performance, and Causal Attributions about the Poorly Performing Student," *Journal of Educational Psychology,* 70(2): 242–247.

——(1979) "Causes of Ineffective Performance," *Proceedings of the Midwest Academy of Management,* Cleveland: 38–48.

Green, S. G., and Liden, R. (1979) "The Effects of Leader Attributions and Company Policy upon Disciplinary Judgments." Unpublished working paper, University of Cincinnati, School of Business.

Green, S. G., and Mitchell, T. R. (1979) "Attributional Processes of Leaders in Leader-Member Interactions," *Organizational Behavior and Human Performance,* 23: 429–458.

Hansen, R. D., and Lowe, C. A. (1976) "Distinctiveness and Consensus: The Influence of Behavioral Information on Actors' and Observers' Attributions," *Journal of Personality and Social Psychology,* 34: 425–433.

Hansen, R. D., and Donoghue, J. M. (1977) "The Power of Consensus: Information Derived from One's Own and Other's Behavior," *Journal of Personality and Social Psychology,* 35(5): 294–302.

Hollander, E. P. (1978) *Leadership Dynamics: A Practical Guide to Effective Relationship.* New York: Free Press.

House, R. J. (1971) "A Path Goal Theory of Leadership Effectiveness," *Administrative Science Quarterly,* 16: 321–338.

Hunt, J. G., and Osborn, R. N. (1978) "A Multiple Approach to Leadership for Managers." In J. Stinson and P. Hersey (eds.), *Leadership for Practitioners.* Athens: Ohio University, Center for Leadership Studies.

Jacobs, T. O. (1971) *Leadership and Exchange in Formal Organizations.* Alexandria, Va.: Human Research Operations Organizations.

Jones, E. E. (1979) "The Rocky Road from Acts to Dispositions," *American Psychologist,* 34: 107–117.

Jones, E. E., and Nisbett, R. E. (1972) "The Actor and the Observer: Divergent Perceptions of the Causes of Behavior." In E. Jones, D. Kanouse, H. Kelley, R. Nisbett, S. Valins, and B. Weiner (eds.), *Attribution: Perceiving the Causes of Behavior.* Morristown, N.J.: General Learning Press.

Kelley, H. H. (1967) "Attribution Theory in Social Psychology. In D. Levine (ed.), *Nebraska Symposium on Motivation* (Vol. 15). Lincoln: University of Nebraska Press.

——(1972a) "Attribution in Social Interaction." In E. Jones, D. Kanouse, H. Kelley, R. Nisbett, S. Valins, and B. Weiner (eds.), *Attribution: Perceiving the Causes of Behavior.* Morristown, N.J.: General Learning Press.

——(1972b) "Causal Schemata and the Attribution Process." In E. Jones, D. Kanouse, H. Kelley, R. Nisbett, S. Valins, and B. Weiner (eds.), *Attribution: Perceiving the Causes of Behavior.* Morristown, N.J.: General Learning Press.

——(1973) "The Processes of Causal Attribution," *American Psychologist,* 28: 107–128.

Kipnis, D. (1972a) "Does Power Corrupt?" *Journal of Personality and Social Psychology,* 24: 33–41.

Knowlton, W. A., Jr. (1979) "The Effects of Causal Attributions on a Supervisor's Evaluation of Subordinate Performance." Ph.D. dissertation, University of Washington, Department of Psychology.

Kruglanski, A. W. (1970) "Attributing Trustworthiness in Supervisor-Worker Relations," *Journal of Experimental Social Psychology,* 6: 214–232.

McArthur, L. Z. (1976) "The Lesser Influence of Consensus Than Distinctiveness Information on Causal Attributions: A Test of the Person-Thing Hypothesis," *Journal of Personality and Social Psychology,* 33(6): 733–742.

McFillen, J. M. (1978) "Supervisory Power as an Influence in Supervisor-Subordinate Relations," *Academy of Management Journal,* 21(3): 419–433.

McMahan, I. (1976) "Relationships Between Causal Attributions and Expectancy of Success," *Journal of Personality and Social Psychology,* 28: 108–114.

Miller, D., and Ross, M. (1975) "Self-Serving Biases in the Attribution of Causality: Fact or Fiction?" *Psychological Bulletin,* 82: 213–225.

Miner, J. B. (1963) *The Management of Ineffective Performance.* New York: McGraw-Hill.

———(1975) *Studies in Management Education.* New York: Springer.

———(1975) *The Challenge of Managing.* Philadelphia: Saunders.

Miner, J. B., and Brewer, J. F. (1976) "The Management of Ineffective Performance." In M. D. Dunnette (ed.), *Handbook of Industrial and Organizational Psychology.* Chicago: Rand McNally, pp. 995–1030.

Mitchell, T. R. (1979) "Organizational Behavior," *Annual Review of Psychology,* 30: 243–281.

Mitchell, T. R., and Wood, R. E. (1979) "An Empirical Test of an Attributional Model of Leader's Responses to Poor Performance," *Proceedings of the National Meetings of the Academy of Management,* Atlanta, Ga.

Monson, T., and Snyder, M. (1977) "Actors, Observers, and the Attribution Process," *Journal of Experimental Social Psychology,* 13: 89–111.

Nisbett, R. E., and Borgida, E. (1975) "Attribution and the Psychology of Prediction," *Journal of Personality and Social Psychology,* 32(5): 532–943.

Nisbett, R. E., Borgida, E., Crandall, R., and Reed, H. (1976) "Popular Induction: Information Is Not Always Informative." In J. S. Carroll and J. W. Payne (eds.), *Cognition and Social Behavior.* Hillsdale, N.J.: Erlbaum.

Omelich, C. (1974) "Attribution and Achievement in the Classroom: The Self-fulfilling Prophecy." Paper presented at the California Personnel and Guidance Association, San Francisco (February).

Orvis, B. R., Kelley, H. H., and Butler, D. (1976) "Attributional Conflict in Young Couples." In J. H. Harvey, W. J. Ickes, and R. F. Kidd (eds.), *New Directions in Attribution Research,* Vol. 1. New York: John Wiley and Sons.

Regan, D. T., Straus, E., and Fazio, R. (1974) "Liking and the Attribution Process," *Journal of Experimental and Social Psychology,* 10: 385–397.

Regan, D. T., and Totten, J. (1975) "Empathy and Attribution: Turning Observers into Actors," *Journal of Personality and Social Psychology,* 32(5): 850–856.

Rosen, B., and Jerdee, T. H. (1974) "Factors Influencing Disciplinary Judgments," *Journal of Applied Psychology,* 3: 327–331.

Rosenbaum, R. M. (1972) "A Dimensional Analysis of the Perceived Causes of Success and Failure." Unpublished doctoral dissertation, University of California, Los Angeles.

Ruble, D., and Feldman, N. (1976) "Order of Consensus Distinctiveness and Consistency Information and Causal Attributions," *Journal of Personality and Social Psychology,* 34(5): 930–937.

Scott, M. B., and Lyman, S. M. (1968) "Accounts," *American Sociological Review,* 33: 46–62.

Shaver, K. G. (1975) *Introduction to Attribution Processes*. Cambridge, Mass., Winthrop.

Soulier, M. (1978) "The Effects of Success, Failure, and Accountability on the Content of Worker Attributions." Ph.D. dissertation, University of Washington, School of Business.

Steinmetz, L. L. (1969) *Managing the Marginal and Unsatisfactory Performer*. Reading, Mass.: Addison-Wesley.

Storms, M. D. (1973) "Videotape and the Attribution Process: Reversing Actors' and Observers' Points of View," *Journal of Personality and Social Psychology*, 27: 165–175.

Strickland, T. H. (1958) "Surveillance and trust," *Journal of Personality:* 26: 200–215.

Walster, E. (1966) "Assignment of Responsibility for an Accident," *Journal of Personality and Social Psychology*, 3(1): 73–79.

Weiner, B. (1974) "Achievement Motivation as Conceptualized by an Attribution Theorist." In B. Weiner (ed.), *Achievement Motivation and Attribution Theory*. Morristown, N.J.: General Learning Press.

Weiner, B., Frieze, I., Kukla, A., Reed, L., Rest, S., and Rosenbaum, R. (1972) "Perceiving the Causes of Success and Failure." In E. Jones, D. Kanouse, H. Kelley, R. Nisbett, S. Valins, and B. Weiner (eds.), *Attribution: Perceiving the Causes of Behavior*. Morristown, N.J.: General Learning Press.

Weiner, B., and Kukla, A. (1970) "An Attributional Analysis of Achievement Motivation," *Journal of Personality and Social Pshchology*, 15: 1–20.

Weiner, B., Nierenberg, R., and Goldstein, M. (1976) "Social Learning (Locus of Control) Versus Attributional (Causal Stability) Interpretations of Expectancy of Success," *Journal of Personality*, 44(1): 52–68.

Wells, G. T., and Harvey, J. H. (1977) "Do People Use Consensus Information in Making Causal Attributions," *Journal of Personality and Social Psychology*, 35(5): 279–293.

Wood, R. E. (1980) "The Effects of Accounts and the Consequences of Behavior on the Attributions of Leaders about the Causes of Subordinate Poor Performance." Ph.D. dissertation, University of Washington, School of Business.

INFORMATION RICHNESS:
A NEW APPROACH TO MANAGERIAL BEHAVIOR AND ORGANIZATION DESIGN

Richard L. Daft and Robert H. Lengel

ABSTRACT

This chapter introduces the concept of information richness, and proposes three models of information processing. The models describe (1) managerial information behavior, (2) organizational mechanisms for coping with equivocality from the environment, and (3) organizational mechanisms for internal coordination. Concepts developed by Weick (1979) and Galbraith (1973) are integrated into two information tasks: equivocality reduction and the processing of a sufficient amount of information. The premise of this chapter is that the accomplishment of these information tasks as well as the ultimate success of the organization are both related to the balance of information richness used in the organization.

Organizations face a dilemma. They must interpret the confusing, complicated swarm of external events that intrude upon the organization. Organizations must try to make sense of ill-defined, complex problems about which they have little or unclear information (Weick & Daft, 1982). Inside the organization, more confusion arises. Departments pull against each other to attain diverse goals and to serve unique constituencies and technologies (Lawrence and Lorsch, 1967). Divergent frames of reference, values, and goals generate disagreement, ambiguity and uncertainty. In response to the confusion arising from both the environment and internal differences, organizations must create an acceptable level of order and certainty. Managers must impose structure and clarity upon ambiguous events, and thereby provide direction, procedures, adequate coupling, clear data, and decision guidelines for participants. Organizations must confront uncertain, disorderly events from within and without, yet provide a clear, workable, well defined conceptual scheme for participants.

How do organizations perform this miracle? Through information processing. The design of organizations—even the very act of organizing—reflects ways to handle information (Galbraith, 1977; Weick, 1979). Managers spend the vast majority of their time exchanging information (Mintzberg, 1973). Specific dimensions of organization structure, such as functional or product organizational forms, and the use of teams, task forces or vertical information systems, all reflect information processing needs within organizations (Galbraith, 1973; Tushman & Nadler, 1978). Several papers have appeared in recent years which focus on information processing requirements as the explanation for observed organizational performance (Arrow, 1974; Porter & Roberts, 1976; Weick, 1979; Galbraith, 1977; Tushman & Nadler, 1978). Consider, for example, the following information processing activities.[1]

City Government. Late in the afternoon of March 13, 1980, a killer tornado bore down on the town of Elkhart, Oklahoma. The tornado cut a swath three blocks wide through the center of town. Everything in its path was destroyed. Several people were killed and scores were injured.

The city administration had prepared for the emergency. Four years earlier, the city council authorized development of an emergency plan. Working with a consultant, city department heads developed specific procedures to follow in the event of tornado, flood, explosion, or noxious gas. The procedures were similar to procedures that had solved emergencies in other towns. A national guard armory had been turned over to the city. Medical supplies were stored in the armory, along with food, water, sanitary facilities, and beds for people left homeless. A communication center to coordinate police, firemen, and utility departments was in one room. Equipment necessary for a temporary morgue was in another room. Space and personnel were allocated for counseling bereaved family members or others in a state of psychological disorientation. The city fathers had thought of everything . . . almost.

The armory was in the path of the tornado. The armory was destroyed. Thirty minutes after the tornado struck, the Mayor realized a new plan would have to be developed from scratch. City councilmen, department heads and the firechief were all called to police headquarters. Individuals toured the community and reported back. The group stayed up all night listening to reports of damage, discussing needs, setting priorities, developing alternatives, and assigning tasks. The administrators were emotionally distraught but by morning the injured had been found and delivered to hospitals, the damaged areas were secure, and a plan for the next week's activities was in place. City officials, working together, carved an excellent plan of action from an unpredicted emergency. They received high marks from townspeople and visiting officials for their effective response to the crisis.

Business College. A new dean was hired to run a large school of business in a major university in the Southeast. The dean initiated a plan to hold aside a portion of the salary increase money to be allocated on top of normal raises—called super raises—for the ten best producers in the college. The department heads met with the dean to recommend top performers from each department and to discuss their relative merits. The purpose of this meeting was to establish a common criterion of performance across departments and to select top performers.

The dean quickly realized that assignment of super raises was going to be difficult. Each professor's record was unique. How did publication in a finance journal compare to publication in a marketing journal? What was the contribution to knowledge of an article, and how was journal quality to be weighted? What was the role of teaching and student learning in the evaluation? The dean simplified the problem by asking department heads to summarize in a single page the record of each individual they recommended for a raise. Seventeen names were submitted with a one page summary of activities. From these the dean had to select ten. He found the decision impossible so he returned the sheets to the department heads and asked them to rate all 17 people on a ten point scale. Professors with the highest average scores received the super raises. In essence, the complexity of each professor's record was first condensed onto a single page, and then into a single number. Several faculty members complained that the best performance in the college had not been rewarded. The following year, the dean and department heads devoted an entire day to discussion and analysis of performance records. Debate was lengthy and heated. Agreement was finally reached, and the outcome was acceptable to faculty members.

Retail Chain. Matthew B. was chief executive of a high fashion retail chain. The chain had 36 stores in 13 cities. Matthew B. hated formal reports. He preferred to discuss matters face-to-face and to reach decisions through consensus and discussion. Staying in touch required extensive travel. He visited stores to see what was selling and to get a feel for store design and layout. He had weekly breakfast meetings with top executives for discussion and planning. He also visited the company's plants and went to fashion shows to stay abreast of new trends.

Following a serious heart attack, Matthew B. retired and James N. became chief executive. He immediately acted on his belief in strong financial controls and precise analysis. He requested detailed reports and analyses for every decision. He relied on paper work and computer printouts for information. He cancelled the breakfast meetings and trips to plants, stores, and fashion centers. Personal contact with others was limited to occasional telephone calls and quarterly meetings. James N. argued that managing a corporation was like flying an airplane. Watch the dials to see if the plane deviates from its course, and then nudge it back with financial controls. Within two years, a palace revolt led by a coalition of board members and vice-presidents ousted him as chief executive. They claimed that the chief executive had gotten hopelessly out of touch with the fast moving fashion environment.

The situations above illustrate ways organizations translate unexpected or complex problems into simpler, workable solutions. For the city of Elkhart, the ad hoc structure seemed to work well. Unclear events were interpreted and a workable course of action was developed. In the business college, the lengthy discussion used to evaluate faculty performance achieved a better outcome than the use of written descriptions or quantitative ratings. A similar thing happened in the retail chain. Management by discussion led to a more satisfactory outcome than managing by formal reports and paperwork.

Purpose of This Chapter

The purpose of this chapter is to propose new theoretical models that explain how organizations cope with the environment, coordinate activities, and solve problems through information processing, as illustrated in the above examples. The concept of information richness is introduced to explain how organizations meet the need for information amount and to reduce equivocality. *The premise of this chapter is that organizational success is based on the organization's ability to process information of appropriate richness to reduce uncertainty and clarify ambiguity.* The concept of information richness is combined with other information concepts to provide an integrated view of the organization as an information processing system. The chapter is divided into four parts.

1. The concept of information richness is presented in the next section and is used to integrate concepts from the information literature.
2. A model of manager behavior is then proposed, based upon the congruence between information richness and information needs.
3. Next, a model of organizations as information processing systems is proposed. Organizations have two information problems to solve: that of interpreting the environment and that of coordinating diverse internal activities. Models based on information richness explain how organizations such as the Elkhart city government and the business school described above resolve both interpretation and coordination needs.
4. Finally, traditional organization concepts, such as bureaucracy, politics, and organic structure are reinterpreted to show how they are associated with richness of information processing. Suggestions for future research are also explored.

DEFINITION OF INFORMATION RICHNESS

Daft and Wiginton (1979) proposed that human languages differ in their ability to convey information. The concept of language was used in the broadest sense to encompass various ways to transmit ideas, emotions, and concepts. High variety languages are those in which symbol use is not restricted and the language can communicate a wide range of ideas. Examples include art, music, and painting, which are subjective in interpretation. Low variety languages have symbols that are restrictive in their use, and the languages communicate a narrower range of ideas. Low variety languages include mathematics and statistics, which convey exact, unequivocal meaning to users. Daft and Wiginton argued that high variety languages were appropriate for communicating about difficult, ephemeral, social phenomena. Low variety languages communicate effectively about well understood, unambiguous topics.

The notion of language variety seems plausible, but it doesn't explain information processing in organizations. Managers typically don't use art, poetry, or mathematics to communicate about organizational phenomena. The range of language used within organizations is typically limited to natural language and simple numbers.

Lengel (1983) proposed a continuum of information richness to explain information processing behavior in organizations. Richness is defined as the potential information–carrying capacity of data. If the communication of an item of data, such as a wink, provides substantial new understanding, it would be considered rich. If the datum provides little understanding, it would be low in richness.

Lengel (1983), building upon the work of Bodensteiner (1970), argued that the communication media used in organizations determines the richness of information processed. He proposed that communication media vary in the richness of information processed. Moreover, communication media were proposed to fit along a 5-step continuum, as in Figure 1. Communication media include face-to-face discussion, phone calls, letters, written documents and numeric documents. The face-to-face medium conveys the richest information while formal numeric documents convey the least rich information.

The explanation for the hierarchy of media richness is contained in Figure 2. Each medium differs in (1) feedback capability, (2) communication channels utilized, (3) source and (4) language (Bodensteiner, 1970; Holland, Stead, & Leibrock, 1976).

Face-to-face is the richest form of information processing because it provides immediate feedback. With feedback, understanding can be checked and interpretations corrected. The face-to-face medium also al-

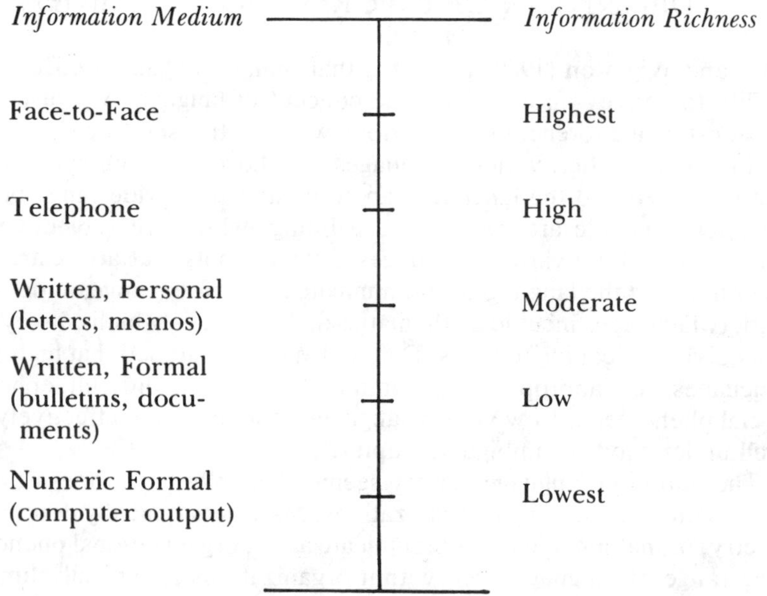

Figure 1. Communication Media and Information Richness.

Information Richness	Medium	Feedback	Channel	Source	Language
High ↑	Face-to-Face	Immediate	Visual, Audio	Personal	Body, Natural
	Telephone	Fast	Audio	Personal	Natural
	Written, Personal	Slow	Limited Visual	Personal	Natural
	Written, Formal	Very Slow	Limited Visual	Impersonal	Natural
Low	Numeric, Formal	Very Slow	Limited Visual	Impersonal	Numeric

Figure 2. Characteristics of media that determine richness of information processed.

lows the simultaneous observation of multiple cues, including body language, facial expression and tone of voice, which convey information beyond the spoken message. Face-to-face information also is of a personal nature and utilizes natural language which is high in variety (Daft and Wiginton, 1979).

The telephone medium is somewhat less rich than face-to-face. Feedback capability is fast, but visual cues are not available. Individuals have to rely on language content and audio cues to reach understanding.

Written communications are less rich still. Feedback is slow. Only the information that is written down is conveyed so visual cues are limited to that which is on paper. Audio cues are absent, although natural language can be utilized. Addressed documents are of a personal nature and are somewhat richer than standard flyers and bulletins, which are anonymous and impersonal.

Formal numeric documents are lowest in information richness. An example would be quantitative reports from the computer. Numbers tend to be useful for communicating about simple, quantifiable aspects of organizations. Numbers do not have the information–carrying capacity of natural language. These reports provide no opportunity for visual observation, feedback, or personalization.

One value of the richness hierarchy in Figures 1 and 2 is that it organizes a diverse set of information concepts. For example, previous research has been concerned with information sources such as human versus documentary (Keegan, 1974), personal versus impersonal (Aguilar, 1967), and such things as files, formal reports, or group discussions (O'Reilly, 1982; Kefalas, 1975). The richness continuum makes sense of these differences, and may explain source utilization. Each medium is not just a source, but represents a difference in the act of information processing. Each medium utilizes differences in feedback, cues and language variety. Richness is a promising concept for understanding information behavior in organizations. In the next section, we show how information richness explains the information processing behavior of managers.

MODEL OF MANAGERIAL INFORMATION PROCESSING

Organizational phenomena confronting managers can vary from simple to complex. Simple phenomena tend to be mechanical, routine, predictable and well understood. Simple phenomena mean that managers typically can follow an objective, computational procedure to resolve problems. When phenomena are complex, however, no objective, computational procedure tells the manager how to respond. These issues are difficult, hard to analyze, perhaps emotion laden, and unpredictable. Managers have to spend time analyzing the situation and thinking about what to do. They will search for information and solutions outside normal procedures. Simple versus complex problems are similar to what Thompson (1967) called knowledge of cause-effect relationships and what Perrow (1967) called analyzability. Managers often experience difficulty seeing into complex tasks to analyze alternative courses of action, costs, benefits, and outcomes.

The proposed role of information media in managerial information processing is presented in the framework in Figure 3. Figure 3 illustrates that rich media are needed to process information about complex organizational topics. Media low in richness are suited to simple topics. The me-

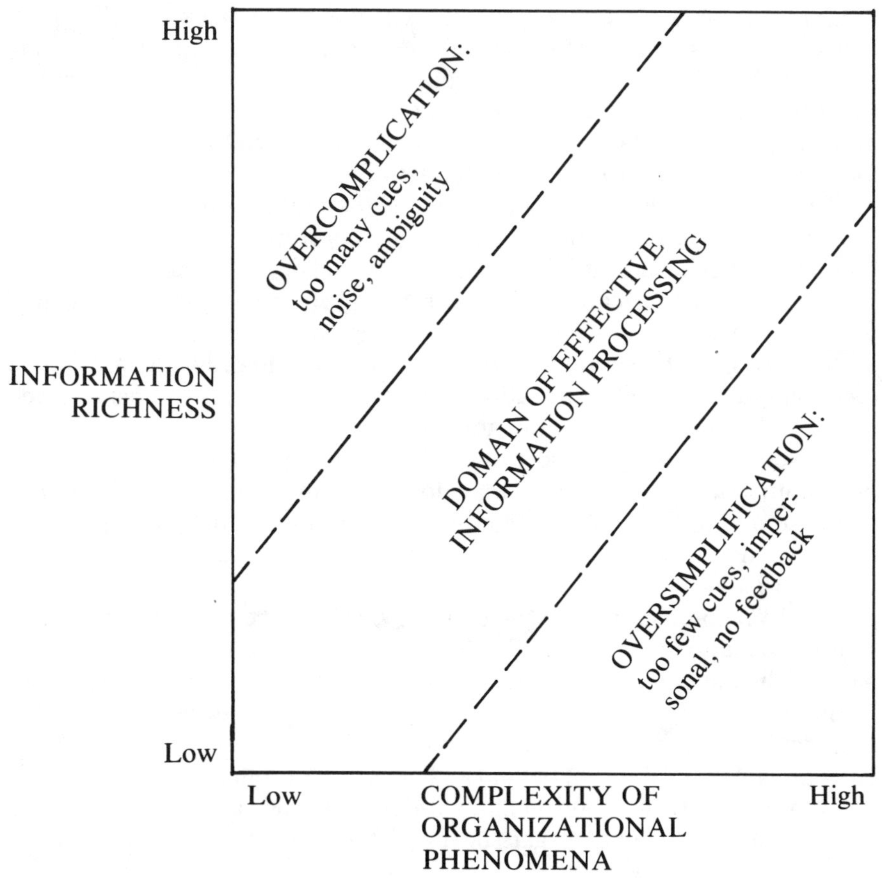

Figure 3. Model of managerial information processing.

chanical side of the organization is normally simple and measureable. Factors such as inventory control or employee attendance are not difficult to conceptualize. Managers can communicate about these phenomena through paperwork and quantitative reports. Other variables, such as organizational goals, strategies, managerial intentions or employee motivation, are intangible. These factors are not clear and discreet, and they can be difficult to interpret. Making sense of these factors requires a rich medium that provides multiple information cues, immediate feedback and a high variety language. Rich information enables managers to arrive at a more accurate interpretation in a short time.

The framework in Figure 3 hypothesizes a positive relationship between information richness and the complexity of organizational phenomena. Managers will turn to rich media when they deal with the difficult, changing, unpredictable human dimensions of organizations. Rich media enable them to communicate about and make sense of these processes. Face-to-face and telephone media enable managers to quickly update their mental maps of the organization. Rich media convey multiple cues and enable rapid feedback. Less rich media might oversimplify complex topics and may not enable the exchange of sufficient information to alter a manger's understanding. For routine problems, which are already understood, media of lower richness would provide sufficient information.

The Figure 3 framework is a significant departure from the assumption that precise, clear information is best for managers. Memos, reports and other written media can oversimplify complex problems. They do not provide a means to convey personal feelings or feedback. These media do not transmit the subtleties associated with the unpredictable, messy, emotional aspects of organizations. On the other hand, extensive face-to-face meetings for simple phenomena may also be inefficient. Face-to-face discussion sends a variety of cues, which may not always agree with one another. Facial expression may distract from spoken words. Multiple cues can distract the receiver's attention from the routine message.

This model, if correct, begins to explain why top managers make little use of formal information in organizations. Managers thrive on informal, personal communications (Mintzberg, 1973). The retail chain chief executives described earlier in this chapter illustrate the role of information media. The executive who used rich media such as store and plant visits, breakfast meetings and phone calls kept well informed on myriad environmental and company issues. The executive who relied on formal reports and financial data got behind and out of synchronization with events. Face-to-face and telephone media, with multiple cues and rapid feedback, are needed to help top managers deal with the complex issues confronting them.

Management scientists, operational researchers, and other staff specialists are frustrated when managers ignore formal reports, systematic studies, and standard procedures. The model in Figure 3 explains why. Those media only work for certain tasks. The reason managers often ignore these sources of information is not personal ignorance, lack of training, or personality defects. Informal, personal media simply are capable of providing richer information to managers about certain problems. Managerial behavior reflects an intuitive understanding of how to learn about things. Many management problems are difficult and complex; hence formal information is not rich enough to convey adequate insight and understanding. Personal sources are more insightful. Thus, managers' information processing behavior may make sense after all.

Research Evidence

Mintzberg's (1973) observation of top managers indicated that each manager is the nerve center for an information network. Managers have extensive contacts both within and outside the organization. They are plugged into channels for rumor and gossip, and are surrounded with formal information systems that provide periodic summaries and analyses of organizational activities. Managers spend over eighty percent of their time communicating. In this section we will review studies of information processing in organizations to determine whether previous research supports the Figure 3 relationship between media selection and problem complexity. This review is organized into three parts: (1) information sources, (2) mode of presentation, and (3) the use of management information systems.

Information Sources. Observations of managers indicate a strong preference for the verbal media. They prefer face-to-face meetings and the telephone. Mail and technical reports are used less frequently (Mintzberg, 1972, 1973). Managers prefer current information and move away from formal reports and quantitative documents.

The information sources observed by Mintzberg represent differences in media richness. Face-to-face and telephone are rich and enable managers to process information about intangible activities. Mail and formal reports are less rich, and usually pertain to well understood aspects of the organization. The majority of manager information is processed through rich media because organizations are often fast changing, and many of the manager's responsibilities pertain to the social, emotional and poorly understood aspects of organization. Our model is consistent with and explains manager behavior such as observed by Mintzberg (1973).

A study by Holland, Stead, and Leibrock (1976) comes closest to evaluating the Figure 3 model of manager information processing. They proposed that individuals working under high uncertainty would use richer media to transfer information than would individuals dealing with relative certainty. Holland, et al gathered questionnaire data from R&D units, and found that interpersonal channels of communication were important when perceived uncertainty was high. They also found a positive relationship between level of uncertainty and the reported usefulness of information sources. Holland, et al concluded that managers experiencing uncertainty should be encouraged to use rich sources of information, even if it meant making long distance telephone calls or traveling. High rich media enabled participants to learn about complex topics in a short time. Written information sources, such as the professional literature and technical manuals, were preferred when task assignments were well understood.

A study by Blandin and Brown (1977) looked at the search behavior of managers. They examined external, formal, and informal information sources and related these to environmental uncertainty. As the level of perceived uncertainty increased, managers relied more heavily on external and informal sources of information. The frequency and amount of time spent gathering information also increased. Thus, both the richness and amount of information increased with perceived uncertainty.

Although only a few studies have compared information source to topic complexity, the findings above do suggest that richer sources tend to be used when managers confront uncertain or complex topics. Less rich sources of information tend to be preferred when issues are well understood and routine. In general, the pattern of findings supports the positive relationship between media richness and task complexity proposed in the managerial information processing model.

Mode of Presentation. Research into the mode of presentation typically presents data in two or more forms to learn how it is perceived and acted on. Nisbett and associates found that case illustrations have stronger impact on people's judgement than hard data (Borgada & Nisbett, 1977; McArthur, 1972, 1976; Nisbett & Ross, 1980). O'Reilly (1980) concluded that humans are more influenced by vivid, concrete examples than by dry statistics, even though statistics represent more systematic evidence from multiple observations. Other studies report that statistical data do have impact, but the case example gets more weight in decisions that appear to be objectively rational (Azien, 1977; Feldman, et al., 1976; Hansen and Donohue, 1977; Feldman & March, 1981; Manis et al., 1980). In a series of studies, Martin & Powers (1979, 1980a, 1980b) provided recipients with written statistical data and with a verbal story to assess which information swayed policy decisions. Stories tended to have more impact. They concluded that organizational reality is not objective, therefore statistical data pretends to report an objective reality which does not exist in the mental model of managers. Statistical data did tend to be influential when used to refute or overturn organizational policy. More precise evidence thus may be required to overturn a decision, while qualitative, story–based evidence is sufficient to support current policies.

Several studies show a strong preference for oral modes of information transfer. Mason and Mitroff (1973) argued that mode of presentation influences information preference. Landendorf (1970) found that interpersonal modes were preferred to written communication because interpersonal modes can be refined, adapted and evaluated to precisely fit the problem. Generally, oral information allows for rapid feedback and resolution of complex problems, and is often easier to gain access to. The importance of oral communication, especially face-to-face, is reflected in the impact of nonverbal signals. Eye contact, body movement, and facial expression communicate meaning beyond the verbal message. In one study of face-to-face communication, only seven percent of the content was transmitted by verbal language. The remaining ninety-three percent of information received was contained in the tone of voice and facial expression (Mehrabian, 1971). A sarcastic versus enthusiastic tone of voice conveys as much meaning as the specific statements processed between managers.

Management Information Systems. Management information systems tend to be on the low end of the richness continuum presented in Figure 1. Most MIS's are formal and use quantitative or written reports.

Many studies designed to evaluate the usefulness of management information systems have attempted to operationalize economic value. Subjects purchase data and make simple decisions. These studies are not very helpful to understanding manager behavior because they employ naive assumptions about how managers use information. These studies are typically conducted in the laboratory, using sterile decision tasks and sterile information. The array of information cues typically available to managers are absent. The generality of these studies is extremely questionable (O'Reilly & Anderson, 1979).

Perhaps the most widely accepted conclusion is that computer-based management information systems are not very useful to managers. The efforts to implement and use these systems have fallen short of providing maximum effectiveness and efficiency (Ackoff, 1976; Deardin, 1972; Larson, 1974; Grayson, 1973; Leavitt, 1975). A number of factors have been cited to explain MIS failures. Management information systems provide data about stable, recurring, predictable events. MIS's provide data that skim over the nonquantifiable detail needed by managers. Management information systems supply quantifiable data. These data do not provide insight into the intangible, social dimensions of an organization.

Brown (1966) noted that information needs may depend upon level of decision. At the operational level in organizations, where decisions pertain to routine technical problems, decision support systems may have greater value. Several other studies support the conclusion that management information systems are most relevant to those managers who work with well defined operational and technical decisions (Dearden, 1972; Dickson, Senn, Cheway, 1977).

A survey of fifty-six organizations in England by Higgins and Finn (1977) examined attitudes toward management information systems. While computer reports could be useful, they found intuitive judgement was used more often than computer analysis in management's strategic decisions. Executives typically drew on a variety of sources of information, weighing each for importance, and then making a final decision. Computer based data could play a role in these decisions, but a small one.

The small role of management information systems is not completely understood, but the primary reason seems to be that they do not convey information that meets managers' needs. MIS's work under the assumption that managers need large amounts of precise data. As managers receive more and more data, they should be able to solve their problems, which is not the case (Ackoff, 1967).

Tushman and Nadler (1977) believe that information designers are more concerned with fitting data to their hardward than with understanding the overall information needs of managers. Information system designers lack a theory about manager needs and behavior. By limiting data to those things amenable to machine hardware, information designers miss the root causes of manager information processing. Most managerial tasks are too ill-defined for quantitative data, yet system designers assume that computer output is sufficient for management decisions. MIS systems are able to capture and communicate about the stable, predictable activities, but not about the important, subjective, ill-defined events relevant to decision making.

Summary. The pattern of findings about managerial information processing tends to support the notion that information richness is a useful explanation for information behavior. Only a few studies have examined managers' utilization of various media, or have related media to specific tasks (Lengel, 1983). Available findings suggest that managerial behavior does reflect media choice based upon the uncertainty or complexity of management problems. When managers work in a highly uncertain context, they rely more heavily on rich media. These media provide a variety of information cues and immediate feedback to interpret and understand the situation. Managerial jobs are fast paced and fragmented, hence they often need to learn about a fuzzy situation quickly. Rich media serve this purpose.

Media of low richness, including formal information systems, seem best suited to well understood management issues. These media are used more often at the bottom of the organization and for problems that are considered objective and quantifiable. The evidence from the literature generally supports the theoretical model of managerial information processing presented in Figure 3. Managers use all media within the organization, and probably should be skilled with each one. Managers move toward rich media for information about difficult problems. They prefer rich media because it meets the information needs associated with the manager's job.

MODELS OF ORGANIZATIONAL INFORMATION PROCESSING

In this section we shift levels of analysis from the individual manager to the organization as a whole. Within organization theory, two theoretical perspectives have had significant impact on the conceptualization of information processing within organizations. These models pertain to what we call the vertical and horizontal information processing needs of organizations.

Two Perspectives

Vertical. The first theoretical view was developed by Karl Weick (1979). Weick focused on the concept of information equivocality. When managers observe or learn about an external event, the information cue is often ambiguous. Managers are unclear about what the event means or how to translate it into organizational action. Weick proposed that organizations are designed to reduce equivocality from the environment. Organizing is the construction of a consensually validated grammar for reducing equivocality (Weick, 1979, p. 3). This means that when managers are confronted with equivocal cues, they must discuss the issue among themselves and gradually arrive at a common interpretation and frame of reference. The equivocality is reduced to an acceptable level, and the common interpretation is then used within the organization and becomes the basis for future action.

Weick's notion of equivocality is intriguing because it demonstrates that organizations must do more than process large amounts of information. Organizational environments can be confusing, impenetrable, and changing. Organizations cannot tolerate too much ambiguity and must cope with equivocal cues in a way that reduces equivocality to an acceptable level so the organization can take action and get things done. The equivocal stimulus triggers information processing within the organization that leads to greater certainty and clarity for participants. Organizations, then, must interpret ambiguous stimuli and reduce them to sufficient clarity for action within the organization. Weick identified this as an important problem that organizing must solve. By processing equivocal information into an agreed upon interpretation, participants can decide what to do. The organization can be reasonably clear about what it is doing and where it is heading.

Horizontal. The other view of information processing was developed by Jay Galbraith (1972; 1973). Galbraith proposed that as the level of uncertainty for managers increased, the amount of information processed should increase to reduce uncertainty. Galbraith argued that the uncertainty confronting an organization was influenced by factors such as diversity, task variability, and interdependence. Diverse products or goals means the organization must process a large amount of information to operationalize and monitor a number of activities. When task variability is high, managers confront unexpected events, so they must process additional information to learn about these events and thereby reduce uncertainty. Interdependence refers to the connectedness of departments. When the activities of one department influence other departments, information must be processed between them to provide the coordination needed for high performance.

The insight provided by Galbraith is that the amount of information processed within the organization explains why certain organizational forms are effective. By diagnosing points of uncertainty confronting the organization, a structure can be implemented that encourages appropriate information exchanges. When interdependence between departments is high, mechanisms can be designed to pass information between those departments. Likewise, when task variability is high, a structural design can be adopted to enable managers to acquire information in response to unexpected events. The selection of an overall structural form, such as product, function, or matrix, reflects the information processing needs of the organization. Each form directs the flow of information within the organization toward the points needed for effective performance. Galbraith provided a framework that explains the amount of information needed within an organization for effective performance. He also described how organizational design provides the correct amount of information where it is needed throughout the organization.

Interpretation vs. Coordination

Weick's theory of equivocality reduction pertains to the interpretation needs of organizations, which is the vertical dimension of information processing. Organizations interpret an ill-defined environment and define with some certainty a course of action for participants. Top managers are involved in the interpretation process. They read cues and then define goals, products, structure, strategy and technology. The vertical dimension of organizational information processing is top down. Upper level managers reduce equivocality to a level acceptable to others within the organization.

Galbraith's discussion of information amount pertains to information for internal coordination, the horizontal dimension of information processing. Horizontal information processing occurs within organizations to coordinate and execute organizational activities. Information is processed as needed for the organization to perform as a coordinated whole. Environmental interpretation is not the concern of people in the core of the organization. These people process large amounts of information when tasks are variable and activities are interdependent.

Figure 4 illustrates the two types of information requirements facing organizations. Organizations must both interpret the environment and coordinate tasks internally. As we will see, these two information needs are resolved in organizations through the use of rich information.

Information Tasks. Within the organization as a whole, a range of tasks are performed. Organizations use a technology to produce goods or services, and organizations work within an environment that is more or less uncertain. Organizational activities—in the broadest sense—impose specific information processing requirements associated with organizational technology, environment, and interdependencies (Poole, 1978). One information task is to reduce equivocality to the point where participants establish a shared view of events. The other task is to process sufficient amounts of information to enable internal coordination and task performance. These two information tasks represent the vertical and horizontal dimensions in Figure 4.

The importance of these two information processing tasks for human organizations can be seen in the comparison to other types of systems that also use information. Boulding (1956) proposed a hierarchy of system complexity that ranged from simple frameworks through control systems, cells, plants, animals, human beings and on to social systems (Pondy & Mitroff, 1979; Daft & Wiginton, 1979). Social systems are the most complex systems in the hierarchy. Figure 5 shows an abbreviated hierarchy of system complexity with 4 levels.

For machine systems at level one, the two information tasks are easy to resolve. Physical systems are usually closed off from the external environment, so little interpretation is necessary. Most knowledge required for performance is built into the physical structure of the system. In a machine system (e.g., clock, assembly line) internal elements are coor-

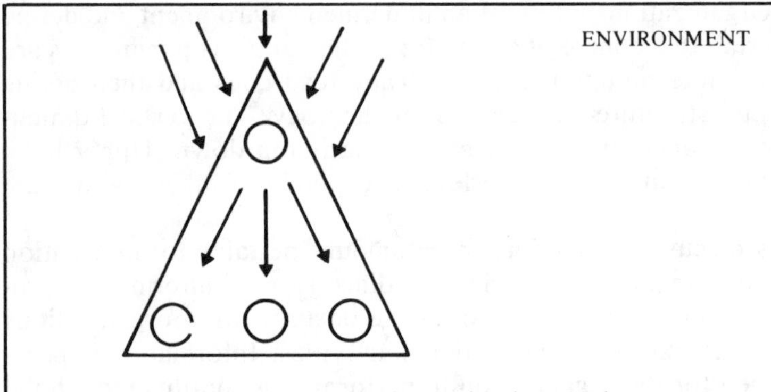

A. Vertical Information Processing: Purpose is to interpret the environment and reduce equivocality.

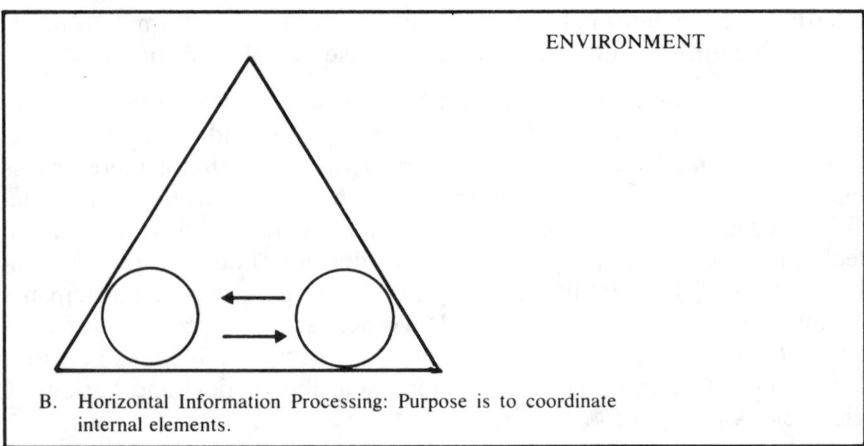

B. Horizontal Information Processing: Purpose is to coordinate internal elements.

Figure 4. Vertical and horizontal information processing in organizations.

dinated through physical linkages. In the case of the solar system, elements are linked by gravity, so that information processing is not required. For control type systems (e.g., thermostat), simple coordination data may be transmitted in response to predefined environmental stimuli (e.g. temperature). But this data is unequivocal and is processed in relatively small amounts compared to higher level systems.

Biological systems (level 2) require a greater amount of information processing than do physical systems. Biological organisms are differen-

	System Type		INFORMATION TASK Amount Processed	Equivocality Reduction
Complex ↑	Social System	Interpretation: Coordination:	High High	High High
	Human Being	Interpretation: Coordination:	High High	High Low
	Biological System	Interpretation: Coordination:	Mod Mod	Low Low
Simple	Machine System	Interpretation: Coordination:	Low Low	Low Low

Figure 5. System complexity and information tasks.

tiated, so data must be communicated among cells, organs and life sustaining subsystems. For an advanced specie, a large amount of data would have to be processed on a continuous basis to enable physically differentiated subsystems to function congruently. Biological organisms also are open systems, so senses are used to interpret the environment. For the most part, however, environmental interpretation is unequivocal. Flowers sense and respond in a predictable way to sunlight. Birds and insects respond in an almost programmed way to environmental changes in weather, seasons, temperature, or location.

The internal information task for the human being (level 3) is similar to biological organisms at level 2. The human being is highly differentiated, so large amounts of data are transmitted among internal systems, although these data are typically unequivocal. Interpretation of the environment, however, is equivocal. In only a few instances, such as putting one's hand on a stove, is the stimulus unequivocal and the response predictable. The majority of stimuli contain ambiguity. The external environment is alive with sounds, observed behavior, music, language, and symbols of all types. Most of these phenomena have multiple interpretations. Knowledge on any single topic is incomplete. People act on scraps of information and form these scraps into coherent wholes (Weick & Daft, 1982). The ability to process and interpret equivocal stimuli from the environment is what distinguishes human beings from lower level systems.

The most complex system of all is the human social system (level 4). The human being is the building block of the social system. The information problem of interpreting the environment is similar to interpretation by individual human beings. Upper-level managers must respond to an uncertain, ill-defined environment, and define with some certainty a course of action for others within the organization.

Human organizations must also process information internally. Internal information must coordinate diverse activities as discussed by Galbraith, which may require enormous amounts of data, especially when the task is uncertain and the organization is complex. Internal coordination in a social system is also equivocal, a point not incorporated in Galbraith's framework. Organizational specialization and differentiation lead to autonomy among subgroups. Group participants have divergent frames of reference. They attend to their own tasks, use common jargon, and pursue group level goals. Information transmitted across departments often is not clear or easily understood. Ambiguities arise, especially when differences among departments is great. Disagreements will occur.

We propose in Figure 5 that critical information tasks in organizations are to meet the need for a large amount of information and to reduce equivocality. The need to process equivocal information both within the organization and from the environment is what distinguishes social systems from lower level systems. Unlike machine or biological systems, internal data can be fuzzy and ill-defined. Diverse goals and frames of reference influence information processing. The organization must be designed to reduce equivocality both from within and without. A model of organizational information processing that treats organizations as higher level social systems should explain the reduction of equivocality as well as the correct information amount. Concepts and models of organization design based on information richness that explain these two information tasks are developed in the remainder of this chapter.

VERTICAL INFORMATION MODEL

Hierarchical Level. The information task of reducing equivocality is a function of hierarchical level. At the top of the organization, the manager's world is subjective. Problems are fuzzy, complex, and poorly understood. Top managers shape reality for the rest of the organization. They decide goals and strategy, and influence internal culture (Pfeffer, 1981). Top managers create and maintain a shared belief andd interpretation system among themselves. They have few objective facts. They must confront uncertainty, make sense of it, and attempt to communicate order and meaning to the lower levels of the organization. Managers use symbols, metaphors, speeches, body language, and other forms of rich information to communicate values, goals and culture throughout the organization.

At lower organization levels, the need to reduce equivocality is minimal. The information task is objective. Employees and first-line supervisors can make use of policies, rules and regulations, formal authority, and the physical requirements of technology to govern their activities. The employees at lower levels work within the defined plans, goals, and technology of the organization. Interpretation is less equivocal. Information can be processed through less rich media and still convey relevant task information.

The equivocal information task along the hierarchy corresponds roughly to media usage, as illustrated in Figure 6. High rich media, such as face-to-face and telephone will dominate at the top management level. Issues here are complex and ill-defined, such as the relationship between the institution and the environment. Middle management works within a somewhat more well defined structure. High rich media will still be used, but paperwork, documentation and other forms of less rich data will also be processed. The lower levels are more objective. People within the technical core, for example, will make frequent use of numeric and written reports. To some extent, all media will be used at each level. But rich media will play a more prominent role in the interpretation of the environment and reduction of equivocality at the top level, while less rich media will play a more important role for lower level employees.

Richness Reduction. The information media used at each level is not random, but reflects the underlying process of organizing. Organizations must reduce subjectivity and equivocality (Weick, 1979). Organizations move from high rich media at the interface with the environment to low rich media within the technical core. Top managers use rich media to

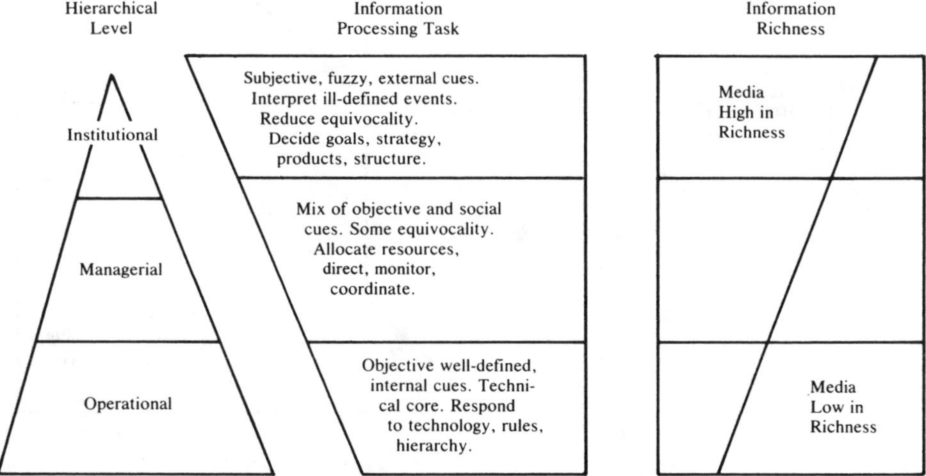

Figure 6. Hierarchical level and information richness.

discuss, analyze and interpret the external environment, and to develop goals and strategies. These interpretations can be translated into less rich policies, paperwork, rules and procedures for use at middle and lower organization levels. *Organizations reduce equivocality through the use of sequentially less rich media down through the hierarchy*. Reducing media richness is one way organizations reduce equivocality. Employees within the organization are thereby given a sense of specific roles, tasks, and purpose and are able to perform efficiently without having to interpret and define messy external issues. When organizations adapt to external changes, or when top managers develop new interpretations, the results work their way down through the organization in the form of new technologies, products, procedures, and reports.

The dynamic of richness reduction is illustrated in Figure 7. Media high in richness are used by top managers to cope with equivocal information processing tasks. Media low in richness are appropriate for the technical core. The diagonal in Figure 7 represents the extent to which the organizational context is objective or subjective. As top managers interpret the

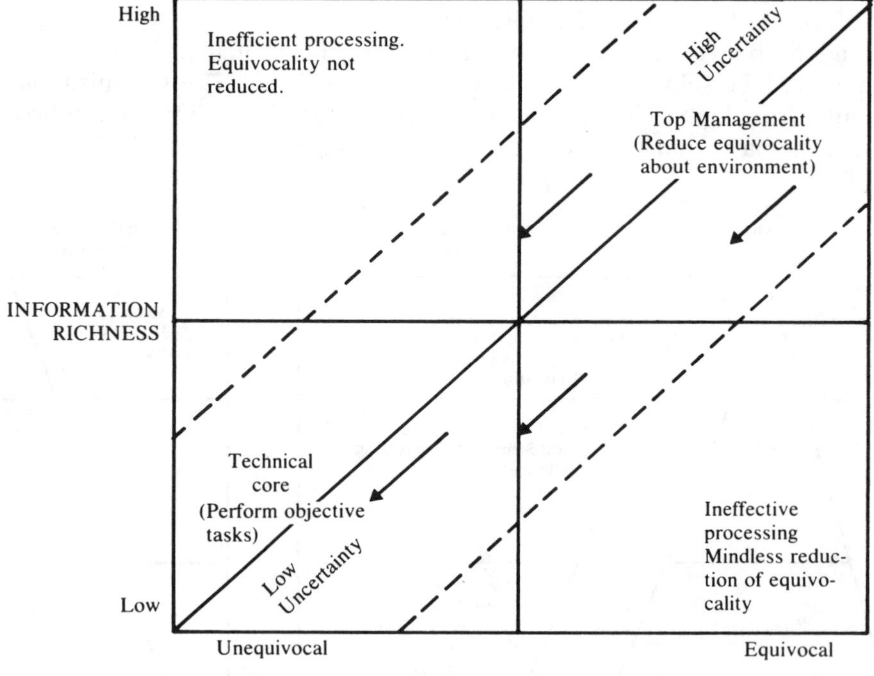

Figure 7. Process of equivocality reduction in organizations.

subjective environment and come to common definitions through the use of face-to-face discussions, they are able to reduce equivocality and provide greater objectivity for lower levels. Richness and equivocality are simultaneously reduced. Information processing inside the organization contains less equivocality and information tasks require less rich media.

The information processing that took place after the tornado in Elkhart, Oklahoma is a perfect example of the richness reduction process in Figure 7. City administrators were hit with an unexpected event that created a highly equivocal information task. They used rich media—continuous fact-to-face discussion and personal observation—to interpret and define the environmental situation. As they began to understand and reach a common definition of the situation, administrators provided a more well defined course of action for volunteers who were assigned objective tasks as the act of organizing progressed. As Weick argued, uncertainty triggers the act of organizing. People cluster around the equivocal event and pool ideas and perceptions. This information should be processed through media of high richness until equivocality is reduced to an acceptable level so that less rich media can be used to communicate specific goals and tasks.

Information processing which takes place outside the diagonal in Figure 7 will not serve the organization well. In those cases where the organizations use rich media to resolve unequivocal issues, the organizing process will be inefficient. Face-to-face discussions to process routine and well-understood events will confound rather than clarify. Participants will feel uninvolved because the equivocality that triggers discussion is not present. Face-to-face meetings will not serve a purpose or help resolve problems. On the other hand, when the organization inadvertently uses media low in richness to process equivocal information, the organization's interpretation will be ineffective. This would be the case when equivocal events are arbitrarily quantified and fed into computers for reports to top management. The equivocality reduction will not reflect the consensus among management, and will not be the outcome of diverse perspectives forged into a common grammar. This is analogous to what happened in the business school example at the beginning of this chapter. A number was assigned to the complex research record of professors. The numbers were assigned prematurely because department heads had not developed a common perspective and evaluation criteria thorough discussion. The richness reduction process was short circuited, and the resulting information was inaccurate.

The implication for organization design is that information media should fit the vertical information task. Environments change. They can be hard to analyze. Organizations should stay open to the environment. They do that by using rich media at the top. Senior managers should maintain personal contacts in key external domains and use personal observation. Within the organization, top management should undertake informal discussions on unclear events. Executives can pool perspectives and build a common interpretation that will guide organizational activities.

As shared interpretations develop, the outcomes can be transmitted downward through less rich media. This creates certainty for lower level participants. Top management absorbs uncertainty through rich media, thereby enabling other employees to concentrate on production efficiency. To have everyone involved in equivocality reduction would be inefficient. Likewise, reliance on paper media by top management would close off the organization from the environment. Media of low richness do not transmit adequate cues to interpret the environment and do not permit managers to establish a common view and grammar.

HORIZONTAL INFORMATION MODEL

Galbraith's (1973, 1977) model of organization design specified structural devices to handle internal information processing. Computers, assistants-to, and information systems can be used to process data within organizations. Galbraith also specified structural devices for horizontal communications, including direct contact among managers, liaison roles, teams, task forces, and full time integraters. Any of these devices might be implemented depending upon amount of information needed within the organization.

We propose that one horizontal information task within organizations is to reduce equivocality, which Galbraith's model did not incorporate. A department in an organization is a system within a system. Each department develops its own functional specialization, time horizon, goals, (Lawrence & Lorsch, 1967), language, and frame of reference. Bridging wide differences across departments is a complex and equivocal problem. The perspectives of marketing and R&D departments, for example, are more divergent than between industrial engineering and mechanical engineering. Coordination devices in the organization must not only match requirements for information amount, but must enable managers to overcome differences in values, goals, and frames of reference.

Information processing between departments has two purposes: reducing equivocality and providing a sufficient amount of information for task performance. Equivocality reduction is required by different frames of reference, which is similar to what Lawrence and Lorsch (1967) called differentiation. The amount of information needed between departments is determined by interdependence. The greater the interdependence between departments, the greater the coordination required. When frames of reference differ, coordination activities also involve equivocality reduction.

Rich information is needed when information is processed to overcome different frames of reference across departments. Managers must meet face-to-face, discuss their assumptions, goals, and needs, and develop a common language and framework with which to solve problems. In the initial stages of a new product, managers from research, marketing, and production would have to resolve their differences and reach agreement through task forces or committee meetings. Once these differences are resolved, less rich media can satisfy information requirements. Progress toward a common goal could be plotted on a pert chart, or data could be communicated with reports or other documents.

The decision process in the business college to give super raises across departments was an example of diverse frames of references. Each department had a different view on research quality. Rich media were needed to resolve these differences and achieve a common perspective for allocating raises. When the business college used face-to-face discussion to achieve a common grammer and perspective, the decision outcome was satisfactory to participants. However, when department heads used media low in richness (written description, numeric ratings) to resolve differences and make recommendations, coordination was not successful. Differences across departments were not integrated into a common grammar. Equivocality had not been resolved to the point where less rich media could be used. Only after a common perspective is established will paperwork and numerical ratings be accurate.

Interdependence determines the amount of information that must be processed between departments. As information amount increases, devices will be utilized that enable large amounts of data to be transmitted. An occasional telephone discussion between managers may be sufficient in the case of low interdependence. A daily meeting of a task force may be required when interdependence is great.

The ideas for horizontal information processing are summarized in Figure 8. Two problems must be faced—frames of reference and interdependence. The need to reduce equivocality is caused by divergent frames of reference that require rich media to resolve. Once a common language and perspective have been established between departments, less rich media such as memos, paperwork, and reports can be used for coordination. As the interdependence between departments increases, devices must be in place to allow sufficient volume of information to be processed, otherwise organizational performance may suffer.

Devices such as full time integraters, integrating departments, and the matrix organization provide both rich media and large amounts of information (cell 2). These structural devices are required when organizational

DIFFERENCE BETWEEN DEPARTMENTS (frames of reference)	Low INTERDEPENDENCE BETWEEN DEPARTMENTS	High
High	1. *High Difference, Low Interdependence* a. Media high in richness to reduce equivocality. b. Small amount of information. *Examples*: Occasional face-to-face or telephone meetings, personal memos, planning.	2. *High Difference, High Interdependence* a. Media high in richness to reduce equivocality. b. Large amount of information to handle interdependence. *Examples*: Full time integrators, task force, project team.
Low	3. *Low Difference, Low Interdependence* a. Media low in richnes. b. Small amount of information. *Examples*: Rules, standard operating procedures.	4. *Low Difference, High Interdependence* a. Media low in richness. b. Large amount of information to handle interdependence. *Examples*: Plans, reports, update data bases, MIS's, clerical help, pert charts, budgets.

Figure 8. Relationship between interdepartmental characteristics and coordination devices.

departments are highly interdependent, yet highly specialized with distinct technologies and frames of reference. When interdependence is high but differences are small (cell 4), information can be processed with less rich media. Written reports, data bases, formal information systems, letters and memos will provide sufficient information for coordination. Clerical staff could be used to process more information through the paperwork system of the organization.

In the case of divergent frames of reference and low interdependence (cell 1), direct contact between departments can be used as needed. Face-to-face meetings would resolve differences, but would only be needed occasionally. Only a small amount of time and data would be processed in this situation. Finally, when differences and interdependence are both low (cell 3), coordination is a minor problem. Standing rules and procedures will be sufficient to accommodate any differences and information needs that exist.

The implication for organization design is that horizontal coordination devices should accommodate the dual needs of equivocality reduction and information amount. Different departmental frames of reference increase equivocality, hence the organization should design devices to process rich information and reduce equivocality in order to facilitate coordination. High interdependence between departments requires a large amount of information, so devices should be designed for sufficient volume of information to facilitate coordination. An organization design that achieves the correct amount of both equivocality reduction and information amount between departments will experience effective coordination, and hence high performance.

RESEARCH EVIDENCE ON VERTICAL AND HORIZONTAL INFORMATION MODELS

In this section we will briefly review research evidence on information processing by organizations. Research pertaining to interpretation of the environment (vertical model) is considered first, then evidence concerning internal coordination (horizontal model) will be discussed.

Vertical Model

One surprise in the literature on interpretation of the environment is that so few studies have been reported. Virtually all writers agree that organizations are open systems that must monitor the external environment. Yet studies of this process are notably sparse (Pfeffer & Salancik, 1978). The specific evidence sought for this section is whether organizations use rich media to interpret the environment, and whether interpretations are then translated through less rich media to provide greater certainty at lower organization levels. The task of equivocality reduction is expected to diminish at lower hierarchical levels.

Hierarchical Level. Parsons (1960) proposed three levels of decision making in the organizational hierarchy: institutional, managerial and operational. These three levels were illustrated in Figure 6. The institutional level is the top of the organization, where the primary task is to set broad goals, and to decide the organization's products, technology, policy, strategy, and relationship with the external environment. The managerial level is the middle level in the organization. The requirement here is to plan and direct the activities of the organization and coordinate tasks laterally. This level is concerned with day-to-day management of organizational affairs. The technical level is at the bottom of the organizational hierarchy. At this level the operational work of the organization is accomplished.

Preliminary evidence indicates that the problems confronting the organization differ by level. Brightman (1978) argued that problems differ in uncertainty, complexity, and political nature. Problems at the top tend to be less programmed than decisions at the bottom. Stimuli at the top are less well structured (Leifer, 1979; Brightman, 1978). While there may be a few routine elements, managers at the top have to deal with economic, legal, political, and social factors that are hard to analyze and define. They also must anticipate the impact of these factors on the organization and consider possible responses. Problems within the organization, although they are sometimes ill-structured, generally reflect a greater proportion of routine and well understood stimuli (Leifer, 1979).

Is the difference in organizational levels associated with information richness? Leifer (1979) argued that inputs at the top of the organization tend to be informational while inputs used at the lower levels are data. Data tend to be more quantitative, objective, and less rich than the personal, subjective information used by top managers. Kefalas and Schoderbeck (1973) found that upper level executives spent more time gathering information about the environment than those at the lower levels. Gorry and Scott (1971) also proposed that information characteristics at the upper level tend to be broad and less accurate. These data are richer than the detailed, well defined, narrow data used at lower levels. Finally, the literature on management information systems reviewed earlier concerning manager information behavior (Dickson, Senn, Cheway, 1977; Tushman & Nadler, 1977; Higgins & Finn, 1977) suggested that the formal systems were not used by top managers. MIS's are a low rich medium, and are more useful for well defined activities at lower hierarchical levels.

Scanning. Scanning pertains to the organization's intelligence–gathering mechanisms. Most environmental scanning takes place at the upper levels of the organization (Aiken & Hage, 1972). The few studies which have actually observed scanning behavior indicated that most scanning utilizes rich media. Aguilar (1967) compared personal to impersonal sources about the environment. He found that personal sources were of much greater importance to executives than impersonal material. Keegan (1967) compared human to documentary sources of information used by headquarters' executives in multinational companies. He found that two-thirds of information episodes were with human sources. The businessmen he studied used a network of human contacts in a variety of organizations to interpret the international environment. Documentary sources, such as the *Wall Street Journal* and the *New York Times*, were read regularly by the executives, but were less influential sources of information.

Bauer, Pool, and Dexter (1964) concluded that to a large degree American business communication is oral or by personal memorandum. Allen (1966) studied information sources for engineering decisions, and found that customers and vendors were the most used information source. Engineers had personal contact with these people to provide information on such things as new product needs. The formal literature, by contrast, was the least used source for this information.

The Keegan (1976) and Allen (1966) studies also indicated that information media reflect the nature of the underlying task. Keegan found that financial executives were more likely to use documentary sources, which is consistent with the well understood nature of accounting systems. General management and marketing, which experienced greater change and uncertainty, made greater use of human sources. Allen found that scientists who were working on well specified research problems made greater use of literature sources than did engineers who were involved in new product development.

Another source of information for top executives is personal observation. This is a very rich medium. It is not unusual for executives to take special tours, which involve face-to-face meetings with subordinates and the observation of facilities (Mintzberg, 1973). Rich media provide greater insight into the organizational needs and problems than would be obtained by relying on letters or formal documentation (Keegan, 1976).

Kefalas (1975) reported a survey of scanning activities by managers in farm-equipment and meat packing companies. He found that upper-level executives devoted more time to scanning the external environment than did lower level managers. The source of scanning information was primarily face-to-face meetings with other people. Moreover, executives spent more time scanning the environment when it was dynamic rather than stable. The dynamic environment represented greater uncertainty and complexity, which was associated with greater use of rich media.

Conclusions reached independently by Keegan (1976) and Kefalas

(1975) revealed the small role played by formal paperwork for senior managers. Keegan's study included fifty executives who each reported three communication incidents. Computer-based or quantitative reports were not reported in a single case as the source of external information. In much the same fashion, Kefalas found tht formal surveillance received very little emphasis in organizations. Many businesses support organized technological and market research activities, but this data is not widely used within the organization. These systems are sometimes haphazardly designed so that information is not always available to the right people. These systems also fail to capture the novel and unstructured aspects of the external environment.

Summary. There has not been a great deal of research on the relationship between media richness and hierarchical level, but a reasonable inference is that the relationship proposed in Figure 6 receives modest support. Upper level management activities differ systematically from lower level activities, and upper level managers make extensive use of rich media to interpret and understand the external environment. Personal contacts appear to be essential for interpreting the external environment and reducing equivocality. Organizations undergo a process of richness reduction from the top to the lower levels of the organization. Rules, procedure, job descriptions, technical reports, and other forms of less rich media are more widely used at lower organizational levels. Rich information media are used for interpretation and decision making at the top, and sequentially less rich media are implemented at lower levels. Variation in media richness helps explain how equivocality reduction necessary for survival and efficient internal performance takes place.

Horizontal Model

A number of studies have examined communication and information processing inside organizations. Research relevant to the information richness models in Figures 7 and 8 are in the categories of technology, interdependence and internal culture.

Technology. Technology is a source of uncertainty for employees within the organization and thus, it influences information processing. Empirical studies have indicated that complex, nonroutine tasks require more information processing than simple, routine tasks. This relationship has been observed in small groups (Bavelas, 1950), simulated organizations (Becker and Baloff, 1969), research and development groups (Tushman, 1978, 1979), and other organizational departments (Van de Ven and Ferry, 1979; Randolph, 1978; Daft & MacIntosh, 1980).

Relevant to the theory presented in this chapter is evidence that media usage is associated with technological uncertainty. Woodward's (1965) seminal study of organizational technology found that communication media changed according to complexity of the task. People in highly routinized mass production organizations tended to rely on written communication and to have extensive formal procedures. Organizations that had less clear technology, such as continuous process or small batch, relied more on verbal media. The complexity of the task was associated with information media richness.

Studies by Van de Ven, et al. (1976) and Daft and MacIntosh (1980) support this general relationship. Van de Ven, et al. found that when task uncertainty was high, managers made more frequent use of unscheduled meetings and other forms of horizontal communications. When task uncertainty was low, rules and plans were the primary means of communicating. Daft and Macintosh reported that when tasks were less analyzable, participants preferred less precise information. Information had greater equivocality and required personal experience to interpret and actual use to solve the unanalyzable problems.

Meissner (1969) found that as technology varied from uncertain to certain, the media used by employees shifted from verbal to objective signs and written communications. Randolph (1978) observed that verbal media were used more frequently as technology increased in uncertainty. He also observed a shift from verbal to horizontal communication. Finally, Gaston (1972) found that nonstandardized tasks were associated with more face-to-face information transfer than were standardized tasks.

The communication patterns associated with technological uncertainty are consistent with our proposed models of information processing. The forms of communication observed by Woodward (1965), Van de Ven, et al. (1976), Daft and Macintosh (1980), Meissner (1969), Randolph (1978) and Gaston (1972) can be interpreted to reflect differences in the continuum of information media. Media high in richness (face-to-face, personal contact) were used when tasks were complex and uncertain. Media low in richness (rules, regulations, written) were used when tasks were simple and certain.

Interdependence. There have been fewer studies of interdependence, but the general direction of findings seems to be similar (Tushman & Nadler, 1978). As interdependence increases, the need for communication between groups increases, so the amount of information processed to achieve coordination increases (Van de Ven, Delbecq, & Koenig, 1976).

Interdependence is also related to media richness. Thompson (1967) argued that when interdependence increased from pooled to sequential to reciprocal, techniques of coordination should change from rules to standardization to mutual adjustment. These coordination techniques are changes in media. Rules do not convey rich information, but mutual adjustment (face-to-face) is very rich. Van de Ven, et al. (1976) also found that communication shifted from rules to meetings as interdependence among employees increased. This finding also fits the richness model in Figure 8.

We theorized that differences in frames of reference across departments would require highly rich media to resolve. This idea receives modest support from the research of Lawrence and Lorsch (1967), who found that personal modes of coordination were used when differentiation within organizations was high. However, their study did not compare personal to impersonal media. The lateral information processing they found was face-to-face, which suggests the need for highly rich media to accomodate divergent frames of reference and perspectives.

Internal Culture. Organizational culture and climate may also be associated with information media. There is intriguing evidence to suggest that myths, stories, and metaphors are effective means of preserving social and emotional aspects of organization (Boje & Rowland, 1977; Clark, 1972; Meyer & Rowan, 1977; Mitroff & Kilman, 1976). Myths, legends; sagas, and stories are prevalent in most organizations. These stories usually pertain to the socio-emotional side of the organization and provide employees with history, background, and meaning for their role within the organization.

Myths and sagas are not written down, and if they were, their usefulness might be lost. A similar finding is true for gossip and the use of the grapevine (Davis, 1953). Information processed along the grapevine generally is of a personal nature and is communicated through rich media. The reason is that stories, myths and gossip pertain to the ill-defined, emotional aspects of organization that are best transfered through informal, personal media. Transmitting myths or gossip through informal, impersonal media would transform the stories into rational facts, and they would no longer pertain to the deeper, emotional needs of participants.

Summary. Once again, evidence from the research literature provides tentative support for the theoretical ideas expressed in this chapter. The findings suggest that rich media tend to be used when tasks are complex, and when differences between departments are great. Task complexity and interdependence are also related to information amount.

Taken together, these findings may mean there is a positive relationship between media richness and amount of information processed, since both seem to increase with task complexity and interdependence. The face-to-face medium, for example, enables managers to process rich information cues. Cues convey more insight, so managers actually acquire more information for understanding a complex issue or developing a new cognitive map. Amount of information may be increased by spending more time communicating or by shifting to richer media. The general conclusion is that requirements for horizontal information processing influence both richness and amount of information. Organizational design should enable the appropriate amount of information to be processed, and should provide managers with appropriate media richness depending on task uncertainty and interdependence.

DISCUSSION AND IMPLICATIONS

Early in this chapter, we proposed that organizational success is related to the organization's ability to manage information richness. Information richness was defined, and three models were proposed. The major points contained in this chapter are as follows.

1. Information is a core construct for understanding organizational form and process.
2. Human organizations, unlike lower level systems, must use information to reduce equivocality.
3. Organizations have two information related tasks, which are to interpret the external environment and to coordinate internal activities. Each of these tasks requires the reduction of equivocality and the processing of a sufficient amount of information.
4. Information richness is an important concept for explaining how organizations perform the task of reducing equivocality to an acceptable level for internal efficiency. Rich media utilize multiple cues, feedback, and high variety language. Rich media enable people to interpret and reach agreement about difficult, unanalyzable, emotional, and conflict-laden issues. Face-to-face discussions lead to a shared language and interpretation. Media of low richness are appropriate for communicating about routine activities within the organization. Paperwork, rules, and computer printouts are accurate and efficient for the transmission of unequivocal messages.
5. Media richness is the basis for the model of manager information processing behavior. For difficult, equivocal topics, managers use face-to-face discussion for interpretation and equivocality reduction. Memos, bulletins, reports and other media of lower richness are used when the topic is specific and better understood. In a sense, there are two sides to managerial communication. Managers use informal, personal, direct contact when problems are ambiguous and unclear. They use formal, paperwork communications for routine matters. Effective managers should have skills with all media and be able to select among them depending on the nature of the problem.

6. Media richness also explains how organizations interpret the external environment, as described in the vertical information model. Media selection enables the organization to learn about an uncertain environment, yet provide a sense of certainty and direction for participants within. Face-to-face and other rich media are used to receive cues about the environment and to define a common grammar for use within the organization (Weick, 1979). The organization reduces media richness as information moves down the organizational hierarchy. Media of low richness can be used to specify goals, policies, procedures, and technology at lower levels, thereby providing clarity and certainty for the efficient performance of routine activities. The key to vertical information processing is to incorporate a balance of media. When the environment is uncertain and equivocal, rich media are called for. Organization design should encourage face-to-face discussion to reduce equivocality and provide certainty within the organization. When activities are stable and analyzable, less rich media should be used.

7. Media richness is also the basis for the horizontal information model that explains how organizations coordinate internal activities. When departments are highly differentiated and interdependent, equivocality is high. When equivocality is high organizations will use rich information media to resolve departmental differences and to reach a common language and perspective. Once differences are resolved and agreement is reached, less rich forms of communication, such as memos and formal reports, will be sufficient for coordination. Media selection within the organization is related to the extent of differentiation and interdependence among departments.

Relationship To Other Frameworks

One outcome of the ideas described in this chapter is that they are consistent with other frameworks in the literature. Current perspectives can be reinterpreted in terms of media richness. Three frameworks—organic versus mechanistic organizations, bureaucracy, and politics—are considered here.

Organic Versus Mechanistic Organizations. The environment is a major source of uncertainty for organizations. Complexity, variability, and rate of change in the environment create additional uncertainty for managers in the organizations. Participants must spend more time finding out about the environment and adapting to changes in the environment.

Perhaps the most widely accepted relationship between organization and environment is that organic structures tend to evolve in uncertain environments, and mechanistic structures are suited to certain environments (Burns & Stalker, 1961). In an organic organization, people are continually redefining and renegotiating tasks. There is widespread discussion about activities. Rules and responsibilities are ill-defined or nonexistent. In a mechanistic organization, activities are more rigidly defined. Rules, regulations and job descriptions are available to control behavior. Task redefinition is nonexistent. Communication tends to be vertical rather than lateral.

We suggest that the principle difference between organic and mechanistic organizations is media richness. The organic structure facilitates communication through rich media. The organization is constantly learning. Changes in the external environment are being interpreted and translated into new roles and internal tasks. Widespread face-to-face discussion enables continuous interpretation and adaptation to take place. The process of richness reduction is minimized in the organic structure because the entire organization is involved in interpretation, discussion and change.

The mechanistic structure makes greater use of media low in richness. Rules, procedures, and job descriptions contain the information necessary for successful task accomplishment within the organization. An extensive reduction in richness from the top to the bottom of the organization is accomplished. A small percentage of people are involved in environmental interpretation. Rules and regulations enable the organization to respond from habit and previous experience rather than through new interpretations. Formal media are appropriate in organizations that have well understood, predictable environments. Of course organic organizations would still utilize some low rich media and mechanistic organizations some high rich media. But rich media are used more extensively in organic organizations where the environment is changing and complex. Media low in richness are used more extensively in mechanistic organizations within stable environments.

Bureaucracy. Research on bureaucratic organizations has indicated that bureaucracy is similar to the mechanistic organizations studied by Burns and Stalker (1961). The literature suggests that as organizations increase in size, bureaucratic traits increase (Kimberly, 1976). Weberian characteristics such as division of labor, rules, and paperwork, are more extensive in large organizations (Blau & Schoenherr, 1971; Dewar & Hage, 1978).

These findings support the idea that richness reduction takes place. In a large organization, communication can be standardized, and relevant information is contained within the formal documentation of the organization. Large organizations develop a niche within the environment so that external conditions are relatively stable. Large organizations learn to take advantage of internal efficiencies by responding through habit or by buffering the technical core when external changes do occur.

Studies that show increased formalization and large clerical ratios with organization size support the idea of reliance on information of lower richness (Daft, 1978; Kasarda, 1974). Formalization is a measure of the amount of documentary data in the organization. Large clerical ratios provide people to process large amounts of paperwork. Small administrative ratios in large organizations means the organization is run with less personal observation (rich media) and more by rules and regulations that act as substitutes for supervision. Media of low richness are substituted for media of high richness during bureaucratization. Even the increasing complexity in large organizations reflects information processing to some extent. An increasing number of departments and specialties is a way to divide the total information base needed for effective performance. Each department can develop a common language and frame of reference that will enable the use of less rich media for task accomplishment.

Politics. Politics is defined as those activities used to obtain one's preferred outcome in organizations when there is uncertainty or disagreement about choices (Pfeffer, 1981). Recent surveys of organizational politics (Gantz & Murray, 1980; Madison, Allen, Porter, Ranwick, & Mayes, 1980) indicate that political behavior occurs most often at the upper levels of organizations and for decisions high in uncertainty.

We propose that political behavior involves the utilization of rich media (face-to-face) to reach agreement when diverse goals and reference frames are brought to bear on uncertain problems. Disagreement is the result of diverse perspectives and goals across departments. Uncertainty is the result of the ill-defined nature of political issues. Politics is a device to encourage face-to-face discussion among a broad group of executives until a coalition is formed that reflects a common grammar and understanding. Media low in richness cannot be used to resolve political issues because paperwork and reports cannot convey the subtleties of power, obligations, and other intangibles. Politics is one vehicle through which rich media are used to reduce equivocality. Politics occurs both at upper levels and across departments when events are uncertain and reference frames diverge.

By contrast, rational models of decision making reflect the use of low rich media to process information and make decisions. The rational model is effective when factors are certain, and when participants agree on desired goals and cause–effect relationships (Pfeffer, 1981). The rational model makes use of documentary sources of information, such as statistics and quantitative analysis. This approach to information and decision making is used more often for operational and technical decisions at lower levels in the organization.

Future Research Directions

The models in this chapter not only relate to the established frameworks above, they also can be the basis for a lengthly agenda of new empirical research. Very little research has been reported on topics such as the selection of media by managers, how organizations interpret the external environment, or the mechanisms used to process information horizontally between departments. A study by Lengel (1983) supports the underlying concept of a media richness and the relationship between media richness and the nature of communication topics. Additionl studies based upon the models presented in this paper and beyond are suggested below.

Media Selection and Usage. The model of manager information processing in Figure 3 might be tested in a number of ways. A large sample of communications typically sent and received via each medium could be obtained and analyzed for systematic differences in content. Managers might be asked to describe critical communication incidents and to describe the medium used. Another approach would be to systematically test the relationship between task complexity and media selection. A sample of communication episodes could be developed according to complexity, ambiguity, conflict, emotional content, and accessability. Then managers could be surveyed to determine their media choice for each episode. Analysis of these data would indicate the extent to which task complexity influences media selection. These data could also be analyzed by manager effectivenss and manager hierarchical level to see if media selection is associated with manager differences. A study could also test these relationships in the laboratory. Specific topics would be communicated through various media, such as telephone, face-to-face, and written. This research would indicate how media influence trust, understanding, and agreement among managers.

Boundary Spanning. Pfeffer and Salancik (1978) proposed that organizations face two problems in their relationship to the environment: (1) how to register needed information about the environment, and (2) how to act upon that information. The first problem is one of boundary spanning. Exploratory case type studies have been conducted by Aguilar (1967) and Keegan (1974), but systematic analyses of external information sources have not been published. An appropriate study would be to interview boundary spanning managers about information topics important to their functions. After two or three critical topics are identified, sources of information on these issues could be determined. External sources such as magazines, personal contacts, and opinion surveys can be identified. The transmission of information into the organizational decision center could also be traced. This study could begin with in-depth interviews of boundary spanning personnel, with a follow up questionnaire survey of information sources for specific topics. The outcome of this study would begin to shed new light on the intelligence gathering activities of formal organizations.

Interpretation and Effectiveness. Weick and Daft (1982) proposed that organizations systematically differ with respect to interpretation style. Interpretation style is an outgrowth of boundary spanning activity, and includes the development of shared perception, goals, and strategies among top managers. In a study of interpretation style, senior managers could be interviewed to identify how they learn about the environment. The role of organization design, such as the existence of a formal department to scan and analyze the environment, could also be examined. The effectiveness of interpretation systems could be evaluated by direct comparison of several organizations in a similar environment. Organizations in the same industry that have differing levels of profit, innovation, or other outcomes can be evaluated for interpretation differences.

Interdepartmental Coordination. Interdepartmental coordination pertains to horizontal information processing in organizations. Van de Ven, Delbecq and Koenig (1976) studied mechanisms used to coordinate members within a department. No studies have been conducted of coordination between departments or between major divisions of a large corporation. Galbraith's (1973, 1977) framework argues that coordination mechanisms reflect differences in information processing needs. A valuable study would examine these coordination processes in more detail. Specific coordination issues could be followed through the organization to learn how coordination was achieved. The model in Figure 7 could be tested by observing the extent to which media richness is related to frames of reference or to the amount of interdependence between departments.

Equivocality Reduction. The theme that underlies this entire chapter is equivocality reduction. Organizations must be able to translate uncertainty to certainty in order to achieve internal efficiency and stability (Skivington, 1982). Equivocality may originate in the external environment or through internal disagreements. Despite the importance of equivocality reduction to organizational interpretation and coordination, we know virtually nothing about it from an empirical perspective. The process of perceiving an equivocal stimuli, evaluating it, discussing it, and coming to a resolution could be the focus of new research. This type of study might be conducted in either the laboratory or in the field. Groups or simulated organizations could be presented with an equivocal stimuli to observe how it is resolved. Specific environmental events might be traced into and through real organizations to learn how an acceptable level of understanding and certainty is reached. Almost any study of equivocality reduction, however exploratory and tentative, would discover significant new knowledge about organizations.

Symbolic Value of Media. Feldman and March (1981) proposed that information in organizations serves as signal and symbol. More information is gathered than organizations use, yet managers may request even more. Formal reports may not influence the rational decision process, but be used to support a course of action previously agreed upon. Feldman and March argued that the use of information is highly symbolic, and that information processing cannot be fully understood by considering only rational communication exchanges and decision making. The selection of media also may have strong symbolic overtones. Face-to-face discussion may be used when a manager wishes to communicate personal interest or to show others that he cares about them. Formal reports might be used to signal that extensive study lies behind a supposedly rational decision. Letters and memoranda convey a sense of the official and symbolize the legitimate role of the organization. The symbolic aspect of media could be assessed by identifying communication episodes and asking managers why they selected a specific medium. The deeper reasons for using media might be elicited through open-ended interviews. Similar interviews might be conducted with people who receive communications through various media. The deeper significance of media in the interpretation of messages could suggest new insights into the types of signals communicated within organizations.

CONCLUSION

This chapter has introduced the concept of information richness and proposed models of managerial information processing, organizational interpretation, and internal coordination processes. The models in this chapter have attempted to integrate ideas and topics from the literature on organizations. These topics include manager preference for personal contact and informal information, sources of information used by managers in various tasks, the observation that organizations must reduce equivocality about the environment (Weick, 1979), and Galbraith's (1973) description of organization structure as a means of directing communication flows. The notion of information richness shed light on all these activities. When the task is complex and difficult, rich media enable successful information sharing. The information richness model provides a way to understand the behavior of individual managers as well as to integrate the notions of equivocality reduction and internal coordination.

Any model involves tradeoffs and unavoidable weaknesses. Probably the greatest weakness in the models presented in this chapter is reflected in Thorngate's (1976) postulate of commensurate complexity. Thorngate states that a theory of social behavior cannot be simultaneously general, accurate, and simple. Two of the three are possible, but only at a loss to the third. The models in this paper are general and simple, and hence are not very precise at predicting details. The models represent frameworks that apply to organizations in general. More specific elaboration of the models can only be developed after additional study and research.

The major conclusion from the paper is the need for organizations to manage information richness. Richness has to reflect the organization's need to interpret an uncertain environment and to achieve coordination within. Organizations are complex social systems that have information needs unlike lower level machine and biological systems. Rich information will have to be processed because environments will never be certain and internal conditions will never be characterized by complete agreement and understanding. Without some level of rich information, organizations would become rigid and brittle. They could not adapt to the environment or resolve internal disagreements in a satisfactory way. The process and outcomes of information processing are a good deal less tidy than would be the case in simpler, machine models of organizations. The ideas proposed in this chapter suggest a new view—perhaps a starting point of sorts—from which to interpret the richness of organizational activity.

NOTES

1. The names in these examples are ficticious, but the examples are based on actual events.

REFERENCES

Ackoff, R. L. Management misinformation systems. *Management Science*, 1967, *14*, 147–156.

Aguilar, F. J. *Scanning the business environment*. New York: Macmillian, 1967.

Aiken, M., and Hage J. *Organizational permeability, boundaries spanners, and organization structure*. Paper presented at the American Sociological Association, New Orleans, Louisiana, 1972.

Allen, T. J. The differential performance of information channels in the transfer of technology. In W. H. Gruber and D. G. Marquis (Eds.), *Factors in the transfer of technology*. Cambridge, MA: MIT Press, 1969.

Arrow, K. J. *The limits of organization*. New York: Norton, 1974.

Azien, I. Intuitive theories of events and the effects of base-rate information on prediction. *Journal of Personality and Social Psychology*, 1977, *35*, 303–314.

Bauer, R. A., Pool, I. S. & Dexter, L. A. *American business and public policy*. New York: Atherton Press, 1964.

Bavelas, A. Communication patterns in task-oriented groups. *Journal of Acoustical Society of America*, 1950, *22*, 725–730.

Becker, S. W., & Baloff, N. Organization structure and complex problem solving. *Administrative Science Quarterly,* 1969, *14*, 260–271.

Blandin, J. S. and Brown, W. B. Uncertainty and management's search for information. *IEEE Transactions on Engineering Management,* 1977, *4*, 114–119. (EM-24)

Blau, P. M., & Schoenherr, R. A. *The structure of organizations.* New York: Basic Books, 1971.

Bodensteiner, W. D. *Information channel utilization under varying research and development project conditions: An aspect of inter-organizational communication channel usages.* PhD Dissertation, The University of Texas, 1970.

Boje, D. M., & Rowland, R. M. *A dialectical approach to reification in mythmaking and other social reality constructions: The P-A-C-E model and OD.* Unpublished manuscript, University of Illinois, 1977.

Borgada, E., & Nisbett, R. The differential impact of abstract versus concrete information. *Journal of Applied Social Psychology*, 1977, *7*, 258–271.

Boulding, K. E. General systems theory: The skeleton of a science. *Management Science,* 1956, *2*, 197–207.

Brightman, H. J. Differences in ill-structured problem solving along the organizational hierarchy. *Decision Sciences,* 1978, *9*, 1–18.

Brown, W. Systems, boundaries and information flows. *Academy of Management Journal,* 1966, *9*, 318–327.

Burns, T. & Stalker, G. *The management of innovation.* London: Tavistock Press, 1966.

Clark, B. R. The occupational saga in higher education. *Administrative Science Quarterly,* 1972, *17*, 178–184.

Daft, R. L. System influence on organizational decision making: The case of resource allocation. *Academy of Management Journal,* 1978, *21*, 6–22.

Daft, R. L., & Macintosh, N. B. A tentative exploration into amount and equivocality of information processing in organizational work units. *Administrative Science Quarterly,* 1981, *26*, 207–224.

Daft, R. L., & Wiginton, J. C. Language and organization. *Academy of Management Review,* 1979, *4*, 179–191.

Davis, K. Management communication and the grapevine. *Harvard Business Review,* September–October 1953, pp. 43–49.

Dearden, J. "MIS is a mirage." *Harvard Business Review,* January–February 1972, pp. 90–99.

Dewar, R., & Hage J. Size, technology, complexity, and structural differentiation: Toward a theoretical synthesis. *Administrative Science Quarterly,* 1978, *23*, 111–136.

Dickson, G. W., Senn, J. A., & Chervany, N. L. Research in management information systems: The Minnesota experiments. *Management Science,* 1977, *23*, 913–923.

Feldman, M. S., & March J. G. Information in organization as signal and symbol. *Administrative Science Quarterly,* 1981, *26*, 171–186.

Feldman, N. S., Higgins, E. T., Karlovac, M., & Ruble, D. N. Use of consensus information in causal attribution as a function of temporal presentation and availability of direct information. *Journal of Personality and Social Psychology,* 1976, *34*, 694–698.

Galbraith, J. *Strategies of organization design.* Reading, MA: Addison-Wesley, 1973.

———. *Organizational design.* Reading, MA: Addison-Wesley, 1977.

Gaston, J. Communication and the reward system of science: A study of national invisible colleges. *The Sociological Review Monograph,* 1972, *18*, 25–41.

Gorry, G. A., & Scott Morton, M. S. A framework for management information systems. *Sloan Management Review,* 1971, *13*, 55–70.

Grayson, C. J., Jr. Management science and business practice. *Harvard Business Review*, July–August 1973, 41–48.

Hansen, R. D., & Donoghue, J. The power of consensus: Information derived from one's and other's behavior. *Journal of Personality and Social Psychology,* 1977, *35*, 294–302.

Higgins, J. C., & Finn, R. The chief executive and his information system. *Omega,* 1977, *5*, 557–566.

Holland, W. E., Stead, B. A., & Leibrock, R. C. Information channel/source selection as a correlate of technical uncertainty in a research and development organization. *IEEE Transactions on Engineering Management,* 1976, *23*, 163–167.

Kasarda, J. D. The structural implications of social system size: A three level analysis. *American Sociological Review,* 1974, *39*, 19–28.

Keegan, W. J. Multinational scanning: A study of the information sources utilized by headquarters executives in multinational companies. *Administrative Science Quarterly,* 1974, *19*, 411–421.

Kefalas, A. G. Environmental management information systems (ENVMIS): A reconceptualization. *Journal of Business Research,* 1975, *3*, 253–266.

Kefalas, A. G., & Schoderbek, P. P. Scanning the business environment—some empirical results. *Decision Sciences,* *4*, 63–74.

Kimberly, J. R. Organizational size and the structuralist perspective. *Administrative Science Quarterly,* 1976, *21*, 571–597.

Ladendorf, J. M. Information flow in science, technology, and commerce. *Special Libraries,* May–June , *61,*

Larson, H. P. EDP - A twenty-year ripoff. *Infosystems,* November 1974, *21*, pp. 26–30.

Lawrence, P. R., & Lorsch, J. W. Differentiation and integration in complex organizations. *Administrative Science Quarterly,* 1967, *12*, 1–47.

Leavitt, H. J. Beyond the analytic manager: I. *California Management Review,* 1975, *17*, 3; 5–12.

Leifer, R. "*Designing organizations for information/data processing capability.*" Paper presented at the National Academy of Management Meetings, Atlanta, GA, 1979.

Lengel, R. H. *Managerial information processing and communication-media source selection behavior.* Unpublished PhD Dissertation, Texas A&M University, 1983.

Madison, D. L., Allen, R. W., Porter, L. W., Renwick, P. A., & Mayes, B. T. Organizational politics: An exploration of managers' perception. *Human Relations,* 1980, *33*, 79–100.

Manis, M., Dovalina, I., Avis, N., & Cardoze, S. Base rates can affect individual predictions. *Journal of Personality and Social Psychology,* 1980, *38*, 231–248.

Martin, J., & Powers, M. E. *If case examples provide no proof, why underutilize statistical information.* Paper presented at the American Psychological Association, New York, 1979.

———. Truth or corporate propaganda: The value of a good war story. In L. Pondy, P. Frost, G. Morgan, and T. Dandrige (Eds.), *Organizational Symbolism.* Greenwich, CT: JAI Press, 1983.

———. *Skepticism and the true believer: The effects of case and/or baserate information on belief and committment.* Paper presented at the Western Psychological Association Meetings, Honolulu, HI, 1980.

Mason, R. O., & Mitroff I. I. A program for research on management information systems. *Management Science,* 1973, *19*, 475–485.

McArthur, L. C. The how and what of why: Some determinants and consequences of causal attribution. *Journal of Personality and Social Psychology,* 1972, *22*, 171–193.

———. The lesser influence of consensus than distinctiveness information on causal attributions: A test of the person-thing hypothesis. *Journal of Personality and Social Psychology,* 1976, *33*, 733–742.

Meherabian, A. *Silent messages.* Belmont, CA: Wadsworth, 1971.

Meissner, M. *Technology and the worker.* San Francisco: Chandler, date.

Meyer, J., & Rowan, B. Institutionalized organizations: Formal structure as myth and ceremony. *American Journal of Sociology,* 1977, *30*, 434–450.

Mintzberg, H. The myths of MIS. *California Management Review,* 1972, *15,* (1), 92–97.

———. *The nature of managerial work.* New York: Harper and Row, 1973.

Mitroff, I. I., & Kilmann, R. H. Stories managers tell: A new tool for organizational problem solving. *Management Review,* July 1975, pp. 18–29.

Nisbett, R., & Ross, L. *Human inference: Strategies and short-comings of social judgment.* Inglewood Cliffs, NJ: Prentice-Hall, 1980.

O'Reilly, C. A. III Individual and information overload in organization: Is more necessarily better? *Academy of Management Journal,* 1980, *23,* 684–696.

———. Variations in decisionmakers' use of information sources: The impact of quality and accessibility of information. *Academy of Management Journal,* 1982, *25,* 756–771.

O'Reilly, C. A. III, & Anderson, J. C. Organizational communication and decision making: Laboratory results versus actual organizational settings. *Management Science,* in press.

Parsons, T. *Structure and process in modern societies.* New York: Free Press,

Perrow, C. A framework for the comparative analysis of organizations. *American Sociological Review,* 1967, *32,* 194–208.

Pfeffer, J. *Power in organizations.* Marshfield, MA: Pitman Publishing, 1981.

———. Management as symbolic action: The creation and maintenance of organizational paradigms. In L. L. Cummings and B. M. Staw (Eds.), *Research in organizational behavior* (Vol. 3). Greenwich, CT: JAI Press, in press.

Pfeffer, J., & Salancik, G. R. *The external control of organizations: A resource dependent perspective.* New York: Harper and Row, 1978.

Pondy, L. R. & Mitroff, I. I. Beyond open systems models of organization. In B. M. Staw (Eds.), *Research in organizational behavior* (Vol. 1). Greenwich, CT: JAI Press, 1979.

Poole, M. S. An information-task approach to organizational communication. *Academy of Management Review,* 1978, *3,* 493–504.

Porter, L. W., & Roberts, K. H. Communication in organizations. In M. P. Dunnette (Ed.), *Handbook of industrial and organizational psychology.* Chicago: Rand-McNally, 1976.

Randolph, W. A. Organization technology and the media and purpose dimensions of organization communication. *Journal of Business Research,* 1978, *6,* 237–259.

Skivington, J. *Strategic planning and organizational stability.* Unpublished manuscript, Texas A&M University, College Station, 1982.

Thompson, J. *Organizations in action.* New York: McGraw-Hill, 1967.

Thorngate, W. 'In general' vs. 'It depends': Some comments on the Gergen-Schlenker debate. *Personality and Social Psychology Bulletin,* 1976, *2,* 404–410.

Tushman, M. L. Technical communication in research and development laboratory: The impact of task characteristics. *Academy of Management Journal,* 1978, *21,* 624–645.

———. Work characteristics and subunit communications structure: A contingency analysis. *Administrative Science Quarterly,* 1979,*24,* 82–98.

Tushman, M. L., & Nadler, D. A. Information processing as an integrating concept in organizational design. *Academy of Management Review,* 1978, *3,* 613–624.

VandeVen, A., Delbecq, A. L., & Koenig, R., Jr. Determinants of coordination modes within organizations. *American Sociological Review,* 1976, *41,* 322–338.

VandeVen, A. H., & Ferry, D. L. *Measuring and assessing organizations.* New York: Wiley-Interscience, 1979.

Weick, K. E. *The social psychology of organizing* (2nd ed.). Reading, MA: Addison-Wesley,

Weick, K. E., & Daft, R. L. The effectiveness of interpretation systems. In K. S. Cameron and D. A. Whetten (Eds.), *Organizational effectiveness: A comparison of multiple models.* New York: Academic Press, 1983.

Woodward, J. *Industrial organization: Theory and practice.* New York: Oxford University Press, 1965.

COGNITIVE PROCESSES IN ORGANIZATIONS[1]

Karl E. Weick

ABSTRACT

Cognitive descriptions of organizations are built on the dual images of organizations as bodies of thought and organizations as sets of thinking practices. Traditional organizational variables such as centralization influence cognitive processes and are themselves shaped by these processes. Viewed as bodies of thought, organizations can be described as recurrent schemata, causal textures, and sets of reference levels. Viewed as sets of thinking practices, organizations can be described in terms of dominant rules for combining cognitions, routine utterances, mixtures of habituation and reflection, nature of rehearsing, and preferences for simplification. Insufficient attention has been paid to the possibility that, for want of a thought, the organization was lost. This essay is designed to redress that analytic imbalance.

An organization is a body of thought thought by thinking thinkers. The elements in that formulation are thoughts (Goodman, 1968), thinking practices (Neisser, 1963), and thinkers (Jeffmar and Jeffmar, 1975). Examination of cognitive processes in organizations involves studying all three.

In reply to the question "what is an organization," we consider organizations to be snapshots of ongoing processes, these snapshots being selected and controlled by human consciousness and attentiveness. This consciousness and attentiveness, in turn, can be seen as snapshots of ongoing cognitive processes or more precisely epistemological processes where the mind acquires knowledge about its surroundings (Bougon, Weick, and Binkhorst, 1977). In these epistemological processes, both knowledge and the environment are constructed by participants interactively.

Given a cognitive orientation, there are distinct ways to talk about organizations. For example, an organization can be viewed as a body of jargon available for attachment to experience just as a person can be viewed as a glossary of labels available for attachment to ambiguous states of arousal (London and Nisbett, 1974; Rodin, 1977). Organizational members vary in their attentiveness to external conditions and suggestibility just as people of varying body weights differ in their external orientation and suggestibility to food cues.

Managerial work can be viewed as managing myths, images, symbols, and labels. The much touted "bottom line" of the organization is a symbol, if not a myth. The manager who controls labels that are meaningful to organizational members can segment and point to portions of their experience and label it in consequential ways so that employees take that segment more seriously and deal with it in a more organizationally appropriate manner (Pettigrew, 1975). Because managers traffic so often in images, the appropriate role for the manager may be evangelist rather than accountant.

Standard concepts in general cognitive psychology (Broadbent, 1971; Reynolds and Flagg, 1977; and Scheerer, 1954) can also be adapted to descriptions of organizations. For example, an organization member's knowledge can be viewed as deductions drawn from a view of the world legitimated within that organization. An organization can be characterized by the specific syllogisms (Jones and Gerard, 1967, pp. 159–162) that are used within it. An organization can be characterized by the contents of the schemata members invoke routinely and through which they size up situations. Organizations can be characterized as sets of weakly held assumptions that are subject to disconfirmation thereby producing the experience of interesting times (Davis, 1971).

To describe an organization as a body of thought is to suggest that collective rather than individual omniscience is the object of interest. That emphasis in turn suggests parallels between organizations in general and scientific communities (Betz, 1971; Ravetz, 1971) in particular. Scientific communities also represent bodies of thought (paradigms), the main difference being that scientific communities reputedly (Brush, 1974) are more detached from and more objective about the thoughts they incorporate. It is conceivable that organizations could be described as scientific communities with self-interest. Organizations have a personal stake in the thoughts they accumulate and transmit, but aside from that their knowing mechanisms resemble those found in scientific organizations.

This essay is about the place of thinking in organizations. We know that people think. We know that in any organization at any moment somebody is thinking. The question then becomes, does that thinking create, accomplish, or displace anything that goes on in that organization? A researcher's job is to spot the thinking people in an organization, see what they're thinking about, and examine how those thoughts become amplified and diffused through the organization or discover why those thoughts remain localized. Much of Mintzberg's (1973) analysis suggests that managers spend little time reflecting. They are active, they act on line, they spend most of their time communicating, they have very little time to themselves, their interruptions are frequent. If they think much at all, their thinking seems to be grooved, or under the influence of the last person they talked to, or abstract and detached from the here and now (Steinbruner, 1974). That portrait, however, is an oversimplification and we will try to show why.

OBJECTS OF ORGANIZATIONAL THOUGHT

Two quotations vividly pose the issue of what is available to be thought about in organizations.

> Defining situations as real certainly has consequences, but these may contribute very marginally to the events in progress; in some cases only a slight embarrassment flits across the scene in mild concern for those who tried to define the situation wrongly. All the world is not a stage—certainly the theater isn't entirely. (Whether you organize a theater or an aircraft factory, you need to find places for cars to park and coats to be checked, and these had better be real places, which, incidentally, had better carry real

insurance against theft). Presumably, a "definition of the situation" is almost always to be found, but those who are in the situation ordinarily do not *create* this definition, even though their society often can be said to do so; ordinarily, all they do is to assess correctly what the situation ought to be for them and then act accordingly. True, we personally negotiate aspects of all the arrangements under which we live, but often once these are negotiated, we continue on mechanically as though the matter had always been settled. So, too, there are occasions when we must wait until things are almost over before discovering what has been occurring and occasions of our own activity when we can considerably put off deciding what to claim we have been doing. But surely these are not the only principles of organization. Social life is dubious enough and ludicrous enough without having to wish it further into unreality (Goffman, 1974, pp. 1–2)

Consider the situation of trial and error.

Trial implies a problematical and alternative result: either the success of the assumption put to trial or its failure. When we ask why this is so, we hit upon the presence of some "controlling" condition or circumstance in the situation—some stable physical or social fact—whose character renders the hypothesis or suggested solution either adequate or vain, as the case may be. The instrumental idea or thought, then, has its merit in enabling us to find out or locate facts and conditions which are to be allowed for thereafter. These constitute a *control upon knowledge and action,* a system of "things." . . . The method of selection by trial and error requires that relative stability, fixity and permanence be discovered in the "control" conditions in the environment, since the genesis of truth lies in the checking off of hypotheses under this more stable control. The truth of a thought may be discovered through its successful working; but we have to consider also the failures, the errors, and indeed the whole situation in which truth and error are alike possible. . . .

I may "bring about" reality perhaps, without this external control, by "willing to believe" in something for which I have no proof or reason, in cases in which this sort of event willed—as, for example, someone else's conduct—may be conditioned upon my act of will. But nature does not take to suggestions so kindly. The will of a general may stimulate his troops and so bring to him the victory he believes in; but such an act of the general's will cannot replenish the short supply of powder or shells, on which the issue of the battle perhaps more fundamentally depends" (Baldwin, 1909, pp. 72–73).

The objects of thought in organizations can be constructions of organizational members (Delia, 1977). But as Goffman, Baldwin, and others (Goldthorpe, 1973; Frankel, 1973) remind us, somewhere in most of those constructions is a grain of truth. The seeds for those constructions exist independent of the observers even though members embellish and elaborate those grains with vigor and originality.

In this essay, we intend to make the environment just as problematic for inquiry as possible. That's where the joining of organization theory and epistemology becomes crucial. Epistemology is concerned with mind and environment relationships and both are actively constructed. To argue that the chief problem of organizational theory is to articulate the relationships between organizations and environments is to miss the point that organizations and environments both undergo considerable construction in the eyes and minds of organizational members (Blumer, 1971). The environment is a problem. One way to deal with the environment is simply to say that it's "dealable." Having imposed that construction on the environment, the actor is enabled to move his world around and make sense of it.

Returning to Goffman's concern with checkrooms and parking lots and Baldwin's about ammunition, in the beginning someone enacted those settings. The trick is to go back far enough to trace that development. The "checkroom" or "parking lot" can also become sites for muggings, arenas for shooting craps, places to pile inventory, personal turf, profit centers, and much more. The thieves that Goffman is worried about certainly impose different definitions on coat rooms than do people who blithely hang their apparel in them.

We want to emphasize that in any situation where people enact their environment there usually are grains of truth that invite elaboration. Enactment isn't a hallucination. Typically it meets the environment half way. But what happens is that the actor in the organization plays a major role in unrandomizing and giving order to the bewildering number of variables that constitute those grains. Through a combination of selective attention, activity, consensual validation, and luck, organizational actors are able to stride into streams of experience where things are mixed together in random fashion and unravel those streams sufficiently so that some kind of sensemaking is possible (Schutz, 1964). In accomplishing that unraveling, people do enact their environments as well as park their cars and hang up their coats. And while doing this enactment these same people often don't assess correctly what the situation ought to be for them because "correctness" is not a dimension that can be made relevant to the situation. Neither can they "act accordingly" when cues are unreliable and instrumentalities equivocal.

Objects of thought in organization are not just enactments, they can also be described in terms of a phrase attributed to Korzybski: The map is not the territory (Hayakawa, 1961). The intent of that assertion is to remind people that their representations of the world are just that, representations rather than the thing itself. We do not take issue with that point of view but do place a different emphasis on it. The map *is* the territory if people treat it as such. That's the thrust of any formulation which talks about a definition of the situation (Ball, 1972). Things are real if people treat them as real and that's the reason why if people mistake the map for the territory, to criticize that action is less crucial than to see how people operate having made that "mistake." Treating the map as the territory also satisfies personal needs for cognition and order (Cohen, Stotland, and Wolfe, 1955).

Maps do structure the territory sufficiently so that someone can initiate activity in that territory, activity that may introduce order. We know that people make do, improvise, and act like *bricoleurs* (Levi-Strauss, 1962, pp. 16–33), which means that a map is sufficient for most people to get a sense of the situation and wade into it. They don't need to know the territory inch by inch to do something about it or in it. So when we assert that the map is the territory we take seriously the facility people demonstrate in taking bits and pieces of information and assembling them into a workable order.

Goffman and Baldwin remind us not to be carried away by images such as "definition of the situation," "negotiation of reality," and "the will to believe." Each of those concepts implies that reality is almost wholly in the hands of the actor and he can make of it what he wants. That's clearly not so. But neither is it the case that parking lots, cloak rooms, and ammunition come clearly labeled (fists can be ammunition), are consensually validated (roofs are floors for cars or ceilings for people), or mean only one thing (parking lot as gymkhana course). Much goes on in organizations after people park their cars and hang their coats and it's those other actions that we're concerned with. Since most of those other actions do involve people, they provide more latitude for invention than Baldwin admits.

The objects of organizational thought oftentimes also are dominated by the prior beliefs among members. Frequently they operate by the maxim "I'll see it when I believe it" (e.g., Gould, 1977; Nisbett and Wilson, 1977, pp. 248–249). As Einstein said, "It seems that the human mind has first to construct forms independently before we can find them in things" (cited in Rosnow and Fine, 1976, p. 63). When we want to examine cognition in organizations, one of the best starting points is to discover the beliefs through which organizational members will examine their experiences.

The importance of beliefs is dramatically apparent in the case of placebos (Bishop, 1977). Placebos are any inactive substance or procedure that is used with a medical patient under the guise of an effective treatment. Repeatedly it has been demonstrated that because the patients believe in these inactive substances or procedures, they actually work. And the amount of symptom relief has been dramatic. How placebos work isn't understood, but that they work is evident and supports the argument that beliefs do play a major role in seeing (Gregory and Bombrich, 1973). The important question for our purpose is what's the organizational equivalent of a placebo? Which beliefs, in conjunction with which innocuous assignments, produce outcomes that are disproportionate in size to those usually associated with such assignments?

One presumption that sometimes is associated with cognitive views is that people are passive. They idly sit around either registering the environment or reflecting on past experiences. In general, these people are interesting only because of their large investment in headwork. That presumption is misleading and should be corrected. The principle object of organizational thoughts is organizational acts. Acts are the raw material for cognitive work in organizations.

One of the big gaps in current organizational theory is that we just don't know much about what happens when acting precedes thinking. That's what much of this essay is about. March and Olsen have recently commented on this oversight: "If we knew more about the normative theory of acting before you think, we could say more intelligent things about the functions of management and leadership when organizations or societies do not know what they're doing" (1976, p. 79).

In terms of my own work (Weick, 1977), enactment processes are viewed as crucial in organizational sensemaking. And as Lou Pondy shrewdly noted, those processes have *never* been labeled "enthinkment." The emphasis is on actions that provide a pretext for thinking, and not the reverse. Most of our analyses elaborate the basic sensemaking recipe, 'How can I know what I think till I see what I say." In that recipe, saying or doing precede thinking and provide the objects on which thinking will dwell. To argue that thinking is detached from action is to miss the point of that recipe.

If we talk about people enacting many of thier own pretexts for sensemaking, several problems come into focus. For example, one of the dominant themes in cognitive approaches to organizations is that people simplify their situations with a vengeance and grasp them with only modest success and thoroughness. From the standpoint of enactment, these people presumably enact and impose simplifications on the world, which means that the world is then sensed as a simple display which can be monitored by attending to a relatively small number of variables. That suggests one mechanism by which Steinbruner's (1974) cybernetic theory of organizations might operate (see also Coulam, 1977). If a person enacts a simple world, it's no great accomplishment to monitor and survive within that simple world. However, the important thing to notice is that simple enactments mingle with those variables that have been ignored, suppressed, or neglected such that the composite sensation will usually be more complicated than what the actor imposed in the first place. People aren't simply presented with their own simplifications of the world. Imposed simplifications that ignore complexities nevertheless interact with those complexities and present a world that is more complicated than the observer.

In summary, when we talk about the objects of thought in organizations we emphasize that though there be grains of truth in the displays confronted by members, grains that become elaborated, additional objects of thought include maps of the organization that are treated as if they are territories, beliefs through which people see the organization, and acts that provide the pretext and raw material for sensemaking. Organizational variables become important as they affect these grains, maps, beliefs, and actions. Whenever one can hypothesize that an organizational variable such as size or formalization or centralization has a demonstrable effect on one or more of these objects of thought, cognitive theory and organizational theory have been joined.

But the causal arrow also goes the other way. Maps, beliefs, and thoughts that summarize actions, themselves constrain contacts, communication, and commands. These constraints constitute and shape organizational processes that result in structures (Berlo, 1977).

ORGANIZATIONS AS A BODY OF THOUGHT

Schemata as Bodies of Thought

The concept of schema (Axelrod, 1973) is a major tool when one wishes to think cognitively about organizations. Schemas have been given a variety of definitions and we will review quickly some qualities of the concept so that its value for the study of organizations can become apparent.

Originally the concept of schema was developed as a way to understand how well-adapted, coordinated movements were possible. When coordinated movement takes place, each successive step is made as if it were under the control of the preceding movements in the series. This implies that the position reached by the moving limb in the last preceding stage somehow is recorded and still functions even though it has concluded. The problem then became to explain how past movements retain current influence. The idea of schema was developed to suggest a standard against which all subsequent changes of posture are measured before they enter consciousness.

Bartlett (1932) used the idea of schema most extensively and the nuances he added are crucial for organizational analysis. Bartlett objected to the static quality implied by the statement that a schema is a standard against which actions are compared. He wanted to emphasize that the standard was actively doing something all the time (not just serving as a static comparison) and that it was developing from moment to moment. Bartlett toyed with the possibility of calling this developing and developed framework an "organized setting" (1932, p. 201), but abandoned that in favor of talking about a schema which he described as

> "an active organization of past reactions, or of past experiences, which must always be supposed to be operating in any well adapted organic response. That is, whenever there is any order or regularity of behavior, a particular response is possibly only because it is related to other similar responses which have been serially organized, yet which operate, not simply as individual members coming one after another, but as a unitary mass. Determination by schemata is the most fundamental of all the ways in which we can be influenced by reactions and experiences which occurred sometime in the past. All incoming impulses of a certain kind, or mode, go together to build up an active, organized setting" (p. 201).

The important thing for Bartlett was that schemata are repeatedly built up on the spot. Literal recall and literal replaying of past responses never happen. Instead the individual uses the past as a point of departure and then reassembles those prior experiences together with new inputs and develops all of this in an active ongoing fashion. People build a version of the past just as they build a tennis stroke afresh, depending on the preceding balance of postures and momentary needs of the game. Every time a stroke is built or a memory is constructed it has some originality. As Bartlett notes, "In a world of constantly changing environment, literal recall is extraordinarily unimportant" (p. 24).

More recently Stotland and Canon (1972) have used schema theory as a way to understand social psychological research. Concerning schema, they observe that

> "persons generate relatively abstract and generalizable rules, called schemas, regarding certain regularities in the relationships among events. Once established they serve as a guide to behavior and as a framework which influences the manner in which relevant new information will be assimilated. Since a schema is an abstraction, a general statement detailing the perceived regular co-occurrence of some categorized events, it tends to be relatively permanent and impervious to change even if a few exceptions to it are noted" (1972, p. 67).

As an illustration of how schemata are used, Stotland and Canon make the following observation:

"It is possible to quite consciously invoke or activate a schema as an assist in dealing with some concrete situation which is being faced. For instance, a person upon finding himself in a new work situation thrown together with a number of unfamiliar people might rather self-consciously turn to his schemata relevant to work, meeting new persons, effective behavior in novel surroundings. These might include such schemata as: persons who talk a great deal are usually leaders, women are easier to get to know than men, an anxiety in a novel situation is lessened by finding some old, familiar elements in it. Self-motivated arousal of such general rules of a relationship would perhaps be useful in suggesting successful ways of coping with a situation. On the other hand, it would be highly likely that schemas of this sort would be operative even though they were not intentionally activated by the person, as they can also be brought into play by external factors" (p. 68).

Thus, a schema is an abridged, generalized, corrigible organization of experience that serves as an initial frame of reference for action and perception. A schema is the belief in the phrase, I'll see it when I believe it. Schemata constrain seeing and one way in which they may do this has been described by Neisser (1976).

Figure 1. Neisser's perceptual cycle.

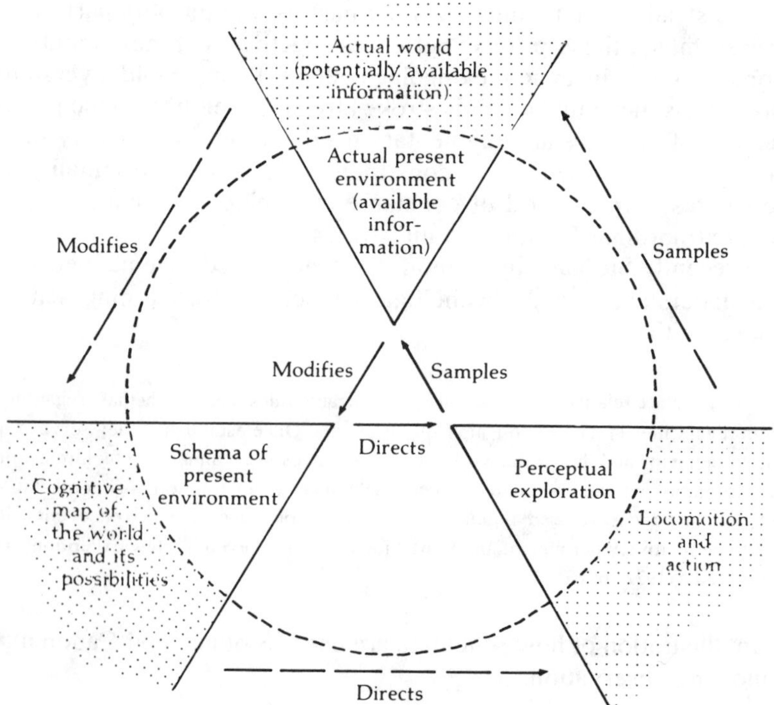

Neisser describes schemata as active, information-seeking structures that accept information and direct action. "The schema accepts information as it becomes available at sensory surfaces and is changed by that information; it directs movements and exploratory activities that make more information available, by which it is further modified" (p. 54). Neisser notes that schemata are analogous to things like formats in computer programming language, plans for finding out about objects and events, and genotypes that offer possibilities for development along certain general lines. Neisser posits a perceptual cycle to illustrate how schemata operate and this graphic provides a useful medium to describe how organizations affect their own cognition.

The perceptual cycle is continuous. A schema directs the exploration of objects, this exploration samples portions of an object, and these samples may modify the schema, which then directs further exploration and sampling, which then further modifies the schema, and this goes on continuously. Notice that the three components of Neisser's perceptual cycle, schema, exploration, and object, correspond rather neatly to the components of thinking, seeing, and saying in the sensemaking recipe, how can I know what I think till I see what I say. On the basis of what a person thinks, he sees different things in his saying and what he sees in this saying then modifies what he thinks and will then single out for closer attention in subsequent saying.

Organization theory can be coupled to schema theory by simply asking the question, given an organization, where in the perceptual cycle does that organization have an effect and how does that effect occur. The organization could directly affect the content of the perceptual cycle and the objects sampled. Less obvious is the fact that organizations could also affect perceptual processing. Imagine, for example, that the arrows associated with the activity of directing, sampling, and modifying are of various widths suggesting tighter and looser coupling among the stages. An organization that has a vision of the world that is highly resistant to change and that runs its life accordingly would have a very strong influence leading from schema to perceptual exploration with relatively looser couplings between exploration and sampling and sampling and modification. In other words, an organization with a world view that is highly resistant to change has a thick, solid arrow at the base of the triangle but relatively weak arrows between any other pair of steps.

Other properties of organizations could be coordinated with patterns of tight and loose coupling in the perceptual cycle. The activity of sampling, for example, takes time. The amount of time available for people to sample objects can have a major effect on the conclusions that are available to modify a schema. Organizations with distinctive competence (Emery and

Trist, 1969) seldom sample their environments and sometimes modify their schemata too late to deal with "sudden" competitors.

While Neisser's formulation describes the directing, sampling, and modification that goes on in just one head, it's important to realize that these activities are dispersed among many people in organizations. Boundary people, for example, are in an ideal position to sample (Aldrich and Herker, 1977, but their sampling seldom gets communicated vividly or quickly to those people who could modify schemata that bind the interpretations imposed by other people in the organization. The dispersal of the various stages of the perceptual cycle throughout an organization serves as another way to describe what an organization is like and to predict how well it will know the world it enacts.

Examples of schemata in organizations are abundant. They may exist as cognitive maps that members infer from their organizational experience (Axelrod, 1976; Bougon, Weick, and Binkhorst, 1977; Stagner, 1977).

The most conspicuous example is the standard operating procedure (Allison, 1971). A standard operating procedure is a schema that structures dealings with an environment. A standard operating procedure is a frame of reference that constrains exploration and often unfolds like a self-fulfilling prophecy (Martin, 1977). SOPs direct attention toward restricted aspects of an object which, when sampled, seemingly justify routine application of the procedure.

Janis's (1972) description of groupthink has overtones of schema theory. The phenomenon of groupthink is important because it demonstrates some of the dysfunctional consequences when people are dominated by a single schema and this domination becomes self-reinforcing. Having become true believers of a specific schema, group members direct their attention toward an environment and sample it in such a way that the true belief becomes self-validating and the group becomes even more fervent in its attachment to the schema. What is underestimated is the degree to which the direction and sampling are becoming increasingly narrow under the influence of growing consensus and enthusiasm for the restricted set of beliefs. As Janis demonstrates, this spiral frequently is associated with serious misjudgments of situations.

Notice that any idea that restricts exploration and sampling by the very nature of that restriction will come to be seen as increasingly plausible. If a person has an idea and looks for "relevant" data, there's enough complexity and ambiguity in the world that support is usually found and the idea is usually judged more plausible. One of the prominent characteristics of schemata is that they are refractory to disproof (Ross, 1977, p. 205).

Neisser would argue that schema are not that vulnerable to distortion and that by and large they pick up real checkrooms, parking lots, and ammunition. It is our contention that most "objects" in organizations consist of communications, meanings, images, and interpretations, all of which offer considerable latitude for definition and self-validation.

Notice that when we coordinated Neisser's perceptual cycle with the sensemaking recipe, the *object* in that coordination was raw talk. It's certainly obvious that saying is subject to numerous interpretations, which means it can appear to support quite divergent schemata. This seeming universal support does not arise from stupidity or malevolence on the part of the actor, but rather from a combination of an intact, reinforced schema and an equivocal object. Actors with bounded rationality presumably are more interested in confirming their schemata than in actively trying to disprove them. Even though people may build up schema anew each time they apply them, they have to start this build-up with something. And it's that something, that assumption, that retrieved portion of the past which can rather swiftly become elaborated into a schema which is like a previous schema and which has a controlling effect on what people perceive.

Thus, diagnosis of organizational schemata is a powerful means for researchers to understand much of what goes on in organizations, how its members arrive at the conclusions they do, and why they persist in conclusions that seem dated. When it is remarked that an organization is a body of thought, that can be restated as, an organization is a body of schemata that direct the exploration of objects. This directed exploration samples features that typically affirm and strengthen schemata, which means they become even more binding as recipes that organizational members apply.

Causal Textures as Bodies of Thought

Environments vary in the ease and accuracy with which cause-effect or means-ends relations can be perceived and enacted in them. This property, labeled causal texture, was described vividly in 1935 by Tolman and Brunswik and later reinterpreted by Emery and Trist (1969). The Emery and Trist work, however, dropped some of the more compelling and valuable features of the original formulation. It is the purpose of this section to revive those original features, because they illustrate how cognitive concepts can be used to diagnose organizational properties and problems. The point of departure for Tolman and Brunswik's discussion of causal texture is the fact that any distant or remote event, both in time and space, is signified with varying accuracy by local representatives. Thus, the likelihood that a manuscript will be accepted for publication may be signified more or less accurately by peer reaction to the paper, composition of the editorial board, books reviewed in previous issues, etc. Both Tolman and Brunswik were interested in the coordination between local representatives and the distant objects to which they might be coupled.

Tolman was interested in the fact that certain means objects have a stronger or weaker possibility of producing certain ends or of reaching certain goals. Working late at the office may be a stronger means to the end of being promoted than graduating from an Ivy League school. Tolman noted that means objects vary in their equivocality, by which he meant that some of them are good ways to achieve goals and other ones are poor. Thus Tolman's contribution to the causal texture notion was the idea that means objects vary in the degree to which they promote goal attainment.

Brunswik's contribution to the causal texture notion was more perceptual. Brunswik argued that means objects themselves are known with greater or lesser clarity on the basis of local signs from which their existence can be inferred. Some cues are good cues that means objects exist, but other cues are less reliable. This means that a member of an organization faces the following complexities. Cues can signify the existence of a means with varying degrees of reliability and the means objects in turn have varying degrees of equivocality when examined as suitable ways to attain ends.

Tolman and Brunswik used the colorful phrase "the lasso principle" (p. 48) to signify individual tries to connect a perceived personal deprivation with some cue, indicating that some means object will produce some

Figure 2. Tolman and Brunswik's categories of causal texture.

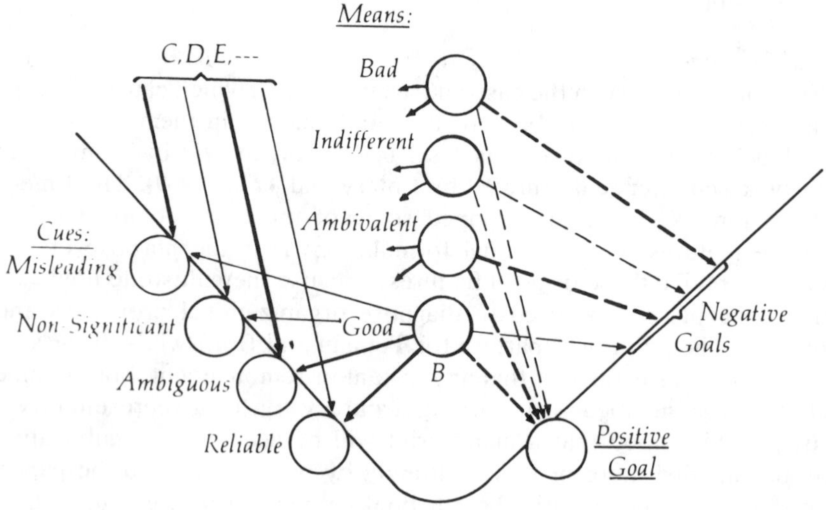

desired goal that will remove the state of deprivation. In other words, the person tries to lasso and couple together a need, a local sign, a means object, and a goal state that will satisfy the need. That seemingly simple lassoing gets complicated because of the problematic ties between means objects and goals and between signs and means objects. The nature of these complexities are depicted in the display reproduced above.

If we focus first on the right side of the diagram, we see that relative to certain goals, means objects such as peer reaction or working late can be characterized in four ways: good, ambivalent, indifferent, and bad. The differences among these four kinds of means objects are shown by the thickness of their connections to positive and negative goals. A good means object is one that leads in a relatively high percentage of cases to a positive goal and in only a small number of cases to a negative goal. An ambivalent means object leads with a relatively high probability to both positive and negative goals. An indifferent means object leads with very little probability to either a positive or negative goal. And the bad means object is one that leads with a high probability to a negative goal and with little probability to the positive goal.

These differences can be illustrated by an exhibit of maze learning. Organizational members are often described as trying to find their way through a maze, even if it is a maze they've enacted for themselves, so use of this illustration is not as ludicrous as it might seem.

Figure 3. The organization as maze.

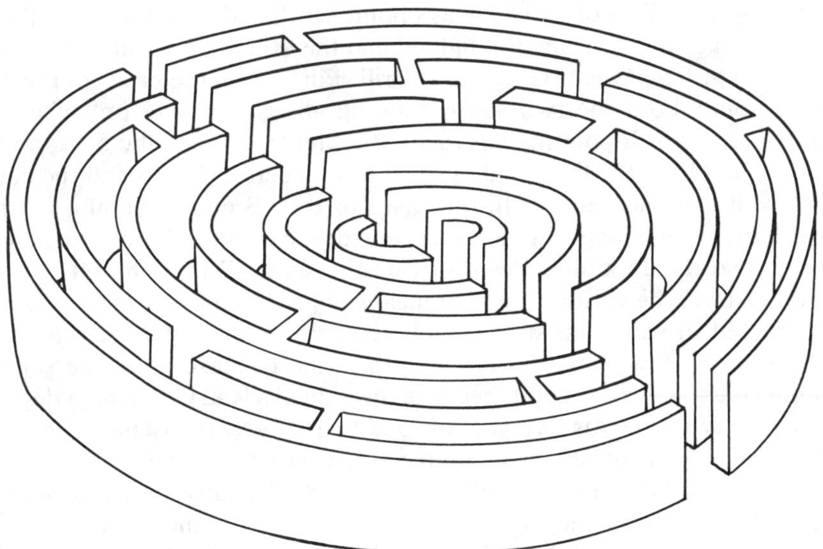

In this illustration, adapted from Tolman and Brunswik, a somewhat unusual maze is used, a maze that has multiple choices at each choice point, making it even more correspondent with choice situations in ongoing organizations. The maze is depicted below and is described in this way:

Figure 4. Tolman and Brunswik's schematic maze.

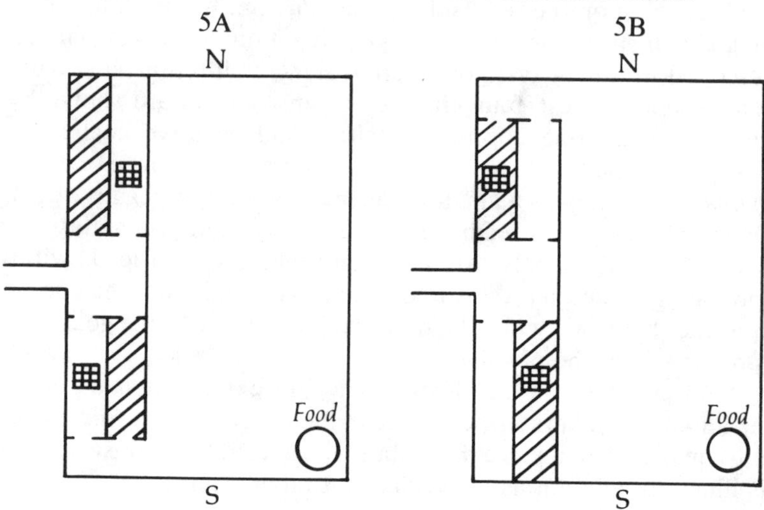

Suppose "that each choice point has four alleys instead of the usual two issuing from it. Two of these always point south and two north. Further, one alley in each pair is always lighted and the other dark, and one has an electrified grill and the other no such grill. Further, in the cases of the 5A choice-points both the two south-pointing alleys will lead on, whereas both the two north-pointing alleys will be blinds. Also in the 5A type of choice-point both the lighted alleys will have electric shocks and the dark alleys will have no shocks. In the cases of the 5B choice-points, on the other hand, everything will be just reversed; the north-pointing alleys will lead on and the dark alleys will provide the shocks" (pp. 58–59).

To illustrate the various kinds of means objects, suppose that a maze is constructed in which most of the choice-points are of the 5A type and there are very few of the 5B type. In this kind of maze all of the south-pointing dark alleys are good, because they always lead with a high degree of frequency to the positive goal of food and they virtually never lead to the negative goal of shock or undue exertion as in a blind alley. The south-pointing lighted alleys will be ambivalent, because they lead with a high degree of frequency both to food and electric shock. The north-pointing dark alleys will be indifferent, because they lead with very little frequency to either the positive goal or the electric shock while the north-pointing lighted alleys will be bad, because they lead with very little probability to the positive goal of food and virtually always to the negative goal of electric shock and a blind alley.

That is the learning problem that confronts a rat deprived of food just as it resembles a kind of learning problem that confronts an organization that is deprived of profit, power, visibility, share of the market, etc. If that organization wants to find a more advantageous position in its environment, it must coordinate certain means objects such as acquisitions and divestitures with more distant positive goals of better positions in an environment and avoid negative goals such as worse positions in the environment.

If we now move to the left side of Figure 2, we can see that there are four different types of cues relative to a single good means object: reliable, ambiguous, nonsignificant, or misleading. Again, the nature of these cues is represented by varying thicknesses of lines between the good means object and other means objects. For example, ambiguous cues are considered to be cues that are caused with a great frequency by both the good object and by other objects that could be potentially disruptive as far as their instrumentality to goal attainment.

Tolman and Brunswik's original description of causal texture provides a valuable means to describe environments that are both enacted and reacted to by organizations. The concepts they propose are manageable and plausible. Thus, we can assert, first, that members impose on their flow of experience the idea that that experience can be differentiated into means and ends. Second, the means they differentiate and superimpose can be good, ambivalent, indifferent, or bad. Third. we can assert that organizational members search in their superimposed world for signs that suggest the existence of reliable paths to good outcomes.

When we embed causal textures in the realities of organizations, we begin to see why it is difficult for organizational members to learn. Because of the fluidity associated with many organizational problems (Cohen, March, and Olsen, 1972) reliable cues for good means objects are transient and rare. They're rare for several reasons. If goals are defined retrospectively rather than proactively, then means-ends coupling will occur after the fact and be loose. In a world of competitors, the value of cues can change swiftly as people try to mislead one another. Reliable cues are scarce in a world where organizations tinker with their own perceptual displays and try systematically to make it more difficult for other organizations to predict what they will do.

Tolman and Brunswik do not neglect unstable causal textures and the problems this creates for lassoing (p. 68). A dark alley which is good in some laboratories can be bad in others. They note that organisms typically bring to any new environment a set of already prepared hypotheses (read Schemata) and these hypotheses are based on the average environments they've encountered in the past. Tolman and Brunswik argue that when people are in a new situation it's crucial that they be able to discover unique features which differentiate this particular maze from the more general case of a normal maze. Once they've made this discovery people have to attach their new set of hypotheses specifically to these unique features of the novel situation. The advantage of this strategy is that people can then use their general hypotheses and schemata in normal environments and invoke specialized hypotheses only when special characteristics emerge.

Tolman and Brunswik conclude that "the wholly successful organism would be one which brings, innately, normal averagely "good" means-ends hypotheses and normal averagely "reliable" perceptual hypotheses; but which can immediately modify these innate hypotheses to suit the special conditions of the special environments; which can note and include in its cue system and in its means-end system the presence of the further identifying features of these special environments. But further, such an organism must also, if it is to become completely successful, be equally able at once to drop out such new hypotheses when the special features as to cues or means are no longer present" (p. 72).

When we argue later that an organization must complicate itself in order to survive, one way to talk about that complication is in terms of a proliferation of hypotheses and heightened sensitivity to the special conditions under which different hypotheses are to be invoked.

It's important to reemphasize that given the shifting nature of organizational goals, given the fact that goals and means are often arbitrarily imposed on ongoing flows of experience, and given the fact that turbulence is often associated with fuzzy cues and loosely coupled means-ends ties (Strauch, 1975), we assume that the combination "reliable-good" occurs infrequently and holds true for relatively short stretches of time and that the other fifteen combinations describe a greater proportion of the cognitive problems that confront organizational members.

We can now see how Emery and Trist borrowed too little. Their four types of environments—placid random, placid clustered, disturbed reactive, and turbulent—are characterized on the basis of the distribution of goals and noxiants and whether similar organizations are present in that environment. Explicit mention of the Tolman and Brunswik categories is made only for the placid clustered environment where it is merely noted that "clustering enables some parts to take on roles as signs of other parts or become means-objects with respect to approaching or avoiding" (1969, p. 247).

Those four types of environments could have been described in terms of which cues and which kinds of means objects were predominant. For example, a placid random environment could be an environment in which there is a high probability that cues will be bad and misleading or an environment in which the cues are indifferent and nonsignificant. Which of those two combinations is chosen as the operationalization of placid random will make sizable differences in how one defines the perceptual problem an organization faces and how one will design a sensing mechanism to solve that problem (Neisser, 1977).

If Tolman and Brunswik's concepts are arrayed in a matrix with the four categories of cues listed along the vertical axis and the four categories of means objects along the horizontal axis, sixteen worlds that organizations confront are depicted, not just the four originally described by Emery and Trist. The problems for organizational action, sensemaking, perception, and cognition differ greatly among those sixteen cells.

The assertion that organizational members have bounded rationality takes on a different meaning if we consider the possibility that many situations in organizations involve strange mixtures of cues and means-objects toward which only hesitant and/or impulsive lassoing is possible. Bounded rationality viewed against that background is something other than one more example of the law of least effort. It is a sound strategy intentionally adopted to deal with recalcitrant, equivocal data.

That way of describing the cognitive problems of organizational members is not common, but it does capitalize more directly on what Tolman and Brunswik said.

One concern of cognitive organizational theorists is to do more fine-grained analyses of the perceptual problems that organizational members face. If an organization is viewed as a body of thought where a substantial portion of that body consists of causal textures with mixtures of cues and means-objects, analysis seems to be enhanced. If we take the assertion that organizations are goal oriented—an assertion toward which we have muted enthusiasm—we see that such an assertion says very little if it neglects the kinds of means objects potentially available for achieving those goals and the clues that people use to determine what means objects are available. Greater usage of the original version of causal texture may reduce the frequency of these oversights.

Reference Levels as Bodies of Thought

William Powers (1973) has written a powerful cybernetic analysis of perception entitled "Behavior: The Control of Perception." The key to his thinking is evident in the book's title. The basic idea is that individuals behave in the interest of controlling their sensory input so that this input remains consistent with some reference level for that sensation. When sensory inputs begin to depart from a reference level, the individual begins to act and does whatever is necessary to bring the sensed input back toward the reference level. The output of any human control system, therefore, is a reference level that is binding on lower-order control systems in the sense that these lower-order systems act to keep incoming sensations consistent with those levels.

Applied to the perception of organizations, the Powers formulation has some interesting consequences. He argues that people have concepts of systems and these figments of the imagination serve as reference signals around which sensations are organized. In response to concepts concerning organization, people act so that sensations are produced that are consistent with these concepts. A person's concept of an organization, in other words, serves as a base line. Incoming sensations are compared against that base line and if these sensations do not deviate significantly from it no action is taken. If the incoming sensations do show some deviation from this principle of organization, the individual acts until the incoming sensations come back into compliance with that base line.

> When a fan is loyal to a baseball team, he is reacting to something that is of a most ethereal nature. In the course of 20 years, a team may change stadiums, managers, owners, coaches, and players—what is left to be loyal to? Only the system concept that made it seem that there was a 'team' in the first place. Since that system concept exists in the . . . perceptions of the fan who was organized to perceive that way, there was no need for the team to have material existence. The fan will perceive it anyway, as long as he wishes rabidly to do so. Many are the stubborn old timers who insist on perceiving the *Brooklyn* Dodgers, who have merely been kidnapped temporarily to a strange state (Powers, 1973, p. 172).

Principles of organization, therefore, are reference signals against which sensations are adjusted. It is that sense in which organizations are figments of the imagination, but they are no more so than any other kinds of elements such as people, families, or ideology.

Ask yourself where is the Duke Ellington orchestra when you watch his son Mercer Ellington conduct it? There is something that is known as the Duke Ellington orchestra in the minds of many people and yet, in watching the present version of that orchestra, it's not easy to spot precisely where the organization is. Over the years personnel and music have changed, yet something persists that transcends any particular sets of charts or people who play them. What persists is the concept of the Ellington orchestra. The concept endures because observers mold whatever assemblage they observe into an entity that produces sensations consistent with the idea of the Duke Ellington orchestra.

Thus, an organization can be a body of thought in the sense that it consists of a set of higher-order reference signals in terms of which people organize their behavior. Organizational behavior then becomes behavior that generates sensations which confirm that the organization is in place and functioning.

If we couple Powers' formulation with Mintzberg's (1973) descriptions of managerial work, it could be argued that what Mintzberg has described are ways in which managers produce sensations that either match or mismatch their reference signals concerning what the nature of the organization is. As the sensed state of the world begins to deviate from these organizational concepts, actions are taken to generate the impression that in fact the organization still exists and is not disappearing. Most managerial actions that Mintzberg has described (e.g., figurehead, spokesman, disturbance handler) could be regarded as efforts to affirm that the organization is alive and well rather than collapsing and disappearing.

ORGANIZATION AS THINKING PRACTICES

Organizations are not just bodies of thought, they are sets of thinking practices that produce those bodies of thought. Some thinking practices have already been implied (schema thinking involves direction, sampling, and modification), but there are other thinking practices that appear in organizations and are responsible for the shape of these organizations and their effectiveness. The purpose of this section is to outline a few of these thinking practices and to suggest by example a means of inquiry that organization watchers should use more widely when they examine organizations.

We want to examine such things as the relations that members impose on unrelated events, the sentences that organizational members utter to themselves, the habits members invoke, the kinds of people they imagine during episodes of solitary activity, and the simplifications they desire.

The Relational Algorithm as a Thinking Practice

Organizational members frequently put cognitions and bits of information into different combinations. Their preferred ways of combining are a good example of thinking practices. A standard definition of creative activity is that it involves new combinations of old elements and old combinations of new elements. How an organization's members do combining, how frequently and elaborately they do it, the variety of elements they have available for recombination as well as the variety of their recombination formats, all can have an effect on the sensemaking that takes place.

Organizations thrive on combinations. Whether members are talking about divestiture, merging, product differentiation, incentive systems, performance evaluations, or how to treat subsidiaries, they are always taking elements and putting them together in some combination. Product differentiation, for example, can involve taking one product in some relation to another product. Take a product "against" a product (the product wipes out the effects of the original product), take a product "after" a product (a second product does a further step that the first product doesn't), take a product "under" a product (our product makes their product work better). The whole exercise of developing incentive systems in organizations is an effort to induce some relationship between a person and financial outcomes. And the same can be said for most other organizational problem solving.

A useful format for recombination is the relational algorithm developed by Herbert Crovitz (1967, 1970). Essentially the algorithm is nothing more than a list of forty-two relational words taken from Ogden's (1934) attempt to boil the English language down to 850 simple words. Crovitz feels that the essence of any idea is a statement in which one thing is taken in some relation to some other thing. The forty-two relational words are operations that can occur between the things and are listed below.

Relational Algorithm

about	at	for	of	round	to
across	because	from	off	still	under
after	before	if	on	so	up
against	between	in	opposite	then	when
among	but	near	or	though	where
and	by	not	out	through	while
as	down	now	over	till	with

Consider the famous Duncker problem: How do you get rid of an inoperable stomach tumor without harming the healthy tissue of the body, by using rays that can be modulated in intensity, and at a high enough intensity that they destroy the tumor? One solution is to take a ray *across* a ray such that the tumor is put at the point where the rays intersect. At this point the energy associated with each ray is summed and this means that the rays can be fairly low intensity so that individually they do not damage the surrounding tissue. If you run through the other forty-one words in the relational algorithm and insert them in the phrase, "take a ray (blank) a ray," you will discover that there are other solutions to Duncker's problem.

Obviously if a problem is described in sufficient detail, there will be a large number of potential domain words (the domain word in the preceding example is "ray") that can be used in the relational algorithm. And some rather massive judgments will be necessary to decide which words to use. But this very judgmental latitude means that informative individual differences in choices among groups in organizations should be evident. Groups with a dominant schema will typically single out the same domain words from every problem and repeatedly run through the same subset of relational words.

Organizational members undoubtedly also differ in the degree to which they duplicate a domain word when trying to solve a problem. In the stomach tumor problem, there are several possible domain words and combinations. Notice that if a domain word is duplicated, as in the case of the X-rays, then the problem becomes more manageable.

It is surprising how often duplicating a domain word and applying all forty-two relations can suggest a solution. For example, the problem of flood control in Japan has been partially solved by taking water against water. The Japanese have come up with a system in which they use plastic bags, fill them with water at the site where the flooding is occurring, and then they pile these plastic bags of water into dikes to control the flood water. In that example a domain word is repeated, the word "against" from the relational algorithm suggests the solution, and the solution occurs because one element is taken in some relation to another element.

There are lots of ways to recombine elements. One of the interesting things in browsing through any collection that is organized alphabetically is that unusual categories, strange suggestions, and novel objects get placed adjacent to one another. This serves as a kind of randomizing or recombination device, just as does leaving material scattered around an office so you keep rediscovering new combinations of those materials.

The point is that organizations frequently analyze their world using combinations. However, factors such as reinforcement, overload, and socialization undoubtedly focus members' attention on a relatively small number of relations present in the relational algorithm. These biases, in turn, seal off many possibilities for new interpretations of organizational events. Assessment of preferred relational words and preferred practices for isolating domain words could suggest how organizations build their bodies of thought and whether they have the resources to rebuild and redefine those bodies of thought.

How Organizations Talk to Themselves

How organizational members execute the sensemaking recipe, how can I know what I think till I see what I say, can affect their interpretation of who they are, what they are doing, and what it means to be effective, given those interpretations. There are several ways in which that basic recipe can be modified and our intent here is simply to illustrate a small number of them.

As it stands the recipe contains only the first person singular pronoun "I". If any one of those pronouns becomes a plural pronoun, we could be inspecting a phenomenon that has organizational relevance. "How can I know what we think until I see what I say" could be a minimal organizational act even if the collective quality of that assertion is modest. It's important to reiterate that organizations can be viewed as entities built up from interlocked behaviors between pairs of people. That interlocking is modest, yet it can occur around any of the four themes implicit in the sensemaking recipe: knowing, thinking, seeing, or saying.

An additional variation of the recipe occurs if the sequence of knowing, thinking, seeing, and saying is shuffled. A basic contention of some newer models of organization such as organized anarchies, garbage cans, and loose coupling is that rational sequences seldom unfold in a rational order. Steps are either omitted or occur at odd points. For example, the standard medical sequence, symptom→diagnosis→treatment in actual practice often becomes symptoms→treatment→diagnosis. On the basis of data about the effectiveness of treatments, physicians can make a diagnosis after the fact, but a priori diagnosis seems to have little to do with treatment effectiveness. Applied to organizations we can ask what kinds of activities in organizations are suggested by these shufflings: "How can we say what I see till I think what I know?"; "how can we see what we know till I think what I say." By altering the sequence of sensemaking activities in the sensemaking recipe, it is possible to characterize both the unique problems that confront an organization and the different styles of thinking adopted by subunits and actors within that organization.

If we look more closely at specific words in the recipe, new possibilities for diagnosing organizational thinking practices and categorizing styles of organizing become apparent. It's not apparent, for example, that organizational members would always want to know *what* they think. People in organizations also want to know how they think, when they think, why they think, and where they think. If we examine those additional questions, we begin to learn something about when people become concerned about seeing what they say.

Inclusion of the word "know" in that recipe has a ring of certainty that may be a luxury in organizations. Instead of saying how can I know what I think, we can imagine the people in organizations settle for how can I invent, intuit, glimpse, discover, get-a-sense-of, grasp what I think till I see what I say. Each of those amendments makes sensemaking more probabilistic and more consistent with the notion of satisficing.

Consider this problem: How can I know what I think because I forgot what I said? The only way the sensemaking recipe works is if people can remember or retrieve what they've said (Krippendorff, 1975). Organizations characterized by cluttered files, empty traditions, or sloppy minutes have poor memories and will have trouble resorting to seeing what they say as a means to understand their existence.

Up to a point faulty memories are functional. Albert Speer, writing about his experiences during the Third Reich, notes that one of the best interventions for improving German industry during the war were the Allied bombing raids. Speer notes that these bombing raids destroyed the filing facilities of factories and also destroyed the traditions and procedures that had been mainstays of those bureaucracies. "Speer was so enamored with the results of these bombing raids that, upon learning of the destruction of his ministry, in the Allied air raid of November 22, 1943, he commented: "'Although we have been fortunate in that large parts of the current files of the ministry have been burned and so relieved us for a time of useless ballast, we cannot really expect that such events will continually introduce the necessary fresh air into our work'" (Speer, 1971, cited in Singer and Wooton, 1976, p. 87).

Moderately faulty memories may lead to healthy improvisation when people look back over their poorly stored words and try to make sense of them. But with no memory whatsoever, virtually nothing is available for people to make sense of.

If members of an organization can know things only a posteriori, that also suggests that how things are said or accomplished will influence the amount and variety of interpretations that can be imposed on them. If organizational members are encouraged to generate complicated sentences that suggest interesting possibilities of what people have been up to, then the lives of the people doing the interpreting should be both more interesting and more adaptive to changing circumstances. If people in organizations, however, are reinforced for uttering the same simple sentences over and over, then their degrees of freedom for subsequent retrospective sensemaking will be curtailed sharply. When people inspect those bland displays, their interpretations will be impoverished, redundant, and potentially nonadaptive.

As a final point, it's probable that organizations vary dramatically in how they stop an episode of sensemaking. It's not obvious when people should stop their saying, start their seeing, conclude that they have a thought in hand, or that they have exhausted the meaning of a display.

A repeated problem in organizational thinking and problem solving is that organizational members think too long and go right past the solution to a problem without realizing they've done so. How organizational members discover when to stop thinking is not obvious, it may distinguish their thinking styles and be responsible for many of the products that come from their thinking practices.

Habits as Alternatives to Thought

Most organizations seem to exist for some time on a small number of ideas, a full array of standard operating procedures, and a handful of well practiced schemata. In any situation where researchers are tempted to examine cognitive processes in organizations, close attention should be paid to the question of whether it's even necessary for thought to occur.

A particularly good essay developing this point is Warren Thorngate's article entitled "Must We Always Think Before We Act?" (1976).

Thorngate argues that people who adopt a cognitive approach seem to neglect two crucial facts. First, thought takes time and mental effort and people try to avoid cognitive strain. Second, most social interactions are redundant either in terms of the situations and people involved, or in terms of the behaviors necessary to sustain the interaction. In the case of most social interaction, familiarity is the rule. Given those costs of thinking, it makes sense to act habitually in most social encounters, because this frees attention and short-term memory for activities such as vigilance concerning events surrounding the interaction and rehearsal of future responses. Control by habit also means that response latencies will be short and responses will be smooth, thereby turning the interaction into a pleasant, self-fulfilling prophecy.

On the basis of these speculations Thorngate induces the general rule that, "If a response generated in an interaction is judged to be satisfactory, it will tend to be reproduced under subsequent, equivalent circumstances from habit rather than thought" (p. 32). Thorngate notes that much cognitive research involves situations where subjects are confronted with unfamiliar environments and are urged to be accurate rather than fast. Given these demands to deal accurately with the unfamiliar, it's not surprising that people have to think in order to manage these complexities. Extrapolating from those situations to organizational situations where people are confronted with the familiar, rewarded for speed, and where gross inaccuracies can be tolerated or rectified is precarious.

Thorngate's concluding comments about future research given these realities are relevant for organizational researchers.

> "To date we have almost no empirical data relevant to assessing the role of habit in social interaction or its relative popularity as a determinant of social behavior. Field research is necessary to determine the redundancy of social interactions across people, topics and situations so that we can estimate how often habits may be invoked. We need to develop methods of distinguishing between thoughtful and thoughtless behaviors in both field and laboratory settings. Studies must be undertaken to determine how often and how quickly behavior shifts from thought to habit, and to determine the relative popularity of various cognitive processes which can be used to generate re-

> sponses in unfamiliar situations. It would also be of some interest to quantify the mental effort associated with various cognitive processes or mental heuristics and to determine the trade-offs between the simplicity or "crudeness" of a heuristic and the number of maladaptive responses it produces in social interactions" (p. 34).

Investigation of the mix between habit and thinking is crucial in any analysis of cognition in organizations. It's important to notice that when people are acting out of habit their attention is focused somewhere and it's important to understand where that attention is focused and with what consequences. Virtually all discussions of thinking in organizations up to now have been concerned with instrumental thought. The concern has been with ideas that are instrumental in solving problems or giving the organization new definitions of itself.

Almost no attention has been paid to consummatory cognitive activities in organizations such as daydreaming and fantasizing (McKellar, 1957). If consummatory cognition accompanies habitual actions it could deflect or accelerate those routines and/or influence the next nonhabitual action the person performs. It does not seem productive to assume automatically that thoughtful accompaniments of habit are irrelevant to the ways in which those habits unfold. The question remains, what happens to thoughts during thoughtless episodes. What people dwell on and what this does to their activities in the next interval are potentially crucial questions when one thinks cognitively about organizations. The question of whether demands for speed undercut reliance on thought does deserve closer attention. Thorngate's automatic coupling of those two into a negative relationship remains to be demonstrated in organizations.

The Invocation of Others in Thinking Practices

Much thinking involves implicit conversations with phantom others. Who those phantom others are, the conditions under which they are invoked, and the vigor of their presumed exchanges with the thinker are all variables that differ among organizational members. The nature of the phenomenon has been described by Lofland (1976, p. 100):

> All encounters involve people in immediate interaction, but not all interactants need be in separate bodies. By means of memory, consciousness, and symbolization, humans summon particular past humans (more accurately, a residue composite of one) and composite categories of persons ("them," "my family," "the government," etc.) into the forefront of consciousness, taking account of what are projected to be their belief and action when dealing with a situation. No other person need physically be present for there to be social interaction in this sense. It is *social* interaction in that the individual is taking other people into account when constructing his own action.

> Moreover, people interact sheerly with themselves, or, rather, different aspects or dispositions of themselves. To the degree that people engage in internal dialogue with themselves, we may speak of self-encounters.

The audience "present" at most episodes of thinking is potentially influential on the way in which that thinking unfolds and the conclusions that come from it. Efforts to diagnose the audience that is invoked during thinking is a crucial aspect of cognitive analyses of organizations. Thinking is never a solitary activity and this means it is important in any understanding of cognition and organizations to discover precisely what people uttering what things keep that organizational thinker from being a solitary individual.

Simplification in Thinking Practices

A substantial portion of the cognitive literature pertaining to organizations can be viewed as variations on the theme that organizational members simplify and vulgarize the data to which they're exposed. Organizational members try to manage uncertainty by imposing categorical inferences rather than probabilistic judgments (Steinbruner, 1974, p. 110), they operate under the constraint of consistency to introduce cognitive economies, they manage inconsistent information by collapsing or stretching time, by wishful thinking, by inferring the impossibility of implied action, or any one of numerous other techniques which have been documented repeatedly (Slovic, Fischhoff, and Lichtenstein, 1976).

It's not evident that cognitive organizational theory is best served by yet one more documentation on the phenomenon of simplification. What we need instead is to cultivate a sensitivity to thinking practices that move beyond simplicity, thinking practices that complicate rather than simplify the world (e.g., Jacob, 1977). We need to understand how people can reverse some of the potential rigidities imposed by schemata. Not much attention has been paid to the issue of how to move beyond simplicity and reverse the tendency of organizations to encourage and operate on increasingly impoverished views of the world.

It's hard to find mechanisms that make organizations smarter, it's easy to find mechanisms that seem to erode their intelligence. Dixon's (1976) recent analysis of military incompetence suggests that there is considerable intelligence scattered throughout military organizations, but that norms of toughness and manliness make cultivation of itnelligent analyses next to impossible. Norms favoring toughness, realism, and doing, summarized in the maxim, "We're all business and mean business," favor simplicity and work against complexity.

People who have been concerned with organizational self-design (Clark, 1975; Kilmann, Pondy, and Slevin, 1976) have noted that organizations seldom have mechanisms for generating new structures that complicate their existence. Most research on groups demonstrates that groups are simplifying collectivities that vulgarize the minds that are in them. When, for example, groups accommodate to the least accomplished member, or foster polarized beliefs, or become solution centered rather than problem centered, potentially complex analyses are excluded from consideration.

Thus it seems crucial to learn more about ways to reverse simplifications. Most organizational researchers are familiar with Bartlett's (1932) serial reproduction situation in which a story is passed along from person to person, details drop out, and the final version of the story is a caricature of the original. Interestingly, nobody has ever sent the story back through in reverse order to see if it *regains* some of its original complexity and then is available for reinspection, reinterpretation, and redefinition.

If we want to make organizational members more complicated and reverse some of the effects of simplification, then somehow we have to make it possible for members to reexamine original rich displays and come away from those reexaminations with different interpretations of what they might mean. If uncertainty can be regenerated as well as absorbed, then theoretically it should be possible to recomplicate original observations that have become simplified. And if original complicated observations can be reinstated, then the organization has the opportunity to reexperience some of those original data and become more intelligent in handling them.

Investigators such as Watzlawick, Weakland, and Fisch (1974) have suggested that intentional confusion is a means to introduce complications and induce insights. Plausible as that suggestion is, it can be double edged. Confusion can also heighten arousal so much that people notice even less about current situations than they noticed before and this, in turn, leads them to rely even more heavily on previous overlearned schemata. The fact that the overlearned schemata do remove the confusion means that they are strongly reinforced right when the intention was to extinguish them. Thus, faced with confusion, the person has become more simplified and more attached to the simplifications that eased him through.

Not much attention has been paid to the ways in which simplifications can be reversed, yet it is not obvious that such reversals are impossible. Research has documented the existence of simplifications but has ignored the question, how can simplifying processes be reversed so that they generate complexities? If, for example, people in organizations were held accountable and rewarded for their success in complicating those who report to them, something other than simplifications should be observed.

CONCLUDING STATEMENT

We have tried to suggest that viewing an organization as a body of thought sustained by a set of thinkers and thinking practices reveals determinants of effectiveness that other formulations miss. Prevailing descriptions suggest that organizational members do many things by standard operating procedures and out of habit, deal with redundant situations with which they are familiar, spend time actively communicating rather than reflecting, argue that "ideas are a dime a dozen" and therefore simple to find, act on the basis of incomplete analyses, and in general seem to get along quite well without much resort to thought. It's the very obviousness of that description which leads us to suspect that we've missed something. The fact that thinking seems so trivial if not impossible under organizational conditions strikes us as all the more reason to look carefully for the places where it occurs, the ways in which it unfolds, and the organizational properties it constrains.

Analyses of cognitive processes in organizations suggest that there are numerous questions which deserve some attention:

1. Precisely what is the nature of the argument that says, if organizations thought more they'd be in better shape? Conceivably organizational members don't need to think more frequently, but rather differently, and on different occasions.
2. How does an organization discover it's ignorant? Should it even try to assess the degree of its ignorance (Schneider, 1962).
3. How do single cognitions generated by a single actor become amplified in organizations? We need detailed case studies of the ways in which single thoughts become diffused through an organization. Subtitle for such an exercise would be, "For want of a thought the organization was lost."
4. If people have bounded rationality and prefer simplification, is it possible to equip them with standard operating procedures that are smarter than they are? It seems no great trick to equip people with smart routines, but the problem is to preserve that complexity and buffer it from the simplifications of operators. Admissions decisions (Dawes, 1976) are a good example of standard operating procedures that can be smarter than their operators.

5. In any analysis of cognition and organizations we can ask, what are the provocations to cognition and who are the provokers? To look at cognition in organizations may be to look at forcing functions rather than at voluntary participation in thinking processes. Many people in organizations throw others off guard and routinely generate inconsistencies. These people can be viewed as provokers of thinking and how they function, where they function, and when they function may be important information.

6. Is cognitive organizational theory basically a tops down view of the organization? When applying a cognitive formulation to organizations, it is easy to argue that the images and thoughts of powerful people are crucial but that images, thoughts, expectations, and sensemakings of less powerful people are not. But, is it the case that lower level cognitions are not inconsequential?

A pair of aphorisms from the excellent collection by Auden and Kronenberger (1966) portray the kind of theoretical tension that potentially is associated with cognitive analyses of organizations and of the way they can enliven our efforts to say interesting things about organizations:

1. "Thinking is more interesting than knowing, but less interesting than looking" Goethe (p. 350).
2. "The world of reason is poor compared to the world of senses—until *or, but, because, when, if, and, unless* populate it with endless possibilities" Kaufmann (p. 342).

FOOTNOTE

1. I am grateful to Rosemary Burke for discussions concerning the content of this paper. This work was supported by the National Science Foundation through Grant BNS 75-09864.

REFERENCES

1. Aldrich, H., and D. Herker (1977) "Boundary spanning roles and organization structure," *The Academy of Management Review* 2, 217–230.
2. Allison, G. T. (1971) *Essence of Decision: Explaining the Cuban Missile Crisis*, Boston: Little, Brown, & Co.
3. Auden, W. H., and L. Kronenberger (1966) *The Viking Book of Aphorisms*, New York: Viking.
4. Axelrod, R. (1973) "Schema theoery: An information processing model of perception and cognition," *American Political Science Review 67*, 1248–1266.
5. Axelrod, R. (ed.). (1976) *Structure of Decision: The Cognitive Maps of Political Elites*, Princeton, N.J.: Princeton University Press.

6. Baldwin, J. M. (1909) *Darwin and the Humanities,* Baltimore: Review Publishing Co.
7. Ball, D. W. (1972) "'The definition of situation': Some theoretical and methodological consequences of taking W. I. Thomas seriously." *Journal for the Theory of Social Behavior 2,* 61–82.
8. Bartlett, F. C. (1932) *Remembering,* Cambridge: Cambridge University Press.
9. Berlo, D. K. (1977) "Communication as process: Review and commentary," in B. D. Ruben (ed.), *Communciation Yearbook,* I, New Brunswick, N.J.: Transaction Books, pp. 11–27.
10. Betz, F. (1971) "On the management of inquiry," *Management Science 18,* B117–133.
11. Bishop, J. E. (August 1977) "Potent non-drugs," *Wall Street Journal.*
12. Blumer, H. (1971) "Social problems as collective behavior," *Social Problems 18,* 298–306.
13. Bougon, M., K. E. Weick, and D. Binkhorst (1977) "Cognition in organizations: An analysis of the Utrecht Jazz Orchestra," *Administrative Science Quarterly 22,* 606–639.
14. Broadbent, D. E. (1971) *Decision and Stress,* New York: Academic Press, Inc.
15. Brush, S. G. (1974) "Should the history of science be rated X?" *Science 183,* 1164–1172.
16. Clark, P. (1975) "Organizational design: A review of key problems," *Administration and Society 7,* 213–256.
17. Cohen, A. R., E. Sotland, and D. M. Wolfe (1955) "An experimental investigation of need for cognition," *Journal of Abnormal and Social Psychology 51,* 291–294.
18. Cohen, M. D., J. G. March, and J. P. Olsen (1972) "A garbage can model of organizational choice," *Administrative Science Quarterly 17,* 1–25.
19. Coulam, R. F. (1977) *Illusions of Choice: The F-111 and the Problem of Weapons Acquisition Reform,* Princeton, N.J.: Princeton University Press.
20. Crovitz, H. F. (1967) "The form of logical solutions," *The American Journal of Psychology 80,* 461–462.
21. ———. (1970) *Galton's Walk,* New York: Harper & Row, Publishers.
22. Davis, M. S. (1971) "That's interesting: Towards a phenomenology of sociology and a sociology of phenomenology," *Philosophy of Social Science 1,* 309–344.
23. Dawes, R. M. (1976) "Shallow psychology," in J. S. Carroll & J. W. Payne (eds.), *Cognition and Social Behavior,* Hillsdale, N.J.: Erlbaum, pp. 3–11.
24. Delia, J. G. (1977) "Constructivism and the study of human communication," *The Quarterly Journal of Speech 63,* 66–83.
25. Dixon, N. F. (1976) *On the Psychology of Military Incompetence,* New York: Basic Books, Inc., Publishers.
26. Emery, F. E., and E. L. Trist (1969) "The causal texture of organizational environments," in F. E. Emery (ed.), *Systems Thinking,* Middlesex, England: Penguin Books, Inc., pp. 241–257.
27. Frankel, C. (1973) "The nature and sources of irrationalism," *Science. 180,* 927–931.
28. Goffman, E. (1974) *Frame Analysis,* New York: Harper & Row, Publishers.
29. Goldthorpe, J. H. (1973) "A revolution in sociology?" *Sociology 6–7,* 449–462.
30. Goodman, P. S. (1968) "The measurement of an individual's organization map," *Administrative Science Quarterly 13,* 246–265.
31. Gould, S. J. (1977) "The continental drift affair," *National History* LXXXVI.
32. Gregory, R. L., and E. H. Gombrich (eds.) (1973) *Illusion in Nature and Art,* New York: Charles Scribner's Sons.
33. Hayakawa, S. I. (1961) "The word is not the thing," in P. R. Lawrence, J. C. Bailey, R. L. Katz, J. A. Seiler, C. D. Orth III, J. V. Clark, L. B. Barnes, and A. N. Turner, *Organizational Behavior and Administration,* Homewood, Ill.: Dorsey, pp. 397–400.

34. Jacob, F. (1977) "Evolution and tinkering," *Science 196,* 1161–1166.
35. Janis, I. R. (1972) *Victims of Groupthink,* Boston: Houghton Mifflin Company.
36. Jeffmar, M., and C. Jeffmar (1975) "A system approach to cognition," *General Systems 20,* 65–69.
37. Jones, E. E., and H. B. Gerard (1967) *Foundations of social psychology,* New York: John Wiley & Sons, Inc.
38. Kilmann, R. H., L. R. Pondy, and D. P. Slevin (eds.) (1976) *The Management of Organization Design* (2 vols.), New York: North-Holland.
39. Krippendorff, K. (1975) "Some principles of information storage and retrieval in society," *General Systems 20,* 15–35.
40. Levi-Strauss, C. (1962) *The Savage Mind,* Chicago: University of Chicago Press.
41. Lofland, J. (1976) *Doing Social Life.* New York: John Wiley & Sons, Inc.
42. London, H., and R. E. Nisbett (eds.) (1974) *Thought and Feeling,* Chicago: Aldine Publishing Company.
43. March, J. G., and J. P. Olsen (1976) *Ambiguity and Choice in Organizations,* Bergen, Norway: Universitetsforlaget.
44. Martin, M. (1977) "The philosophical importance of the Rosenthal effect," *Journal for the Theory of Social Behaviour 7,* 81–97.
45. McKellar, P. (1957) *Imagination and Thinking.* New York: Basic Books, Inc., Publishers.
46. Mintzberg, H. (1973) *The Nature of Managerial Work,* New York: Harper & Row.
47. Neisser, U. (1963) "The multiplicity of thought," *British Journal of Psychology 54,* 1–14.
48. ———. (1976) *Cognition and Reality,* San Francisco: W. H. Freeman and Company Publishers.
49. ———. (1977) Gibson's ecological optics: Consequences of a different stimulus description," *Journal for the Theory of Social Behaviour 7,* 17–28.
50. Nisbett, R. E., and T. D. Wilson (1977) "Telling more than we can know: Verbal reports on mental processes," *Psychological Review 84,* 231–259.
51. Pettigrew, A. M. (1975) "Towards a political theory of organizational intervention," *Human Relations 28,* 191–208.
52. Powers, W. T. (1973) *Behavior: the Control of Perception,* Chicago: Aldine Publishing Company.
53. Ravetz, J. R. (1971) *Scientific Knowledge and its Social Problems,* New York: Oxford University Press.
54. Reynolds, A. G., and P. W. Flagg (1977) *Cognitive Psychology,* Cambridge, Mass.: Winthrop Publishers, Inc.
55. Rodin, J. (1977) "Research on eating behavior and obesity: Where does it fit in personality and social psychology?" *Personality and Social Psychology Bulletin* 3, 333–355.
56. Rosnow, R. L., and G. A. Fine (1976) *Rumor and Gossip,* New York: American Elsevier Publishing Co., Inc.
57. Ross, L. (1977) "The intuitive psychologist and his shortcomings: Distortions in the attribution process," in L. Berkowitz (ed.), *Advances in Experimental Social Psychology,* Vol. 10, New York: Academic Press Inc., pp. 173–220.
58. Scheerer, M. (1954) "Cognitive theory," in G. Lindzey (ed.), *Handbook of Social Psychology* Vol. 1, Reading Mass.: Addison-Wesley Publishing Co., Inc. pp. 91–142.
59. Schneider, L. (1962) "The role of the category of ignorance in sociological theory: An exploratory statement," *American Sociological Review 27,* 492–508.
60. Schutz, A. (1964) "The stranger: An essay in social psychology," in A. Schutz, *Collected Papers,* Vol. 2. The Hague: Martinus Nijhoff. pp. 91–105.

61. Singer, E. A., and L. M. Wooton (1976) "The triumph and failure of Albert Speer's administrative genius: Implications for current management theory and practice," *The Journal of Applied Behavioral Science 12,* 79–103.
62. Slovic, P., B. Fischhoff, and S. Lichtenstein (1976) "Cognitive processes and societal risk taking," in J. S. Carroll & J. W. Payne (eds.), *Cognition and Social Behavior,* Hillsdale, N.J.: Erlbaum, pp. 165–184.
63. Speer, A. (1971) *Inside the Third Reich,* New York: Avon Books.
64. Stagner, R. (1977) "New maps of deadly territories" (review of Structure of decision by R. Axelrod (ed.), *Contemporary Psychology 22,* 547–549.
65. Steinbruner, J. D. (1974) *The Cybernetic Theory of Decision,* Princeton, N.J.: Princeton University Press.
66. Sotland, E., and L. K. Canon (1972) *Social Psychology: A Cognitive Approach,* Philadelphia: W. B. Saunders Company.
67. Strauch, R. E. (1975) "'Squishy' problems and quantitative methods," *Policy Sciences 6,* 175–184.
68. Thorngate, W. (1976) "Must we always think before we act?," *Personality and Social Psychology Bulletin 2,* 31–35.
69. Tolman, E. C., and E. Brunswik (1935) "The organism and the causal texture of the environment," *Psychological Review 42,* 43–77.
70. Watzlawick, P., J. Weakland, and R. Fisch (1974) *Change,* New York: W. W. Norton & Company, Inc.
71. Weick, K. E. (1977) "Enactment processes in organizations," in B. Staw and G. Salancik (eds.), *New Directions in Organizational Behavior,* Chicago: St. Clair pp. 267–300.

Evaluation and Employment in Organizations

Edited by **L.L. Cummings** and **Barry M. Staw**

CONTENTS: Performance Appraisal: A Process Focus, *Daniel R. Ilgen and Jack M. Feldman.* **Self-Assessments in Organizations: A Literature Review and Integrative Model. A Process Analysis of the Assessment Center Method,** *Sheldon Zedeck.* **Sex Bias in Work Settings: The Lack of Fit Model,** *Madaline E. Heilman.* **Understanding Comparable Worth: A Societal and Political Perspective,** *Thomas A. Mahoney.* **The Meanings of Absence: New Strategies for Theory and Research. Employee Turnover and Post Decision Accommodation,** *Richard M. Steers and Richard T. Mowday.* **The Effects of Work Layoffs in Survivors: Research Theory and Practice,** *Joel Brockner.*

1990 256 pp. LC 90-4533 Paper $19.50
ISBN 1-55938-219-8

Personality and Organizational Influence

Edited by **Barry M. Staw** and **L.L. Cummings**

CONTENTS: Personality and Organizational Behavior, *Howard M. Weiss and Seymour Adler.* **Interactional Psychology and Organizational Behavior,** *Benjamin Schneider.* **Toward a Theory of Organizational Socialization,** *John Van Maanen and Edgar T. Schein.* **The Politics of Upward Influence in Organizations,** *Lyman W. Porter, Robert W. Allen, and Harold L. Angle.* **Principled Organizational Dissent: A Theoretical Essay,** *Jill W. Graham.* **Power and Personality in Complex Organizations,** *Robert J. House.* **Organizational Structure, Attitudes, and Behaviors,** *Chris J. Berger and L.L. Cummings.*

1990 326 pp. LC 90-4524 Paper $19.50
ISBN 1-55938-217-1

All articles are reprinted from: **Research in Organizational Behavior,** Edited by **Barry M. Staw,** *School of Business Administration, University of California, Berkeley* and **L.L. Cummings,** *Carlson School of Management, University of Minnesota*

JAI PRESS

J A I

P R E S S

Work in Organizations

Edited by **Barry M. Staw** and **L.L. Cummings**

CONTENTS: Motivation Theory Reconsidered, *Frank J. Landy and Wendy S. Becker.* **Activation Theory and Job Design: Review and Reconceptualization,** *Donald G. Gardner and L.L. Cummings.* **Toward an Integrated Theory of Task Design,** *Ricky W. Griffin.* **Of Art and Work: Aesthetics Experience, and the Psychology of Work Feelings,** *Lloyd E. Sandelands and Georgette C. Buckner.* **The Expression of Emotion in Organizational Life,** *Anat Rafaeli and Robert I. Sutton.* **"Real Feelings": Emotional Expression and Organizational Culture,** *John Van Maanen and Gideon Kunda.* **Work Values and the Conduct of Organizational Behavior,** *Walter R. Nord, Arthur P. Brief, Jennifer M. Atieh, and Elizabeth M. Doherty.*

1990 296 pp. LC 90-4474 Paper $19.50
ISBN 1-55938-216-3

Leadership, Participation, and Group Behavior

Edited by **L.L. Cummings** and **Barry M. Staw**

CONTENTS: Leadership: Some Empirical Generalizations and New Research Directions, *Robert House and Mary Baetz. Charisma and its Routinization in Two Social Movement Organizations, Harrison Trice and Janice M. Beyer.* **Participation in Decision-Making: One More Look,** *Edwin A. Locke and David M. Schweiger.* **Workers Participation in Management: An International Perspective,** *George Strauss.* **The Meeting as a Neglected Social Form in Organizational Studies,** *Helen B. Schwartzman.* **Understanding Groups in Organizations,** *Paul S. Goodman, Elizabeth Ravlin, and Marshall Schminke.*

1990 386 pp. LC 90-4529 Paper $22.50
ISBN 1-55938-220-1

All articles are reprinted from: **Research in Organizational Behavior,** Edited by **Barry M. Staw,** *School of Business Administration, University of California, Berkeley* and **L.L. Cummings,** *Carlson School of Management, University of Minnesota*

J A I P R E S S

The Evolution and Adaptation of Organizations

Edited by **Barry M. Staw** and **L.L. Cummings**

CONTENTS: Organizational Life Cycles and Natural Selection, *John Freeman.* **Even Dwarfs Started Small: Liabilities of Age and Size and Their Strategic Implications,** *Howard Aldrich and Ellen R. Auster.* **The Political Environments of Organizations: An Ecological View,** *Glenn R. Carroll, Jacques Delacroix, and Jerry Goodstein.* **Managerial Discretion: A Bridge Between Polar Views of Organizational Outcomes,** *Donald C. Hambrick and Sidney Finkelstein.* **Organizational Evolution: A Metamorphosis Model of Convergence and Reorientation,** *Michael L. Tushman and Elaine Romanelli.* **Behavior in Escalation Situations: Antecedents, Prototypes, and Solutions,** *Barry M. Staw.* **A Model of Creativity and Innovation in Organizations,** *Teresa M. Amabileand Jerry Ross.* **When a Thousand Flowers Bloom: Structural, Collective, and Social Conditions for Innovation in Organization,** *Rosabeth Moss Kanter.*

1990 320 pp. LC 90-4525 Paper $19.50
ISBN 1-55938-221-X

All articles are reprinted from: **Research in Organizational Behavior,** Edited by **Barry M. Staw,** *School of Business Administration, University of California, Berkeley* and **L.L. Cummings,** *Carlson School of Management, University of Minnesota*

JAI PRESS INC.
55 Old Post Road - No. 2
P.O. Box 1678
Greenwich, Connecticut 06836-1678
Tel: 203-661-7602

J A I P R E S S

Also Available !

Corporation and Society Research:
Studies in Theory and Measurement
Edited by **Lee E. Preston**
1990 306 pp. LC 90-4604 Paper $19.50
ISBN 1-55938-222-8

International and Comparative Corporation and Society Research
Edited by **Lee E. Preston**
1990 302 pp. LC 90-4567 Paper $19.50
ISBN 1-55938-223-6

Business and Politics:
Research Issues and Empirical Studies
Edited by **Lee E. Preston**
1990 322 pp. LC 90-4473 Paper $19.50
ISBN 1-55938-224-4

Business Ethics:
Research Issues and Empirical Studies
Edited by **William C. Frederick** and **Lee E. Preston**
1990 280 pp. LC 90-4468 Paper $18.95
ISBN 1-55938-225-2

Government Regulation and Business Response:
Research Issues and Empirical Studies
Edited by **Lee E. Preston**
1990 302 pp. LC 90-4490 Paper $19.50
ISBN 1-55938-226-0

All articles are reprinted from: **Research in Corporate Social Performance and Policy,** Edited by **Lee E. Preston,** *University of Maryland, College Park*